D0423832

LIVING ABROAD IN
FRANCE

AURELIA D'ANDREA

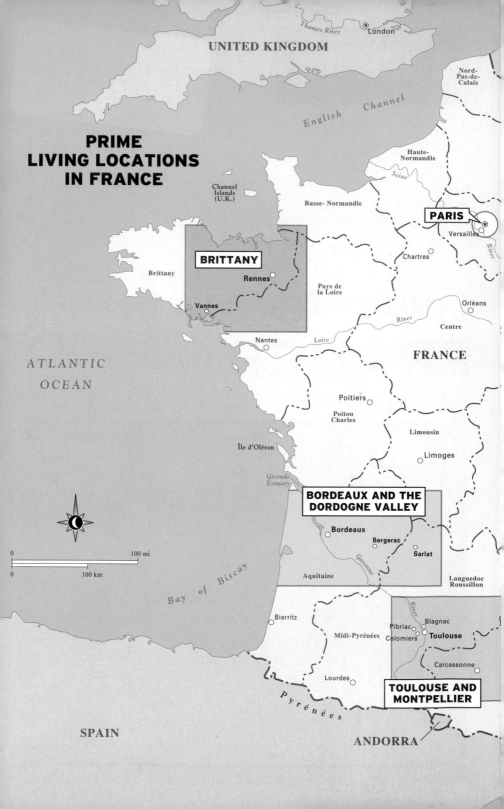

PRIME LIVING LOCATIONS IN FRANCE

UNITED KINGDOM

London

Thames River

English Channel

Nord-Pas-de-Calais

Haute-Normandie

Seine

Channel Islands (U.K.)

Basse- Normandie

PARIS

Versailles

River

Chartres

BRITTANY

Brittany

Rennes

Vannes

Pays de la Loire

Orléans

ATLANTIC OCEAN

Nantes

Loire

River

Centre

FRANCE

Poitiers

Poitou Charles

Limousin

Île d'Oléron

Limoges

Gironde Estuary

BORDEAUX AND THE DORDOGNE VALLEY

Bordeaux

Bergerac

Sarlat

Aquitaine

Garonne

Languedoc Roussillon

Bay of Biscay

Biarritz

Midi-Pyrénées

Pibriac

Colomiers

Blagnac

Toulouse

River

Lourdes

Carcassonne

TOULOUSE AND MONTPELLIER

Pyrénées

SPAIN

ANDORRA

0   100 mi

0   100 km

Contents

At Home in France

"The chief danger about Paris," cautioned poet T. S. Eliot, "is that it is such a strong stimulant." The same wonderful warning can be applied to all of France, where the everyday sensory experience borders on extravagant. Throughout the country, breathtaking architecture that stretches back to the Middle Ages sets the fairytale tone. Add the luscious scent of warm bread rising in a *boulanger*'s oven, toss in the sound of a distant church bell ringing, and finish with a smattering of outdoor markets bursting with all the colors of the rainbow, and you have a solid sense of the sort of stimulation l'Hexagone has to offer.

As worthy of superlatives as this complex country may be, France is much more than a delicious carnival for the senses. For the roughly 150,000 North American expatriates who call France home, at least part of the country's allure is its renowned quality of life: relaxed, engaged, and fine-tuned to simple pleasures. The French way of living isn't perfect, but it's pretty darn close.

On any day in hundreds of hamlets, villages, and urban metropolises throughout the country, you can follow the yeasty aroma of baking baguettes down a crooked cobblestone alleyway and wind up standing before a dazzling display of culinary wizardry: shiny fruit tarts — their buttery crusts pinched to perfection — sitting in neat little rows between caramel-and-whipped-cream *religieuses* and meringue-topped *tartes au citron*.

Your eyes feast on the tempting patisserie until a familiar melody from a distant accordion coaxes you out of your sugary reverie. Drifting away

on an éclair-scented cloud, you hear the music grow clearer and louder. Rounding a corner, you spy the source: a mustachioed man in a striped fisherman's sweater, tapping and squeezing a heartstring-tugging rendition of "La Vie en Rose," a beret at his feet awaiting the toss of a few coins.

Up the street, past the *fleuriste*, the *crémerie*, and the 13th-century cathedral, the warm glow of a café summons you indoors. From behind the zinc bar, the owner calls out, "Bonjour, mademoiselle!" (You can always tell if he's flirting by whether he addresses you as "mademoiselle" or "madame.") You make a beeline for the terrace to take in the last rays of sunshine on this fading spring afternoon.

Sipping your tipple and relishing the parade of impeccably dressed grandmothers pulling plaid *chariots* up the street toward the twice-weekly *marché*, you eavesdrop on the lively football (soccer) debate being hashed out at the table next to you, and marvel at two children quietly drawing with crayons while their father nurses a foamy *demi* and skims today's edition of *Le Monde*.

A hyperbolized rendering of a day in your French life? As disarming as it may seem, the truthful answer is a definitive *"non."* Even as it struggles to adapt to 21st-century growing pains – an aging population, stagnant birth rates, and burgeoning unemployment – France rises to the challenge while retaining the traditions that give the country its flavor. Stimulating? *Absolument.* Survey the expatriate community, and odds are people will tell you that the "danger" Eliot warned us against is a risk worth taking.

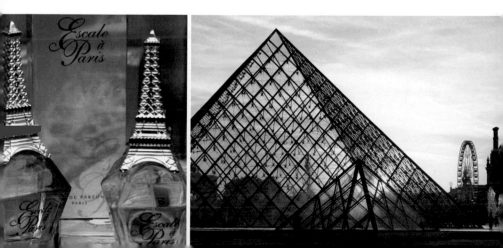

► WHAT I LOVE ABOUT FRANCE

- Mastering the myriad meanings of the beloved expression *"oh la la."*

- Watching strangers helping strangers lug suitcases, *poussettes* (baby strollers), and grocery bags up and down those seemingly endless Métro stairs.

- The way kids — from toddlers to teens — greet you with a *bisou* (kiss) on each cheek when meeting you for the first time (and each time thereafter).

- Those silly ceramic garden gnomes peering out from window displays at the pharmacy, hardware store, and neighborhood bookseller.

- The outdoor produce market in autumn, when summer's ripe peaches and cherries give way to earthy mushrooms, fresh hazelnuts, and crisp Normandy apples.

- *Brocantes* (secondhand sales), *marchés aux puces* (flea markets), and *vide-greniers* (rummage sales), where scoring secondhand treasures is a popular yet casual weekend sport.

- The perfectly quaffable €2 glass of Côtes du Rhône available at any French café.

- Leaving gray and rainy Paris on the morning TGV and arriving in warm, sunny Nice just in time for a prix fixe lunch at a bustling outdoor-terrace café.

- The way my neighborhood *boulanger* reaches for the *tradition graine* baguette as soon as I walk in the door.

- Buying hot chestnuts and mulled wine from street vendors at Christmastime.

- The unabashed topless septuagenarians sunbathing at the public swimming pool.

- Salivating over the schoolchildren's lunch menu posted outside every *école élémentaire.*

- The fact that chocolate — in the form of *tartine* spread, cereal, a stuffed croissant, or a hot drink — is an entirely acceptable way to start the day.

WELCOME TO FRANCE

INTRODUCTION

There are many ways to describe 21st-century France, but the most fitting might be "traditional." The French cling to their customs with an unrivaled tenacity for reasons as mysterious to foreigners as they are to the locals themselves. Ask why, and you're likely to be met with a rote *"C'est comme ça"*—that's just the way it is. Progress can wait, the French seem to be saying. What's the big hurry?

Change tends to make the French feel a bit uneasy, so forward motion takes place at an Operation Escargot pace. But the same timeless, traditional values attract many foreigners to France. The French have earned a global reputation for having mastered the art of living, and they deserve it. In a manner that elicits envious sighs around the world, they continue to show us that balancing work and home life isn't just a dream. Here, the motto seems to be "work to live, and live *la belle vie."* This is particularly evident at lunchtime, when construction crews and suited-up office workers from Picardie to Provence file into homey brasseries to relish their perfectly quotidian three-course lunches—*with* wine. You also see it in the healthcare safety net that guarantees 90 percent of the population is covered by comprehensive medical insurance. And you feel it during the month of August, when entire cities empty out as locals flock to the seashore and the countryside to enjoy their luxuriously long summer vacation. In France, *relaxation* is definitely not a dirty word.

This country of 64 million may have nailed the quality-of-life thing, but there are still a few areas of the French modus operandi that could use a modern makeover. The customer is most certainly *not* always right in France, so even the most mundane tasks—opening a bank account, getting your electricity connected—can serve as an exercise in frustration that will test the patience of the most laid-back émigré. The French are also a guarded bunch, with a very distinct line separating public and private life. Many an American expat laments never having been invited to a French person's home. This is the norm, not the exception, and it's not worth getting offended about. Give your new French friend time—five or six years, perhaps—and you just might just find yourself on the receiving end of that most mysterious, coveted dinner invitation.

What seems to matter most in France is family, as reflected in the social system. Even before a child is born, the social benefits kick in: parents-to-be are entitled to special grants for having a child through biological means or adoption. From 11 days' paternity leave for new fathers (new moms get 16 weeks) and subsidized childcare for preschool-age kids, adding to the population is rewarded rather than punished. France consistently ranks at the top of the global charts when it comes to the scope and standard of healthcare, and a government subsidized "family allowance" is given to all families with two or more children, regardless of income. Also regardless of income, housing benefits are doled out to all families with children under the age of 20. To the uninitiated, these social benefits might seem excessive, but French voters consistently say "yes" to the established welfare system.

Yet in spite of France's deeply held traditional values, there is a sense of transition in the air. This change is due in part to the Internet, which continues to open up the French consciousness. Traditionally valued institutions such as marriage are waning, but civil unions—including same-sex unions—are one the rise. English is more widely spoken than ever before, and multiculturalism has reached an unprecedented level. Immigrants from North and West Africa, Eastern Europe, and Asia continue to alter the look, feel, and flavor of France, taking the edge off the homogeneity that has long defined the French ethos.

As private, traditional, family-oriented France slowly adapts to its changing landscape, it continues to attract an expatriate community that fortifies itself on those timeless, easily accessible attributes that have stood the test of time: dazzling architecture, towering snowcapped mountains and picture-perfect seashores, unrivaled cuisine, a fascinating history, and an unsurpassed quality of life. There's never been a time as prime as now for letting this seductive country make its everlasting imprint on the adventurous Francophile. Welcoming, wonderful France awaits.

The Lay of the Land

The largest country in Western Europe, France—nicknamed l'Hexagone for its distinct six-sided geometry—occupies a particularly strategic and resource-rich piece of the European pie. Hemmed in by Belgium, Luxembourg, and Germany to the north and northeast; Switzerland and Italy to the east; and Monaco, Andorra, and Spain to the south; metropolitan France is a bountiful bouquet of geographic diversity, boasting world-renowned beaches, rivers, valleys, and mountain ranges.

To the east, the French Alps lay claim to Western Europe's tallest peak, Mont Blanc. The 15,770-foot-high mountain attracts many thousands of skiers, bikers, climbers, and daring outdoors enthusiasts of every stripe each year, making it the third-most-visited natural monument in the world. To the south, a magnificent cluster of dormant volcanoes forms the Massif Central, a giant swath of rugged, millennia-old mountains and plateaus dotted with thermal hot springs, a reminder that the volcanoes are merely dormant, not extinct.

Butting up against Spain in the far south, France's second mountain range, the Pyrénées, acts as a natural border separating the Iberian Peninsula from the rest of mainland Europe. Like the mountains of the Massif Central, the Pyrénées are punctuated by hot springs, around which spas both fancy and utilitarian have been built, each touting the naturally curative benefits of their waters to ailing bodies. (*La sécurité sociale* even covers the cost of some thermal hot springs "cures.") Winter sports are popular here, and in summer, hiking enthusiasts come in droves to tackle the 500-mile Mediterranean-to-Atlantic footpath known as the GR 10.

The Gallic landscape is crisscrossed by hundreds of rivers that meander between mountains, flow across great stretches of verdant farmland, and wend their way through some of the most picturesque, châteaux-rich valleys in all of Europe. The fabled Seine is surely the best known of all France's *fleuves,* twisting majestically through Paris on its way to the seaport of Le Havre,

Love the great outdoors? You'll adore the French Alps.

where it billows out into the rocky waters of the English Channel. However, the Seine is neither the longest nor the most important of the country's waterways. The swift-moving Rhône has served as France's primary internal trade route since Roman times; and, at 620 miles long, the Loire claims the title of France's longest waterway.

At its northernmost point, France meets Belgium on the brutish North Sea, but the coastline relaxes as you travel south, moving along the English Channel and finally to that swath of Atlantic coastline known as the Bay of Biscay, which reaches clear down to the Spanish border. This expanse of windswept land where sea meets sand is flat and marshy, and because of its easy proximity to France's most famous wine-growing region, it's extremely popular for French vacationers during the month of August.

France is blessed with exceptional natural beauty, but the country's prize jewel is easily the Mediterranean coast—more specifically that exclusive stretch of sundrenched seashore called the Côte d'Azur. Notorious for its 300 days of sunshine per year and more yachts per capita than any other region in the world, the Riviera serves up razzle-dazzle with substance. Over the centuries, the region has played host to waves of invading armies and migrating crusaders, plus a famous artist or two, including Pablo Picasso, Marc Chagall, and Henri Matisse, whose paintings reflect the special flavor of their temporary home base.

Jutting out of the turquoise Mediterranean 100 miles off the Provençal coast is Corsica (known as Corse in French), a rugged explosion of jagged mountains

MIND YOUR MANNERS

Snobby. Rude. Elitist. These are some of the nicer adjectives folks who haven't even visited France will casually bandy about to describe an entire nation and its inhabitants. Maybe even be a person or two who *has* set foot on French soil will substantiate the pejorative name-calling with an anecdote or two, likely based on a hurried weekend trip to Paris armed with little more than a loud Midwestern accent. Give the country's 64 million people half a chance, however, and they'll show you that the negative stereotypes are unfounded.

What many mistake for snootiness is actually an ingrained social formality that, from an outsider's perspec-

What to Say	What It Means
Bonjour, madame/monsieur	Hello, madam/sir
Bon journée, madame/monsieur	Have a nice day, madam/sir
Bon soir, Madame/Monsieur	Good evening, madam/sir
Bon soirée, madame/monsieur	Have a nice evening, madam/sir
Au revoir, madame/monsieur	Goodbye, madam/sir
S'il vous plaît	Please
Merci bien, madame/monsieur	Thank you very much, madame/sir
Excusez-moi, s'il vous plaît	Pardon me, please
Je suis désolé(e) de vous déranger, mais...	I'm so sorry to bother you, but...
Merci, vous etes très gentile	Thank you, you are so nice
Je suis très désolé(e), mais je ne comprends pas	I'm so sorry, but I don't understand

and red-tile rooftops. Though closer to Italy than France—and culturally distinct, with its own language and culinary customs—Corsica is considered no less French than any other mainland region. As well as being a major tourist hub, the island is an important agricultural zone, producing many warm-weather fruits (those delicious little Clementine oranges in particular) and vegetables sold throughout France at open-air *marchés* and standard supermarkets.

COUNTRY DIVISIONS

Metropolitan France, or what the locals refer to as La Métropole, is carved into 22 culturally distinct regions, including the island of Corsica. Each of these regions is further divided into 96 *départements,* and, in the manner of Russian dolls, each department contains *arrondissements, cantons,* and *communes.* For the day-to-day practical purposes of the expat, knowing your regions and departments is what matters most.

tive, can feel very old-fashioned. People still greet their neighbors with a cordial *"Bonjour, madame"*; never forget to say *"Au revoir, monsieur"* at the pharmacy, wine shop, and post office; and always hold the door for the person behind them, regardless of gender. A certain attention to dress – nice shoes, for instance – is almost universal in French cities, and only recently has the casual sartorial approach (sweatpants, white gym shoes) inched its way into the fashion sphere. If you want to make a good first impression and feel like a local *tout de suite* (immediately), commit these phrases to memory and employ them liberally.

When to Say It

When entering any shop, restaurant, or business during the day

When leaving any shop, restaurant, or business

when greeting shopkeepers and others after dark

When saying goodbye to shopkeepers and others after dark

When leaving any shop, restaurant, or business (often combined with *bon journée* or *bon soirée*)

Before approaching strangers for help, before placing your order at a restaurant, and when trying to get someone's attention

At the close of any transaction

When asking strangers for directions or other information

When you want to lay it on thick in the gratitude department

When you're especially grateful for something

When you want to elicit sympathy and possibly an English-language response

Departments are numbered alphabetically, beginning with Ain (01) and ending with Val d'Oise (95). Corsica is the one anomaly, with two departmental codes—2A and 2B, representing Corse du Sud and Haute Corse—standing in for 20. In the same way that all French phone numbers begin with a two-digit sequence that indicates the region, French license plates bear the two-digit departmental number at the end of the seven-character alphanumeric sequence. This indicates where that car was registered and makes for a great game during long-haul road trips.

Each department has its own elected officials and an administrative capital known as a *préfecture*. The *préfets*—the places to go to register a birth, report a death, acquire a driver's or a marriage license, or register a new address—are responsible for carrying out national law on a local level. This system, first instituted under Napoleon I, allows local administrative hubs to function with a certain degree of autonomy within the centralized French government.

Préfectures are also the primary public administration zone most foreign nationals get to know on an intimate level; expect to spend hours here waiting in line, having your dossier scrutinized, and ultimately registering your legal status as a temporary resident in France.

POPULATION DENSITY

Until the 1950s, half the French population lived rurally. Today, the majority resides in urban areas, with Paris topping the charts as the most dense, accounting for a full 3.5 percent of the country's population. With approximately 64 million inhabitants, France is the fourth-largest country in Europe, falling behind Germany (82 million) and just ahead of the United Kingdom (62 million). In only a few major cities—Paris, Marseille, and Lyon in particular— and their suburbs will you feel the suffocating glut of overcrowding, and usually just at rush hour or during one of the many annual public festivals.

France differs from North America in that its suburbs, or *banlieues,* are often as densely populated as the urban centers they skirt. This is a symptom of poor urban planning; to meet the needs of a growing immigrant population in the '70s and '80s, enormous concrete housing developments called *cités* were hastily erected, intended as temporary dwellings to house a population that was expected to return "home" at some point. Some of these *banlieues,* most notably to the north of Paris but also on the periphery of Marseille,

© SOPHIA PAGAN/WWW.SOPHIAPAGAN.COM

Cafés add to the liveliness of the streets in France.

BISOU BREAKDOWN

Everyone's heard of a French kiss, but the voracious tongues-and-all method isn't the standardized variety carried out in *la belle France.* From the moment you step off the plane or alight from your train, you'll see what French kissing is really all about (and, perhaps, what it *isn't* about: tongues). The art of the *bisou* begins with identifying who's on the receiving end: If you're of the female persuasion, you'll dole out kisses to everyone. Ditto if you're a child. (They start 'em young here.) Men are typically exempted from kissing other men, unless they're family or extremely close friends. Step two is all about the action: Lean in toward your intended with your right cheek, allowing your respective cheeks to touch gently and momentarily while you make a kissing sound. Step three involves pulling back slightly and repeating the gesture on the left cheek. One or both hands can rest gently on the kissee's shoulders or an arm, or simply keep your mitts to yourself. In some parts of France, this act can be repeated for a total of four kisses; let the Frenchie take the lead if you're uncertain of the local protocol. So what about that other French kiss practiced the world over? Yes, they do it in France, too, but here they call it *un bisou avec la langue* – a kiss with the tongue.

have been the sites of police clashes and rioting. In 2005, a weeklong series of riots in the northern Paris suburbs, replete with burning cars and Molotov cocktails, made international headlines and drew attention to the racial issues that had previously been ignored by the mainstream media. Marginalized populations—often discontent second-generation immigrant youth caught between two cultures—are credited as the source of the suburban "problem," but humanizing the structure of suburban communities through better urban planning is seen by many as one possible solution.

Generally, French streets tend to feel lively and functional rather than clogged. Cities and towns usually have a commercial center where you'll find basic necessities, including a post office, a café, a *boulangerie,* and other services. Many towns have user-friendly squares or parks with benches, picnic tables, and children's play areas. Whatever the season and the weather conditions, you're bound to see silver-haired grandmothers out buying bread, fathers ushering their children to school, working women cycling to their offices, and beret-sporting old men out walking their dogs.

After a long spell of declining birthrates, the numbers have charted a steady increase over the past decade, evening out at roughly two children per woman of childbearing age. This increase is due in large part to the continued creation of family-friendly social policies and financial incentives. Lifespans in France tend to be on par with the rest of Western Europe: 77.9 years for men, and 84.4 years for women—not bad, considering the number of cigarettes inhaled by the general population. (One quarter of all French women smoke, and a full third of men.)

WEATHER

It's safe to say that France is a four-season country, but the winter you get in Paris is definitely not the same one you'll experience in Nice (winter in the capital is guaranteed to be considerably colder and a few shades grayer than in its southern cousin). Often referred to as having a temperate climate, France actually claims four distinct climatic zones wherein the proximity to oceans and mountains dictate the amount of heat or cold you'll experience throughout the year.

The north of France holds the honor of that oft-touted temperate climate, with cool springtime temperatures; warm summers; cold, wet winters; and a mild autumn. You can also expect year-round rain showers—summer in the capital may mean dramatic thunderstorms and spirited downpours, while Brittany and Normandy are a veritable wetfest throughout the winter, which makes for a verdant paradise.

The climate along the Atlantic coast stretching down to Bordeaux is classified as "maritime," meaning the sun shines nearly as bright year-round as it does along the Mediterranean, but the North Atlantic Drift moderates the temperatures so it's never extremely hot nor cold. The further you inch along the sandy white beaches toward the Pyrénées, the more rainfall you can expect in winter. The maritime climate also plays host to the "June gloom" phenomenon, which socks those pretty beaches beneath a blanket of fog for the first half of summer.

A mountain climate reigns in the Alps, ushering in bitterly cold winters with generous and predictable snowfall; cool, wet springs; mild summers; and a nippy autumn. Ski resorts see avalanches regularly in the wintertime, and the southeastern river valleys experience an occasional flash flood in the warmer months.

The renowned Mediterranean climate, consisting of year-round sunshine and mild winters, is tempered by the Mistral, a relentless wind that whips down through the Rhône River Valley most winters and often through the spring. You can see the Mistral's legacy in the cypress trees hugging the Provençal coastline, hunched over like old crones trying to escape the brunt of the wind. While the punishing nature of this unique meteoric phenomenon is known to keep the locals locked indoors for days on end, the wind is, in part, what gives the Mediterranean its prized climate. It blows all the detritus from the air and sucks the moisture out with it, leaving the terrain sun-drenched, dry, and clear.

Giant whirling wind turbines, towering high on the hills above the Western Mediterranean coast, harness the mighty Mistral winds and generate power for the region, but they're a source of contention among locals. Are they an environmentalist's answer to an impending energy crisis or an eyesore marring the pristine landscape? It depends entirely on whom you ask.

FLORA AND FAUNA

Before the industrial revolution in the mid-19th century, when forests and woodlands were razed to lay the foundation for industrial agriculture and an emerging urbancentric way of life, France teemed with diverse wildlife and plant species. Now untamed wilderness has given way to structured farming, formal parks and gardens, and concentrated urbanism, but within the man-made order you can still find natural pockets of biodiversity.

Plane trees dominate the picturesque Parisian streetscape, lining up majestically along the Champs Elysée and every other major thoroughfare in the French capital. But oak, beech, poplar, and chestnut trees are the scene stealers throughout the rest of France. In the mountainous eastern regions, coniferous pines and spruce stretch skyward against an evergreen backdrop, and in the spring and summer, the Alps explode in a riot of wildflowers, inviting the intrepid rambler to take a nature hike among them.

France is an important flower-growing region for the world's perfume industry; the perfume capital of the world is inarguably the Provençal city of Grasse. Lavender, jasmine, and roses are cultivated here, and the city hosts two important flower festivals each year in honor of the aromatic blooms. If you're prone to allergy flare-ups, you can expect them here and elsewhere along the southern coast in the springtime, when the bright yellow mimosa and other pollen-heavy flowers begin to blossom.

© AURELIA D'ANDREA

The food shopping experience is an important part of daily life.

To visit an outdoor market in France is to experience the country's edible bounty in miniature. Mushrooms—from the legendary black truffles to woodsy morels and bright yellow girolles—grow wild in every corner of the country and are a point of culinary pride. But don't think about harvesting any you stumble upon without seeking permission. French law dictates that mushrooms belong to owner of the land they grow on, so getting the all-clear before harvesting will help circumvent any unnecessary visits to the *préfecture de police.*

The most beloved crop grown in France is surely the grape, with dozens of varieties produced for both *la table* (table grapes) and for that bottle of *vin rouge* you'll be sipping with your next meal. At outdoor markets, it's customary to sample the wares before buying; just ask for *un petit goût*—especially if the heavenly purple Muscat grapes are on offer. Apples are the most popular fruit consumed in France, and, like grapes, they are also transformed into beverages; in this case, cider and that potent elixir Calvados, both of which have been produced in Normandy for nearly 500 years.

Despite a long tradition of hunting in the countryside, wild boar and deer still manage to survive in French forests, but the wildlife you're most liable to stumble upon throughout the country is the ubiquitous *lapin.* Rabbits have proven to be particularly adaptable creatures, burrowing holes along the runways at Charles de Gaulle airport and proliferating with healthy vigor in urban parks from coast to coast. The farther you move away from urban centers, the more likely you are to spot the foxes, badgers, and martens that also make their home here.

Migrating birds—ducks and geese—make temporary pit stops in France along their migratory routes, and pheasant, partridge, and gulls linger as year-round residents. In the southern river delta known as the Carmague, there's even a rare species of pink flamingo that's flourishing, thanks to a bountiful =plankton growing in the brackish waters. For those who prefer a more animal-friendly sport than hunting, birdwatching is a good option, with plentiful opportunities for the would-be ornithologist.

Social Climate

Several years into the global financial crisis, France is feeling the economic strain as much as the rest of the world. Unemployment is up, petty crime is on the rise, and creative responses to social problems are becoming more common—the wave of bossnappings by factory workers fearful of losing their

LINGUA FRANCA

Language helps define a culture, but what happens when a culture defined as "French" speaks multiple languages? The official language of France may very well be French, but dozens of ancient regional dialects are alive and well here, from Alsacien and Breton to Gascon and Lyonnais. You'll also hear Flemish near the Belgian border, German and Swiss in the east, Italian on the Riviera, and Arabic in every city throughout the country.

For centuries, these "second" languages were subject to government-sponsored censorship, specifically through exclusion within the centralized education system as a means of retaining cultural dominion. But the powers that be needn't have fretted – the population of metropolitan France has reached 64 million, but French is spoken by more than three times that many people worldwide. Today, foreign languages and regional dialects are taught in public schools, but there's still a bit of resistance toward the effect of globalization on this component of French culture.

In 2010, the government held a contest inviting students to invent new French-sounding replacements for the current crop of Anglophone buzzwords impinging on French youth vernacular. Those up on the chopping block included the threatening "buzz," "chat," and "newsletter." The winning stand-ins were determined to embody a more French-ish *je ne sais quoi*. Do they? You be the judge:

Out with the Old English	In with the New French
buzz	*ramdam*
chat	*éblabla*
newsletter	*infolettre*
talk	*débat*
tuning (slang for customizing your car)	*bolidage*

jobs is testament to that. Even though union membership is waning, the tradition of the non-violent *grève* (strike) lives on. The masses—young and old, male and female—take to the streets several times a year to protest the rising retirement age and other threats to the French lifestyle. To the untrained eye, it sometimes looks as if France's social order is spiraling out of control, but it's really just par for the course in a country with a long history of social action and galvanizing for a cause.

Ever since Nicolas Sarkozy was inaugurated as president of the republic in 2007, he has moved forward on his campaign promises to curb crime and combat illegal immigration. His push to send Paris's Romany population back to Eastern Europe in the summer of 2010 was met with worldwide accusations of racism, as well as cheers from anti-immigration hardliners. But for some, these center-right maneuverings aren't enough. Far-right political factions—most notably the Front National party—continue to capitalize on France's growing pains and social stumbling blocks, using a handful of isolated incidents to promote a nationalistic agenda. However, the party's shrinking numbers hint at a failed effort.

Thankfully, it's not all doom and gloom in the land of the Gauls. In spite of a sluggish economy, free enterprise is finally catching on here as an idea, and newly relaxed tax laws for small businesses have spawned a wave of entrepreneurship. As foreign immigration continues to change the face of France, it is also reshaping ideas inside contemporary art, politics, and social policy, building onto an already impressive foundation. Could the collective chokehold on the past be slowly loosening its grip? Time will tell for certain, but all the elements are in place for a modern French renaissance.

The next presidential election, which will take place in April 2012, is likely to see current president Nicolas Sarkozy making his second bid for the office against his close contender from the last election, Socialist Party candidate Ségolène Royale, as well as Jean-Marie Le Pen of the Front National, whose party numbers have been declining steadily over the last decade. Backlash against Sarkozy's right-leaning policies may translate into a strong show of support for the left-leaning Royale, who has historically structured her platform around bridging the gap between the classes and expanding the state-sponsored welfare system.

FRANCE AND FOREIGNERS

For centuries, foreigners by the boatload have flocked to France in search of political exile, freedom of artistic expression, and unfettered adventure. Writers from Ernest Hemingway to Adam Gopnik have parlayed their fabled expatriate experience into a literary canon that continues to enthrall and entice new generations of immigrants, but it's easy to focus on the fantasy and forget the reality of moving abroad. In France, the success of your individual experience hinges greatly on whether or not you make an effort to assimilate quietly into the local culture.

Most French men and women will tell you that their country is a place where tolerance is exercised—if you play by the rules. Tune into the local frequency, and you'll feel the sense of "sameness" that permeates French society, from the standardized education model to the way public parks are designed to the uniform manner in which people dress. Uniqueness isn't a prized quality here in the same way as it is in North America; in France, upholding the status quo means maintaining order, and that's the way the French like it. This commitment to homogeneity is palpable on many levels, and it sometimes comes cloaked in

EXPECT THE UNEXPECTED: CULTURE SHOCK

Name: Karin Bates
Age: 42
Hometown: Denver, Colorado
Current city: Paris

Karin moved to France for love – not for love of the country, but for a fellow American who has made his home here for 20 years. Karin's experience adapting to the French way of life is an ongoing process, and nearly three years later, she's still settling in.

In her own words: "One thing I did not anticipate before moving to France was experiencing culture shock. I'd lived and worked in China before, and while I felt culture stress there, I think what hit me in France was more profound than what I experienced in China. This probably had more to do with my age and stage in life than about uprooting and moving to another country, but it was a challenge I didn't expect. One way I helped myself though the transition was by starting a blog. Getting out and experiencing Paris, facing my fears, and then writing about it has benefitted me the most. It's also helped me connect with my fellow Parisians and develop a support system of friends.

On a pragmatic level, getting ordinary things done can be challenging here. Some of this is due more to big city living than it is to being 'French,' but sometimes it's frustrating that I can't just pull my car up to Super Target, load up, drive it all home, and be done with shopping. Instead, Paris living means going to three or four stores to get everything I want – some stores have product X, while others have Y; there is no easy way to get it all in one place. Also, getting laundry done with French-style washers (and dryers, if one has one, which we don't) is a hassle. I sometimes really miss dryer-dried towels. I handle this by learning to accept that life here is just a different way of living – and also by complaining about it with other expats when it gets too tiresome."

© SOPHIA PAGAN/WWW.SOPHIAPAGAN.COM

Get used to store-hopping to buy everything on your shopping list.

the separation-of-church-and-state veil. In a notable example, the 2004 ban on headscarves in French public schools stirred heated public debate, prompting some pundits to call it an act of "neocolonialism."

Since the early 20th century, France has developed repatriation schemes loaded with seductive promises of all-expenses-paid travel and cash bonuses to those willing to commit to quitting the country for good. The truth is that most of these programs target specific populations—unskilled workers, illegal migrants, and other candidates perceived as taking advantage of a generous public welfare system— while immigrants from the United States and other developed nations aren't generally regarded as part of the problem.

the Americanization effect seen on a café menu board

© JENNIFER PICKENS/BLACKBIRDPHOTO.COM

Politically, the French public view of the United States shifted with the departure of George W. Bush back in 2009. With the new American Democratic regime came a updated take on foreign policy, which heralded a newfound sense of solidarity between the two countries. Culturally, France has long resisted the Americanization effect inherent in globalization, but there's no denying the presence of Starbucks and "McDo's," as well as the popularity of long-running television shows like *The Simpsons* and *Friends*.

Since the French are purveyors of public politesse, you probably won't sense it if they *aren't* in the mood to welcome foreigners. If you swagger into town with a purple mohawk, tattoos, and a face full of piercings, you're likely to garner some down-the-nose looks (this is especially true in Paris)—but for the most part, your new neighbors will keep their thoughts about your appearance to themselves. The key to ingratiating yourself with the locals is as easy as learning a few key words of the language and always remembering to say *"merci"* (thank you) and *"s'il vous plaît"* (please). If you adopt the unifying national characteristic of formal politeness, the French will warm up to you in no time and will help ease the shock of transitioning to a country that is, indeed, very different from your own.

HISTORY, GOVERNMENT, AND ECONOMY

Wherever you are in France, you are never more than a few paces from some landmark that recalls the rich and illustrious France of antiquity. Triumphal arches conjure memories of great battles and conquests, majestic cathedrals recall the legends of martyred saints, and those turreted châteaux stand as reminders of the rise and fall of the French monarchy. Signs of more recent history are evident at every turn, too. It's hard to step across a rough patch of road that reveals a cluster of cobblestones without remembering the student uprising of 1968 and its famous freedom cry, "Beneath the paving stones, the beach"; plaques commemorating World War II feature prominently in most provincial towns. In other words, finding a corner of the country that doesn't overflow with profound historical significance is next to impossible.

Tucked among the symbolic remnants of yore are emblems of modern France that hint at what sort of potential the future holds. In multicultural urban

© CAROLECASTELLI/123RF.COM

metropolises, thriving art scenes driven by the younger generations continue to propel France to the forefront of the avant-garde movement. Daring culinary experimentation is staking its claim amid the old-guard, *très* traditional *cuisine Française* in cutting-edge restaurants, and France keeps surprising the rest of the world with the realization of novel ideas from wine vending machines to the public bicycle system, Vélib'.

Above all, the French themselves represent the spectacular convergence of old and new. Immigrants in traditional West African boubous and dashikis mingle at the markets with men in djellabas and women in hijabs, modern-day reminders of France's colonial past. A population in flux means more diversity: gay, straight, Muslim, Jewish, old, young, conservative, liberal. Active participation in politics, as evidenced by high voter turnout—the last presidential election drew 84 percent of eligible voters, versus 63.6 percent in the U.S.—reflects an empowered population with a vested interest in creating a 21st-century society that meets the basic needs, and quite often the wants, of every citizen.

History

PREHISTORIC FRANCE

In 1940, four teenage boys spelunking in the bucolic town of Montignac, in the Dordogne Valley, accidentally discovered an ancient treasure trove that put France on the map as an important source of prehistoric riches. The cave paintings of Lascaux, dating back nearly 20,000 years to the upper Paleolithic period, feature larger-than-life-size renderings of horses, bison, bears, and other animals, hinting at the hunter-gatherer civilization's two preoccupations: sourcing an adequate food supply and avoiding becoming someone else's *déjeuner*.

Beyond providing clues about the eating habits of early humans, these vivid murals support the theory that Cro-Magnons were not just modern humankind's closest ancestors but possibly the earliest French aesthetes; decorative objets d'art ranging from primitive statuettes to more ornate pottery have been discovered in many French cave dwellings. Fashion before function? Indeed. Damage from human traffic prompted officials to close the Lascaux caves in the early 1960s, but an artificially re-created Lascaux II, complete with reproduction murals, opened 20 years later and now welcomes thousands of visitors each year.

The early hunter-gatherer civilization that thrived throughout southern

France, from the Dordogne to the Mediterranean, fed on the abundant plant and animal life that flourished along the waterways. Homo sapiens mastered the art of tool-making for hunting and ultimately evolved their tools to adapt to a more sedentary agricultural society that followed the hunter-gatherer epoch. It was during this period that *Canis familiaris*—hunter, protector, and friend—was domesticated in France, solidifying its status within the French family structure.

THE CELTS AND THE ROMANS

On the outskirts of the tiny seaside village of Carnac, in the far west region of Brittany, rows upon rows of lichen-covered stones rise up from the grassy fields, looking very much like an army of frozen soldiers standing sentinel over the windswept terrain. These Celtic megaliths, known as menhirs, date from the Neolithic period. They are not as well known as their celebrated neighbors at Stonehenge, but their historical significance in France is on par with that of their British counterparts. How the heavy stones, each of which weighs tons, got there is an unsolved mystery—but the historical consensus is that they were arranged here by the early Celts, who settled in France beginning as early as 8000 B.C. Debate continues about the stones' original purpose, but it was most likely related to astrological forecasting or religious worship.

© SOPHIA PAGAN/WWW.SOPHIAPAGAN.COM

Rome or Nimes? Relics of ancient civilizations abound throughout France.

Mysterious origins aside, modern France has embraced its ancient Celtic roots through music festivals, literature, and efforts to keep the Breton language alive. Even the fictional character Obélix, from the beloved comic book series *Asterix,* is a menhir sculptor by trade, often depicted lugging around one of the giant stones on his enormous back.

Skip forward a few millennia from the Neolithic period to the 1st century B.C., when Julius Caesar and his massive army of 65,000 men marched into France with an eye on transforming the country into the newest corner of the Roman empire. In 49 B.C., after nine years of near-constant battle, their conquest was complete. Their legacy was sealed with the introduction of a newly revamped centralized political system, the introduction of the Latin language, and an art-and-architecture overhaul that gave France a distinctly Roman aesthetic. In the southern city of Nimes, the "Rome of France," a well-preserved amphitheater hosts gladiator reenactments for enthralled crowds of tourists, and other relics—aqueducts, arches, forums—remind the contemporary population of the lasting influence of the Roman reign.

STORMING OF THE BASTILLE AND THE REVOLUTION

Long before a mob of angry men marched toward the Bastille prison on the infamous gray and dreary afternoon of July 14, 1789, discontent had been brewing among the French common class. While the First Estate (nobility) and Second Estate (clergy) were essentially exempted from taxation, the Third Estate—the bulk of the population, made up of middle-class merchants and farming peasants—was left to pay the price for an overindulgent parade of kings, beginning with Louis XIV and ending with Louis XVI and his queen, Marie Antoinette.

As the country sank into bankruptcy, the commoners of the Third Estate felt the sting the sharpest. The price of bread, their primary food staple, had risen so high that the average family spent 80 percent of its income just to feed itself. Unemployment had reached frightening highs of nearly 50 percent, and the burden of heavy taxation showed no signs of ebbing. Meanwhile, Madame Deficit, as the spendthrift queen was nicknamed, continued to indulge in her excessive shopping habits while her king struggled to keep all the segments of French society in a state of relative calm.

When the alienated public learned that they would be denied voting privileges at a representational meeting of the Estates General, social discontent reached a fever pitch. Instead of sulking, the people formed a new national assembly and, when the king saw he had no hope of wielding his absolute power against the growing legions of discontent citizens, he struck a deal: We'll make it formal, he suggested, with a newly established National Assembly, wherein each Estate will have equal representation. Sovereignty of the people in, absolute monarchy out. This was the first revolutionary act. The storming of the part-prison, part-munitions warehouse known as the Bastille was next.

While the events of July 14 were more symbolic than truly revolutionary—there were only seven prisoners being held at the Bastille at the time, and the amount of arms collected was negligible—it is recognized as such because it returned power to the people after a long spell of rather tyrannical rule. Not long afterward, King Louis XVI relinquished his governing power, though he was left with the honorary title of King of the French. He held this new post until being tried and convicted of treason, then guillotined in front of a public audience in Paris's Place de la Révolution (now Place de la Concorde) in January 1793. His wife of 23 years, the reviled Marie Antoinette, was beheaded in the same spot nine months later.

Less than a month after the Bastille drama unfolded, a 17-point blueprint for a new constitution was drafted. The Declaration of the Rights of Man—a pastiche of ideas borrowed from the Declaration of Independence and the English Bill of Rights—proclaimed that the law exists to support and carry out the idea that every French citizen is born equal and with inalienable rights; that man is entitled to freedom of speech and freedom of religion; and that he is innocent until proven guilty. The 10-year revolutionary period was marked by brief changes in control, juggled in turn by the middle-class liberals, the radical revolutionaries, and the counter-revolutionaries whose champion, Napoléon Bonaparte, helped cement France's future as a global powerhouse. On September 21, 1792, the French royalty was abolished and, amid much celebration by the people, the First Republic, founded on the principles of *liberté, égalité,* and *fraternité,* was born.

NAPOLÉON BONAPARTE AND THE FIRST REPUBLIC

Even before he became emperor of France, in 1804, Napoléon Bonaparte reigned as a well-respected military leader in the French Revolution whose ambition for power matched his skill at war. Throughout his adventurous life, he earned a reputation as both a misogynist and a genius, but there's no debating the petite corporal's legacy as a reformer in the areas of education, religion, and government.

Before the monarchy was dissolved, education was a privilege extended primarily to the wealthy. Napoléon believed that developing a strong, unified population began with education—for boys in particular—and under his leadership, a uniform system of post-elementary schools called *lycées* was established. Through these education hubs, which most closely resemble North American high schools, a unified body of thought could be transmitted to generations of moldable minds. This is still the basis for today's highly centralized French public school system, which continues to preach loyalty to the republic and dictates which path a young student will follow later in life.

Revamping the dominant role of the Catholic church became an obsession for Napoléon I, who began this project at his coronation, which was completely

detail of Jean-Pierre Cortot's *The Triumph of Napoleon in 1810* on the Arc de Triomphe

devoid of any religions pomp and circumstance. He bucked tradition by deny-ing Pope Pius VII the honor of crowning him the new emperor, but he wasn't anti-church. Napoléon saw the power that religion had in the lives of French citizens, and he merely wanted to seize control of that. With the signing of the Concordat, Napoléon got his wish, gaining the right to choose bishops and take control of land previously belonging to the church.

Not long after being crowned emperor, Napoléon made one major restruc-turing move: The constitution, known as the Rights of Man, was transformed into the Napoleonic Code. For some, this was a distinct advantage: Special privileges and feudal advantages for the wealthy were effectively abolished, which was good for the 99 percent of the population that fell into the common class. Religious freedom was also guaranteed, as was the right to a trial before being sentenced for a crime. For others, the changes weakened their status. Women and children were essentially deemed the property of their husbands and fathers, and women were stripped of the right to buy or sell property. The freedom of the press suffered, too, with Napoléon famously proclaiming that "if the press is not controlled, I shall not remain in power three days." But it's probably safe to say that Napoléon's good deeds outweighed the bad. The public works projects he commissioned—wide boulevards, shipping canals, and the famous Arc de Triomphe—are the modern-day symbolic reminders of the diminutive leader's vision of France.

FIRST AND SECOND WORLD WARS

When Archduke Franz Ferdinand was shot and killed by a Serbian assassin in Sarajevo on June 28, 1914, the Austro-Hungarian government didn't waste any time before declaring war on Serbia. Soon, one country after another was at war with its enemy, but World War I wasn't *officially* called until Austria's strongest ally, Germany, declared war on Russia.

As a Serbian ally, France was drawn into the mix, but there was no widespread public support for this war. Speaking on behalf of the pacifist community, French Socialist Party leader and lefty newspaper publisher Jean Jaurès called for peace, but he was silenced by a bullet fired by an overzealous pro-war French nationalist on July 31, just a month after war was declared. Four years later, on November 11, 1918, the signing of an armistice agreement put an end to the long, catastrophic conflict.

The final tally of France's dead reached nearly 1.4 million, and the number of wounded a staggering three million. Birthrates dropped, the national debt exploded, president Napoléon III was ousted, and a third French Republic was declared. It took years before France recovered, and when it did, it didn't get much of a breather before being thrust back into the cold embrace of another devastating world war.

No event in modern history has had as profound an effect on the French national psyche as World War II, especially in the way it has shaped modern French identity and solidified the necessity of social unity. In 1939, after Germany invaded Poland, France (a Polish ally) and Great Britain jointly declared war on Germany. By 1940, France had surrendered to the Germans, who began a humiliating occupation of France that lasted four years.

On October 24, 1940, after the French had already surrendered to German forces, a new regime took control of the country, collaborating with the Nazis but still retaining some small level of autonomy. The Vichy Government, led by marshal Philippe Pétain, was merely a French extension of the Nazi establishment, and the effects of this collaboration spawned its own post-traumatic stress disorder: the Vichy Syndrome.

Through the hardship of occupation and war, a sense of solidarity grew among the greater French community. Thousands of men and women joined together to form the French Resistance, and volunteer armies from North and West Africa sprang up to fight alongside the French army. Mini-armies began to sprout, too. The most significant of these independent brigades were the *maquis,* small groups of men and women who worked in concert with the resistance movement against German forces. Rather than be conscripted into the

German workforce, they took to the hills with their guns and ammunition, battling long and hard in their signature Basque berets.

In 1944—the same year in which French women earned the right to vote—the Allied Forces, at long last, liberated France from Germany's iron grip. After a triumphant promenade down the Champs-Élysées, general Charles de Gaulle addressed his fellow citizens in a celebrated speech thanking them for their concerted efforts, closing with a fervent *"Vive la France!"*

The memory of occupation is never far from the modern French person's consciousness, yet there isn't a palpable sense of melancholy rooted in those memories either. *C'est la vie,* say the French, but let us not forget completely *les années noires.*

MODERN FRANCE

The Fourth Republic sprung up on the heels of World War II, with general Charles de Gaulle, France's trusted and revered wartime chief, serving a brief stint as head of the provisional postwar government. He stepped down not long after his appointment but was elected president of France more than 10 years later, in 1958, marking the beginning of the fifth and current republic.

After a successful first term, he was reelected to the country's top post, which he served until retiring from politics in 1968, when his viewpoints were falling out of favor with the young postwar generation. The end of his political career was punctuated by a wave of social unrest throughout France, beginning at the universities and ending at the heart of the industrial sector: the factory.

In the spring of 1968, what started as a couple of small student protests against comingling of the sexes in student housing at the University of Nanterre and Paris's Sorbonne quickly morphed into something out of a fictional police drama: students and armed riot police going toe-to-toe on the streets; hundreds of young men and women being thrown to the ground and arrested; tear gas shot from cannons, filling the air with a thick haze. Three days later, on May 6, more than 20,000 students, professors, and supporters marched through the streets of the capital to call public attention to the overzealous response by the police to a simple, nonviolent campus protest—and again were met with baton-wielding riot police, tear gas, and violent arrests.

The great *manifestations* (political protests) lasted for days, virtually halting all normal activity in Paris and its close suburbs. Brick throwing and Molotov cocktail tossing brought the city to a standstill. Students, borrowing ideas from anarchist ideology and using language tinged with Marxist rhetoric, demanded social change to benefit the people rather than the powers in charge.

Events took a turn for the worse when a 17-year-old high school student was

© SOPHIA PAGAN/WWW.SOPHIAPAGAN.COM

Police morph into riot squads during *grève* (strike) season.

killed by riot police in Paris's Latin Quarter on June 10; reverberation was felt acutely during the following weeks. Simultaneously, discontent that had been percolating in France's automobile factories reached a boiling point, prompting a frustrated labor force to engage in both sit-ins and walkouts. Workers at Renault, Citroën, and Peugeot voiced their own demands for a set minimum wage, salary increases, and reduced work hours. At a Peugeot factory, two workers were killed by police, prompting another wave of discontent to ripple through the country. Walkouts at banks, public transportation hubs, department stores, and even hospitals paralyzed France. An estimated 10 million *grèvists* (strikers) from Toulouse to Saint-Nazaire took to the streets in protest throughout May 1968, and made their thoughts about France's old-school, outdated political direction known in their cry: *"Adieu,* de Gaulle!"

The government reacted with tough-guy posturing, threatening an official state of emergency if things didn't simmer down. They finally did. The government met the demands of the automobile unions, offering a shorter work week, increased salaries, and an increased minimum wage, which the unions accepted, and students returned to their university lecture halls. Yet as daily life settled back into a state of normalcy, the days were numbered for de Gaulle's government. The aftereffects on French society were still being registered decades later, with political analysts referring to the period as "a revolution" with many of the same attributes of revolutions past. A body of rebel artwork—graffiti, protest posters—produced during the era survives in archival galleries as testament to the social upheaval.

In the decades that followed, France underwent several presidential shifts: Georges Pompidou ('69–'74), Valéry Giscard-d'Estaing ('74–'81), socialist François Mitterrand ('81–'95), and former prime minister and Paris mayor Jacques Chirac ('95–'07). Mitterrand's presidency marked the first time a leader on the political left had taken that office, and during his tenure he abolished the death penalty and initiated a moratorium on nuclear testing.

Chirac, who founded the center-right RPR (Rally for the Republic) party, led France with a more conservative vision, but he will probably always be remembered in North America for taking an active stand against the U.S. invasion of Iraq. (Remember "Freedom Fries"?) The French supported his opposition to the war, but his domestic policies left much to be desired among French voters, who ranked him the most unpopular president of the Fifth Republic in 2007.

Chirac's successor, former minister of the interior Nicolas Sarkozy, was voted in as the sixth president of the Fifth Republic on May 7, 2007. The son of a Greek-Jewish mother and a French-Hungarian father, the former lawyer promised to give France a good kick in the pants to bolster the economy, get tough on immigration, and reform the social welfare system. Part of his reform agenda included tightening access to foreign student visas, which he saw as an easy ticket for potential ne'er-do-wells to obtain residency status. Now facing dismal popularity figures in his fifth year as president, Sarkozy can still look back on his career with a sense of pride. He accomplished many of the goals he set out for himself: passing a law restricting two-term presidential limits, easing taxation to encourage entrepreneurship, and ending the 35-hour workweek.

Government

As a representative democracy, the Republic of France is ruled by a president who is voted in by the public and eligible for a maximum of two five-year terms. The president appoints a prime minister and a cabinet to help run the show, but there's no question who holds the top spot—and with it the larger burden of responsibility for ruling the country. In addition to ensuring that the constitution is upheld, the president enacts French laws, oversees the military, and has the ability to dissolve the French parliament. The president must also solicit the signature of his prime minister for every official document he signs, with the exception of dissolving parliament.

On the legislative end, parliament is made up of a 577-member lower house called the National Assembly, whose representatives, called deputies, are elected directly by the public to five-year terms. The 321-member upper parliament, or senate, is voted in by an electoral college representing each of the 92 departments, overseas territories, and French citizens living abroad; each member serves six-year terms. Together, the two houses meet for nine-month sessions that begin in October and end in June, voting on issues as varied and

THE FIFTH REPUBLIC'S HONORARY ODD COUPLE

He's a diminutive yet powerful politician and orator, and she's a former supermodel with skyscraper legs and a trail of ex-boyfriends that reads like a who's who of alpha males: Mick Jagger, Eric Clapton, Donald Trump. Judging by appearances, they're a bona fide odd couple, but after a whirlwind courtship and multiyear high-profile marriage, French president Nicolas Sarkozy and his first lady, Carla Bruni, have managed to keep the flames of passion burning.

It was love at first sight for "President Bling-Bling" and blue-eyed Bruni, who were introduced at a dinner party in late 2007 by mutual friend Jacques Séguéla, who thought the single singer-model and the Fifth Republic's new president would make a dynamic pair. He was right. That night, the duo left the party à deux, giving the tabloid media something juicy to chew on as the country adapted to its new leader.

Bruni, who bears more than a passing resemblance to Sarko's second wife, Cécilia Attias, was born in Italy in 1968, the daughter of a pianist mother and a composer father who was also the heir to a tire fortune. When Bruni was eight years old, she and her family moved to Paris, where she spent her formative years studying at elite private schools before launching her modeling career and cultivating her maneater reputation in the 1980s.

Sarkozy, 13 years his wife's senior, began his career in politics in the 1970s, when he served as mayor of the Parisian suburb of Neuilly-sur-Seine. He married young and had two sons with his first wife, Marie-Dominique. While they were still married, Sarko began an affair with Cécilia, who was his wife's best friend. Their marriage, the second for each, lasted 11 years and produced another son, Louis.

Three months after their first date, Sarkozy and Bruni swapped "I do"s at the Elysée Palace before jetting off on an Egyptian honeymoon. Since then, Bruni had grown into her role with a graceful ease, launching an eponymous foundation dedicated to ending child illiteracy and fighting AIDS (her brother died of the disease), and holding her own among world leaders at state functions. But despite these good works, readers of the French magazine *VSD* voted Madame Sarkozy the most irritating woman in France in 2010.

Irritating or not, Bruni and Sarkozy's relationship looks durable several years into their marriage. The pair is regularly photographed – he on tiptoe to compensate for the four-inch height difference – looking very much in love and very much the image of sexy, modern France.

contentious as gay marriage (which received a *"non"* vote in January 2010) and voluntary euthanasia (also voted down in 2010).

France has a multiparty system that spans the spectrum from the extreme right to the extreme left, but a few parties dominate, including Sarkozy's UNP (Union pour un Mouvement Populaire); the left-leaning Socialists, the far-right Front National, and communists and greens pick up the remaining seats in parliament. Regional elections are held every four years, departmental representatives and city council members are elected every six, and elections are always held on Sundays, which helps ensure a solid voter turnout. The French take the voting process quite seriously, and the rules governing campaign advertising and the prognostication of results on the day of the election are tightly controlled.

If no candidate wins more than 50 percent of the vote in a presidential election, a runoff election is held. The 2007 election pitted Socialist party candidate Ségolène Royal against the UNP's Sarkozy, with Sarkozy ultimately winning with 53.04 percent of the vote.

Though President Sarkozy is eligible for reelection, his future looks a little iffy. In the March 2010 regional elections, his party lost a number of parliamentary seats, while the Europe Écologie and Socialist parties picked up control in a number of regions. There's no telling whether Sarkozy's center-right administration will compel French voters to swing further to the left or to the right in the 2012 presidential election, but the results of a 2011 opinion poll published in French daily newspaper *Le Parisien* show that 46 percent of those polled are "completely in disagreement" with the ideas proffered by the Front National.

Economy

After World War II, France boomeranged back into shape with unrivaled optimism and vitality. Those three fruitful decades even earned a special moniker: les Trente Glorieuses, or the Glorious Thirty. Under de Gaulle's leadership, an initial five-year plan was put into place, launching public works projects and creating a climate ripe for new industries. French factories were overhauled, churning out products for a postwar population that skyrocketed to numbers not seen for more than 100 years. This baby boom sparked a cycle of production and consumption that helped keep the economy moving. New motorways were built to keep up with the number of new cars on the roads, and by 1960, the French owned more automobiles than refrigerators.

The big shift from rural to urban that took place in the 1960s and '70s translated to overcrowding in the major cities. To meet the needs of this expanding population, giant housing developments mushroomed outside the clogged metropolises, and the *banlieue* was born. The sense of France in transition was palpable nationwide.

With the establishment of the European Union and the introduction of a single currency, trade barriers were torn down and competition increased, generating new revenue streams that flowed throughout Europe. But the latest global economic crisis has done a lot to destabilize the French economy and the faith of the French people with regard to their future economic security. To ease the strain of the current crisis, the Sarkozy government has passed a number of stimulus packages, but France still faces high unemployment (10 percent) and public debt (for which the government is trying to compensate by curtailing politicians' wine-fueled, expense-paid lunches).

Among the most critical issues facing French voters today is coming to terms with the idea that the social safety net that has supported them for so long may sink under its own weight. Throughout September 2010, *grèvists* again took to the streets of cities and towns throughout France to protest Sarkozy's proposed revamp of the country's cushy pension plan. Without a workforce to pay for the system, said Sarkozy, there will be no money left in the coffers for retirees to pull from. The public didn't buy it, and over the course of several weeks, students, unionists, and office workers alike waved banners of protest in the streets, halting commuter traffic, disrupting fuel deliveries, and causing delays at airports and train stations nationwide. On October 23, 2010, much to the public's dismay, parliament passed Sarkozy's pension reform bill, raising the minimum retirement age to 62 and the full pension age to 67.

PEOPLE AND CULTURE

France is fertile ground for cultural stereotyping. Those tenacious mental renderings of a beret-clad, baguette-hugging, bicycle-riding population have been etched into our collective unconscious via film, fashion magazines, and yes, even holiday snapshots. More than anything, perhaps, the French are known 'round the world for their way of life, which focuses on maximizing sensual pleasures. The truth is, they do love their wining, dining, and song, but surprisingly, not a whole lot more than their European neighbors. Over the years, the French have abandoned some of their legendary habits in favor of newer, healthier ones (*le jogging,* anyone?).

Per capita wine consumption has plummeted by more than 50 percent since 1970, when the average Jacques quaffed 103.6 liters all on his own each year. The French do guzzle more booze than the Poles, the Dutch, or even tipplers in the UK, but Jacques still throws back fewer drinks than his Irish counterpart. The amount of bread consumed per day by the French has steadily dwindled over the last century (though you'd hardly know it from

Not a cliché: The street accordianist fills French *rues* with music.

the number of *boulangeries*), but the amount of yogurt, brie, and crème fraîche consumed has nearly doubled since the 1970s. Stroll down the dairy aisle at the nearest *hypermarché,* and you'll get a solid sense of how important the role of dairy is in the French diet. But an entire culture can't be distilled into a food-and-wine caricature.

Like their country, the French are complex, idiosyncratic, and a tad mysterious, which makes them all the more interesting. "French" has come to mean something different in the 21st century than in previous eras: It now means Algerian, Tunisian, Malian, Moroccan, Senegalese, and even American. Each of these immigrant populations has left its mark on the standard culture, producing something of a multicultural patchwork that gives France its special flavor.

Ethnicity and Class

One of the ideas propelling the French Revolution was that the social playing field could—and should—be leveled. Members of the proletariat, mostly working-class farmers and peasants, were fed up with being taxed while their upper-class comrades were exempt, and the clergy had had enough of the royals' having access to all the wealth. These issues germinated and sprouted into a rebellion, and subsequently the class system was abolished as members of the National Assembly renounced their class privileges.

No longer would the middle and lower classes be held liable for taxes that they could ill afford while the nobility class and clergy skirted by without paying a centime. The revolution gave birth to a new constitution, the cornerstone of which was the Declaration of the Rights of Man. This critical rulebook defined the future of the Republic, setting forth the novel idea that all men are created equal. In subsequent decades, the leadership grappled with the inconsistencies of that basic assertion, particularly in light of the fact that slave ownership was alive and well in the French colonies and the role of women remained subordinate to men. The declaration has been rewritten over the years (and renamed the Constitution), but its fundamental assertion remains a critical component of French identity.

Today, the issue of national identity is a hot topic in France, especially in light of the impending 2012 presidential election. The Front National's newest leader and candidate for the top spot, Marine Le Pen, inherited her father Jean-Marie's passion for a very, well, "French" version of France, and she has put the issue at the front and center of her party's platform. The Front National promulgates the idea that a more homogenous France can be restored with measures that include expulsion of certain populations—primarily Arab Muslims—and shoring up immigration laws to prevent what the party believes to be unbridled waves of unworthy foreigners. The Front National motto, "France for the French!", says it all.

Customs and Etiquette

One of the first things you'll notice about life in France is the distinct sense of politesse that pervades daily interactions. Neighbors greet each other with a friendly *bonjour* and *au revoir*, sales clerks will always refer to you as *madame*, *mademoiselle,* or *monsieur,* and most of the time, drivers will actually slow their Citroëns and Renaults down to a stop at crosswalks for pedestrians—which may or may not be a direct result of the Ministry of Transportation's efforts to establish a Day of Courtesy. More important than mimicking the French

CULTURE OF PESSIMISM?

Living in the land of camembert, champagne, and croissants is no insurance against the blues. Not only is France home to more antidepressant-poppers than any other country in the world, but it recently earned yet another not-so-coveted title: Most Pessimistic Nation. In a Gallup poll published in 2011, 61 percent of French respondents saw nothing but gray clouds in their bleak futures – a darker outlook than prognosticated by even their Afghan and Iraqi counterparts who participated in regional polls. This can be explained, psychiatrist Serge Hefez told reporters at *Le Parisien,* by the social welfare system. The broader the safety net, the greater one's fear of losing it all, and with recent cuts in government spending to curb the national deficit, panic and depression are beginning to rise. So what's a French person to do? Move to Vietnam, it seems, where the reported level of optimism remains among the highest in the world.

version of Emily Post is to simply treat everyone you encounter with respect. Do as the locals do and be liberal with your pleases and thank-yous. When boarding a train or a bus, step aside from the doorway to allow others to exit first. Offer your seat to older men and women, pregnant women, and parents juggling one or more children. The friendly smile and sincere thanks you'll get in return are worth it, and they contribute to the social order.

LINE JUMPING

One annoying exception to the standard French trend toward politeness is line jumping. It happens each and every day at Disneyland Paris, the local post office, and regional *hypermarchés:* A silver-haired granny or twentysomething hipster will glide in ahead of you, occasionally with cash in hand to announce the guaranteed swiftness of the impending transaction, with nary a glance in your direction, lest eye contact be made and guilt established. Fussing about this is rarely worth the effort, though it's very annoying.

PDAS (PUBLIC DISPLAYS OF ANGER)

The French are quirky, so it follows they would have quirky customs, many of which foreigners find simultaneously befuddling and charming. The tradition of the *bisou*—kissing on each cheek as a form of greeting—is so ingrained that kids in diapers are practically pros by the time they reach the Terrible Twos. The French are not entirely immune to the urge to flip out in horn-honking traffic, but road rage isn't practiced here the way it is in other countries. If you want to react in a manner befitting the locals, you'll learn to puff out your cheeks, throw up your hands, and say *"Oh la la la la"* like the rest, while leaving the shouting and aggressive driving maneuvers to the uncivilized world.

TIPPING

Many North Americans are pleased to discover that tipping is not mandatory or even expected in France. Restaurant work is a profession with a modicum of prestige attached to it, and because waitstaff earn a living wage and are entitled to full benefits, they aren't motivated to perform any better in expectation of a monetary bonus. However, at cafés, it's customary to leave any small coins floating around in your pocket on the table or counter, and many diners—if they feel like it—will leave a euro or two after a restaurant or brasserie meal. These little acts of generosity are entirely voluntary, and you shouldn't feel obligated to leave anything beyond what's tallied up on your *addition*.

INVITATION ETIQUETTE

Here are a few rules of thumb to commit to memory, just in case you are lucky enough to earn a coveted invitation to a French person's home. Many expats report never having received a party invitation, let alone a dinner invite, even after years of working with someone or decades of daily chats with the next-door neighbor. This is less about you and more about the separation of public and private life—a cultural idiosyncrasy that is sacrosanct to the French. But when that elusive invitation comes, arrive at your host's home 15 minutes late, bring flowers instead of wine (they've already selected the wine to drink that evening), and don't be afraid of "awkward" silences; think of them as food-enjoyment pauses instead.

Food

Some tourists come to France almost exclusively for the food, and no wonder: They really know what they're doing here when it comes to creating culinary magic. Standard, everyday French fare tends to fall into the "honest" category: What you see is what you get, with the unique selling point of being exceptionally well prepared and made with good-quality ingredients. Fancy, no; delicious, yes. From humble brasseries to revered Michelin-starred eateries, restaurant menus tend to reflect seasonal produce while adhering to a perennial list of *plats principals* (main courses): *poulet roti* (roast chicken), *steak frites* (steak and french fries), *steak tartare* (raw minced beef, sometimes mixed with

Bio (organic) food has become an important consideration in France.

Say "nay" to horse meat by skipping the *chevaline* butcher, identifiable by the horse head over the door.

egg and onion), *porc roti* (pork roast), *salade de chèvre chaud* (green salad with slices of warm goat cheese), and a variety of pasta dishes.

A lot of the meats served in France fall into categories many North Americans would file under politically incorrect. If eating baby animals is your thing, you're going to love dining in France: Veal is a popular meat, as is lamb. Foie gras, which translates as "fatty liver," is a specialty of the southwestern region; it's created by forcing a tube down a duck's or a goose's throat and pumping in an excessive quantity of grain. This causes the liver to inflate at an artificially induced rate. Expect to see lots of foie gras around the winter holidays, when it is marketed as a celebratory treat. Horse meat can still be found on restaurant menus, and butchers who sell it can be identified by the horse head mounted above the door, but overall its appeal is waning. That old culinary cliché, escargots, is alive and well, but oysters and mussels are more popular among French diners.

French fast food resembles its North American counterpart, though McDonald's offers wireless Internet, table service, and made-to-order burgers. A more traditional fast food is the crêpe. In big cities and small towns, look for stands, both permanent and mobile, where you can order sweet crêpes topped with everything from sugar and lemon juice to a thick slather of Nutella, or savory versions topped with *un oeuf* (an egg), *fromage* (cheese), *jambon* (ham), or any combination thereof. In Nice, they turn out a delectable local version of the crêpe made with chickpea flour, water, and olive oil called *socca*. Sprinkled with a bit of salt and pepper, this humble street food is elevated to heavenly status.

Vegetarians, vegans, and people with food allergies won't have trouble sourcing comestibles for home-cooked meals, but eating at restaurants can sometimes pose a challenge. Most restaurant staff doesn't understand non-religious dietary modifications or restrictions, and it's almost not worth explaining. Making food substitutions isn't part of the French dining-out style,

KING OF CAKES

It happens every year after the Christmas holiday, just as it has since the 15th century: *Boulangeries* throughout France set up their homogenous display of circular tarts, the shiny brown crusts topped with a golden crown signaling to passersby that Epiphany is just around the corner. For Christians, these *galettes des rois,* or kings' cakes, are symbolic reminders of the visit of the Magis to the infant Jesus. For the rest of us, they're just a delicious wintertime treat.

What makes these sweet confections so special isn't necessarily their decadently creamy frangipane interiors redolent of butter and almonds, but the other pleasant surprise they hold: the *fève.* Baked inside every *galette* is a tiny porcelain figurine – in the old days, they used a dried fava bean – that entitles you to wear the paper crown for a day, should you be lucky enough to find it in your slice.

Something about that *fève* brings out the cheating impulse in people, and many Frenchies admit they've sought out the slice with the most noticeable bump as a shortcut to earning the royal headpiece. (A well-prepared *galette,* any baker will tell you, will reveal no such telltale signs.) Holiday rule makers have found a way to encourage fair play: The youngest child at the Epiphany soirée decides who gets which slice of cake.

The frangipane-filled variety gets the most play, but the Provençal version of the *galette des rois* is worth a mention (and a taste). The crown-shaped ring of brioche is studded with candied fruit and coarse sugar, and, like its flat counterpart, also contains a *fève.* Besides the calories involved, there's only one downside to indulging in this annual tradition: Whoever earns that crown has to buy the next cake.

© SOPHIA PAGAN/WWW.SOPHIAPAGAN.COM

Galettes des rois, or kings' cakes, appear in *boulangerie* windows at Epiphany.

so if you have a wheat allergy, you're better off ordering things you know to be wheat-free. Vegans will need to master *"sans fromage, s'il vous plaît"* ("no cheese, please") when ordering pizza and sandwiches.

Gender Roles

As quick as the authors of the French revolution and the Declaration of the Rights of Man were to espouse *liberté, égalité,* and *fraternité* as the founding principles of the new republic, they kind of forgot a big hunk of the population: women. Women's rights and the ideas supporting them didn't really enter mainstream French discourse until fairly recently. The country's earliest outspoken feminists and women's rights advocates—such as Olympe de Gouges, who also advocated on behalf of minorities—were simply silenced by the guillotine for their uppity ideas about equality. Those early rabble-rousers brought the idea of gender equality to the forefront in the 18th century, but women were not given the right to vote until 1945.

World War II altered the male-female dynamic in profound ways, for better and for worse. During wartime, traditional gender roles took a back seat as women and men crawled through the trenches side by side in the resistance effort, bearing arms with equal strength and commitment to both personal survival and the protection of their country. When the war ended, society fell into recovery mode, followed by a slow and steady rebuilding of the economy. The shift from rural to urban and from agriculture to industrialization fostered a new middle class. After decades of declining birthrates, the postwar message broadcast toward women from the church, the government, and the media echoed loud and clear: "Stay home and have babies." Women listened; between 1943 and 1965, there were 14 million new additions to the French population. Thus began a return to the traditional family structure, with men reengaging in the burgeoning industrial workforce and women staying home, dutifully raising children, cooking meals in their shiny new kitchens, and otherwise presiding over the domestic realm.

In 1949, five years after women were given the right to vote, writer-philosopher Simone de Beauvoir penned *the* manifesto on French gender equality theory, *The Second Sex,* which is often credited for kick-starting the modern feminist movement in France. Her writing encouraged women to examine their role in society, to consider themselves as autonomous agents rather than merely inferior sidekicks to the dominant male power, and to "aspire to full membership of the human race." De Beauvoir's work heralded a new way of thinking that laid the groundwork for significant improvements in gender equality. In 1967, birth control was finally legalized in France, and the roaring baby boom slowed down considerably, beginning to rise again only in the early 21st century. This allowed women to consider their work potential outside the home.

France has sort of made up for its female-unfriendly past by bestowing specific social benefits on women for doing the one thing their male counterparts can't do: Bear children. Women are entitled to everything from a four-month federally mandated maternity leave (in contrast, employers in the U.S. are not required by law to offer any leave) to postnatal "vaginal rejuvenation therapy." (Really.) Those perks aside, women in France still have a long way to go before they reach true equality. Most medical school graduates are female but the majority of hospital heads are male, and women still earn 75 cents for every euro a man earns. Though they invest as many hours in working outside the home as men do, women carry the heavier burden in the domestic sphere. Women are still the primary caregivers for children and devote a larger chunk of time to housekeeping, grocery shopping, and other household chores.

GAY AND LESBIAN CULTURE

In the early 20th century, France—Paris in particular—attracted a wild and woolly lot of characters who defined themselves as "artists." Many of them also called themselves "gay." Even though the Assemblée Nationale didn't vote to decriminalize homosexuality until 1982, the closet door swung wide open throughout the early 20th century, and artists, intellectuals, and everyday

Paris's gay pride festival draws hundreds of thousands of participants and spectators.

DON'T ASK, DON'T TELL, DON'T QUESTION

Name: Owen Peery
Age: 39
Hometown: Syracuse, NY
Current city: Toulouse

Owen, a technology and e-learning consultant, moved to Toulouse with his French boyfriend in 2007. Before moving, the pair registered their relationship at the French embassy in Washington, DC, and secured "PACS" (Pacte Civile de Solidarité) status. Owen's thoughts about the French and their attitudes toward gay people are mixed. On one hand, France offers progressive social benefits, and on the other, old-fashioned mores seem to hold firm here – even within the gay community.

In his own words: "We were PACSed in 2007, and the most immediate benefit was that I *could* have come to France on a regular long-stay visa and be covered by Assurance Maladie, the national health insurance plan. However, if I'd gone this route, I wouldn't have been able to work – so instead I applied for a student visa. After my second year, I was able to convert my *carte de séjour* to a *vie privée familiale*, which expanded my ben-efits and gave me the right to work full-time.

Another benefit to being PACSed is that, in theory, it lowers your tax rate, but that supposes you earn enough to have to pay taxes. Up until 2010, that hasn't been much of a benefit because we haven't had much work. This past year, I had to pay about €175 in taxes. That's good news because it means I earned more money.

Generally, the gay community in Toulouse seems to be about 30 years behind the times, and that's being kind. Here's an example: One night, my boyfriend and I went out on the town in Toulouse with another gay friend of ours and his sister, who was visiting from out of town. We tried to go to a gay bar, but before we could get inside, we were stopped and told that no women were allowed in. I couldn't believe it. 'Only on Sundays,' they said. I'd never heard of such a thing! Apparently it's legal if it's a 'private' club, but in reality, it was just a neighborhood bar that managed to obtain private-club status, ostensibly to get around antidiscrimination laws. Still, it was very, very, very shocking to me."

folk resisted the urge to hide their sexuality from the judgmental eyes of the world. Gertrude Stein and her longtime partner, Alice B. Toklas, lived out and proud in Paris's Left Bank, as did Sylvia Beach, the respected proprietor of landmark bookstore Shakespeare & Company. Oscar Wilde, the great Irish writer entombed beneath a majestic headstone in Paris's famous Père-Lachaise cemetery, sought sanctuary in France after a horrible episode in which he was imprisoned in England for the crime of being gay. World War II was a dark era for gays and lesbians, who were shipped off with Jews, gypsies, and other "deviants" to concentration camps. But a lot has changed since then.

In 1999, the Assemblée Nationale passed a law to protect individuals in civil unions and extended this coverage to gay men and lesbians. PACS (Pacte Civile de Solidarité) allows gays and straights alike to register their partnerships and share in some of the social benefits and protections extended to married heterosexual couples. The PACS union is so popular that it's well on its way to eclipsing traditional marriage as the bond uniting most straight couples. In 2009, more than 170,000 French couples were "PACSed." In that same year, 200,000 couples married. In theory, based on the French constitution, France only recognizes *citoyens*; special rights are not accorded to these citizens with relation to their gender, sexual orientation, and religious preference.

Each June, gay pride festivals throughout France draw hundreds of thousands of participants and spectators. In Paris, openly gay mayor Bertrand Delanoë usually makes an appearance at the rainbow-heavy funfest as it weaves through the city, blasting techno music to enthusiastic crowds; and the city's gay hub, the Marais, begins to resemble a gay Disneyland in all the best ways. One way to get a sense of French ideas on homosexuality is by watching films with gay themes. Some of the most interesting, entertaining, and popular among the international crowd are *Côte d'Azur, Defense d'Aimer, Donne-moi le Main, Drôle de Felix, Entre Nous, French Twist, Je t'aime…moi non plus, Ma Vie en Rose, La Naissance de Pieuvres, Presque Rien,* and *Les Témoins.*

Religion

When the Romans conquered Gaul, in 58 B.C., they claimed their territory using an age-old approach: religious conversion. The tactic worked. More than 2,000 years later, Roman Catholicism is still the most widely claimed religious group in France, though it's difficult to say for sure—in 1872, the government banned the gathering of both religion- and ethnicity-related statistics. All information collected today is via voluntary polls. Recent figures point to the not-so-surprising fact that Roman Catholics are the reigning religious group; they claim 85 percent of the population, though most are largely thought to be nonpracticing, with a mere 12 percent attending mass on a regular basis. Muslims, Protestants, and Jews split the remaining 15 percent, and for the most part, everyone coexists peacefully.

THE JEWISH COMMUNITY

France is currently home to the largest Jewish population in all of Europe, with 600,000 members. Nearly two-thirds of those live in Paris, and smaller Jewish communities thrive in Marseille, Lyon, Toulouse, and Strasbourg. During the 1950 and '60s, the population grew when more than 200,000 Sephardic Jews from North Africa abandoned their homes in an extended exodus kickstarted by the Six-Day War. Settling primarily in the French capital, where a solid Jewish infrastructure including synagogues, *cacher* (kosher) restaurants and Hebrew schools was already in place, they formed new communities and assimilated into existing ones. Jewish artists Amedeo Modigliani and Marc Chagall came to France to work and live, and their creations are celebrated in art institutions nationwide, such as the Musée d'Orsay and the Paris Musée d'Art Moderne.

THE MUSLIM COMMUNITY

France also houses Europe's largest population of Muslims—more than six million, a full 10 percent of the population. In big cities such as Paris, Marseille, and Lyon, the

the minaret at Paris's largest Muslim mosque

© TAOLMOR/123RF.COM

distinctive, throaty chatter of Arabic fills the air, and street scenes are alive with women in hijabs, bustling halal butcher shops, and kebab joints. Fast food chains—notably Quick Burger, the French equivalent of Burger King— offer halal hamburgers to observant Muslims, to the chagrin of some political groups who see expanding menus as "preferential kowtowing." This is one of the selling points used by the Front National to promote its anti-immigration platform, suggesting that specialized menus create a sort of divide that isn't in line with "French values," in particular the separation of church and state. Despite these challenges, hundreds of mosques throughout the country help solidify a sense of community, and they often serve as all-in-one centers with hammams, daycare, and meals.

THE ROMAN-CATHOLIC TRADITION

At major Christian holidays, such as Christmas and Easter, you'll be reminded that this country is still Roman Catholic at heart, at least superficially. Christmas is celebrated with an endless parade of fanfare: Town halls are kitted out

France claims to be secular, but the government-sponsored Christmas trees indicate otherwise.

with giant Sapins de Noël; the *rues* and boulevards are strung with colorful lights; shops bust out the bows, balls, and flocking spray and go to town. Best of all, the *boulangeries* and patisseries churn out seasonal treats that people of all religious persuasions enjoy. The *bûche de Noël,* a cake baked in the shape of a log, is often decorated with tiny wintertime scenes, and the *galette des rois,* a frangipane-filled pastry eaten in celebration of Epiphany, comes with a hidden trinket and a paper crown that lets one lucky indulger be king or queen for the day.

The Arts

The earliest creative expression in France can be found in the now notorious caves in the verdant river valleys of southern France. The art of the homo sapiens zeroed in on the important issues of the day: food, shelter, and threats to safety. Rendered in rudimentary paints and chalks, these primitive pictures offer a glimpse of the more refined art to come. Millennia later, France has transformed into a cultural nirvana. Fine arts, architecture, music, sculpture, and literature are just some of the arenas in which France boasts a disarming number of highly skilled denizens. So beloved are these contributors to the artistic canon that streets, hospitals, and schools throughout the country bear their names: Voltaire, Balzac, Renoir, and even Gainsbourg.

To say that the French place an extremely high value on the arts would be an understatement. In this country of 64 million, 30,000 are registered "dramatic artists" and dancers, and an equal number are registered musicians. The country boasts 1,200 museums, 288 yearly arts-related festivals, and an annual arts-and-culture budget that tops €12 billion. This investment clearly pays off: Every year, millions of visitors come to Paris to ogle the Mona Lisa, peer up at the Tour Eiffel, and take in a feathers-and-sequins show at the Moulin Rouge, pumping in billions of dollars to the local economy. The government has even created a special dole just to support the new generation of artists, who are guaranteed a living wage should they find themselves unable to find work in their craft.

IMPRESSIONISM

France has given birth to numerous art movements, but none whose global impact has been as profound as Impressionism. It began with Édouard Manet. After being turned away from the great Paris salons sponsored by the government-run École des Beaux Arts in the late 19th century for expressing ideas on canvas that were too avant-garde and nonconformist, Manet rallied together a few other rejected painters eager to show their work to an interested audience. Together, Manet and his artistic consorts developed an alternative salon featuring work focused on everyday life, much as their Cro-Magnon predecessors had: on the streets, in the home, at lively cafés, at work in the fields, and at play on the *plage*. The movement began in Paris and spread south to Provence, where Auguste Renoir and Paul Cézanne lived and painted.

The work of Renoir, Camille Pissarro, Edgar Degas, and Cézanne evoke a specific vision of France, one where distinctive brushstrokes and reflected light combine to dazzle the eye. Considering the era, the movement was very progressive—and it was also short-lived, petering out in just 10 years, but paving the way for the post-Impressionists. Always in high demand, Impressionist paintings from the great French museums are often loaned to art institutions outside of France, but the Musée d'Orsay's permanent exhibit is a perennial go-to for a broad cross-section of art lovers.

ARCHITECTURE

Walk down any street in France, and you'll undoubtedly encounter the past. Maybe it's one of those troglodyte houses built into a hillside in the Loire Valley, its chimney jutting out from an earthen roof; or a medieval château whose towers cast tall shadows over an empty moat now harboring a lush green lawn. In Paris, it's said, you're never more than 10 paces from a view onto that iconic monolith, the Tour Eiffel, but it's the broad avenues hemmed by manicured trees and tidy apartment buildings that your gaze will surely settle on time and again. The City of Light wasn't always the bright and airy *ville* it is today; those beautiful sand-colored buildings, with their giant, wooden double doors and ornate metal balconies festooned with potted geraniums, are the work of baron Georges-Eugène Haussmann, a 19th-century architect and urban planner commissioned by Napoléon III to revamp Paris's cramped, unsanitary *rues* and transform them into broad, beautiful boulevards.

Beginning in 1852, Haussmann took to his task of modernizing Paris and making it easier for the bourgeois class to partake in their preferred pastime: strolling. In Haussmann's distinctive style, which made great use of straight lines, the streets were widened, groomed parks were constructed, functional squares were designed and built, and those sometimes confusing star-shaped roundabouts were put in place. This regimented style was fraught with de-sign restrictions that defined the height, width, pitch, and color of all new construction. In 1870, Haussmann completed his work of transforming the Paris of the past into the Paris of the future. Today, the architects behind the design are acknowledged for their work by an engraved stamp on the front of many private and public buildings throughout the capital.

Charles-Édouard Jeanneret, better known as Le Corbusier, is Swiss by birth, but he is easily France's second-best-known architect. Like Haussmann, he was engaged by the government to design aesthetically pleasing urban housing that would offer function and design at once. Many of his ideas didn't make the cut—there are, for instance, no 60-story tower blocks in central Paris, as he proposed—but the structures that did come to life have stood the test of time, including the boxy, beehivelike Maison de Fada in Marseille and the Notre-Dame-du-Haut cathedral in Ronchamp. Simultaneously loved and loathed for his modern, hard-edged style, Le Corbusier is credited with ushering in the prevailing aesthetic of contemporary French design.

LITERATURE

Their reputations are so heady and their work so iconic they need only one name to be recognized: Balzac, Camus, Colette, Flaubert, Molière, Proust, Zola. France's premier contribution to the arts might very well be its body of litera-ture, even if the majority of Americans have never read from it. The heyday of French literature peaked in the 19th century, when Jules Verne pumped out his sci-fi body of work and Flaubert titillated readers (and irked early censors) with

Madame Bovary. French students begin studying the great writers in elementary school and have read many of the classics by the time they finish *lycée*.

French literature has had an interesting cultural impact on the rest of the world as well: Alexandre Dumas' stories have been made into ballets—*The Nutcracker*, for starters—and his *Trois Mousqueteers* was co-opted by Disney (and morphed into Mousketeers, if you recall), as was Victor Hugo's famous *Hunchback of Notre-Dame.* Hugo is also responsible for one of Broadway's longest-running musicals, *Les Misérables.*

ESCAPE ARTISTS

For more than a century, North Americans have migrated to France in search of creative freedom, heady inspiration, adventure tinged with a seductive accent, and a slice of that celebrated joie de vivre. It's no wonder that writers, musicians, actors, and especially painters are drawn to this country where the arts are seen as a right rather than a privilege. From the Lost Generation to Gen X, meet some of the daring dreamers who shipped off across the pond to hone their craft in *la belle France*.

Josephine Baker	Adam Gopnik	Cole Porter
James Baldwin	Ernest Hemingway	Ezra Pound
Art Buchwald	Langston Hughes	Molly Ringwald
Belinda Carlisle	Washington Irving	Jean Seberg
Sofia Coppola	Henry James	David Sedaris
R. Crumb	Diane Johnson	Nina Simone
Johnny Depp	Aline Kominsky	Gertrude Stein
John Dos Passos	Carson McCullers	Alice B. Toklas
Ernest Hemingway	Henry Miller	Tina Turner
Feist	Jim Morrison	Edith Wharton
F. Scott Fitzgerald	Charlie Parker	

WIKIMEDIA COMMONS/PHOTOGRAPHS: PARIS YEARS, 1922-1930

Ernest Hemingway poses with his son in Paris, 1927.

Jean-Paul Sartre won the Nobel Prize in Literature in 1964 but famously declined the honor, saying that were he to accept it, he would be in some sense beholden to the awarding institution and thus compromising his artistic integrity—a risk that he believed no writer should feel compelled to experience. Writers who have gladly accepted the award include Albert Camus, who won the prize in 1957 for his contributions to the field of modern literature.

Modern French writers who have also cracked the global literary scene include Faïza Guène, whose 2006 book *Kiffe Kiffe Demain* (*Kiffe Kiffe Tomorrow*), about life in a contemporary suburban housing project, has been translated into more than 20 languages; and 2002's *The Sexual Life of Catherine M.,* a saucy memoir by Catherine Millet that details the between-the-sheets (and open-air) exploits of a liberated, middle-aged Frenchwoman.

FASHION

Vogue Paris editor Carine Roitfeld made waves in 2010 when she announced her departure from the glossy fashion magazine after 10 years of savvy sartorial forecasting. Who, then, would keep the world informed of what steps we should all be taking toward a well-heeled future?

For the past 100 years, France and fashion have been synonymous. Blame Gabrielle "Coco" Chanel, who began her career as a milliner; she put Paris on the fashion map with her signature tweed jacket that combined a masculine edge with a ribbon-trimmed feminine sensibility. A century later, the Chanel brand—and the cut of that jacket—is still a coveted symbol of high style. In the 1950s, Christian Dior reigned over the glamorous world of couture party dresses, ball gowns, and stylish prêt-a-porter suits, giving French women a fashion prototype to emulate (or at least to admire on the pages of fashion magazines). In the 1960s, the house of Courrèges altered the fashion landscape with an ultramod aesthetic that married bright white dress suits with shiny patent boots that hinted at fashion's space-age potential.

When revered couturier Christian Dior died in 1957, a very young Yves St. Laurent took over as head designer at the fashion house, giving the brand a modern makeover. In the '70s, the Algerian-born designer revolutionized the sartorial scene with Le Smoking—a structured, menswear-inspired jacket that became one of the harbingers of the gender-neutral fashions of later decades. St. Laurent's designs have been showcased in popular exhibitions in both French and American museums, and several years after his death, he remains one of France's most beloved fashion icons.

Chanel, Dior, Céline, and Chloé still attract the world's deep-pocketed pretty people to high-end boutiques on Paris's Avenue Montaigne and beyond.

© SE SA BERNARD/WWW.MAKINEN.FR/SUSA/WORDPRESS

High-fashion hounds will want to make a beeline for Paris's chichi Avenue Montaigne.

But as if the incessant television commercials don't give it away, designer perfumes are reeling in the most cash for French fashion houses, to the tune of billions of dollars each year.

As for the mystery question above? Emmanuelle Alt, named Roitfeld's successor at *Vogue Paris,* heralds in a beautiful new era in 2011.

Sports

When France lost to Mexico 0–2 in the first team match of the 2010 World Cup in South Africa, the mood among French sports fans turned somber. Instead of screaming in anger at the television or sharing conciliatory slaps on the back with fellow sports fans packed inside cafés and brasseries, the French sulked in silence before the big screens, staring into their pints of Pelforth with a mixture of shame and denial.

Some analysts called the sporty comedown a metaphor for the social problems plaguing French society: Both, they say, are mired in ego, strained relations among minorities, and the refusal to accept blame for failure. To others, football—what Americans refer to as soccer—is just a game. Everyone in France, however, has some sort of opinion on the country's most popular sport. Football is played in minor and major leagues throughout the country, packing stadiums and luring multiple generations of fans. When the home team wins, packed stadiums vibrate with the stomping of feet, waving of flags, and the chanting of thousands of vociferous spectators.

Paris's Parc des Princes and St. Denis' Stade de Paris—with more than 100,000 seats between them—play host to the most international football games. If there's one place you don't want to be stuck in your car, it's near the choked arteries around these arenas, especially if the home team has lost. For an authentic local experience, regional stadiums in smaller cities and towns are the places to be to see a match. Expect up-close views of the action that allow you to see the subtle nuances of the game and to feel part of the local community every weekend, year-round (or almost year-round—like the rest of the country, football takes a two-month summer holiday).

Like football, France's cycling culture reaches back to the 1800s, when Vélodromes drew crowds (Ernest Hemingway was a fan) for dizzying races that sometimes lasted six days, ending for some fatigued riders in a bloody pile on the wooden racetrack. It's the sexy Tour de France, though, that has earned the most international attention when it comes to the two-wheeled sport. Every July since 1903, racers from around the world have pedaled a circuit that takes them up and over some of the country's tallest peaks, down through picturesque medieval villages, and finally up the Champs-Élysées for a final lap before hundreds of thousands of whistling, cheering, clapping fans.

PLANNING YOUR FACT-FINDING TRIP

It's easy to fall in love with the surface image of France, but there's only one way to find out if the French personality meshes with yours—whether a long-term relationship is possible—and that's to come visit and stay awhile. You'll want not only to explore the cities, towns, and villages where you might settle down, but also to attune yourself to the rhythms of your potential new home before making a commitment.

The sedate vibe of rural France is kilometers away from the urban bustle, but each offers something special worth checking out. The most important part of your reconnaissance mission is to veer off the tourist trail: Skip the hotel next to the Eiffel Tower and park yourself at a neighborhood auberge in a less touristy arrondissement. Outside Paris, you'll benefit by skipping the budget chain hotels near the freeway and looking for accommodations (independent or otherwise) in the center of town. Give yourself at least a few days

© EKATERINA POKROVSKY/123RF.COM

to *really* get to a know a place: when and where the nearest outdoor market is held, which of the handful of cafés feels most like home, and who your future neighbors will be.

Bring your sense of adventure, your best manners, and your French phrasebook, and don't be afraid to ask questions—even if you don't always understand the responses. Reaching out will let the locals know you've got nothing to hide, and will give you the opportunity to see what the local mores and attitudes are toward foreigners. Eat out, visit the post office, shop at the local grocery store, and imagine what life will be like in your adopted hometown.

Preparing to Leave

It's true that France is a large country, but the (relatively) fast and efficient train system means no major hub is more than a five-hour journey away. If you'll be venturing into smaller towns not connected by rail service, it's worth booking a car rental in advance to take you off the beaten path and into those quaint pockets tucked into valleys and on hilltops. You'll find rental-car agencies at train stations—but, like much of France, they take a midday break for lunch, so try to schedule your arrival time before noon or after 2 P.M. Cheapie air companies have made the move into France as well, so if your time—and the amount of baggage you're carrying—is limited, consider Easy Jet, Ryan Air, and other low-cost carriers. Advance bookings can turn up some pretty amazing deals, like the yes-it's-really-true €5 flights.

The Internet is a traveler's best friend, but be wary when pulling out your smartphone in big cities; Paris has seen a rash of handheld-device thefts lately, and you don't want to become a statistic when you're supposed to be out enjoying an exploratory adventure. Do as much of your sleuthing as possible in advance, and keep your written details in an old-fashioned notebook or on a computer printout. Guidebooks are also good travel companions and can point you in the direction of a dependable hotel, restaurant, or sightseeing spot without your having to weed through the never-ending possibilities that the Internet is so good at providing.

When narrowing down regions to explore, consider your needs, wants—and, yes, your dreams. It's helpful to rank your list in terms of importance. What comes first: work, play, or family? If you're moving without a job and need to find work right away, big cities are the obvious choice for the sheer variety and number of employment opportunities. Ditto for rental housing. Don't mind the winter cold but can't live without sunshine? Focus your exploration in the south instead of the north, where winters can be gray as all get-out. If you're a retiree on a limited budget, you'll want to consider some regions where housing is a bargain but where you'll still have access to cultural amenities—and a *boulangerie*. Be realistic as you begin your search, but don't deny your dreams. A happy medium does exist!

WHAT TO BRING
Passport

Before you book your travel plans, make sure your passport is up-to-date, and ideally that it will be valid for six months beyond your expected return date. Make two copies of the first few pages of your passport, then leave with a trusted friend or relative back home and stick the other in your travel bag. If your passport is lost or stolen, you'll be able to take a copy to the American embassy in Paris or to the U.S. Consulate in Marseille and have a new passport issued, usually within 24 hours. While you definitely need to carry your passport with you, if you're staying in France for less than 90 days, you won't need a long-stay visa. Keep in mind that many travelers bend the rules and stay longer than 90 days without any problems, but it's always best to err on the side of the law and play by the rules, lest you risk being sent home with a mysterious red mark scribbled into your passport.

Money and Credit Cards

Credit and ATM cards are widely accepted in France; a sticker system, usually posted on the doors or windows of businesses, indicates exactly which cards you can use at a specific establishment. Some shops—most often small grocery stores and many restaurants—have minimum-purchase requirements that hover around €10 or €15, in which case a sign will be posted at the register or another easily visible spot. There is a major difference between U.S. credit cards and French ones, and that's the *puce*. Embedded inside French cards is a tiny microchip containing a variety of data. If your credit card doesn't have one, you won't be able to purchase Métro tickets from some vending machines or rent a Vélib' bike in Paris or Vélo'v in Lyon. But as long as the credit card machine has the side swipe feature (you may need to help the person behind the counter with this—it's not every day they see a non-European card), your card will be readable and therefore usable. Keep in mind that *boulangeries* and small mom-and-pop shops still aren't outfitted with credit card machines, so it's wise to carry at least €10 in change at all times for those little necessities like your morning *café* and croissant.

Before your departure, check in with the banks that issue your credit and

ATM cards to let them know you'll be travelling and to expect foreign transactions to appear in their computer systems. If you forget to do this, you may find your account suspended after the first foreign purchase, and undoing this damage from a continent away can be a frustrating challenge. If you forget to make the call in advance of your trip, do so immediately after your memory is jogged. Some banks, such as Wells Fargo, and credit card companies, such as Visa, charge a commission or a one-time transaction fee for every foreign purchase or cash withdrawal. These 2 and 3 percent charges on purchases and up to $10 fees for each withdrawal are annoying and can definitely add up, so your best bet is to withdraw the maximum amount of cash possible from an ATM to use for your purchases. If your bank account has a per-day withdrawal limit, ask about increasing it before you leave.

Driver's Permits

International driver's permits are not required by car-rental agencies in France, but it can't hurt to have one just in case you need an extra piece of ID, or if the rules suddenly change overnight (which is altogether possible), or if you're stopped by the *police routière* and want to show what a good citizen you are by having an "official" document translated into French. International permits are valid for one year can be purchased by licensed drivers at AAA offices, where they cost $15, or through private companies acting as intermediary agents that generally charge twice as much. You'll need one passport-size photo and your U.S. driver's license to complete the transaction.

Communications

The value of a French phrasebook cannot be underestimated. If you're polite and apologetic, it is very likely that the person you're attempting to communicate with will break into English (don't ruin your chances by immediately asking, "Do you speak English?"), but attempting to speak the language— even if you're reading straight from a guidebook and sound like an uneducated automaton—will make the French more inclined to help you when you need it most. Many smartphones and other handheld devices now have foreign phrasebook applications, so for the light traveler, this may be the way to go. Many people who aren't yet conversational in French find making telephone calls nearly impossible. Still, if you can't live without your phone for the duration of your stay, check with your carrier to see if your mobile roaming privileges extend to France. If not—or if the costs are prohibitively exorbitant—you have other options.

If you own a late-model cell phone, you can buy a France-friendly SIM card to temporarily replace your American SIM card. Companies selling them online include www.callineurope.com and www.cellularabroad.com. Cell phone rentals are not necessarily cheap, but they do exist; look for kiosks at Charles de Gaulle Airport or rent one at home before you leave. You might also consider purchasing a pay-as-you-go phone once you arrive; they usually cost between €30 and €50. Recharging the phones is easy: You simply visit the nearest *tabac* and ask for *une carte recharge*. You might be asked whether you want the more cost-effective SMS (texting) option, and you'll certainly be asked how much credit you want, usually a minimum of €5 and increasing in increments of €5 or €10. Keep in mind that phone credit has an expiration date—usually one or two weeks from the date of purchase.

Electronics

The power animating all those electric hair dryers, microwave ovens, televisions, and other appliances in France courses through the wires at 220 volts—double the U.S. and Canada's 110 volts. Some machines—laptop computers, digital camera battery chargers, cell phone chargers—are designed to run on both voltages, so they simply need a cheap and easy-to-find outlet adapter. If you can't live without your iPod docking station or your electric razor, you'll need to source a transformer. They come in different shapes, sizes, and degrees of reliability. For a dependable experience, invest in one or two of those rather industrial-looking transformers. They aren't worth the extra weight or investment for a short trip, but you'll definitely want to consider them if and when you make the move.

Even if you don't see one in your room, hair dryers are available at most hotels in France. Ask about availability when you check in, or send an email inquiry in advance. Online language converters such as www.freetranslation.com can help you get your question across in a way the recipient will understand.

Medication and Personal Items

One of the hardest things to get used to in France is learning which products are and are not available at the supermarket or drugstore. Everyday items like multipurpose contact-lens solutions and good ol' Advil can be found only in pharmacies, and often they're stashed behind the counter, requiring you to practice your French yet again to get relief from that headache. Prices are comparable to the U.S. ones, though some items are noticeably cheaper than in the U.S. or Canada, including homeopathic remedies and many prescription medications. Mostly, though, you'll find that discount-price goods are hard to come by. Expect to pay around €10 for a bottle of contact-lens solution,

€3 for a box—yes, a box—of ibuprofen or acetaminophen (which is called Paracetamol in France), and €3 or €4 for sore-throat lozenges.

The French are known as the world's leading consumers of prescription drugs, so tracking down your prescription medication at the pharmacy shouldn't pose a problem. But for convenience's sake, you're still better off carrying your prescriptions from home. If you must get a refill while you're here, make sure to bring the brand name, generic name, dosage, and doctor prescription with you.

Clothing and Accessories

If you want to look like a local, then it helps to dress like a local—and in France, that means black, black, and more black. Women, men, and children tend to take a formal approach to dressing, and the style is easy to mimic with a monochromatic ensemble and a few nice accessories. Parisians in particular tend to shy away from too much color, sticking to black from their berets right down to their stiletto boots. Wearing your nice shoes might not be the most comfortable route, but if possible, leave the bright white running shoes at home and opt for something with a lower, darker profile. And flip-flops? Well, save those for summer on the Riviera, if you must. Men might find it difficult to trade in their baseball caps for an empty head, but if you want to blend in, leave the sportswear at home.

France is a four-season country, so you'll want to pack gloves, scarves, and hats for wintertime travel, as well as for early spring and late fall. These items are easy to find at French chains like Monoprix and in little shops throughout the country, but if you have them already, stuff them in your suitcase, just to be safe (and warm).

The most indispensable year-round item to carry with you is an umbrella; with the exception of the Côte d'Azur, which is predictably rain-free in the summer months, showers can erupt without warning in any season. Umbrellas are easily acquired once you're here, but even the cheapest models aren't that inexpensive by American standards. Expect to pay €15 for a small travel umbrella at a department store or pharmacy.

Until recently, the French really didn't do sunglasses. They're becoming more common with each passing year, but people still rarely wear them in winter, on overcast days, or even during the summer. If you're a sunglasses devotee, consider bringing an extra pair, as they aren't as easy to find as they are in the United States and Canada.

WHEN TO GO

You'll find France a welcoming destination at any time, but there are seasonal idiosyncrasies to keep in mind when planning your trip. Weather can certainly impede travel—as it did in the winter of 2010–2011, when flights in and out of the country were cancelled because of snowstorms, and trains were delayed by as long as several days—and some towns shut down for the low season, making it a challenge to find accommodations. (In cities, you'll be fine.) During the month of August, when the entire country goes on vacation, you will also find signs affixed to the doors and windows of many businesses announcing closures for *"congés annuels"* or *"fermé pour les vacances,"* often accompanied by a very apologetic note explaining where in the neighborhood you'll be able to find similar baguettes/chocolate/shoe repair services/haircuts, as well as the business's reopening date. During the winter and spring school breaks, you'll find that many tourist hubs—especially the ski and seaside resorts—are full of Frenchies, who often grab the best deals on accommodations months in advance. If you plan to travel at these peak times, it's a good idea to book in advance, too.

Aside from requiring you to bundle up to ward off the cold, winter can be a festive time of year to make your investigative visit. Every city in the country gets itself dolled up in a manner befitting the yuletide, upping the charm factor tenfold; getting a reservation at the hotel and restaurant of your choice is usually easier, too. If you're focusing your search on cities, expect most everything to be open for business. In Paris, more businesses are actually open on Christmas than on New Year's Day, so you won't go hungry or thirsty just because it's a major holiday. In smaller towns, however, you'll be lucky if the *boulangerie* is open for a couple of hours in the morning, if at all.

Spring and autumn offer the mildest temperatures and possibly the best glimpses of "real France," without the vacationing hordes to impede your view. If you want the Côte d'Azur all to yourself, head south in late September, when the last of the tourists have packed up and left but the sun is still warm and sea still swimmable. Pack layers—shirt, jacket, trench coat, scarf, hat—and be sure your umbrella makes its way inside your suitcase.

Summer has the most predictable temperatures, which tend to fall into the warm range. But it can get scorching hot in the south, and some of us have been known to turn on the heater on oddly nippy July mornings in the north of France. Remember that late July and the entire month of August are national holiday periods, as well as the standard vacation time for much of the rest of Europe, so some destinations can feel quite crowded with a mix of international and local tourists. Men: If you'll be staying in the Paris, Lyon, Toulouse, or Nice areas and want to make use of the affordable and accessible public swimming pools, pack your Speedo: They're mandatory. For everyone: If you've got a swimming cap, bring it along. Otherwise, you can purchase suits and the requisite caps in special vending machines inside public pool lobbies.

Arriving in France

If you're flying into France from North America, you'll mostly likely land at Charles de Gaulle, the country's primary international airport that sits roughly 27 kilometers northeast of Paris. The airport is connected to bus, train, taxi, and private-car services that can ferry you to other destinations—including Orly Airport, south of Paris, where you can catch flights elsewhere within France and Europe.

VISAS AND PASSPORTS

The customs experience is generally a no-fuss exercise requiring little more than standing in line for 10 minutes, followed by a friendly *"bonjour"* as you hand over your passport for stamping. In France, appearances do matter, so to make your experience as smooth as possible, trade in your Juicy sweats for dark jeans and a nice jacket, tuck your purple mohawk inside your beret, give your shoes a spit shine, and be prepared to offer a friendly "hello" and "thank you" in French. There is always a slight chance you'll be pulled aside to have your luggage rifled through unceremoniously. Officials are looking for contraband items, so it's best not to pique their curiosity by smuggling in your favorite fresh fruit from home (you'll find it in France!) or your beloved Venus flytrap.

TOURIST BOON

Whether you're a bona fide, just-off-the-TGV tourist or have actually moved to France already, the office of tourism should be one of the first places you visit in any French town. The people who greet you from behind the desk are locals – multilingual ones at that – whose job is to provide you with information on the area. Hotel bookings, sightseeing suggestions, detailed neighborhood descriptions, restaurant recommendations, ideas on places to avoid, and free local and regional maps are just a few of the things you'll have access to here. Day-use lockers, bathrooms, transport passes, and mini-museums are other onsite possibilities. To find the tourist office, ask at the train station *guichet*.

Be mindful of the duty-free import restrictions, which are clearly outlined in your airline's in-flight magazine and on the customs form you're required to fill out before landing. When in doubt, ask a flight attendant, a fellow passenger, or the person behind the counter in the duty-free shop. Once you've cleared customs, the real adventure begins.

TRANSPORTATION

There are multiple options for getting away from the airport and toward your final destination; which one you choose depends on where you're headed. Want to address your jetlag by going to sleep immediately? Consider taking a shuttle bus to a nearby airport hotel and starting fresh in the morning after a little shut-eye. Shuttles are free, and there are many bargains to be found within 10 minutes of the airport, from budget-friendly chains to cushy five-star digs.

If you're headed to Paris, the possibilities abound. One of the simplest is Roissybus, which runs every 15 to 20 minutes, depending on the time of day. The extra-long bus—two cars with an accordion-style middle section—costs less than €10 per trip and drops you off in the heart of Paris, behind the Opéra Métro station. You can pay with cash or a credit card once you're on the bus, and there are pickup locations at every airport terminal. During rush hour, the journey can take more than an hour; on a good (no-traffic) day, the trip takes about 30 minutes.

The RER B is a regional train line that connects the airport to Paris and its suburbs. For roughly the same price and same time commitment you'd invest in Roissybus, you can hop aboard a train and arrive at one of three central Paris train stations: Gare du Nord, St. Michel, and Denfert-Rochereau. If you're staying in Paris's popular Latin Quarter, the St. Michel station is your stop. Tickets can be purchased from the agents staffing the station kiosks (ideal if you're paying with a card), or you can use an automated vending machine (best if you're using cash).

Shuttle buses are a newly emerging alternative to Roissybus and the RER, but they're more expensive and offer a somewhat clunkier experience, since you have to call the company—albeit on a toll-free number accessible from an airport pay phone—to let them know you've arrived. To get the best deals, it's imperative you book your pickup in advance. Try www.bluvan.fr, www.supershuttle.fr, or www.parisshuttle.com, each of which offers English-language options on its website.

If money is no object, or if you just want to get to your hotel or apartment with a minimum of hassle, taxis are the way to go. Expect to pay between

WELCOME TO FRANCE

© BRIAN JACKSON/123RF.COM

If you missed the last Métro, bus, or train, take a taxi.

€65 and €100 to ride from the airport to your front door, depending on traffic. Though tipping isn't standard in France, an extra 5 percent on top of the fare makes sense if the driver helps with your baggage or otherwise makes your journey easier and more comfortable.

Practicalities

ACCOMMODATIONS

One of France's best-kept secrets is its value-for-money lodgings. Who needs a fancy €1,000-per-night suite at the Plaza Athénée when, for a fraction of the price, you can relax for a night or two in a comfortable room with free wireless Internet *and* a view of the Eiffel Tower? Bargains aren't limited to Paris or to hotels—you'll also discover great deals on bed-and-breakfasts, *gîtes,* and short-term apartment and villa stays—from the top of the country to the bottom and from east to west—offering clean comfort for the night. France holds the distinction of having a counterintuitive cheaper-on-the-weekends hotel policy, so if you're flying in on a Friday, Saturday, or Sunday, you'll likely get your room for an even better rate.

If you're going the good old-fashioned hotel route, it's helpful to know what those stars posted at the hotel entryway mean. The French government has instituted a rating system that the majority of establishments adhere to, with the number of stars clearly visible outside, usually affixed to a blue sign on the wall adjacent to the front door. The number of stars doesn't reflect quality per se, but it does correspond to the amenities available to guests, which may act as an indicator of quality. A hotel with five stars might have a swimming pool and a refrigerator full of booze and bottled water, but that doesn't mean it's immune from the dreaded cockroach. What you *can* expect at the bottom level is a no-frills room with a bed, a TV, and a bathroom equipped with a tiny shower stall. There may or may not be an *ascenseur* (elevator) to take you to your fourth-floor room. Budget chains include Kyriad, Etap, and Formule 1, which offer a uniform aesthetic with predictable, midlevel quality and comfort. Further up the starry ladder are the Ibis, Novotel, and Mercure chains, which fall into the three- and four-star range. Only a handful of French hotels reach five-star status.

So what can you expect to pay, and what do you get for your euro? In a small village in the Dordogne Valley, you might find a family-run place situated above a café-brasserie, where your second-floor room will set you back €40 a night and give you enough floor space do your yoga exercises in the morning. For €50, you could easily find a quaint room overlooking a castle in the Loire Valley, within walking distance of a number of restaurants and sightseeing destinations. For €60, you could rest your head on a fluffy pillow in a homey bed-and-breakfast on the Brittany coast, then spend the afternoon collecting seashells on the shore before turning in for a glass of sherry in the B&B lounge. In Paris, you could find a chic little boutique hotel with a cut-rate room priced at €100, with a Métro stop a two-minute walk out the lobby

© JENNIFER PICKENS/BLACKBIRDPHOTO.COM

The number of stars at your hotel indicates the breadth of amenities, not cleanliness or comfort.

B&B FOR (ALMOST) FREE

In France, San Francisco-based Air BnB has become the budget traveler's best friend. How it works: Private parties list their available room(s) on the Air BnB website (www.airbnb.com), you surf the listings for the city or town you'll be visiting, and, with luck, something pops up that's right in your budget bracket. In Paris, double rooms can be had for €36 per night; in Nice, for €30; and in Lyon, for as little €20 per night. No matter what you spend, you're guaranteed to meet interesting people (a high percentage of those identifying themselves as artists offer rooms this way), get a feel for living in a specific neighborhood (access to a kitchen allows you to shop at the local markets and prepare your own meals, if you want), and possibly save a lot of money. But if Air BnB is still a budget breaker for you, there's always CouchSurfing (www.couchsurfing.org).

door and a *boulangerie* on the corner where all of your brioche-for-breakfast dreams can come true. In other words, there's a lot of variety, and the prices aren't bad either.

If you're securing a place to stay on the spot rather than booking in advance, ask to see a room before committing. In France, you always pay at checkout and you'll be asked for your passport at check-in, at which time they might decide to hold on to your passport for the duration of your stay. Accommodations run the gamut from thrifty to fancy, and while the room you get may not exactly match the description precisely, you can be sure of quality, safety, and a good night's sleep.

Paris

The French capital is loaded with options for accommodations, from short-stay apartment rentals and niche B&Bs to swanky upscale hotels and family-run one-star dives. Craigslist is a great place to start your search for a temporary apartment rental, but beware of anyone who asks you to wire money in advance (though if they accept PayPal, you're safe). Veering off the tourist path will lead you to more bargain digs than you could ever hope to find near the Champs-Élysées and will give you the chance discover neighborhoods worth considering as your new home.

On a quiet but interesting street near the Gare de Lyon, **Le Mistral** (3, rue Chaligny, tel. 01/46 28 10 20) offers cozy comfort at a bargain price. For €60, expect a double room with TV, heat, hairdryer, and free wireless Internet.

Just over the *périphérique* in a quiet, family-oriented neighborhood, Emoke Tarnay, a bubbly Hungarian expat, offers a **private B&B** in her modern, comfy Boulogne-Billancourt apartment (21, quai Alphonse de Gallo, tel. 01/41 31 01 49). The price is right at €40, and she makes a mean boiled egg for breakfast.

For something on the hip end of the spectrum, try **Hotel Le Citizen** (96, quai de Jemmapes, tel. 01/83 62 55 50), in the city's trendy Canal St. Martin neighborhood. Rooms begin at €160 and include big fluffy pillows, flat-screen TVs, and free iPad use during your stay.

Brittany

RENNES

Beautiful, laid-back Rennes has some beautiful, laid-back hotels in the city center. One of the comfiest is **Hotel des Lices** (1, place des Lices, tel. 02/99 79 14 81) just off the busy weekend-market square, Place des Lices. This 48-room hotel offers soundproof sleeping quarters with balconies and prime access to all the old town has to offer: restaurants, markets, parks, shopping, the Métro, and people-watching. Chic doubles run €65 to €88.

Closer to the train station is **Hotel le Sevigne** (47, avenue Janvier, tel. 02/99 67 27 55), where a clean, spiffy double room decorated in bright, cheery colors starts at €67. Special weekend rates are usually available, so it's worth building your *séjour* around a Friday- or Saturday-night stay.

VANNES

An hour away by train is Vannes, where nearly all the town's hotels are within walking distance of the *gare*. At the **Hotel Ocean-Manche** (31, rue de Lieutenant Colonel Maury, tel. 02/97 47 26 46), you'll be welcomed by a convivial staff who'll make you feel at home *tout de suite* (right away). From here, you can walk to the old city in five minutes and the port in 15, and access the seashore in half an hour on a groomed walking trail. Doubles, which begin at €52, are spacious and comfortable.

Near the *mairie* and the historic ramparts of the old city, **Hotel Le Bretagne** (36, rue de Mené, tel. 02/97 47 20 21) offers cuteness and quaintness in one well-placed hotel. Double rates run €44–59, depending on the season. Not that unlike at most hotels in France, dogs are *interdit* (prohibited) here.

Bordeaux and the Dordogne Valley

BORDEAUX

Bordeaux's beautiful and historic city center boasts a broad spectrum of hotels, but if you're coming and going by train, you might consider resting up for your exploration near the train station.

At the **Etap** (60, rue Eugène le Roy, tel. 08/92 70 02 39) directly across from Gare St. Jean, you'll find spartan but comfortable rooms for two or three beginning at €48. From there, it's a five-minute tram ride or a 15-minute walk to the city center.

If you prefer to stay where all the action is, the very cute (in a 1950s sort of way) **Hotel de la Presse** (6–8, rue Porte-Dijeaux, tel. 05/56 48 53 88) is ideally situated a two-minute walk from the Place de la Bourse, right in the thick of the pedestrian shopping promenade, rue Sainte-Catherine. Rooms range €69–112.

BERGERAC

Whether you arrive in Bergerac by car or by train, you'll be able to get to the city center by following the signs to *centre ville*. If you meander to the small, quaint old quarter of town, just beyond République near the covered market, you'll discover **Hotel le Family** (3, rue du Dragon, tel. 05/53 57 80 90), a no-frills, clean, and comfy hotel attached to a traditional Périgourdine restaurant. Double rooms start at just €35.

Edging closer to the Dordogne on a pretty tree-lined street is **La Bonbonnière** (15, place de la Mirpe, tel. 05/53 61 82 04), a B&B run out of an authentic medieval abode by a friendly French couple. Simone will make you breakfast, with homemade jam to slather on your warm bread and strong coffee to get you through a day of sightseeing.

SARLAT

Martine and Patrice, the proprietors of **Le Petit Mas** (22, rue Gabriel Tarde, tel. 05/53 30 34 09), offer charming rooms for rent at their comfortable home a 10-minute walk from the Disneyesque medieval town center. Expect to pay between €35 and €60, depending on the room, season, and number of people.

If you prefer a one-minute walk to the heart of Sarlat, **Le Couleuvrine** (1, place Bouquerie, tel. 05/53 59 27 80) is run by another husband-and-wife team who offer food, accommodations, and a cozy little bar. Rooms are hard to secure in the summer without a reservation, but if you land one, you'll pay between €58 and €78 for a comfortable, vintage room with bathroom, wireless Internet, and TV.

Toulouse and Montpellier

TOULOUSE

Toulouse is a big city with oodles of hotels, hostels, and *chambres d'hôtes* in every price range. But first you have to decide what part of the city you want to stay in. In the center near the train station, a short walk from place Victor Hugo, is **Hotel Beauséjour** (4, rue Caffarelli, tel. 05/61 62 77 59). This friendly, no-nonsense hotel has great prices and a good location. Doubles start at €40.

Not far from here is the three-star **Grand Hotel Raymond IV** (16, rue Raymond IV, tel. 05/61 62 89 41), where a double room will set you back €75 in the low season. For that kind of cash, you'll get access to room service and amenities like dry-cleaning service.

MONTPELLIER

Montpellier is a popular convention destination, so don't make the mistake of rolling into town and expecting a comfortable bed for the night, just to discover that the French Medical Association is holding its annual conference and every last hotel is booked solid for the week. (But if you do find yourself in this predicament, most hotels will help book you a room in a neighboring town.) With advance planning, you could stay in the heart of the city a block from the magnificent place de la Comédie at the 46-room **Royal Hotel Montpellier** (8, rue Maguelone, tel. 04/67 92 13 36). Chic, comfortable rooms run €80–120, and the location couldn't be more central.

For more pedestrian comfort, try the **Hotel Colisée-Verdun** (33, rue de Verdun, tel. 04/67 58 42 63). Right around the corner from the main train station and a short walk to the historic center, it offers cheap, clean rooms. Doubles range from €34 (with shower down the hall) to €62, and all rooms have wireless Internet and TV.

Provence and Côte d'Azur

AIX-EN-PROVENCE

In Aix-en-Provence, you might find yourself so charmed by the terra-cotta-colored Provençal architecture and plane tree–shaded boulevards that you forget to take note of the hotel situation. If it's easier for you, the nice people at the rather dated-looking tourist office will happily book you a place to stay. Or you can BYOR (book your own room) at the quaint little **Les Quartre Dauphins** (54, roux Alphéran, tel. 04/42 38 16 39), on a side street in the center of old Aix. It's within walking distance of the *gare* and all the terrace cafés, bookstores, and picturesque squares your heart could fancy. Doubles range €65–85, slightly more in high season.

Deeper in the heart of Aix is **Hotel des Augustins** (3, rue de la Masse, tel. 04/42 27 28 59), whose dramatic, somewhat regal foyer belies its midrange prices. Doubles range €99 to €250 year-round.

ANTIBES

Antibes has a small-town feel about it, and the limited number of hotels in the *centre ville* lend credence to that notion. Visit in the off-season and you'll feel like you have the place to yourself, but not so much in the summer. Close to the port at **Relais du Postillon** (8, rue Championnet, tel. 04/93 34 20 77), you'll find fair prices and a friendly welcome in the cozy, fireplace-lit reception room and bar. During the low season (October 1–April 30), spacious rooms—some overlooking the park across the street—range €49–104 per night.

A few blocks farther inland in the pedestrian quarter is the simple but comfortable **Modern Hotel** (1, rue Fourmilière, tel. 04/92 90 59 05), with double rooms going for €66 per night in the low season, €82 in high season.

NICE

You'll have a lot to choose from in Nice, and you can even find charming little hotels for less than €100 across the street from that turquoise wonder, the Mediterranean. The trick to landing the perfect accommodations in the heart of town is booking in advance—way in advance—if you plan to stay in town during the busy summer months. Off-season, you can walk into most hotels and secure a room on the spot.

Just two blocks from the sparkling sea sits **Hotel Felix** (41, rue Massena, tel. 04/93 88 66 73), perfectly positioned on the main pedestrian promenade in the Carré d'Or (Golden Square). You'll get a decent-size room with a small balcony, wireless Internet, and that French hotel-room rarity, the hot-water kettle for morning tea and coffee, for between €50 and €65 per night.

Down the street and around the corner is the two-star **Hotel Paradis** (1, rue Paradis, tel. 04/93 87 71 23). Half hostel, half hotel, this affordable spot offers shared rooms beginning at €16 per night and private doubles beginning at €50. Beach mats are available for borrowing, and breakfast is served all day for €5.

Lyon and Grenoble

LYON

Lyon is a pretty city with a fitting number of pretty hotels to choose from. If you haven't made reservations, visit the tourism office on place Bellecour, where the staff will book you a room in your price range for no extra charge. Easy access to all the action in Lyon can be found in that sliver of the city sandwiched between the Saône and Rhône Rivers, where tramlines, the Métro, and bus service crisscross, taking passengers in different directions. Within walking distance of Gare Perrache (with direct trains to Paris) is chain hotel

Kyriad (24, quai Perrache, tel. 04/78 37 16 64). Standard rooms fall into the affordable category at €47, including nice amenities like bath gel, hair dryers, and complimentary coffee, tea, and biscuits in your room.

At the foot of Fourvière, in the überadorable St. Paul neighborhood, **Hotel Saint Paul** (6, rue Lainerie, tel. 04/78 28 13 29) offers a cozy welcome to travelers in its purple lobby. Rooms are painted with equally colorful panache, with doubles beginning at €66. The Renaissance-period building is equipped with modern conveniences, including free wireless Internet and cable television.

GRENOBLE

Grenoble is one of many potential home bases for snow enthusiasts who've come to this corner of the country to tackle a mountain or two. The tourism infrastructure is well established, and there are many accommodations to choose from as you scope out the city and its neighborhoods. Smack in the middle of town is Grenoble's oldest hotel, **Hotel de l'Europe** (22, place Grenette, tel. 04/76 46 16 94), where clean, modern double rooms—some with a fireplace—range from €35 to €88 per night. After pounding the pavement looking for that perfect apartment, you'll appreciate the hotel's sauna and fitness room.

On the southern end of town, walking distance from the tramway, is **Citéa Grenoble** (41, rue Maruice Dodéro, tel. 04/38 21 17 00), which falls into the "aparthôtel" category. If you're going to stay a few days and want to save money by shopping at the *marché* and cooking meals at home, staying in these studio and one-bedroom apartments is a good bet. The area's not the prettiest, but it's safe and there's parking. Studios start at €70 per night, with discounts for longer stays.

FOOD
Paris

If Parisians aren't the dining-out champions of the world, then who could it possibly be? In even the most quiet neighborhood, every street seems to have at least two restaurants, one of which is guaranteed to be hopping with happy patrons. Do like 62 percent of Parisians do, and eat in the quartier you call home—if only temporarily. Don't know where to look? Start with this short list, but know that you really can't go wrong at any of the city's thousands of brasseries and cafés.

Not far from the infamous Bastille neighborhood is **Les Funambules** (12, rue Faidherbe, tel. 01/43 70 83 70), an überpopular café specializing in gigantic, meal-in-a-bowl salads. Sit on the outdoor terrace and watch all the well-groomed locals stroll by as you eat.

Chez Gladines (30, rue Cinq Diamants, 13e, tel. 08/99 69 63 59) offers no-frills, Basque-influenced cuisine in a festive atmosphere. While you wait for your table at the bar, scour the menu, which features such favorites as cassouletand escargots, and choose your €15 bottle of wine.

In a friendly, authentic Parisian neighborhood near the Gare de Lyon is a friendly, authentic Italian eatery, **La Toscana** (94, blvd. Diderot, tel. 08/99 23 47 31). Expect simple but delicious pizzas, pastas, and *pichets* of *vin rouge* that really hit the spot after a day of exploration.

In an unassuming neighborhood in Paris's far northwest corner, the scent of roasting coffee beans signals your proximity to **Menelik** (4, rue Sauffroy, tel. 01/46 27 00 82). At this lively Ethiopian eatery, every guest is greeted with a complimentary glass of *kir,* and everyone leaves utterly sated and happy.

Brittany

RENNES

Once you've settled into your hotel, it's time to mosey over to the **place des Lices** for a slice of the weekend-market action. In between the market's two covered *halles,* fast-food vendors dole out hearty crêpes, roast chickens, and Thai noodles from mobile carts. Get in the longest line, and you can be assured whatever you order will be delicious.

If meandering through the market with a crêpe in hand isn't your cup of tea, work your way through the vegetable stalls and the flower vendors and over to **place Rallier du Baty,** where a bustling terrace hums with diners from three different restaurants on the square. Grab one of **La Luppa's** (10, place Rallier du Baty, tel. 02/99 79 31 15) tables and order a thin-crust, wood-fired pizza and a *pichet du vin,* and you'll have all the fuel you need to explore the city afterward.

VANNES

In Vannes, you'll have to resign yourself to the fact that this is crêpe country. Give in to it, and soon you'll be addicted. Some of the best examples are at **Crêperie Saint-Exupéry** (8, rue Orfèvres, tel. 02/97 47 28 18), on a cobbled corner of a medieval street in the old town. The buckwheat galettes (savory crêpes) are thin and tasty, and if you want fries with that, they've got you covered.

For comparison's sake, take a stroll down to the water's edge approximately half an hour from the city center, where you'll find three crêperies on the little harbor at **Conleau.** Whichever one you choose, you can be sure of a cheap and tasty lunch, accompanied by a *bolée de cidre,* and a lovely, sunshiny view of the small harbor.

Bordeaux and the Dordogne Valley

BORDEAUX

In Bordeaux, it's all about the tapas. And the couscous. And the kebabs. And the curry. You definitely won't go hungry in this town, no matter your food preferences—and if you happen to be vegetarian or vegan, you'll be glad to know about **Le Samovar** (18, rue Camille Sauvageau), a funky teahouse and café in the St. Michel quartier that serves cheap, tasty *plats* for the bargain price of €4 (€7 for an extra-large helping), bowls of steaming soup for €2, and tea and coffee for a range of prices. The hearty vegetable tart, which comes with bread and salad, comes recommended.

Vegetables not your thing? Perhaps you're better off hitting one of the many tapas bars in town. One of the tastiest, **Meson La Venta** (17, place Meynard, tel. 05/56 91 59 80), sits smack across from the daily *marché aux puces* on place Meynard. Sit inside or out and dig into a buffet of small plates, including a Spanish tortilla, cheese-stuffed peppers, and potatoes with aioli, and wash it all down with glasses of tangy sangria.

BERGERAC

Bergerac is a humble little town with a nice community feel that's reflected in the food offerings about town. Sure, there are the handful of Michelin-star-type restaurants, but if you want to eat like a local, skip the fancy places and head straight for the pedestrian. **La Pataterie** (81, rue Neuve d'Argenson, 05/53 61 38 52) has a T.G.I. Friday's vibe, and that's not necessarily a bad thing. Baked potatoes are the specialty, but you can also load up on big salads, greasy meat plates, and booze (mojitos are always the drink du jour).

If you're not feeling that festive but still want a nice meal, you might try the slightly more refined **Restaurant le St. Jacques** (30, rue St. James, tel. 05/53 23 38 08). The proprietors, who are originally from Holland, serve traditional French food based on what's in season—which, if you're lucky, will be some sort of mushroom. Eat in the cozy main dining room if it's raining, or choose the pleasant outdoor courtyard in summer.

SARLAT

In Sarlat, you can always get a croque monsieur or a slice of quiche lorraine for a few euros at a *boulangerie,* but this is truffle country, so let yourself be seduced by the myriad menus proffering these treats. Truffled omelets seem to be the perpetual *plat du jour;* if you're feeling eggy and a little bit spendy, you might want to splash out on the €27 version served at **Restaurant La Rapière** (place de la Cathédrale, tel. 05/53 59 03 13), in the heart of the medieval old town.

Not feeling that *riche*? The traditional €15 lunch *formule* is a three-course treat that's a bit lighter on the old wallet. If a wood-fired pizza is more to your fancy, visit **Pizza la Romane** (3, côte de Toulouse, tel. 05/53 59 23 88), where a vegetarian special and tiramisu await.

Toulouse and Montpellier
TOULOUSE
If you aren't tempted to try the cassoulet in Toulouse, the locals might wonder what's wrong with you. To taste this regional specialty, bring your empty stomach to **À la Truffe de Quercy** (17, rue Croix Baragnon, tel. 05/61 53 34 24), near the Musée des Augustins. The menu is a mélange of traditional and Spanish cuisine, so if you're not feeling the cassoulet, you might try the paella instead.

North of the city center, a short walk from the Canal du Midi Métro stop, is **Les 2 Pachas** (52, avenue Honoré Serres, tel. 05/61 63 99 28). This is Toulouse's prime spot for authentic Moroccan couscous, tajines, and deliciously savory eggplant salad.

MONTPELLIER
Montpellier is student central, and where there are students, there are cheap and filling restaurants. At the **Bol d'Or** (8, rue du Clos René, tel. 04/67 58 43 34), between the *gare* and the place de la Comédie, you can choose between Chinese and Vietnamese dishes; fill up on that tasty relic, chop suey; sample the crab noodles; or choose a dish from the full vegetarian menu.

At **Le Kreisker** (3, passage Bruyas, tel. 04/67 60 82 50), a bit farther north on the other side of the place de la Comédie, filling up on Breton crêpes is as easy as *un deux trois*. The staff is friendly, the atmosphere convivial, and the tables squeezed in tight, so you'll get to know your neighbors while tucking into your galette.

Provence and Côte d'Azur
AIX-EN-PROVENCE
Aix is another student's paradise: coffee shops, bookstores, and affordable eateries abound in the old town and beyond. At **Eqwi** (13, rue d'Italie, tel. 04/42 53 23 79), a quick-serve joint specializing in healthy food to go, you can choose between tasty and affordable bagel sandwiches, wraps, and soups. Vegetarian, gluten-free, and dairy-free items are clearly marked, and both wine and fresh-pressed juices are on offer.

For history-loving arty types, a meal at **Les Deux Garçons** (53, cours

Mirabeau, tel. 04/42 26 00 51), on the lovely tree-shaded street, is a must. This is where everyone from Cézanne and Zola to Piaf and Picasso used to hang out back in the day—and you can hang here, too, beneath the green awning on a summer's day. Expect to pay a pretty penny for that entrée and *plat,* or, if you want the ambience without the astronomical price tag, sip *une bière pression* instead.

ANTIBES

In pretty little Antibes, tucked into the old town behind a salmon-colored façade, sits **Chez Helen** (35, rue des Revennes, tel. 04/92 93 88 52), a *mignon* restaurant specializing in vegetarian cuisine. Helen, a native of England, serves up homey meat-free versions of traditional fare like bangers 'n' mash, lasagna, and chili. Tea, beer, and wine are also on tap.

At the more traditionally French brasserie **La Terrase** (1, Place Guynemer, tel. 04/93 34 56 77), sip your rosé with a salty *apéro* delivered on the house, or come for the morning sunshine backed by a croissant and a café express.

NICE

Nice is famous for *socca,* but when you tire of eating that delicious local specialty and want a complete change of pace, pop into **Delhi Belhi** (22, rue de la Barillerie, tel. 04/93 92 51 87) for a memorable evening meal. No, not *that* kind of memorable (they really should change their name); this authentic North Indian restaurant offers oodles of ambience and delectable curries at reasonable prices. Everything you try will be delicious, but the naan and *aloo baji* are particularly tasty.

If you're ravenous and in the mood for something napped in tomato sauce, **Pasta Basta** (18 rue de la Préfecture, tel. 04 93 80 03 57) is your place. Huge plates of pasta, gnocchi, and pizza await you, but you might have to wait for a seat—this place is popular with a capital *P*.

Lyon and Grenoble

LYON

Ask gourmets which city is the food capital of France, and they'll inevitably say Lyon. If you want a taste of no-frills French food cooked to perfection and served in a homey atmosphere, get thee to the old town, spin yourself around, and walk into the first *bouchon* you bump into. These traditional Lyonnais restaurants serve food like Grandma used to make, if Grandma happened to live in the Rhône-Alpes region and wasn't a vegetarian. Meaty dishes like goose-liver terrine, duck cooked in cognac, and chubby pork sausages take center stage at *bouchons,* so remember to bring your heart meds.

For something on the lighter end of the spectrum, **Wasabi** (76 rue d'Anvers, tel. 04/37 28 08 77), on the other side of the Rhône River in the university district, serves Japanese fare that will leave you sated but not belly-ache full. Sushi, miso soup, and Korean-style *bulgogi* are on the menu, as are special *formules* for children and vegetarians.

GRENOBLE

The mist-shrouded, mountainous landscape around Grenoble brings to mind Alpine resort foods, like fondue and cheesy raclette. You actually will find those dishes here, but that's so predictable. How about going for southeast Asian instead? Grenoble has a sizeable Vietnamese community, with bountiful authentic restaurants catering to those locals. Near the Tuesday–Sunday *marché* l'Estacade, **Saveurs d'Asie** (3, boulevard Gambetta, tel. 04/76 84 41 32) serves up traditional Vietnamese favorites like *pho,* rice-paper rolls, and *bahn xeo.* When you're full up, you can shop for condiments at the nearby Asian grocery stores.

For another taste of South Asia, try one of the masala *dosas* at **Lanka** (49, cours Jean Jaurès, tel. 04/76 86 06 61), or go nuts and have the *thali* for a hearty lunch.

Sample Itineraries

Even if you only have a week, you can pack a lot of exploration into your fact-finding experience, thanks to France's marvelous public transportation system. Two weeks will provide you with a cursory sense of what to expect when you land permanently. If you have a month to spare, consider yourself an honorary local. Before you leave, you'll want to get familiar with the national railway website, www.sncf.fr, for making online reservations for trains, cars, and flights. Once you're here, try to imagine yourself as a resident. Hit the neighborhood cafés, visit the cinema or the theater, take in a musical performance, picnic in the neighborhood parks, and above all, sample the wares at the local *boulangeries;* there's no underestimating the importance of a good baguette.

ONE WEEK: THE PARIS COMMUTER
Day 1

Once you've settled into your temporary **Paris** digs, you need to get out there and explore. Use your first day to orient yourself to the city and its major landmarks as you shake your jet lag. Pick up a free city map at a tourist office or invest in a Michelin guide of the city; it's indispensible if you're going to make Paris your home.

Today is also a good day to secure your travel passes. If you plan to use a combination of public transportation and walking, spend €12 on a *carnet* of 10 tickets good for the Métro and city buses that will last the duration of your stay—if you limit your travel to one or two rides a day and walk the rest. For about €40, you can splash out on an unlimited Navigo pass that'll get you to and from the airports on the RER, as well as the suburbs of Versailles and Fontainebleu, if you choose to voyage out and about. Less expensive but more restricted Navigo options are also available; all can be purchased from kiosk vendors in train stations, some Métro stations, and many tabacs.

Days 2 and 3

Now that you're familiar with the layout of the city, get to know some of the quartiers you're considering settling in. Outdoor markets are a good way to get a feel for the neighborhood. See who's shopping there, who's selling, and *what* they're selling. Stop in to the friendliest-looking café for a glass of wine or a coffee, pick up a baguette sandwich from an inviting *boulangerie,* find a bench in a park or square that's perfect for people-watching, and tuck in.

Along the **Canal St. Martin** in the 10th arrondissement, you can join the others lounging in the sun along the water, sharing an afternoon picnic. Farther north, near **La Chappelle,** take in an Indian thali, then walk it off heading toward **La Villette,** where joggers, cyclists, and parents pushing strollers make good use of the open green spaces. If it's a Saturday morning, mosey over to the lively **Batignolles** neighborhood, where a weekly *bio* (organic) market is in full swing. While you're here, stop into every *immobilier* (real estate office) you pass and pick up a copy of its latest listings.

From here, hop on the Métro and migrate south toward **Parc St. Cloud,** where you can look back at Paris and admire the view, as Marie Antoinette and Napoleon III once did, while getting a taste of what suburban Paris has to offer. Crossing the *périphérique* back into Paris proper, head toward the **Alésia** neighborhood in the 14th, visit the cool (and kind of creepy) catacombs, then pick up a copy of *Particulier à Particulier* at the nearest *La Presse* kiosk, tote it to an inviting terrace café, and enjoy the last rays of the sun while perusing your collection of apartment-rental listings.

Days 4 and 5

You have a feel for the city now, and you've even prowled a few prime neighborhoods. It's time to brave the French-speaking sphere by making phone calls and arranging visits to some of those Parisian abodes you've been scoping out. If you don't have a phone or a phone card, pick one up. It's as easy as a visit to Phone House (there's one in nearly every arrondissement), where €25 will get you a *portable,* a SIM card, and calling time to make those vital connections. Don't forget to check out Craigslist and FUSAC for both housing and job leads.

If you're leaning toward a certain neighborhood, this might be a good moment to explore your banking options and even open a French bank account. Whatever branch you select will become your "home" branch, so be thoughtful in your choice—changing banks isn't impossible, but like every other bureaucratic process, it is time-consuming and a tad draining. If you're planning to buy rather than rent, consider discussing mortgage prospects with your banker, too.

Spend a bit of time exploring the campus of the Sorbonne, or visit any private language school you're considering. With a little planning, you could also hit a Meetup (www.meetup.com) to get to know some of the locals before you make the big leap.

Day 6

Spend your penultimate day in Paris exploring the close **suburbs** and enjoying a spot of relaxation while you're at it. To the east, over the *périphérique,* the Montreuil flea market (Saturday through Monday) is worth a stop before you head into town to explore this affordable alternative to Paris. One town over and a short walk or Métro ride away is St. Mandé, with its old-fashioned downtown and close proximity to the beautiful Bois de Vincennes. Pick up your comestibles at the open-air market, then head to the 1,000-hectare park for lunch in a verdant setting. As you relax beside Lac Daumesnil, synthesize your experiences and make a mental checklist: What neighborhoods can I really imagine living in? What job prospects deserve further consideration? Do I need to make another visit?

Day 7

With all the real-estate information, business cards, email addresses, and phone numbers of new friends tucked safely into your suitcase, you can enjoy your final breakfast of a croissant, *thé,* and *Le Parisien* before heading to Charles de Gaulle for the flight home.

TWO WEEKS: THE WEST COAST JAUNT

You've done the Paris region, and now it's time to broaden your horizons westward and southward to see what life could be like outside France's largest metropolis.

Day 1

Begin with a train ride from Paris's Montparnasse station to **Rennes,** the gateway to Brittany. After checking into your hotel, mosey over to the university town's liveliest square, **place des Lices,** with its colorful half-timbered buildings, crowded cafés and brasseries, Saturday-morning market, and generally lively tempo. After you purchase your fill of fresh apples and snack on the requisite crêpe from a market stand, visit the tourist office, where the friendly staff will supply you with maps and answer all your questions about Rennes' history and its varied quartiers, and offer you tips on where to dine and sightsee. Spend the afternoon strolling along the canal and exploring the pedestrian walkways and parks before heading back to the place des Lices for dinner of pizza and wine at an outdoor eatery.

Day 2

If it's a sunny day, get yourself a day pass for the Vélo Star, Rennes' public bike-share program, and start exploring the neighborhoods of this flat, cycle-friendly city. Check out the two University of Rennes campuses—you might be working or attending classes here at some point—and pick up a copy of *France Ouest,* the local daily, to get a read on life in Western France. After a long day cruising the city, roll over to O'Connell's Irish Pub, Rennes' unofficial Anglophone hub, and just *try* not to make a new friend or two over your pint of Guinness.

Days 3, 4, and 5

A bit more than an hour away by bus, iconic **Mont St. Michel** beckons as a fun day or overnight trip. Middle Ages architecture and fairytale ambience reign in this corner of France, where awe-inspiring ocean views and Romanesque churches compete for your attention. From here, you can hire a rental car and drive south to **Vannes,** a pretty little medieval town on the Morbihan coast. Check into your hotel and then hit the streets, where a walk through the pedestrian-friendly *centre ville* works up a craving for crêpes and cider. Indulge! You'll need food to fuel your walkabout. Vannes is small enough to get to know on foot—unless you're interested in "rural" Vannes, in which case a cruise in your rental car is a great idea. Market days are Wednesdays and Saturdays, and everyone in town turns out for the shopping experience—you should, too. Meandering by foot gives you plenty of opportunity to collect real-estate brochures and pop into agencies to ask questions, and don't be shy about talking to local shopkeepers about the way of life here.

A 20-minute drive southwest brings you to **Carnac,** where stone megaliths as far as the eye can see offer visual reminders of Brittany's ancient Celtic roots. The *fleur de sel* (sea salt) produced in this region is among the most coveted by epicures, and regional treats—from buttery caramels to locally harvested sea beans—conjure up the salty flavor of the ocean. Driving back into Vannes, take in the sea air. Does this feel like a weekend-getaway destination or a dig-in-your-heels-for-the-long-haul kind of place? To take the live-like-a-local experience a step further, try a yoga class or catch a live musical or theatrical performance at the Théâtre Anne de Bretagne.

Day 6

Breathe the word "bordeaux," and it's hard not to visualize that ruby-red elixir of the gods. This is indeed the gateway to one of France's most celebrated wine-growing regions and most vibrant urban communities. Getting here from Vannes involves a six-hour train ride, leaving you with enough time to catch up on sleep, finish that novel you've been toting, or delve into all the job- and house-seeking materials you've gathered.

Assuming you arrive in Bordeaux in the late afternoon, check into your hotel, don your walking shoes, and make a beeline for the Garonne River and its pedestrian-friendly promenade. Take in the vistas and the atmosphere, then head back across the street toward a lively shopping street, Sainte-Catherine, and settle in for a meal at one of the many nearby tapas restaurants.

Days 7, 8, and 9

You'll need at least one day in Bordeaux just to get the lay of the land. Pick up a bus pass or *carnet* (10 tickets good for the bus and tramway), and set off exploring, making sure to cross the river into the emerging neighborhood of La Bastide to visit the botanical gardens. Head north to Le Lac for a bit of sunbathing and people-watching if the weather is warm, and explore several centuries'-worth of old churches in between. Take time to stroll on foot, and to examine the *"à louer"* (to rent) and *"à vendre"* (to buy) listings.

Weekdays are prime for scheduling home-viewing appointments; after you've visited a few *immobiliers,* perused online listings, and made a few phone calls, your day should include several hours of home-scoping, leaving you enough daylight to visit the sprawling Université de Bordeaux campus and meet with potential employers.

If one of your Bordeaux days is a Sunday, lucky you: It's market day, and the offerings range from fresh-cut flowers to oysters on the half-shell. You've earned a day of relaxation, so consider a visit to one of the city's many museums. Move from the past to the present at the Musée des Arts Décoratifs, or zoom straight into the eclectic 21st-century at the Musée d'Art Contemporain. Finish your final day in Bordeaux with a *verre de vin* at an outdoor café in the Chartrons district, overlooking the river.

Day 10

When your inner Bacchus begins to stir, pick up a rental car or catch a train at Gare St. Jean and head east toward the beautiful wine-growing region of the **Dordogne Valley.** Independent wineries punctuate the landscape; if you're traveling by car, stop for a sip and maybe pick up a bottle to enjoy later. Pop into **St. Emilion** before heading to **Bergerac,** and if there's enough daylight left, wander the compact old town, visit an art opening, and stop for a pizza at a homey restaurant.

Day 11

If you've made arrangements with local real-estate agents to view properties for sale, book your appointments for the morning so you'll have time for

© JENNIFER PICKENS/BLACKBIRDPHOTO.COM

Take time to explore the medieval village of Sarlat.

an afternoon boat ride on the river before making the 60-kilometer journey to **Sarlat.** On your way, pass through the medieval villages of Milandes, Lanquais, and Montbazillac. In **Les Eyzies,** stop at the national museum of prehistory to see what the first Frenchies were up to all those millennia ago.

Days 12 and 13

After getting situated in Sarlat, explore the pretty village. Don't forget to visit the covered market (where you can pick up the local specialty, truffles) with its sky-scraping metal doors and Disneyland atmosphere. Stop for *un verre* at a café on the place de la Liberté and soak it all in. In the summer, expect music, art, and theater in the streets. The rest of the year, similar cultural activities move indoors. Take a sculpture- or jewelry-making class, and get to know some of the locals who may soon become your new neighbors.

It's a great idea to dedicate a day to exploring housing possibilities; after cruising the surrounding countryside, you may be thinking that a more rural living situation is right up your alley. Allow enough time to meet with several different agencies and explore all your options—setting aside an hour or two to visit the *mairie* and the chamber of commerce would also be wise, especially if you plan to open a business here and have questions about how to do so.

Day 14

Before heading for the airport, train station, or highway in your rental car, take one last spin through town and pick up some of the locally produced treats, including a bottle of the heavenly walnut wine. If you haven't visited the tourist office yet, pop in and pick up any brochures you may have missed, and ask any final questions about the area. Oh, and that truffled omelet? This is now-or-never time.

FOUR WEEKS: SEA, SUN, AND SNOW

With a month to amble around *la belle France,* you'll not only come away with a solid sense of the varied geography, but you'll have time to relax and absorb the unique characteristics of each region.

Weeks 1 and 2

Even with all this time on your hands, it still makes sense to begin your adventure in Paris. From here, you can move either clockwise or counter-clockwise. Following our route west and south, you could hit Rennes, Vannes, Bordeaux, and the Dordogne Valley, or do a bit of hopscotching to reach the areas that hold the most appeal to allow time for in-depth exploration.

Weeks 3 and 4

The capital of the Languedoc region, **Toulouse,** is a sprawling, sophisticated metropolis settled by the Romans way back in 120 B.C. You'll also find a cosmopolitan blend of people here—Anglophones among them—drawn by the area's thriving high-tech and aerospace industries. Meander the medieval back streets of the old city; visit France's largest cathedral, the Basilic de St. Sernin (pray that the organist is in session); and relish a steaming dish of cassoulet in the local tradition.

If you want to meet friendly locals, go to the English in Toulouse Meetup that takes place every Friday evening. Walk or ride the Canal du Midi path, and spend a day or two gallivanting about town and getting to know the neighborhoods.

Farther south, as you migrate toward Montpellier, make a side trip to the fortified city of **Carcassonne,** where the bougainvillea clinging to rough stone edifices signals your proximity to the Mediterranean. Explore the fairytale old city; take in a jousting match at the castle; and visit the thrice-weekly market, where local vendors peddle honey, cheese, and other locally produced goods.

When you arrive in **Montpellier,** you can abandon your rental car and rely on trains to move you around the Mediterranean coast. If the sun is shining—which it most likely will be—mosey over to place de la Comédie, the city's pedestrian plaza, and find a terrace café beneath the palm trees to sip a cool glass of rosé and watch the world go by. The tourist office on the northwest edge of the *place* is a hotbed of activity and information: Stop in here to ask questions, collect brochures, and make theater reservations. You'll also find rental-housing information and brochures for Anglophone real-estate agents here.

Next, take the train or drive 130 kilometers to the quintessential Provençal college town of **Aix-en-Provence.** Make it your southerly home base for a few days to explore the region that inspired painters from Cézanne to Van Gogh. Don't forget to stop into the Book in Bar bookshop and make use of their English-language resources for newcomers. The bulletin board and friendly staff are just the beginning; the books, muffins, and tea are the icing on the cake.

Back along the coastal route, make **Antibes** your home for a day or two. Walk the cobbled city streets within the ramparts and admire the pleasure boats in the harbor; bike, walk, or drive around Cap d'Antibes; look at some of the rental possibilities for sale; and take a dip in the sea if it's between June and October. Next stop: **Nice,** where it really is nice, and a lunch of *socca* and sauvignon blanc awaits beneath bright blue skies. Get a short-term bus pass and explore Monaco, Menton, and the tidy, sun-dappled streets of Nice's diverse neighborhoods. Real-estate agencies by the boatload beckon on nearly every *rue,* so make good use of them—and don't miss the tourist office, in a dated building on the promenade des Anglais. The staff can point you toward the next ski bus headed for the Alps or book you a hotel room in the city center.

When you grow tired of the seafaring views and sunshine, head north toward **Grenoble,** where the palm trees give way to pines and the snow-capped Alps come into focus. Hemmed in by mountains, Grenoble is prime outdoor-activity territory, the place to give in to your urge to commune with nature. After you've settled in to your *chambre d'hôte,* hotel, or by-the-week apartment, hit the hiking and biking trails to breathe in the delicious, conifer-scented air.

A visit to one of Grenoble's daily markets will give you a sense of the city's varied population and will introduce you to all the wonderful produce and other edibles at your disposal. If you're here on a Tuesday, visit the Open House Grenoble Meetup and talk to other expats, who'll share their wisdom and experience to help make the transition into life here easier and smoother. If you have an interview at one of the many American companies with French offices here, you'll likely meet someone at one of these events who'll be able to share information on office culture, too.

A 90-minute train ride from Grenoble puts you in **Lyon,** France's second-largest city and the country's gastronomic capital. Big but not intimidating, Lyon deserves at least a few days. Ride the funicular to the top of the hill overlooking the city and take in the broad-reaching panorama, across red-tiled roofs and two rivers. Visit the famous basilica and the beautifully preserved Roman amphitheater, then eat a meal—or two or three—at a *bouchon,* where humble Lyonnais cuisine rules.

Once you've scoped out the housing situation and investigated the local job market, you might as well dive right into the networking scene. Anglophones at Lyon's social get-togethers offer a chance to mingle with a youthful, enthusiastic group of expats who are ready to welcome you into their fold and share tips and suggestions. An exploratory visit to a few of Lyon's many French-language schools might factor into your plans, too.

DAILY LIFE

MAKING THE MOVE

No more postponing the dream. You've decided to make the move to France and integrate baguettes, berets, and cafés into your everyday life. Yes! What's more, you've already made a reconnaissance trip or two, decided where you want to live, and begun researching the area for schools, employment opportunities, and housing. Now comes the tricky part: how to make it all happen. Visas, *cartes de séjour,* residency permits—what do they all mean, and what exactly do you need to make this big leap a success? There's a lot to consider, but with a bit more planning and a lot of moxie, the transition can be practically pain-free. Stumbling blocks are bound to appear, but don't let the bureaucratic sludge drag you down. Follow the rules and somehow, thankfully, it all comes together. Excited? You ought to be! Just a few more hurdles and you're on your way.

Horaire / Time	Destinations	Vol / Flight	Vol / Flight	Terminal	
1120	MINSK	B2 866		2B	ON TIME
1120	CHICAGO	UA 943		1	DELAYED
1125	MONTPELLIER	AF 7680	AZ 3680	2F	ON TIME
1125	DOHA	QR 022		1	ON TIME
1125	ISTANBUL	TK 1822		1	ON TIME
1130	TOKYO-NARITA	AF 272		2E	ON TIME
1130	ATHENS	OA 202		1	ON TIME
1130	ANTALYA	OHY 646		3	ON TIME
1130	LOS ANGELES PAPEETE	TN 007		2A	ON TIME
1130	AJACCIO	U2 3717		2B	EXPECTED 11:40
1135	ABU DHABI	EY 032		2A	ON TIME
1135	DUBROVNIK	OU 477		1	ON TIME
1140	FRANKFURT	LH 4215	UA 9073	1	ON TIME
1140	MONASTIR	TU 7561		3	ON TIME
1140	PHILADELPHIA	US 755		1	ON TIME
1145	DALLAS	AA 049	GF 6649	2A	DELAYED
1145	BRUSSELS	SN 3634		1	ON TIME
1145	MOSCOW	SU 250	AF 2044	2E	ON TIME
1145	RIYADH	SU 168		1	BOARDING
1145	BASTIA	U2 3723		2B	EXPECTED 12:00
1145	ALICANTE	UY 8244	IB 5797	3	ON TIME
1150	BAKOU	J2 074		2B	ON TIME
1150	CATANIA	U2 3885		2B	EXPECTED 13:05

Horaire / Time	Destinations	Vol / Flight	Vol / Flight	Terminal
1235	BRUSSELS	AF 7183		2T
1235	NANTES	AF 7724	MK 9096	2D
1235	ROME-FIUMICINO	AZ 333	AF 9846	2F
1235	SOFIA	FB 432	AF 2786	2B
1240	WARSAW	AF 2346		2F
1240	RABAT	AF 2458	DL 8695	2F
1240	NAPLES	AF 2578	AZ 7819	2F
1240	LUXEMBOURG	LG 8014	AF 4602	2D
1245	STUTTGART	AF 2008	AZ 2656	2D
1245	MOSCOW	AF 2244	SU 450	2E
1245	OVIEDO	AF 3242	UX 3426	2G
1245	BREMEN	AF 5532	DL 8372	2G
1245	PAU	AF 7772	AZ 2964	2G
1255	BARCELONA	AF 1648	UX 3648	2F
1255	DUSSELDORF	AF 1906	MK 9366	2D
1255	PRAGUE	AF 1982	DL 8590	2D
1255	MANCHESTER	AF 2268	UX 3503	2E
1255	COPENHAGEN	AF 2350	DL 8426	2D
1255	GOTHENBURG	AF 3222	AZ 3708	2G
1255	DUBLIN	AF 5006	AZ 3574	2E
1255	BILBAO	AF 5964	KL 2166	2G
1255	MARSEILLE	AF 7664	OK 3782	2F
1255	NICE	AF 7714	MK 9088	2F
1255	DJERBA	BIE7246		3

Immigration and Visas

As a citizen of Canada or the United States, you don't need a visa for stays of fewer than 90 days. France is a signee of the Schengen Agreement, which means it shares a flexible internal border-control system with fellow Schengen countries and a stronger border-crossing process with non-Schengen countries, such as the United Kingdom. Passport checks are rare between, say, France and Belgium, but they're a given if you're traveling to the UK. Your free 90-day visa is valid throughout the Schengen zone, but don't mistakenly believe that to extend your stay you just need to Chunnel on over to England, get your passport stamped, and resume another 90-day sojourn in France. Unfortunately, it doesn't work like that. If you want to stay legal, you can make only one 90-day visit within any six-month period. When in doubt, apply for a long-stay visa or accept the risks involved in overstaying your welcome.

The first step in determining what kind of visa to apply for is to ask yourself how long you plan to be in France. If you're subletting your flat back in Minneapolis and just want to try a three-month trial run, that's considered a "short stay"—as is any stay shorter than 90 days—and a valid passport is all you need. But if you're planning on a year (a school year or an actual calendar year), you'll need to begin the visa application process *tout de suite* (right away). Even though it probably won't take this long, give yourself a good two months to make it all come together.

DOSSIER 101

Dossier. OK, let's try saying that out loud the French way: "DOH-see-yay."

You'll want to practice this a few times to get the hang of it, because you're going to use it a lot. You'll need a dossier for every step of the way on your move to France, beginning at the consulate, and ending with – well, it never ends in France. You'll create a dossier for the *préfecture*, the bank, the real-estate company, the movers, your university, your children's school, the gas company, the veterinarian, the doctor, and just about everything else you can think of.

The dossier is simply a file containing documents relating to whatever business is at hand. The foundation of nearly every dossier is a copy of your passport or other ID, plus your gas bill or other proof of residence (often an *attestation* written by the person hosting you, complete with his gas bill and copy of his *carte d'identité*). Then, like a bureaucratic buffet, each agency adds on a series of additional must-haves that give your dossier its special flavor.

Though most expats find the dossier system tiresome, each pile of paperwork you create makes building the next one that much easier.

Step two is figuring out what you're going to do when you get here, to help you zero in on which long-stay visa to apply for. Maybe you've always fantasized about living in France and just want an extended vacation to relax, study independently, or meet a handsome Frenchman or -woman and see where the relationship takes you. If so, you'll need money in the bank to show you can support yourself for the duration of your stay. Do you have a brilliant idea for a new business that *has* to be launched in France? There's a visa for that. It also requires evidence of your means of support, plus detailed information on how you plan to carry out the project, and you must prove that the idea itself fills a void in France to be eligible for approval. Maybe you're a college student who wants to study abroad for the semester or a nanny (or manny) who just landed an au pair job through an agency. Whether you're an artist, an entrepreneur, an intern, or a student, there's a long-stay visa with your name on it. Now getting that visa will take a bit of elbow grease and perseverance, but armed with willpower and solid resolve, you can make it happen.

WHERE AND HOW TO APPLY

Submitting your visa application must be done in person, but not every state or province in the United States and Canada has a French consulate. If your region does not, you'll have to make the trip for a scheduled appointment. One appointment is all you need: Follow-up requests for documentation can be mailed or faxed in, and your passport—with or without a shiny new visa inside—can be mailed back to you in the prestamped express-mail envelope you provide at the time of your appointment. To find the consulate closest to you, visit www.ambafrance-us.org (United States) or www.ambafrance-ca.org (Canada).

THE LONG-STAY VISA

Visa laws have been relaxed in the past few years, so most long-stay visa holders don't need to visit the *préfecture* on arrival, as had long been standard protocol. (An exception to this rule is the Carte Compétences et Talents, which still necessitates a visit to your local prefect. More on that below.) Instead of schlepping yourself and your dossier full of paperwork to endless appointments, the streamlined system allows you to register with the French Office of Immigration and Integration (OFII) by mail within three months of your arrival.

Registration involves submitting copies of your passport pages that show your photo and expiration date; the entry stamp for your arrival in France; and the visa issued to you by the French Consulate. You'll also need to include a completed Demande d'Attestation OFII form, which you'll receive from consular officials when your passport is returned to you with your new visa. (If you don't automatically receive this form, ask for one or visit the OFII website to download a copy: www.ofii.fr.)

These items must be sent via *letter récommandé*, which is essentially a registered letter that the recipient will sign for. Once your documents are received, you'll receive a notice of receipt from the OFII, which serves as temporary proof of your legal right to stay in France. Within three months, you'll be called in for the requisite medical exam, which includes lung X-rays and blood-sugar analysis, at which time you'll also pay for your *timbres* (tax stamps)—which, depending on your status, will vary between €55 and €340. Once this process has been completed, you'll receive the final passport stamp in the visa-acquisition process: a *vignette* stamp alongside your French visa. Now, a big sigh of relief!

STUDENT VISA

Probably the most popular of all move-to-France visas is the student visa. French universities are open to anyone of any age who has earned his or her high school diploma or equivalent. Because it's a relatively straightforward point of entry into France that also gives the holder the right to work part-time, this is an attractive option for getting your foot through the French front door.

Students used to have to apply for a visa even if they intended to stay for fewer than 90 days, but that's no longer the case: Your American or Canadian passport is sufficient if you'll be living and studying in France for less than three months—say, a summer study-abroad course. However, because students who hold a *carte de séjour* are entitled to work part-time during their stay, you might consider jumping through those more challenging hoops to get the long-stay visa even if you don't plan to stay for the entire duration, just for the added perk of being allowed to work legally.

If you'll be studying for more than three months, you'll need to apply for a long-stay student visa, which first requires you to register online with Campus France, an intermediary agency that handles the initial phase of your visa formalities. Here, you'll create the first of many *dossiers,* so consider it a necessary evil. Whether you're a Canadian or an American citizen, you will be expected to have your Campus France ID number at the time of your appointment at the consulate, as well as a long-stay visa application, travel itinerary, and proof of financial means of support while you're away. You may also be asked for several other documents, making for a multivisit experience before you've even left the country. (If you live out of state or out of the area, you'll be allowed to fax or send in supplemental documents.) You'll need several passport-size photos during the process, so have a set made and carry them with you to each appointment in your home country and in France.

Once you arrive in France with most types of visa, you'll need to follow the OFII registration procedure outlined in the long-stay visa section above. If, after your first year in France, you'd like to renew your residency permit, you'll have to do so at the prefecture two months before your current residency permit expires.

WORK VISA

If you're one of the lucky ones who has already received a job offer in France, you'll have to apply for a visa before you can receive your work permit. But before that happens, the company sponsoring you must file all the necessary paperwork on its end with the French labor department (DDTEFP). (The exception to this is the work contract for 90 days or fewer; no visa is needed for short-term workers, but your employer must still file paperwork on your behalf to make the arrangement legal.) Once it's approved, you can start cultivating your own paper trail.

CARTE DE SAY WHAT?

Name: Jennifer Kildee
Age: 48
Hometown: Camarillo, CA
Current city: Paris

Jennifer moved to France in 2008 with a flourishing business as a French translator. As an independent contractor whose business was established in the United States, Jennifer doesn't have to pay French taxes, but she's not exempt from the annual trip to the *préfecture* to (hopefully) renew that all-important document, the *carte de séjour*.

In her own words: "When I first arrived in France, I lived in the suburbs outside of Paris. My first encounter with French bureaucracy was when my boyfriend and I went to the *préfecture* to get the *carte de séjour* process rolling. We waited for hours outside, and once we made it to the reception desk, we were handed a sheet of paper listing all the documents I would need to bring to my *carte de séjour* appointment. We took a number and waited at least another hour. When my number finally came up, the official told us what papers I would need to bring to my *carte de séjour* appointment. So basically, four hours were spent just to get the same piece of information twice. Everything you've heard about French bureaucracy and inefficiency are true. Once I moved to Paris, it became more efficient because now I deal with Cité, the main Paris *préfecture*. It's still big and impersonal, but they take appointments and there is less waiting time.

The first couple of times I had to deal with French bureaucrats, I was very nervous. It was so bad that at my medical screening, one of the doctors asked about the *'boutons'* on my skin. Sure enough, I was covered with red blotches. I don't deal with uncertainty well, and whether your application gets approved

DAILY LIFE

Don't have a job offer yet? Start scouring the employment opportunities on sites like FUSAC (www.fusac.org), Craigslist, the UN, OECD, and UNESCO. Note that high-level, well-paid positions are in high demand among future expats, and the pool of qualified applicants will be full and competition stiff. Be honest with yourself when submitting your résumé: If you don't have a college degree, the likelihood you'll land one of the coveted positions with an international NGO or multinational with offices in France is slim. The odds aren't impossible, but they're not great. The more well-rounded your educational qualifications, the better your chances for getting a sponsored gig. Ditto for your language skills. If you aren't equipped with at least conversational French, you may have a tough time landing your dream job with a company that will sponsor your visa. (See more about working in France in the *Employment* chapter.)

If you work at a company in the United States or Canada with offices in France, explore transfer opportunities. Many banks, high-tech companies,

or denied largely depends on who reviews your case. You have no control over that. I've heard horror stories about nasty officials who deny applications over the most trivial thing. Fortunately, everyone I've encountered has been pleasant. The last time I had to renew, I was much less nervous. It has gotten to the point now where I figure that even if something goes wrong, I will just deal with it and come back later. They're not going to kick me out of the country if I fail to fill out a form completely.

Here are some tips for dealing with French officials, based on experience:

• Appearances are very important to the French, so I always dress for a *carte* appointment as if I were on a job interview. I've often heard that if you smile too much, it will be read as a sign of weakness. It's OK to be friendly during your appointment, but don't give the impression that you can be pushed around.

• Go over your list of required documents several times and make sure you have everything. I have seen people turned away after waiting for hours because they were missing one sheet of paper out of their entire file. Bring extra copies; it's better to have too many copies than not enough.

• The French don't mess around with their language. In every dealing you have with an official, including the mandatory medical screening, you will be expected to understand and speak French. Out of the dozens of personnel I encountered during my medical visit, maybe one or two spoke a few words of English. If you feel you aren't sufficiently proficient in the language, bring a friend."

and fashion-related organizations have set up shop here and offer first-consideration privileges to those who have been on their employment rosters for at least three months. As a final option, you can hit up your French friends to "hire" you to work for them. If a good friend or family member is willing to climb the bureaucratic Mt. Blanc on your behalf, this could be your ticket. As with any endeavor that attempts to skirt the standard procedure, there are inherent risks involved; still, this sort of creative problem-solving is not unheard of. Approached with a modicum of professionalism, it can be a successful way to move to France and secure legal permission to work.

CARTE DE SÉJOUR COMPÉTENCES ET TALENTS

In theory, this new "skill and talents" card is a dream come true for independent, creative types who want to live in France but don't fit into any of the other visa categories. The idea is that you come up with a project you'd like to work on in France that fits within your professional and educational experience. The tricky part is that it must in some way function as a means of bridging the cultural relationship between France and your home country. Perhaps you own a bicycle shop in Portland and teach mountain-biking clinics on the weekend; you may want to parlay your experience into a business that teaches children how to ride downhill in the Alps. Or perhaps you're finishing up your PhD in 20th-century American literature and want to start a tourism business that takes travelers on a journey along the path of the Lost Generation in Paris and beyond. There are countless ideas, but this visa still in the experimental phase. There are no exact parameters on what the powers-that-be are looking for, and therefore no guarantees that they'll accept your idea To boost your chances, invest time in creating a solid business plan before presenting it to French consular officials. Get creative with your powers of persuasion, pull out all your credentials (letters of recommendation, diplomas, and certificates), and really sell yourself and the lasting contribution your project will have on the French public.

When applying for a *carte de séjour compétences et talents,* you'll need to prepare yourself for the number of trees that will be sacrificed to meet the demands of consular officials: long-stay visa forms, letters from your bank, a police record release or FBI clearance form, résumé, proof of insurance, proof that you have a place to stay in France, flight itineraries—all in duplicate.

If you are granted this visa, you are entitled—again, in theory—to a renewable three-year *carte de séjour* that allows you to work in your chosen profession. If you are married, your spouse will receive a *vie privée et familiale* card that entitles him or her to work as well. But don't get too excited just yet. Even if you're granted this visa, you can still expect to jump through a lot of hoops to get your *carte* once you arrive in France. Expect to spend many hours over several days, weeks, and even months at the *préfecture*. You will be asked to produce supplemental material—notarized translations of specific documents, French-language copies of your rental agreement, proof of address, copies of your passport, photographs—and even then you may be told that they're only going to give you a one-year *carte* "to see how it goes" before allowing you to renew.

FOREIGN TRADER'S CARD

Some people are born with an entrepreneurial spirit. If you want to start a business in France, it will help to be equipped with both that spirit *and* the patience of a saint. You've heard a bit about French bureaucracy, right? Well, it hits its zenith at the business-launching phase. The good news is that tax laws have been relaxed in the last few years, making it easier for startups than ever before. But before you start thinking about applying for this special *carte,* be sure to do your research and have a solid business plan ready. In addition to your long-stay visa application, you'll be asked to provide budgets, proof of funding, and other documents that support your assertion that you know what you're doing and have the backing to carry out the project. Pull out all the stops: Got an aunt in Brittany you haven't seen in 20 years? Call her up and ask if she'll act as a *garante* (financial guarantor). If you have a bank account established in France already, ask the bank to write a letter attesting to your solid financial history and line of credit. Most of all, pitch your idea by touting all the wonderful ways in which it will benefit France, fill a major void, and better serve the community. Your education, experience, connections within France, and ability to communicate in French will all be taken into consideration by the consulate.

VISAS FOR ACCOMPANYING SPOUSES AND CHILDREN

Depending on the type of visa you've applied for, your children and spouse will likely be authorized to join you, provided you've all filled out the necessary forms and provided the required paperwork. Before you begin the process, make sure you have copies of your marriage license, spouse's birth certificate, and birth certificates of your children. If you or your spouse has children from a previous relationship, a notarized letter from the other parent granting permission to move to France will also be required.

For the *carte de séjour compétences et talents,* your spouse also receives permission to work, though there may be limitations, such as part-time only. Workers being sponsored by an employer need to ensure that the "accompanying family member" paperwork is being taken care of by said employer.

OTHER VISAS

Visas for nannies, researchers, interns, and retirees also exist, and the steps for applying for each are similar to the aforementioned visa application processes. And if you've met a French national and want to marry and move to France, there's a visa for you, too. If the visa you are applying for is likely to be denied for some reason, you will probably be notified of this at the time of your consular appointment. There's a chance that your visa request will be outright refused, in which case you have the right to reapply. If you don't hear back from the consulate within two months, this means the rejection is firm.

Beyond the Visa

When asked to sign formal documents at the *préfecture,* you will often be required to ink your John Hancock into a little rectangular box. Note that this box has very specific boundaries, and if your signature extends beyond any of the four sides of said box, you have effectively ruined the entire document and will have to start over from scratch. So remember to write between the lines—seriously.

Before you are granted any kind of official *carte,* you will be given a temporary Récépissé de Demande de Carte de Séjour, a small rectangle of paper with your photo attached to it and an official seal and an expiration date stamped on it. Before you trade in the interim paper in for the official pink laminated version, you'll be required to undergo a quick health screening at a public clinic. The government foots the bill for this—which seems appropriate considering that you'll have to get naked from the waist up while a stranger photographs your lungs to ensure they're free of tuberculosis.

Depending on where you decide to settle in France, your experience can vary vastly. Expats report shorter waits at *préfectures* outside Paris city limits, as well as generally less muss and fuss when it comes to the bureaucracy. In a city of any size, you can expect long lines—sometimes to the tune of a five-hour wait—and even then, you might not get in the building before they close for lunch or, worse, for the day. Inside, you'll need to pull a numbered ticket from the little machine and wait your turn. Expect line-jumping—lots of it. It's annoying, and you can choose whether or not to pitch a fit. But whatever you do, do not lose your cool with a staff member. Even if you feel as if your brain will explode with frustration after a daylong wait and ruthless line-jumpers, you must keep a calm and composed demeanor when face to face with the people behind the desk if you want to have a successful experience.

Though it may seem superficial, it helps to take extra care with your personal appearance on the day of your *préfecture* visit. Wearing chic, stylish clothing—don't forget to polish your shoes and groom your hair—and having your dossier neatly organized in a professional-looking attaché case will convey to the authorities that you've got your act together, even if that's the furthest thing from the truth. Some people report getting to bypass certain steps, such as providing proof of funds, and credit the fact that they dressed the part of the professional, upstanding citizen.

RESIDENCY

Visas and *cartes de séjour* have temporary residency periods built into them. Your visa buys you a finite amount of time, and your *carte* gives specific time parameters with renewable options. After three continuous years, holders of the *visiteur, salarié, étudiant, vie privée, commerçante, scientifique* or *artistique cartes* visas are eligible to apply for a 10-year residency permit, which gives you the luxury of returning to the *préfecture* only once a decade.

French immigration laws are prone to change with disarming regularity. Keep reviewing the consular websites for new updates and changes, and keep a flexible attitude if at all possible.

Moving with Children

Getting your children to France with you is fairly straightforward, and once you're settled, you'll discover that France is an extraordinarily kid-friendly country—hardly surprising, considering the central role that the family plays here. The first stop in your children's move-abroad adventure is securing your own visa; if you're in, they're in. Like you, they'll need specific documents for the consular appointment: two photos, a long-stay visa application, a copy of their birth certificates and passports. If you are a single father or mother traveling without your child's second parent, you'll also need to bring a notarized letter of authorization signed by him or her.

SCHOOL-AGE CHILDREN

Parents of school-age children will need to begin thinking about enrolling them in some sort of academic institution, and your options are contingent in large part on where you live. *Écoles privées* (private schools)—from Montessori and Waldorf to good old-fashioned Catholic schools—exist throughout the country, and like elsewhere, you'll have to pay tuition. The cost varies

France is an extraordinarily kid-friendly country.

from school to school, but it's generally less expensive than private schools in the U.S. International schools, which are basically American in concept and function, are also available and provide a familiar academic structure at a premium price. Unlike other countries, where "state-run" anything has negative connotations, French *écoles publiques* (public schools) are of uniformly high quality and are a good way to begin your child's integration into French culture. Just like back home, schools want to see a child's academic records and inoculation history, so don't forget to bring copies of those.

CHILDCARE

If your child is younger and you want to consider daycare, it's helpful to register with your local *crèche* (state-run daycare center). These agencies follow the standard academic cycle and generally accept new wards only in September and occasionally in January. Children as young as three months are welcome, and the staff are highly trained and qualified. In Paris and other big cities, you will see brigades of nannies, often from former French colonies in West Africa, pushing prams full of infants. You too can find a nanny via word of mouth, Craigslist, FUSAC, an agency, or a referral from your local *mairie* (city hall).

RESOURCES FOR FAMILIES

As with any major life change, there is bound to be an adjustment period for your child. Kids are generally more adaptable to new situations—and definitely have an edge up on older family members when it comes to the ability to learn new languages—French culture is different from North American culture, and all the unfamiliarity can be unsettling. Fortunately, there is a lot of support here for you and your family.

Families who settle in the Paris area will want to check out MESSAGE (www.messageparis.org), a support network of fellow Anglophone parents and parents-to-be whose aim is to help you and your family integrate, adapt, and adjust to life in the City of Light. They produce a quarterly magazine with information about regional child- and family-friendly events and activities, host social events, and offer a slew of parenting resources. They charge annual membership dues, but you can find valuable information on their website without having to join officially. Another website worth frequenting for information, forums, and articles on a wide range of topics is www.expatica.com, which is particularly comprehensive when it comes to children and family issues. Any question not answered on the site can be posed to the helpful audience in their various forums, and chances are you'll be received warmly and given plenty of helpful information from people who've been through it all already.

Moving with Pets

© SOPHIA PAGAN/WWW.SOPHIAPAGAN.COM

Most cafés have a "dogs allowed" policy.

One of the most common complaints among expats who move to France with their companion animals is how they were allowed to just breeze right in with their pet after going through all the trouble and expense to secure health certificates and other travel documents. "Don't you want to see my paperwork?" is the common newcomer's cry, and "Nope! Welcome to France!" seems to be the official response.

This doesn't mean you should skip the health check; your airline might request documentation supporting your assertion that your cat or dog has no diseases. For dogs and cats, a microchip will be required, as well as current rabies vaccinations.

Your vet back home will have the necessary animal-export forms to be stamped by the USDA, the agency that oversees domestic-animal import and export. France does not have an open-door policy for some breeds of dog categorized as "dangerous": pit bulls, rottweilers, and dogs in the mastiff family. If your dog falls into any one of these categories, you'll have to check with the consulate to confirm the import legalities.

FLYING WITH YOUR PET

Some airlines—United and Air France are two—allow cats and dogs who meet certain weight restrictions to fly in the cabin with you, under your seat. This does not apply to flights coming in and out of the UK, where stringent anti-rabies policies are in place (complete with quarantine) and all animals must be flown in the plane's cargo hold. If you're traveling with your dog or cat, do your best to book a direct flight. The shorter the trip, the less stressful it'll be for your pet—and therefore for you.

It's not generally recommended to sedate your pet because the risks outweigh the benefits. If your four-footed friend reacts badly and looks sick on arrival, customs officials can hold the animal for observation and evaluation by a state-sanctioned veterinarian. Better to time your flight for the evening (or your pet's normal downtime), and if he or she is particularly prone to travel stress, consider a milder approach, such as Bach Flower Remedies' Rescue Remedy, which many pet people swear by. (It reportedly works for stressed-out humans, too.)

CARING FOR YOUR PET

Once you're here, you'll have many veterinarians to choose from, and it wouldn't be a bad idea to visit one and establish a dossier for your pet. This way, you can keep up on necessary vaccinations and have a place to go if your pet should ever fall sick. Don't be surprised if your vet writes you a prescription for Fluffy's antibiotics at the local human pharmacy; many pharmacies throughout France do double-duty vending veterinary and human medical supplies. Pet food is easy to get in France through a number of sources: at grocery stores, natural food stores, dedicated pet-supply stores, veterinarians' offices, and online. Depending on the type of food your pet eats, you may want to shop around to see who offers what and at what price. You'll find premium brands at vets (such as Science Diet and Eukanuba), and if your pet happens to be a vegetarian, chains like Naturalia vend plant-based dry and canned food.

Though France is home to more than 18 million dogs and cats, suggesting a country of animal lovers, some antiquated attitudes toward their care still exist

Follow the arrows to find the dog *toillette* area.

here. It's not uncommon to see dogs out "walking themselves," even in big cities like Paris, and when you find a lost or injured animal on the street, it can be a challenge finding an agency willing to accept responsibility for its care. In theory, you should be able to take the animal to the local *commissariat,* which acts as an intermediary between the public and the SPA (Société Protectrice des Animaux); but in practice, you'll most likely find yourself shouldering the responsibility of taking a found animal to the nearest animal protection agency.

What to Bring

The three most stressful events in a person's life are death, divorce, and moving. To take some of the stress out the already stressful shift from there to here, it's a good idea to begin planning at least six months in advance. This gives you enough time to decide whether to ship your stuff, store it, sell it, or leave it in a sublet. It also gives you enough time to decide what you really need, what you really want, and how to reconcile the two.

HOUSEHOLD ITEMS

With a few minor exceptions, everything you could hope to procure in North America is equally procurable here: furniture, clothing, knick-knacks and tchotchkes, appliances, automobiles, bicycles, jewelry and watches, houseplants, garden furniture, lawnmowers. While most of us don't want to add to

SHIP HAPPENS

Name: Jeff Rogers
Age: 49
Hometown: San Francisco, CA
Current city: Paris

When Jeff was planning his move to Paris with his wife and their small dog, he wasn't convinced that they should ship all of their belongings. It would be expensive, after all – more so than buying a new apartment's worth of Ikea furniture, anyway. But in the end, his collection of bicycles – nearly 10 of them – was the deciding factor that container shipping was the way to go.

In his own words: "Because of the uncertainty of how long we'd be living in France – it could be one year or as many as six – we had to carefully weigh all the options. Storing everything would have been relatively affordable at approximately $350 per month, but after the first year, the financial advantages would have been negligible. The fact is that we are fond of our things – art, vinyl records, old rugs – and I am particularly attached to my bicycles. Since shipping them via FedEx or regular post would have cost about $400

per bike, it just didn't seem worth it to go that route.

After a bit of research and, honestly, at the very last minute, we found a company that would ship the contents of our one-bedroom apartment – and all of my bikes – for about $5,500. We decided to bite the bullet. A week before move day, we started packing everything up. When the moving guys came, they packed the fragile items and the oversized ones and hauled it all away in a U-Haul-type truck.

Less than two months later, a man in a truck with a giant container on the back pulled up to our apartment and said, "OK, here you go!" We were a little surprised that no movers were here to help, since the service we paid for was supposed to include that. Thankfully, the guy felt bad for us and offered to chip in and help. We got the job done within an hour and tipped him handsomely for his hard work. If I had to do it all again, I would have shopped around more and found a shared shipping container, and I'd have packed it myself. It would have been a lot cheaper."

the landfill problem by needlessly throwing away things we already have just to turn around and replace them, that's definitely one option. (And if you have a garage sale or sell your stuff on Craigslist, you might even earn enough money to cover the cost of replacement or the cost of shipping what's left.)

Many items for sale in French stores seem a lot pricier than they do back home, but often they're made better and therefore worth the investment. Tools, for example, can be very expensive, so pack your wrenches, hammers, and screwdrivers if you can't live without them. Your teenage son (or inner teenager) might be disappointed to learn that video games tend to cost about twice as much as they do in the U.S., so if you're a grade-A vidiot, pack your games.

If you settle near one of the big cities—Bordeaux, Marseille, Grenoble, Lyon—you'll be within driving distance of an IKEA, whose goods seem to fill half of all French homes these days. It's no wonder: The store offers handsome, modern design at bargain-basement prices. In Paris, a city where people come and go like the seasons, you'll find Craigslist and FUSAC full of ads posted by folks looking to unload their things at great prices. You can easily furnish your entire apartment or *maison* with quality secondhand goods.

For small household items, like washcloths, dish drainers, kitchen towels, and sewing supplies, try the Chinese- and South Asian–owned markets in the big cities. They're treasure troves for all those little knick-knacks you forgot to pack. At *marchés aux puces* (flea markets), you'll also find stalls selling new items—cutting boards, bars of soap—and wallet-friendly buys can be had if you keep your eyes open.

ELECTRONICS

When packing, consider whether or not to replace your electronic items. If you choose to bring them with you, you'll need a series of transformers and adapters to make them work in France, and you'll always run the risk of overloading your appliances' electrical circuits. As many of us have learned the hard way, all transformers are not created equally.

Electricity in Europe comes through the wires at 220 volts, double the amount of power that surges through standard U.S. and Canadian lines. In order to whittle the energy down to something your appliances can handle, you'll need a heavy-duty step-down transformer. This is not the kind you'll find in most travel shops—those are designed for small appliances, like electric razors—and should not be confused with the little adapters you'll be able to use to plug in your laptop, cell-phone charger, and camera-battery charger. A transformer is a solid, square, brick-size metal box that converts those 220 volts into 120. This is generally considered safe for things like televisions, DVD players, and small kitchen appliances.

Regional standards may also affect your decision on whether or not to pack your U.S.-configured electronics. You won't be able to play French DVDs in your American DVD player, for instance; you'll need a PAL (Phase Alternating Line)-compatible DVD player, which costs about €50 new at electronics specialty stores like Darty, to watch all those straight-to-video releases.

If you have a computer with a DVD drive, you can watch any old video, provided you've switched the region settings to the European standard. The only tricky part is that most computers have restrictions on how many times you can make this regional switch; five is the norm.

If you've packed your PlayStation to play games and run Blu-Ray Discs, be aware that there are three disc-playing zones—A, B, and C—and the European standard is Zone B. When renting or buying Blu-Ray Discs, look for Zone A on the back of the box; changing the region settings on your machine isn't possible, so anything other than Zone A discs will be unreadable.

Considering that you'll need one of those bulky, expensive transformers to run most American electronic gadgets, on top of having to futz with regional codes and standards, it really makes more sense to sell your electronic goods before you leave and replace them with European versions once you get here, especially if you plan to live here for any length of time. Sadly, electronics such as computers and televisions have essentially become disposable goods after a year or two of rigorous use.

If you are particularly attached to your lamps, it is possible to convert them to the French standard by purchasing a 220-volt plug (and 220-volt light bulb to match), available at just about every *quincaillerie* (hardware store) in the country. If you're feeling DIY-ish, you can easily splice this new plug onto your existing electrical cord and, if you end up returning to North America, repeat the conversion process by splicing a 110-volt plug on the end when you get back home.

SHIPPING OPTIONS

If all this talk of electrical currents and step-down transformers hasn't scared you away from packing your life up and shipping it across the ocean, then it's time to consider your transport options. If you've decided to start fresh and just pack your clothes, toothbrush, and passport, good for you! You'll be more mobile that way and will have a lot more flexibility in terms of where you live. For most of us, paring life down is not so simple. It's hard to let go. If you're taking everything with you, your best bet is to send it by sea in a shipping container. Prices vary depending on where you're shipping from and to, how much space you'll need in a container (measured in cubic feet or meters), and whether or not you share your container with someone else. But the first step is finding a company to help you make it all happen.

To find a qualified moving company, start with FIDI (www.fidi.com), the international nonprofit agency representing moving companies worldwide. Shipping companies who are part of the FIDI alliance have met a series of quality standards that put them in a league above the rest, but that doesn't mean that if you choose a non-FIDI mover, you'll have a lesser experience. Another place to look for moving-company references is at the consulate, which should be able to provide you with a handout with some good leads. Do your research, ask for testimonials or reviews, and give yourself enough time to shop around so you're not stuck with the only company that's available when you need to move.

Peak moving season in the northern hemisphere begins in mid-May and ends in September. It might not be possible for you to arrange your move at any other time, but you'll have more options if you can be flexible with the date. Though you'll want to start your research six months in advance, if you're trying to budget your move with care, you'll want to book your moving reservation no sooner than one month before departure. Why? Freight charges fluctuate—sometimes drastically—from month to month, based on a number of factors including the value of the dollar and the price of oil. So the figure you're quoted could change significantly, usually in the direction you don't want.

Moving companies offer a range of services, from we'll-do-it-all-for-you to we-just-ship-and-that's-it and everything in between. There are a couple of approaches you can take to sort out all of the details.

If you're lucky enough to be transferred by your company, chances are they'll be handling (read: paying for) all the details of your move, in which case you can just kick up your heels and start plotting the adventures you hope to see unfold in your new French life. For the rest of us, there's a bit of decision-making involved. Do you want to go the cheapest route possible? Then get a shared "groupage" container, but expect it to take anywhere from one to four months for your goods to arrive. The shipping company sends movers to pick up your stuff in a truck, deliver it to the loading docks, and either put it in a container that already has someone else's (or several someone elses') belongings in it—or put it in a container and wait around for another shared load to arrive to fill the container space. This costs about half—sometimes less than half—of what you'll pay for an exclusive container. To bring the cost down further, you can deliver the stuff to the container yourself.

The next cheapest option is direct shipping, meaning your stuff goes inside your own dedicated shipping container; no shared space. The shipping company will either send movers over to pick up your packed goods and deliver them to the shipping port, or they might actually bring your shipping container right to your front door and load it there, sealing the doors afterward with a plastic security band that you will later snip open when your container is delivered.

Armed with the basics, you'll want to visit FIDI online or use *bouche-à-oreille* (word-of-mouth) references and make a few calls. Shipping containers come in two sizes, 20-foot and 40-foot, so expect to be asked how many cubic meters' worth of goods you have. The shipping company should send a representative over to make an assessment. Once you've been given an estimate that works for you—and it's definitely worth shopping around, since prices can vary by thousands of dollars—you'll be asked to submit a down payment, with the rest payable upon delivery.

CUSTOMS

Customs is a relatively straightforward process, but you won't necessarily know that if your shipping company contact isn't well informed. You'll have to fill out a customs form that your shipping company will submit to the *douane* (customs) agents at the port of entry, but unless your cargo is made up of brand-new electric items that look like they might be ready for immediate resale in France, you won't have to pay an import fee. You will be asked to attest on paper to the fact that you have lived in your country of residence for the last 12 months and that the items you are shipping are older than six months. (Items purchased less than six months before your ship date are subject to import fees.) If you can solemnly swear that this is true, you won't need to pay any fees.

One important consideration is the storage fee. If your shipping dossier is not in order at the customs agency at the port of entry in France—this usually happens when you do your paperwork yourself or use an underqualified moving agency with little overseas shipping experience—your container may have to be "stored," with daily fees in the realm of €250. To avoid getting saddled with hefty fees, confirm with your shipping company that your paperwork is in order, and that there will be no hidden and unwarranted customs fees. You or your shipping agent should have collected in your dossier the following papers:

- a copy of your passport
- pay stubs or other proof that you have lived in the U.S. or Canada for at least six months
- a copy of your rental agreement and/or proof of current residence in France (an electricity bill works)
- a French customs inventory form
- a signed letter attesting that the purpose of importing your goods is not to resell them upon arrival
- a Representation en Douanes form.

HOUSING CONSIDERATIONS

From crumbling cottages covered in vines to chic Left Bank flats furnished in fancy Louis XIV fashion, housing runs the gamut in France. Exactly where you decide to live is surely contingent on work, school, and budget, but once you've sorted out those fundamentals, you'll be ready to embark on your hunt for the perfect home. Finding a place to live is best reserved for when you actually arrive; as alluring as online ads can be, making a decision from afar isn't really practical. If you'll be spending more than six months in your new abode, you'll want to ensure that the neighborhood meets your standards, that the advertisement in square meters matches the spatial picture you had in mind (and that your antique dining-room table will fit in the *salle à manger*), and that you'll have access to transportation and other amenities. It's hard to judge this accurately without a visit. Once you're here, there's a lot to see, so bring your phrasebook, comfy walking shoes (but not the sporty white ones), and your sense of humor.

The French Housing Market

In 2010, French housing prices finally began to rebound after a two-year slump, making it more of a seller's than a buyer's market. Paris is the one exception, having remained virtually untouched by housing-market fluctuations in other parts of the country. Buyer optimism is at last on the mend, thanks to a strengthening economy, and banks have begun lending again after a temporary dry spell related to the most recent economic crisis rattling through Europe and the rest of the world.

France has long been a popular place for foreign investors and second-home buyers; the British especially have done a number on the real-estate industry here, snapping up properties to fix up and rent out or fix up and live in, if only for part of the year. In some pockets of France—particularly in Brittany, where housing prices are among the cheapest in France and access to the UK by ferry, Chunnel, and plane is quick and easy—Anglophones outnumber Francophones. This is the clearest evidence of the British invasion that peaked in the '00s, when the pound was strong against the euro and the cost of living in France was drastically less expensive than in the UK. The economic parity that is now settling in between the two countries means there isn't a feverish race to the realty finish line, and there are more options for those interested in buying now.

Even with the dollar weak against the euro (the exchange rate is a dismal €1 = $1.41 at the time of writing), Americans will find French housing prices to be an incredible bargain. After all, in how many places in the United States can you find a livable home for less than $50,000? Not many. Throughout France, low-cost options abound, but expect your €20,000 bolt-hole to require at least a bit of work—maybe a lot. On the other end of the spectrum, million-dollar Parisian apartments and country châteaux are out there for the taking for people with money to burn.

Renting

Renting has its advantages over buying, the most obvious being a much lighter initial investment. For the French, housing laws that favor the tenant over the landlord make renting a safe and secure option. Even if you don't pay your rent, a landlord can't kick you out in the winter, for instance. But as a foreigner entering the rental market, you won't necessarily have all the same

CLASSIFIED INFORMATION

Scouring the want ads for the perfect place to call home can be a fun pastime that helps you better imagine yourself living your French dream. If your language skills aren't up to snuff, though, it can become frustrating drudgery. Don't know your *cuisine* from your *cave?* Bone up on the essential real-estate lingo before you hit the *immobilier* (real-estate agency) to know exactly what you'll be investing those hard-earned euros in.

à louer/location for rent

ascenseur elevator

à vendre for sale

bail à ceder for lease

cave cellar

chambre room, usually referring to a bedroom or main room in a studio

charges supplemental charge for water, garbage, maintenance, and sometimes electricity

chauffage heating

chauffage collectif radiator-style heat collectively turned off and on

chauffage individuelle heating that you can control in your own home

colocation shared rental unit

couloirs hallway

cuisine kitchen

dépot garantie security deposit

2ème étage second floor

deux pièces standard one-bedroom

disponible available

equipée furnished (usually describes a kitchen with refrigerator and stove)

escalier staircase

gardien onsite manager

honoraire finder's fee to the agency

hors charges not including charges

immeuble building

immeuble ancient/neuf old/new building

jardin garden

loué already rented

meublée furnished

mezzanine elevated area, often a DIY loft space for sleeping that frees up floor space

pièce room

une pièce/studio studio

pierre/pierre de taille stone

placard closet

renové renovated

rez-de-chaussée ground floor

salle d'eau washroom

salle de bain bathroom with tub or shower

sans vis à vis an unobstructed view

séjour living room

toilette toilet

T1/T2 studio/one-bedroom apartment

tout compris, cc, or ttc all inclusive

vendeur seller

vendu already sold

vide empty

© SOPHIA PAGAN/WWW.SOPHIAPAGAN.COM

Don't forget to look up when launching your home search.

advantages extended to you, which is one reason why French homeowners seek out foreign tenants.

Paris rental laws are particularly strict, and it's technically illegal for owners to rent to anyone—foreign or not—for periods of less than one year. To do so legally would require owners to change the status of their property from private to commercial, and securing the coveted commercial status is next to impossible. Theoretically, the law was intended to ease Paris's shortage of affordable housing; you'll often hear the story of the lifelong Parisian sent packing to the suburbs because he can no longer afford the city's astronomical rents. The law is easy to skirt, however, as evidenced by the number of ads offering short-term "furnished" accommodations. "Furnished" is a loose term that can mean anything from a bare room save a single chair or bed to a decked-out space with all the mod cons in place: microwave, television, sofa, etc. Short-term rentals bring in far more income for owners than long-term rentals, so flying under the radar and hoping not to get caught is a risk many landlords are willing to take.

French bureaucracy doesn't end at the front door of your new house or apartment, which can make finding a place to live a challenge, particularly if you are short on time or funds. If possible, rent a short-term place for a month while you look for your permanent housing, which will buy you enough time to find something that will feel like a true home and not force you into something less—or more—than you'd hoped for. You can find more affordable options for short-term and long-term rentals on Craigslist and FUSAC. More expensive possibilities are also available via dozens of short-term rental agencies (again, check out the FUSAC magazine online), but they will charge higher rents and also include a supplemental fee for finding you a place to live that could either be a percentage of the overall rental period or the equivalent of one month's rent. If you want to avoid the hassles of combing the want ads altogether, this is a viable option even for the long term, but note that nearly all rentals will come in varying degrees of "furnished." So if you're expecting a cargo container to arrive with all of your belongings, you'll need to make sure you have the room for it or risk paying hefty storage fees.

You're already familiar with the dossier, and you'll be needing one to rent a house or apartment from either an agency or a private party. Your dossier should contain:

- copies of your passport
- your last three bank statements
- your last three pay stubs (French or otherwise)
- proof of insurance (if you have it)
- an *attestation* from a *garant* or *cautionnaire* saying you'll be covered if you can't pay your rent
- personal letters of recommendation (in French, if possible!)

Without these, it's unlikely you'll find any standard real-estate agency that will rent to you long term. Even familiar North America–based companies like Century 21 have rigid policies that will exclude you based on missing documents in your dossier. The tricky part is that this rule doesn't always hold. If you have time and tenacity, 1 out of 20 agencies you visit or speak with by phone (or email) might be willing to look the other way on missing documents if they like you, or more likely, like your bank statement. If you make a break-through and actually get someone to show you an apartment (be forewarned that some agents won't even consider showing you a place until they've seen your paperwork), and you fall in love with the place, work those negotiating skills and see what happens. Some expats have reported that homemade brownies work as a form of bribery, but simply being personable and connecting genuinely with the person you're hoping to impress is probably the best route to take. Their bottom line is, "Will she be able to pay the rent?" If you can convey a sense of trust and reliability, you're halfway there.

In Bordeaux, a one-bedroom rents for less than €500 per month.

FINDING THE RIGHT PLACE

When you launch your home search, it helps to put *all* your feelers out—all of them! This is not the time to be a wallflower. Check the bulletin board at your local chapter of the Alliance Française back home for possibilities, scour Craigslist and FUSAC to get a sense of the rental climate in the town you're moving to, ask everyone you know if they have friends-of-friends-of-friends who might have a place to rent in France, and visit sites like Se Loger (www.seloger.com) and Particulier à Particulier (www.pap.fr) to start getting a feel for French-language rental ads. The more familiar you are with the lingo and the more questions you formulate before you leave, the better prepared you'll be for your next challenge.

When you get here, get out there and start networking. Join expat groups, venture out to Meetups (www.meetup.com), and read every bulletin board you lay your eyes on. As much as you want to integrate into French society, your best bet for finding a place to live is through word-of-mouth within the Anglophone community, so cast your net as wide as it will go.

It takes many North Americans some time to get used to the size of French dwellings. Unless you're looking at a château or a modern apartment, you'll find traditional French rooms to be a little on the small side (and often plastered with outdated wallpaper, which can make a room feel even smaller). And that oversize sofa you packed? Good luck squeezing it into an elevator (which most building *syndicats* don't allow anyway) or wrangling it around the twisty stairwell. You'll need to hire a special moving *elévateur* to lift it up and through the window.

Short-Term Rentals

If you don't have someone with very strong ties to France arranging your move for you, you're probably going to need to give up on the notion of finding an unfurnished rental. They do exist, but they're very hard to get your hands on as a solo-flying expat on a non–corporate executive's budget. For the short term, it's usually preferable to set up in a furnished place anyway, since you'll just need something in the interim until your cargo container arrives or while you scope out a permanent place to live. And if you're only staying for a brief period, a furnished rental unit makes a lot of sense.

Your options for short-term rentals are vast and varied. You can go through a big agency that will likely charge you a big fee or a mom-and-pop business offering the same service but charging less, or you can bypass surcharges altogether by working directly with a landlord, who might himself be a subtenant to another landlord. There is a bit of risk involved in the latter option on both the landlord and tenant's sides; you are being entrusted to someone else's property, and you're handing over your hard-earned cash to someone you hope is on the up and up. Odds are they will be, but always trust your instincts—if something doesn't feel right, don't feel obligated to follow through. In any situation, it is advisable to always leave a paper trail and to draft a lease, even if the person renting to you doesn't think it's necessary or, more likely, didn't think of it.

TIPS FROM THE TOP

When Scotsman Ross Husband moved to France in 2005, he had a hard time finding a long-term rental for his family. The process proved so frustrating and time-consuming that he and his wife, Karin, decided to launch their own business to help people find rental housing. Ross, Karin, and their daughter, Anna, now live in the Pyrénées and continue helping others find their little swath of *la belle France* through their company, Rent a Place in France. Here are Ross's top five tips for finding that perfect rental.

1. Research. Thoroughly research the area you're thinking of moving to in France and what type of property you'll require.

2. Visit. If possible, view the property prior to committing to a long-term rental; you don't want any unwelcome surprises.

3. Toe-dip. Don't sign up for a three-year rental unless you have already experienced local life for a few months. It may not live up to your expectations.

4. Double-check. Ensure that facilities at the property are in adequate shape and functioning order, especially heating systems. Winter temperatures can be cold, even in the south of France.

5. Crunch numbers. Calculate a budget for your total monthly expenditure, including bills. Be realistic!

Within the law, short-term rentals of a year or less that don't come with a lease are supposed to be rented only to tenants who have a primary residence other than the one being rented. This would be a challenge for anyone to disprove, and rarely is it an issue in terms of the law cracking down on you, but the person renting to you may ask you to sign a paper stating as much to cover his or her tail.

For a nice cross-section of short- and long-term rentals throughout France, try www.rentaplaceinfrance.com. The friendly owners, Ross and Karin Husband, are English speakers originally from Scotland who will help you find a place to live and answer all of your questions. The American Chamber of Commerce in France also offers recommendations for short-term rental agencies at www.amchamfrance.org.

If you're looking for a temporary sublet, summer is a great time to check out Paris and other big cities while the locals flee to the sea and countryside for their multiweek escapes. You will have lots of room to negotiate, since people don't want to get stuck paying all their rent while they're away, and you'll get to experience what it could be like to live in a real French home (versus a sterile short-term rental unit).

Long-Term Rentals

A long-term rental has lots of advantages: It allows you to get to know a place before buying, lets you feel more integrated in a community knowing you won't have to pick up and leave in three months, and often is a lot less expensive than a short-term arrangement. The only problem is *finding* a long-term rental, though that isn't necessarily a problem if you have the luxury of time.

As with short-term rentals, it's possible to go through an agency whose specialty is expatriate rental services, but you will pay a premium, usually in the form of a "finder's fee" surcharge amounting to the equivalent of one month's rent or a percentage of the rent you'll pay over the months (or years) you'll be staying. It's also possible to go through an *immobilier,* a real estate agent who often deals in rental units as well as selling homes. The tricky part will always be to meet the dossier demands, which generally require three French pay stubs proving that you earn several times the amount of the rent, a *garant's* attestation, and more.

It's no secret that French landlords like renting to North Americans. They know you'll be leaving for your "real" home at some point, and therefore won't be taking advantage of the tenant-friendly laws that essentially guarantee you can't be forcibly evicted. This also allows many landlords to get around the law that says empty units must be rented under a three-year lease; many North

Americans are staying only for a year or two, so the landlord won't be locked in a long-term situation. You're also generally considered more financially stable than your French counterparts, making you prime tenant material.

Renting directly from the owner gives you a lot of flexibility; you can negotiate the removal of existing furniture, open a discussion about filling voids—for example, if your "furnished" apartment doesn't come with a TV or washing machine, you may be able to persuade the *proprietaire* that these are necessities. (As always, ask nicely and be prepared to make a convincing argument if necessary.) Sometimes you can negotiate both the rent and the length of your stay. So there's a lot to be said for finding your home this way. Even though it's not as popular in France as in North America, Craigslist is a good place to start your search, especially if you'll be settling in Paris. You'll find a broad variety of possibilities, and the people advertising are almost

DAILY LIFE

THE *GARANT,* AND WHY YOU MIGHT NEED ONE

If you've moved house in the last 10 years, you know the renter's drill: Arrive early to the showing to beat the crowds, have your credit report and application ready, and – if you're feeling spunky – bring a bribe in the form of fresh-baked cookies to really grab the real-estate agent's attention. Well, in France, it's going to take a bit more effort to land that perfect apartment, and we're not talking about swapping out the cookies for chocolate *moelleux*. If you don't have a job contract and three months of pay stubs to demonstrate your fiscal stability, you can kiss that cute 18th-century walkup *au revoir*. Even a bank account loaded with euros won't help you here. Rules are rules, and what the folks renting to you require are those pay stubs, showing earnings equal to three times your monthly rent – or, if you can't pull that off, a *garant*'s attestation. *Garant? Attestation?* What's all this, you ask?

A *garant* is someone with income or assets greater than your own who acts as a financial guarantor in case you default on your rent. This person is expected to provide a dossier full of documents similar to those you're unable to provide: proof of residence, proof of monthly income equal to three times the amount of your rent, and copies of her own rental agreement or real-estate tax forms. Employers occasionally extend this perk to staff, but not always. If you're lucky enough to have a wealthy aunt in France who's willing to put three years' worth of rent into a "hold" at the bank, rental agencies will consider that in place of a *garant*.

Recently, public *garant* agencies have sprouted up, offering their services to desperate would-be renters, but not all rental agencies will accept this sort of arrangement. If those options fail, there's still hope: Enroll in a university (students are usually exempt from the *garant* rule) or rent straight from the owner (try Craigslist and Particulier à Particulier), a deal that usually allows for a more flexible negotiation process.

always Anglophones. One thing to be wary of: There have been some scams popping up on Craigslist lately, and they almost always involve 1) a deal that's too good to be true (such as a luxury apartment for €750 per month) and/or 2) a request for money transfers or wires before you've even seen the place. Don't sign anything, and *don't* hand over a euro until you've seen the place—and the person renting it—in person.

Particulier à Particulier (www.pap.fr) advertises apartments and houses directly from the owner, so if your French skills are up to snuff, you can probably circumvent the challenges inherent in working with an agency—namely, a rigid set of dossier requirements. In addition to the website, PAP publishes a thick, oversize journal every Thursday. Pick it up at newsstands for €2.95, and you'll have access to thousands of ads. Brush up on your French and be prepared to pick up the phone to get the best deals. If your French isn't that good but you have a friend who's fluent, have her make the call for you.

Shared Rentals

Finding a *colocation* (shared rental) situation in France is relatively simple, particularly in university towns with large student populations. The site to visit to find your next roommate situation is www.colocation.fr, but it will benefit you greatly if you speak French. You *do* want that €100 living situation, *don't* you? The downside to this otherwise wonderful site is that to access the contact information of your potential new roommate, you have to pay for the access number; usually the fee is less than €2, but if you're calling more than a handful of people, it adds up. A no-cost option is www.recherche-colocation.com—also in French, but at least membership is *gratuit* (free). If you're still most comfortable with an English-language publication, head straight for the old tried-and-true FUSAC and Craigslist.

RENTAL AGENTS AND LEASES

Before signing on the dotted line, you'll want to have some sort of contract in place, even if it's just a simple form you downloaded off the internet 10 minutes before your hand-over-keys meeting. (You and your landlord wouldn't be the first.) What you sign and what kind of information it contains hinges on what you're renting and the landlord's level of professionalism. Let's say you're renting a furnished apartment in Nice directly from an owner who takes the matter rather seriously and has taken steps to keep the transaction on the up and up. In this case, you can expect to be presented with a lease contract or rental (*bail à loyer* or *contrat de location*) containing the following information:

- Name of the owner, contact information, and rental address
- A description of the rental: floor, door, dimension in square meters
- A mention of communal access and services: a courtyard, bike parking, elevator
- A definition of purpose: whether the space is for living or working
- The length of the contract and whether it's renewable or not
- An outline of the charges—rent, *taxe d'habitation,* electricity—and when they are made payable
- The amount of your security deposit
- An outline of any proposed work to be done on the dwelling, including dates and whether less or more rent will be charged as a result
- A statement indicating that the renter will leave the space in the same state it was rented out in to guarantee you get your deposit back.

A short outline of the owner's obligations to the renter and the renter's obligation to the owner is also part of the contract, and often a *clause pénale* will be inserted declaring what will happen if the renter fails to pay his rent. But it's almost guaranteed that the contract you sign will be much simpler than the one outlined above, if you're actually offered a contact at all.

In keeping with the up-and-up theme: Even if you're not asked to provide a full-fledged dossier, you may be asked to provide proof of renter's insurance and income. Paying your last month's rent up front is not legally mandated, but landlords *are* legally entitled to ask for a deposit equal to one month's rent. They have two months to return it to you once you've moved out. You, on the other hand, can ask your landlord-to-be for a *certificat de ramonage,* which certifies they've had the chimney swept so you can have a cozy little fire roaring in the fireplace.

Buying

If you've never visited a real-estate website, consider yourself warned: They're deliciously addictive. There's nothing quite as tantalizing as poking around cyberspace and popping in and out of other people's *maisons*—homes that might soon be your own (if only in your fantasies). From a rural 17th-century cottage perched on the edge of a grassy glen to a riviera *pied-à-terre* equipped with a sunlit balcony built for two, a version of your French dream awaits you in the wonderful world of virtual real estate.

It takes a village to buy a home in France, and you can expect all kinds of seemingly superfluous individuals to become part of the transaction: *notaires, mairies,* insurance agents, and even doctors. For some mortgages, you'll need to ensure that you'll live long enough to pay for your little piece of France—this is solved with the addition of a life-insurance policy, which you can't purchase until you've had a blood test and possibly an electrocardiogram, the results of which are supposed to indicate a life span beyond the terms of your mortgage. No, this is not a joke. If you want to bypass all that, you can always pay cash. (And plenty of people do—especially for those €50,000-and-under bolt-holes.)

You're bound to find yourself looking at one or two "fixer uppers" throughout the process, and one thing you'll notice right away is that no two are alike. Some "fixer uppers" are veritable shacks with dirt floors and a resident family of pigeons. If the ad says the 20,000 euro cottage is *à renover* (to renovate), be prepared for the worst, and maybe, just maybe, it won't be that bad. The "to renovate" possibilities could simply mean they haven't yet installed the sunken bathtub in the master bath.

FINDING THE RIGHT PLACE

So where you should you begin cultivating your French roots? Before sorting that out, you'll need to be firm about what sort of use you have planned for your place. Will it be strictly somewhere for you to live, or are you envisioning an income-generating rental property? Maybe you just want to let it sit empty until you come for your two months of vacation each summer, and let friends borrow it for vacation otherwise. Buying into a retirement home where you can spend your golden years isn't a bad idea, what with the high quality of life here and the top-notch health system. But don't make the mistake that many of your predecessors have: Buy a place and plan to rent it out without considering how many others have done the same thing—and how many others are that much closer to the Mediterranean. You will have a much more challenging time finding short-term tenants for your "vacation rental" if it doesn't have quick access to leisure activities: a beach, a swimmable lake or river, or at the very least a *piscine* (pool) in the backyard. This is what people seek in a vacation home—not a one-room cottage in the middle of nowhere, the nearest *boulangerie* a 20-kilometer bike ride away. Hold on to the dream, but don't let practicality fall by the wayside.

REAL-ESTATE AGENTS AND CONTRACTS

The most cursory Internet search points to an overwhelming reality: There are scads and scads of French real estate sites. The good news is that many of them cater to English-speaking shoppers. If your French is solid, even better: You'll be able to pull into any small town during your information-gathering trip, pick up the local real-estate magazine from the news rack outside the *immobilier*'s office, and get nearly instant gratification by stepping inside to inquire about that charming stone *longère* covered in a tangle of wild roses that caught your eye.

Like so much else in life, it all about who you know in the French real-estate world. Ask around for references before settling on an agent. Some are nicer than others, and some charge heftier fees. You'll also need to engage the services of a *notaire* (more on that below) and a mortgage company. If you've got the resources, you can hire someone to see you through every step of the process and make the arrangements with notaries and bankers on your behalf. If you're flying solo—which is entirely possible to do, and definitely a money saver—and your language skills still aren't up to snuff, bring a good friend who speaks French to all your official rendezvous to help translate.

You'll need a French bank account, since most mortgage companies are going to want to debit the mortgage payments directly from that account. (To learn more about opening a bank account, see the *Finance* chapter.)

The French home-buying system is fraught with bureaucratic peculiarities, but the oddest of all is that bit about the blood test. If your mortgage is approved and you'll be borrowing more than €200,000, you'll be required to take out a life-insurance policy that will cover the remaining cost of your mortgage if you're, say, suddenly swept away by a tsunami while sunbathing on the Côte d'Azur. To qualify for that policy, you'll need a blood test and possibly a urine test. Oh, and we mustn't forget about the electrocardiogram. Yes, really.

PURCHASE FEES AND TAXES

One person you'll get to know well during the property-purchasing process is the *notaire*. This is an independent contractor who acts as the official hand representing the state in your home-buying transaction. The stamps, seals, and signatures the *notaire* applies to your *contrats* make a document official, and the buy/sell transaction cannot be completed without this authorizing signature. The *notaire*'s fees are not low, but they don't all go into her pocket. The bulk of what you pay to the *notaire* is actually local and national taxes, with the remaining fraction divided between the *notaire*'s actual employment fees (a fixed rate determined by the government) and expenditures for things like paperwork and travel. In terms of real estate transactions, *notaires* collect 5 percent of the fee on sales of up to €46,000, and 2.5 percent after that. It's worth budgeting in that extra expense as you determine what you can afford to spend in France. To find a *notaire,* try the word-of-mouth route or visit www.notaires.fr to search an online directory in English.

Once you've found a place you love and are ready to commit, you can set the process in motion by following these steps:

- Find a *notaire* and secure her services.

- Sign the *compromis de vente* that binds the seller to the transaction and pay a deposit of 10 percent of the purchase price.

- Mull it over and decide whether or not you have buyer's remorse within seven days (you can pull out without penalty before then).

- Apply for a mortgage. If you are rejected, try again and save the rejection notice. If you are unable to secure a mortgage, you can pull out of the agreement without penalty.

- Contact your *notaire* to say your mortgage has gone through and the transaction can be completed.

From start to finish, count on a good three months or more for the transaction to be completed.

French inheritance laws favor children over spouses, so if you want to ensure that any greedy offspring don't snatch up and sell your property after you die, leaving Pa or Ma out in the cold, bring this up to your *notaire,* who can use the right paperwork to help ensure that doesn't happen.

BUILDING AND RESTORING

As you know by now, no transaction involving the French bureaucracy is ever a cake walk. This holds true when it comes to rebuilding, renovation, and starting a housing project from scratch. Expect a long, dossier-encumbered process—but one that might be very much worth the effort if it means getting the house you've always wanted.

When scouring the real-estate ads, you'll often stumble upon land for sale. If there is a "permission to build" clause built into the sale deed, you're in luck: One major hurdle has been cleared. Otherwise you'll need to solicit permission to build on your own, starting at the *mairie*'s office with a *certificat d'urbanisme.* This should be done *before* you make your land purchase. With permission to build in hand, you'll need to start beefing up that dossier with some more paperwork: architectural drawings from an officially recognized architect, building estimates, and construction contracts.

Your local *mairie* can help you along the way by directing you to free services that will ease the burden of DIY. The Conseil d'Architecture d'Urbanisme et de l'Environnement (CAUE) is one such valuable resource. To find a builder, good ol' word of mouth works best, but you can also ask for recommendations at the *mairie* or visit the website of the builder's union, Union Nationale des Constructeurs de Maisons Individuelles (UNCMI), for direction (www. uniondesmaisonsfrancaises.org).

French contractors do things at their own pace, so it helps to know who you're hiring before you hire them. You can expect long lunch breaks, regular vacations (just like everyone else), and a "What's the big rush?" attitude on the job, but it'll eventually get done. If you're a Mr. or Ms. Bricolage (handyperson), you might consider taking on some of the work yourself.

Household Expenses

Once your new title of French homeowner is etched in *pierre* (stone), you'll want to start gussying up your new place and making it feel homey. But not so fast. First, you need to make sure there's running water, electricity, and—if you're way out in the boondocks—a *fosse septique* (septic tank). Many houses are sold in deplorable states of as-is, and it's up to you to know what you've gotten yourself into before you take the plunge.

If your adorable 300-year-old farmhouse has a *fosse septique,* you may be required by your local *mairie* to convert to *mains drainage,* otherwise known as the municipal sewer system. This comes at a price, so be sure to factor that in before you buy. Electricity is not a given either; if you're not already hooked up, you'll have to put a call in to state-owned Electricite de France (EDF) to see what kind of magic they can make down on the farm. To get started, you'll need proof of sale of your home, called an *attestation;* ask your *notaire* for a copy.

There are three taxes you will be responsible for as a new French homeowner: *taxe d'habitation, taxe fonciere,* and *redevence audiovisuelle:* the TV tax. The first is your residence tax, the second is your homeowner's tax, and the third is self explanatory. If you lived in your home on January 1 of the given year, then you are responsible for *taxe d'habitation.* If someone else lived there, they are responsible for paying it—so if you moved in on January 2, you're off the hook. Landlords can also pass this fee on to their long-term tenants, but this should be outlined in a rental agreement first. The tax is determined by the powers-that-be in your community and vary from city to city. You will receive a *facture* (bill) in the mail from the local government when tax time draws near.

Plan to tune into French TV? Don't forget to budget for your annual TV tax.

If you are over 60, lucky you! You don't have to pay this one. Families with children are taxed at a reduced rate. You'll receive your €121 bill for the TV tax at the same time (and yes, you're off scot-free if you don't have a TV).

Taxe fonciere, on the other hand, is a property owner's tax, and what you pay is again set by local authorities and relates to the value of your home as a rental property on the open market, minus cost-of-living fees. Like the other taxes, it hinges on a January 1 ownership date. Many types of properties are exempted from this tax, including homes remodeled for energy efficiency and new construction, so you'll want to check with your local government to see if your property is exempted.

UTILITIES

The primary supplier of electricity, Electricite de France (EDF), offers notoriously expensive power for those who live on the grid. North Americans by the droves have stood slack-jawed over their first wintertime electricity bill, expecting a two-digit number like the ones they used to see back home.

The good news is that you can choose the kilowatt supply that comes to your home and effectively reduce the figure you write on that check every two months. First, though, you have to open an account at the EDF, which can be done in person or online at http://bleuciel.edf.com. As with most French bills, you can arrange to go paperless on this one and have the money debited directly from your bank account.

Getting water running through the pipes involves a similar process. If the previous tenant had water services engaged, you can have the billing information transferred to your name. If you need to start from scratch, you'll need to visit your local government to find out who your water supplier is before making contact.

One thing you can't help but notice is the quality of water throughout France; though quite potable, it is extremely calciferous, with telltale white flecks often visible in your glass after drinking. This may or may not explain the French love affair with bottled water, but it's perfectly OK to consume, though you might be interested in a filter system. The calcium build-up will affect the look of your water kettle, your dishwasher, and your coffee maker, but anti-calcium tablets that will dissolve the problem are readily available in supermarkets and hardware stores.

Telephone landline options are many and and a veritable bargain, thanks to deregulation in the telecommunications sector. (Deregulation has not been good for everyone—restructuring and layoffs are said to be the culprit behind France Télécom's high rate of employee suicide: nearly 50 since 2008.) Usually your phone fees are bundled together with your Internet and cable television fees. Companies including SFR (www.sfr.fr), Bouygues (www.bouyguestelecom.fr), and Orange (www.orange.fr) offer packages as low as €30 per month, and you can make all the arrangements for hookup online.

DAILY LIFE

LANGUAGE AND EDUCATION

It's a little-known fact is that approximately 99.9 percent of all French people know at least a word or two of English, and many are darn near fluent. You'd hardly know it, though, given the way you're often left struggling to puzzle together the simplest request (*"Où est la WC, s'il vous plaît?"*), only to be met with a remarkably English-sounding response ("The bathroom? In fact, it's right over there.").

It's certainly possible to get by in France without speaking French—many an expat has done it, sometimes for years on end—but language restrictions will resign you to life in a bubble that only floats on the surface of a genuine French experience. At least part of what brought you here was your fondness for the rich culture, right? Language is the biggest cultural marker you'll find, so it makes sense to give it a shot and break free of the insular and—let's face it—superficial Anglophone-only experience. Plus, there's nothing quite as satisfying as ordering your first meal at a restaurant in French and having your request processed without quizzical looks and excessive head-scratching on the part of your waiter. Even more wonderful is the (relative) ease with which you'll glide through your *carte de séjour* and other official processes when armed with working French.

From Alsacien to Provençal, regional dialects abound, but it isn't imperative that you become fluent in the local *langue*. The mother tongue—plain old French—is all you really need to assimilate into your new community and boost your own confidence along the way.

Learning the Language

DAILY LIFE

If you were clever enough to have studied French in high school or college, you're lucky: That foundation will give you the confidence you need to get started. One of the most difficult things for non–French speakers to get used to is the feeling of vulnerability that comes with not being able to communicate effectively. For some, those insecurities are compounded by the genuinely-trying-to-be-helpful French person who corrects your grammar (I promise they're not doing it to make you feel bad), often in public and loudly enough for others to hear. It's a challenge for us control freaks, but now is the time to let go and embrace the linguistic fumbling and stumbling. Relaxing a little

---

WORDY WISDOM

French and English have *beaucoup de* cognates in common – that is, words that share the same etymological roots – but don't jump to the conclusion that just because certain words look and sound similar, they have the same meaning in both languages. For instance, a tampon has a particular meaning in the U.S. (you're familiar with that one) and another in France – it's a stamp for making documents official. Here, a list of common cognates and their unexpected meanings.

- *baskets* tennis shoes
- *chat* cat
- *collège* middle school
- *culte* religion
- *fantaisie* imagination
- *fart* ski wax
- *magasin* store
- *parole* song lyric
- *préservatif* condom
- *retard* late
- *roman* novel
- *salé* salty
- *sensible* sensitive
- *tampon* stamp
- *tube* hit song

will help you—and that ego of yours—move on to experimental chatting phase that will ultimately benefit you immensely.

If you've seen the film *Paris, je t'aime,* you'll probably remember the vignette featuring Carol, an American postal clerk who takes her dream trip to the City of Light, narrating her experience in heavily American-accented French. She charms us with her earnestness—and an extraordinarily flat delivery where rolling *R*s ought to have been. When you start out, go the postal-clerk method and focus on just speaking, rather than speaking with a perfect accent. You'll have time for that later. Besides, when you have a good accent, people assume you speak fluently or at least conversationally and will begin yakking at you in rapid-fire French that you're not equipped to handle—yet.

BEFORE YOU LEAVE

Whether or not you've studied French before, as soon as you even begin thinking of moving, you should also start thinking of enrolling in a language class. You'd be surprised how many resources there are out there—something for everyone, no matter your budget or lack thereof. From Alabama to Winnipeg and everywhere in between, the nonprofit Alliance Française awaits your enrollment in one of its many classes, from structured beginner courses to more relaxed conversation groups. This isn't the most affordable option, but it might be the most fun: The AF also hosts events—art shows, film screenings, speaking engagements, mixers—with a French twist. One of the benefits of membership is access to the library of books, DVDs, and CDs, making for an all-in-one cultural immersion program minus mandatory exams and pesky report cards.

If you live near a community college, this is an excellent, budget-friendly option. For the cost of lunch at a French restaurant, you can take a semester's worth of classes in a structured environment with fellow beginners. The downside to college classes is that they tend to be heavily grammar-focused, and it often takes several semesters for you to work up to anything resembling a conversation level.

Private classes are another possibility. Look at the bulletin board at your local AF, troll the halls of the nearest university and look for the language department there, or ask the consulate for a list of references. Look for one-on-one lessons offered by French students at American universities or by Francophone expats looking to earn a bit of spending money on the side. These personal sessions tend to emphasize conversation rather than grammar, and this approach can be a really great introduction to the colloquialisms and idioms you'll likely begin hearing as soon as you land.

Many people swear by the pricey audiovisual experiences offered by Rosetta Stone and Fluenz. For around $400, you can pick up one of these programs at the bookstore or online and study in the comfort of your own living room. The philosophy and approach to teaching languages differ significantly between the two (the former applies an immersion approach, while the latter feeds you morsels of the language one at a time), but both allow you to go to school whenever and as often as you like. For couples studying together or for those who don't have time to attend conventional classes, this option makes a lot of sense.

The most affordable of all your language-learning possibilities is the Meetup (www.meetup.com). While technically not classes, Meetups are social-networking groups that share a common interest, which, in this case, is the French language. Expect culture-oriented get-togethers—museum outings, gatherings at wine bars, French cinema rendezvous, cheese tastings—that all serve as fun vehicles for ameliorating your language skills *ensemble* (together). These sessions are often great networking zones where you'll meet not only other Anglophones but also honest-to-goodness French people. The casual ambience of most Meetups will relax you enough to loosen your chat mechanism and help fuel enthusiasm for your upcoming move.

LEARNING IN FRANCE

Not surprisingly, France is a hotbed of language-learning possibilities, so even if you arrive with French skills in the negative values, you'll be OK: A learning institution that meets your budget and experience will be available in your newly adopted country. Always begin by word of mouth—your friends, colleagues, and even the people standing in line at the *préfecture* will be able to weigh in on their experiences learning the language in France. If you land in Paris, visit your local *mairie,* where the staff will gladly offer you a list of references for municipally run classes in your quartier. The government-sponsored Française Langue Étrangère (French as a Foreign Language) classes are a veritable bargain at €60 per 180-hour, two-semester course, and when it's said and done, you'll have yourself a handy-dandy diploma or certificate to show for your hard work.

Shorter summer sessions are also available, though they cost slightly more (€80). Expect a diverse student body, lots of structure, and a thorough introduction to the language. Similar state-sponsored classes are available in cities throughout France; to find the one nearest you, visit www.fle.fr, an online portal with an extensive list of schools. The information is available in English and includes not only public institutions but also courses offered by nonprofits,

STUDY SKILLS

Name: Cedric Holz
Age: 18
Hometown: Grand Marais, MN
Current city: Lyon

Cedric came to France in 2010 in search of adventure – and to do his French-born mother proud by beefing up his language skills. He found opportunities to follow both pursuits in Lyon, where he attends a private language school three hours a day, five days a week. Here, Cedric recounts his experience searching for – and ultimately deciding on – a school.

"I came to France in September of 2010 to gain an adventure and a language, and it's been going fantastically so far. I chose France specifically because I have family here; my cousins asked if I wanted to stay with them in Lyon, and after traveling around Europe for a while and having no other plans, I said 'Why not?' and came.

There wasn't really a set study plan to begin with, but when I got here I decided going to school would be the best way to learn French, make friends, and become part of some sort of community. I had heard of two French schools here in Lyon and I checked them both out. I couldn't meet the professors because I arrived while everyone was on vacation, so really, I had to make my choice based on the school's ambience.

The first school had plain halls and not a lot of windows. Inflexyon (www .inflexyon.com) had paper snowflakes and colorful decorations all over. Inflexyon won. It was the right choice, too. It's a great school: The teachers are extremely friendly, and it's a really good place to meet other internationals who could be your friends for the rest of your life (and who offer the added benefit of a free place to stay when you want to go visit their cities).

The student body changes just about every month, when new internationals come and others leave. The students' ages range from 18 to about 30, but there are exceptions, because you are admitted here no matter your age. The average age is about 25. Tuition for one month, 15 hours a week, costs €420; you should expect to pay around €500 a month no matter where you go.

I spend three hours every day in class, which is usually divided among two different classes. I study French pretty much whenever I'm at home, so it can be anywhere from an hour a day to maybe five hours, depending on what's happening after school. The teachers here are amazing. Because it's a French school and because everyone is specifically here to learn the language, the teachers know we are all serious about learning – so there isn't that bitter resentment from the teachers, which I became accustomed to in American schools. They make jokes and laugh and sometimes they even go out drinking with the students.

If I was going to advise a fellow American on what steps to take before coming to France to study, it would be to save up money. Everything is extremely expensive on this side of the pond – especially beer, which is an important part of student life."

such as the Alliance Française. Prices can vary dramatically from organization to organization; at the Sorbonne, you can expect to pay €1,600 for your semester-long French class, and a private study center in Sarlat, with housing and meals included, goes for as much as €1,000 per week.

One of the best and perhaps most obvious ways to learn French is by getting out there, interacting with the locals, and trying your best to speak in their native tongue. At the supermarket, post office, and *bibliothèque* (library), you will find a surprisingly patient audience who will hear you out as you stumble along in elementary French, gently correcting you as you go. Don't miss these valuable learning opportunities by insisting that everyone speak English; you'll make friends and win hearts with a bit of earnest effort. Slightly more formal opportunities for interaction with Francophones can be found at local language-exchange groups, some of them cleverly disguised as English conversation groups. Don't be fooled: It's almost always a 50-50 French-English exchange, often over drinks with an eclectic international crowd. In Toulouse, try English in Toulouse (www.englishintoulouse.com) for weekly chat sessions over tapas and wine with a friendly Anglo- and Francophone group. In Paris, the Big Ben Club (www.bigbenclub.eu) meets up every Thursday for French-English exchange at that Left Bank bibliophile's institution, Shakespeare & Co. Nominal dues will be solicited, but they resemble pocket change more than mortgage payments.

Education

Founded on the principles of *liberté, egalité,* and *fraternité,* the French education system is considered one of the better socialized-learning institutions in the world. Every child in France has access to a high-quality education—between the ages of 6 and 16, they are required to attend. Today, parents can choose between public, private, and home schooling, but it wasn't always this way.

During the Dark Ages, the importance of education in France fell by the wayside and didn't pick up again until the enlightenment period, when Holy Roman Emperor Charlemagne introduced a centralized education model. Primarily religious in focus, the system was geared toward the elite and expanded through monasteries, later called "church schools." Catholic leaders, worried about losing their control to the professors at these schools, began hiring only those who were sanctioned by Catholic bishops to teach, thereby ensuring dogmatic, uniformly Catholic-oriented pedagogy.

Paris became the center for learning in the country in the 16th century, at which time Latin was supplanted by French as the lingua franca in universities and other learning institutions, but the Catholic church was still the controlling force behind the educational system. Reform continued throughout the 18th century with the development of *écoles centrales* and later *lycées*—a sort of middle-and-high-school amalgamation for the 11- to 18-year-old set. With a pedagogical model built on a well-balanced diet of math, science, literature, and the arts, each school was also decreed to have a library, garden, and natural history collection. During this period, teacher salaries were determined by the centralized government, but later this duty fell under the responsibility of the local departments, who still oversee regional educational institutions.

In the early 19th century, Napoléon overhauled the education system yet again, giving elementary schoolchildren a standardized education while 12-and-ups were given two options: a civil servant's education or a military-bound secondary education. This blueprint is not too far off from today's model, wherein students are groomed for a specific career path that's usually determined by a test, the *diplôme national du brevet,* taken during a student's first year at *lycée.* The test is the deciding factor in whether a student pursues further studies and a subsequent career in science and math, economics, or the arts or follows a trade-school path.

Under Napoléon's rule, women—long excluded from the education process—were finally admitted to study, but their education was limited to religious studies while a more rigorous academic training was the exclusive terrain of the men. That's changed a bit since Napoléon's time: Today, girls not only receive an equal education but outnumber boys in the *baccalauréat* path leading to careers in economics and the arts. They also attend institutes of higher learning at higher rates than their male counterparts.

EDUCATIONAL LEVELS

One the surface, the French education system looks a little more complicated than the North American one, but once you understand the naming convention, the stages begin to look a lot more familiar.

Children are eligible for *crèche* (subsidized daycare) when they are three months old and *maternelle* (preschool) at two years old. They don't enter *école primaire* (primary school) until the age of six. *École primaire* is the French equivalent of elementary school. Kids begin at roughly seven years old, working their way up through five years of classes focused on reading, writing, math, geography, history, and occasionally a foreign language, including English.

When American kids look forward to graduating to middle school, their

The elementary school set spends its days at the *école maternelle*.

counterparts in France move up to *collège,* four years of pre–high school academic training that begins with level six (*sixième*) and ends with level three (*troisième*). Here, they study more of the fundamentals, plus French literature, music, and up to two languages, including English, German, Spanish, or Italian. Students are taught in the same classroom all day, with a rotation of teachers coming in to instruct. Each year, two students from each class are nominated to act as liaisons between the students and the teachers, facilitating dialogue and helping make decisions that affect their fellow students, from scrutinizing academic performance to weighing in on disciplinary action.

A child's entrance into *lycée* marks the beginning of the French high-school equivalent, which some might be glad to know lasts only three years. Counterintuitively, the first year of *lycée* is the *séconde,* and the second is the *première.* The third and final year is known as *terminale.* The last two years are spent focusing on a specific track of academic training. Kids following the science path can expect to take plenty of math, physics, and chemistry classes; humanities students will focus on foreign languages, including the classics, plus literature, philosophy, and history; economics students will study social sciences and math.

ENROLLING IN FRENCH SCHOOLS

If you are planning to enroll your child in the French school system, it's important that he has a language foundation to help him through the rough world of being the new kid in school. For high-school students in particular, the ability to assimilate, make friends, and thrive in any new environment is contingent on a basic ability to communicate; the better her language skills, the more successful your child will be at adapting. The younger the child, the more adaptable to the new language she will be. But if you throw a *lycée*-age teen into an all-French class without any preparation, the outcome could be disastrous: depression, failing grades, and worse.

Before being placed in a class, your child will be given an entrance exam to determine which school level is best. Even for the brightest students, repeating a grade to compensate for language deficiencies could be a reality. A handful of public schools throughout the country—in Paris, Bordeaux, Nice, Lyon, and Rennes, among others—offer special "international" sections for North American students entering the system without a solid foundation in the language. These unique curricula differ from the standard education model; they are designed especially to facilitate the integration of foreign

TEACH YOUR CHILDREN WELL

Name: Sheila Johnson
Age: 41
Hometown: Spooner, WI
Current city: Toulouse, Pibrac

In 2005, after dating *very* long distance for a year, Sheila moved to Toulouse to be with her French boyfriend – bringing the cat and her two children, then six and eight, along for the adventure. Adjusting to life in France was a struggle for everyone, but the move was definitely toughest on her kids. French schools don't seem to have much in common with their American counterparts, something to which Sheila and her kids can attest. Here, Sheila shares her words of wisdom to help parents and children survive their *entrée* in to wild and woolly world of the French public education system.

"Even though the French love arts and music, schools here aren't very kind to the right-brained. There's very little patience for free-thinking, creative students.

Even grade-school art classes have strict instructions to follow (and, for the creative but untalented, what can seem like cruel grading). Your child, if used to the American school system – even a strict parochial school – might be shell-shocked by the sudden responsibility for being organized and having homework be neat and perfectly formatted (they do drafts, then re-write). Even grade-school kids turn in homework in pen.

Recalibrate your idea of what a "good" grade is. Kind of like getting used to temperatures in Celsius, grades are totally different, too, and they can't be converted so easily. We're used to looking at percentages and seeing 60 percent as an F. Grading here is much tougher, and perfect 20s are rare. A 13 out of 20 – although only 65 percent – isn't really considered a bad grade.

Get a French person to help you figure out the list of school supplies you'll need. I didn't, and I ended up in tears of frustration.

students into the French system. (They also work to prepare French students for living abroad in other countries). Students can expect an extra six hours per week of French study, as well as a lot of time spent with their noses embedded firmly in books.

PRIVATE EDUCATION

As in the United States and Canada, private schools can be found throughout France, including parochial schools, Waldorf and Montessori schools, and elite international schools with annual tuitions that rival the cost of a new car. Despite the generally high standard of public education throughout France, parents opt to enroll their children in private schools for the same reasons parents everywhere do: higher teacher-to-student ratios, safety, religious purposes, proximity, or to give children the advantage of being instructed in their native tongue.

And don't forget to have a few extra fountain pens and cartridges at home for spares, because kids never fail to lose them, and you're left having to run to the *tabac* before school.

Make the acquaintance of a parent or two in the class. Ask the teacher to pass your name and number to someone who might *parrine* (foster) if you need the extra help. It's a lifesaver when your child can't read the homework assignment he has copied in his agenda, or when you have questions about notes the teacher sends home.

Even if you think you won't need daycare, sometimes there are strikes and the school isn't open. Have a backup plan in case you aren't comfortable leaving your child home alone and must work or have other commitments. The public *garderie* is one possibility. Complete the dossier in advance so that you can simply call to register as a drop-in when the need arises. Also, having the numbers of other parents of your kid's schoolmates are handy for coordinating the sharing of care on strike days.

This sounds so American, but the toilets in every school I have visited have been awful. Even during the H1N1 scare, they didn't have soap or paper towels because the 'kids just mess the place up with that stuff.' Toilet paper is a rarity in my daughter's school. Kids develop the bad habit of trying to 'hold it' until they get home. Have your kid keep a germ gel in his backpack and packet of tissues in his pocket, just in case.

Even if your child doesn't have vision trouble, ask that she be seated near the front. It is easier for kids who aren't 100 percent fluent yet to be able to read the instructor's mouth and facial expressions. The teacher can also take better visual cues from your child, in case something isn't being understood. Lots of copying from the blackboard is expected, and sitting closer will make that easier as well."

DAILY LIFE

French private schools fall into two camps: *sous contrat* (under contract) and *hors contrat* (outside contract). Teachers at *sous contrat* schools are paid by the state, and tuition fees are generally on the low end of the spectrum. Curricula mirror those of public schools, and the academic calendar follows the same schedule. *Hors contrat* schools, because they aren't state-funded, are free to set their own curricula and tuition fees, and they run on an academic calendar of their own design.

The type of private education you choose for your children depends largely on your personal preferences, but your employer in France may affect your decision. Some employers offer new hires the option of enrolling their children in nearby international schools attended by the children of other international staffers. This may not provide the sort of enriching cultural exchange you'd envisaged for your child, but the assimilation process at an international *collège* or *lycée* will likely be smoother at an international school than at a French public school. To explore your options for French private schools, visit two online databases: www.enseignement-prive.info and www.fabert.com.

FRENCH UNIVERSITIES AND *GRANDES ÈCOLES*

There are two tiers within the French university system: the *université* and the *grande école*. The former are standard-issue universities that accept all who apply, as long as they meet the base criteria of having completed *lycée* (and survived the *baccalauréat*). Tuition fees are set annually and standardized throughout the country. For 2011, the annual tuition fees range from €174 to €567.

Grandes écoles are elite schools, not unlike American Ivy League colleges, which accept only the best of the best and charge tuition fees that run higher than the national average. Expect to pay between €3,000 and €10,000 per year if you or your child is accepted into one of these institutions, and also expect to earn a well-paying job at the end of your education. Whichever academic path you take, you can expect a long semester of it's-up-to-you-to-study independence, followed by a big make-it-or-break-it exam at semester's end. France has a relatively high university enrollment rate that's matched by a high dropout rate, due in large part to the stress of this virtually all-or-nothing system.

STUDY ABROAD

French universities roll out the welcome mat to 250,000 foreign university students every year, making France one of the most popular study-abroad destinations in the world. Coming into the French university system as an

American college student is a significantly different experience than entering as a French *lycéen,* beginning with the fact that you won't have had to take the dreaded *baccalauréat* exam. Semester-abroad programs allow foreign university students to ease into the system; this is one of the most popular avenues for obtaining long-stay visas and *cartes de séjour,* which give students the right to work part-time. But first you must meet a few criteria.

To enroll without showing an *international baccalauréat,* you'll have to have two years of college under your belt already. Next, you'll have to decide if you want to study independently or through your university. The former is generally less expensive but requires more effort on your part.

You begin by contacting the school of your choice—a list can be found on the government-sponsored education portal www.enseignementsup-recherche. gouv.fr—then creating a dossier that you submit online directly at the university website. You will not be asked to show transcripts or grades; the onus will be on you to determine whether or not you're up to snuff, educationally speaking. Unless you are studying the French language exclusively, you will be asked to take a French-language proficiency exam or show a certificate attesting to your language skills.

Tuition at French universities is surprisingly affordable and varies slightly according to your academic goals. Here are the 2011 tuition costs: For a standard undergrad diploma, students pay €174 annually; for masters programs, the annual fees jump to €237; doctoral students pay €359 per year; and students pursuing a *diplôme d'ingénieur* pay €564 per semester. Certificate programs, including those that allow you to bypass the French-language proficiency tests, cost considerably more; expect to pay between €800 and €3,000 per four-month semester for the luxury of being instructed in English. Private school tuition is, not surprisingly, higher still: Don't be shocked if that exclusive private business school asks you to fork over €10,000 a year to earn your MBA. But it might still be cheaper than its American equivalent, so if you're seriously considering this route, invest in some French classes and start your research *tout de suite.*

One final word of caution: A unique difference students will notice between the French and American university education is the level of responsibility that falls on the student's shoulders. Don't expect surprise quizzes, weekly assignments, or even midterms—but do expect cumulative exams at the end of the semester that will determine your final grade. To learn more about your options as an American or Canadian student studying in France, visit www. campusfrance.org or check with your university.

HEALTH

In the 2007 documentary *Sicko,* director Michael Moore used the French healthcare system to illustrate its American counterpart's many flaws. This cinematic tactic proved effective, earning the film an Academy Award nomination and prompting the viewing public to critically examine the issues that stirred such heated debate. But what stood out more than the U.S. healthcare system's startling deficiencies was that a humane, affordable, reliable government-run medical system is possible. In France, as it ought to be everywhere, medical treatment (and preventive care) is a right, not a privilege.

Consistently ranked the number-one healthcare system in the world, France's Assurance Maladie, part of the Sécurité Sociale system, is available to everyone who lives here legally and supports the government-sponsored system by paying taxes. People earning little or no income pay little or nothing. The rest of us pay according to our means. For the roughly 12 percent of the population that is self-employed, other forms of government-subsidized insurance is available. Even if you're not here legally, you won't be denied affordable

Médecin

healthcare: Low-cost public hospitals are at your disposal, and mobile doctors will even make house calls to those unable to get to a hospital at any time of day or night.

If you play by the rules, you will have confirmed that you are insured before you arrive in France, since this is a required component of most visa applications. You're asked to submit proof of insurance, but experience proves that consular officials don't always fact-check the documents you provide, and you aren't likely to be asked to provide proof again once you get here. Maybe you went ahead and purchased a traveler's policy that covers you in case of catastrophic illness or injury or reimburses you for travel expenses should you need to fly home to see your own doctor. If you're a student, it's likely that your school provides coverage for study-abroad programs. Or maybe, just maybe, you came with nothing at all, and suddenly that tooth with the wonky old filling is starting to give you grief. If that's you, you don't have to suffer in silence.

Types of Insurance

There are several types of health insurance available to expats in France, the first being the aforementioned Assurance Maladie offered by the state. Supplemental insurance coverage, called *mutuelle,* is popular among the French, who use it to offset the already small (by American standards) deductibles, copays, and other types of care not covered by regular system (cosmetic dentistry, for instance). Finally, there are private insurance options you can purchase in the U.S. or in France that provide different sorts of coverage—inpatient or outpatient or both, maternity, dental—at moderate prices. Which one you choose depends largely on your financial means and the kind of coverage you require for your own sense of security.

ASSURANCE MALADIE

The French public healthcare system is supported by the tax-paying public, which contributes approximately 20 percent of its income to prop up the system. It functions in a pay-as-you-can manner, which many tag as "socialist" because those who earn the most pay the most, and those with little pay less. (And those with no income pay nothing.) Even if you don't contribute taxes, you are entitled to Couverature Maladie Universelle (CMU) if you come from a country (like the U.S.) that doesn't offer universal coverage and will be residing France for more than three months, or if you are on a limited income.

The system is stressed after years of seeing the contributor population dwindle. Retirees no longer contribute, and the birthrate has been low in France for decades—meaning there may not be enough new citizens to support the healthcare system in the future.

It's possible to come to France and sponge off healthcare, but this is not advisable. You don't want to be the proverbial straw that broke the camel's back, nor the scapegoat for the failure of a generous, relatively smooth-running

ONE NATION, UNDER PAPERWORK

If you're an independent contractor willing to pay into the French healthcare system, thus earning eligibility to reap its benefits, be prepared to work for it, especially when it comes to building your *carte vitale* paper trail.

Step 1: Assemble your documents.
You'll need to have the following on hand:

- downloaded and completed forms from the Assurance Maladie website (www.ameli.fr)

- a photocopy of your passport

- your bank account information

- a photocopy of your foreign tax return for the previous year

- a photocopy of proof of residency for the past three months

Step 2: Try to find out where to take your paperwork.
Not all of Assurance Maladie offices process these applications. In Paris, you'll go to the bureau at Folie Méricourt (1 bis rue de la Pierre Levée), in the 11th arrondissement. Expect befuddled looks from the staff before someone finally relieves you of your dossier and tells you they'll call you.

Step 3: Wait patiently.
Within a few months, you should receive a letter saying you've been accepted and that coverage will be made retroactive to the date you submitted your dossier. Also, you will likely be sent a form requesting more information and a photo for your *carte vitale*, which will arrive a few weeks after you send of that paperwork.

Step 4: Keep track of your income.
You'll need to know how much tax to pay – based on a percentage (8 percent at the time of writing) of your income – and when taxes are due (the first day of each quarter).

Step 5: Photocopy your *carte de séjour* each time it's renewed.
You'll be expected to send in a photocopy of your *carte de séjour* every year. Failing to do so will result in the cancellation of your coverage, which means starting again from scratch.

system. With more than €10 billion in debt, it can't take much more stress, something that political leaders are struggling to address. Recent attempts to overhaul the system have resulted only in upsetting the safe, predictable way of life for the locals. (The passing of a law to raise the French retirement age in 2010 is one recent example.) Paying into the system will help keep it—and the other people who help run it—operating.

After applying for your CMU, you may need to wait a few months to get approval and ultimately your Carte Vitale. If you have to visit a doctor or pharmacy, save your receipts; the coverage is usually retroactive to the date on which you submitted your documents. The cost of your annual premium is determined by your income—expect to pay 8 percent of whatever income you declare—and is due in quarterly installments.

Once you have your bright green Carte Vitale in hand, you can rendez-vous with your doctor of choice and visit hospitals, clinics, pharmacies, and laboratories. Produce your card when you pay for your goods and services up front, then submit your receipts to Assurance Maladie, which reimburses you a percentage: 70–100 percent of what you paid for services and 15–65 percent of what you paid for prescription medicine. Your reimbursement takes about two weeks and is deposited directly into your French bank account. Sound complicated? It might seem that way at first, but like all things French (and therefore heavy on bureaucratic ritual), it's easy to get used to.

MUTUELLE

By American standards, the full cost of medical treatment at a French public hospital borders on a bargain; depending on the treatment you receive, an overnight stay with regular nursing care and medications at a public hospital could set you back just €100—a whole lot less than it would at any public or private hospital in the U.S. Most drug costs are lower here, too. These two factors combined have resulted in some expats scheduling full-fare medical procedures in France. But for regular folks who simply want basic coverage, Assurance Maladie is a good start. Next, you might consider *mutuelle,* the supplemental insurance coverage that most French people opt for. It covers the cost of deductibles and all the little things that add up when you need them: ambulance costs, private hospital-room fees, and cosmetic dentistry, for instance. You can choose from a number of configurations, depending on your needs, and the price will reflect what those needs are. Want to make sure your deductibles on any future hospital stays are paid for? Identify that concern when making your *mutuelle* purchasing decision.

In addition to all the private agencies offering *mutuelles,* the government also offers this additional coverage to families and individuals of limited means through the CMU website (www.cmu.fr). The information is in French, so if your language skills are still at the work-in-progress phase, you'll want a French friend to help you with the technical translating.

PRIVATE INSURANCE

All you need to feel totally overwhelmed by the private insurance policy process is type in "expatriate health insurance" into your favorite search engine. You'll be met with links to dozens of companies, each offering similar but different insurance options that span a frighteningly broad financial spectrum. So which do you choose? The best bet is to go by word of mouth. Ask friends who've already made the move, post queries on expat forums, and check with the American Embassy in France, which offers a downloadable list of companies on its website (www.france.usembassy.gov). HCC Medical Insurance Services (www.hccmis.com) has earned high marks from some expats, with coverage in the US$600 to US$800 range annually.

MATERNITY MANIA

Name: Mariel Chatman
Age: 30
Hometown: Berkeley, CA
Current city: Paris

Mariel, an attorney from the San Francisco Bay Area, moved to France in 2009 after falling in love with a Parisian. She and her partner, Thibaut, discovered they were pregnant in early 2010 and decided to give the local healthcare system a try. The experience was harrowing, but healthy baby Noèmie made it worth the 25 hours of labor and subsequent C-section.

In her own words: "As soon as we found out I was pregnant, we registered at a public hospital. It wasn't until later that we realized there was a *maternité* – a private clinic for low-risk births – right on our street. Because of the convenience, we decided to see if I could get in there. Even though it was several months into my pregnancy and

you're supposed to secure these details the moment you discover you're pregnant, we were put on a list, and eventually someone called to say a spot had opened up.

At a public hospital, when you go into labor, you get whatever doctor happens to be on duty at the time. And though you spend more money for care at a private *maternité* than you would at a public hospital, we liked that were able to choose our own OB/GYN who'd be with us straight through delivery. When my water broke, we took a taxi to the *maternité*. When we got there, I was ushered into a tiny room (with nowhere for Thibaut to sit), strapped to a hospital bed, hooked up to a monitoring machine, and was told not to move – even to use the bathroom.

"The nurse didn't encourage me to walk around, and when I suggested it, she got very angry with me. 'These are the rules,' she said.

Also worth a gander are www.expat-medical-insurance.com and www.health careinternational.com.

UNINSURED

Nearly everyone who's lived in France for any amount of time has one health-care story or another; it usually ends with "I couldn't believe how small the bill was/how short the wait was/how friendly the staff was." Even if you have no health insurance coverage, you will be treated respectfully and without palpable bias or hostility. You will not be asked to show proof of insurance before you are treated, and you will not be denied care in the emergency room because of lack of funds. (You aren't even asked for a credit card or other payment during the course of your treatment; a bill will be mailed to you once your treatment is completed.) If you have no insurance and find yourself at the emergency room with a broken big toe or at the dentist's office with a faulty filling, be prepared to pay the bill when it arrives a week or two later, and expect the costs to be significantly less than if you were to have the same

You *should* be able to walk around and let gravity take its course, but every time I suggested it, there just wasn't any room for discussion. After 15 hours if labor, they induced me and gave me an epidural that was so strong it numbed my whole body. After 25 hours, I went in for an emergency C-section. Thibaut wasn't allowed in the operating room, and after Noèmie was born, they took her away, Thibaut was gone, and I was all alone.

I think I had an unusually bad experience – none of the mothers in my circle of friends experienced anything they'd consider to be traumatic like this, but I feel like I have post-traumatic stress disorder. For new moms and dads to-be who are considering giving birth in a French hospital, here are some things to consider beforehand:

Be your own healthcare advocate. If you want something, whether it's a drink of water during labor or an early discharge from the hospital, learn your rights and be firm and clear with the hospital staff.

Make sure your dossier is complete. It is your responsibility to carry all of your own medical documents, including X-rays and lab results, to every doctor's appointment. You may be turned away if forms are missing.

Thoroughly examine the differences between the private *maternité* and a public hospital. Remember that you'll be paying between €5,000 and €8,000 up front for *maternité* care – some of which will be reimbursed – or you can opt to pay nothing at a public hospital.

Remember that your partner will not be able to stay overnight with you at the *maternité* or hospital. This may affect your decision to stay the standard five days at the hospital after giving birth (seven days for C-sections)."

treatment back home. Remember to save your receipts, in case you sign up for Assurance Maladie; the program is retroactive and may cover a good portion of your out-of-pocket expenses.

PUBLIC HOSPITALS VS. PRIVATE CLINICS

Only one third of all French *hospitaux* (hospitals) are privately run; the rest are nonprofit public institutions run by the government, which sets fees for medical services rendered by any institution or individual medical professional on the government payroll. For example, on January 1, 2011, the cost of a visit to a family physician in France increased by €1, from €23 to €24.

Of the public institutions, many are *centres hospitaliers universitaires,* or research hospitals affiliated with a university. These are not the funky institutions that might come to mind when you hear "government-run facility." They are as warm and friendly as any hospital, and the care you'll receive is on par with private facilities. Expect the usual amenities in the rooms—toilets and televisions—and maybe even something more: Some hospitals post their menus online, so you can plan your overnight stay for a Saturday to benefit from the Sunday-morning croissants.

There are two different types of *cliniques* (private hospitals) in France—for profit and not-for-profit. The American Hospital of Paris, which is actually in the well-to-do suburb of Neuilly-sur-Seine, belongs to the latter category, and

THE DOCTOR'S HOUSE CALL GOES MODERN

It's 2 A.M., and you haven't stopped coughing since 2 P.M. Your throat is seared and your eyeballs feel like dried raisins. Are you dying of some mysterious tropical disease, or is it a simple case of the 24-hour flu? If you don't have the strength to haul yourself to the nearest hospital, you're in luck. When you call SOS Médecins, an honest-to-goodness doctor will be knocking on your door within the hour, medical kit in hand, ready to diagnose what ails you and offer you a soothing balm – or at least an aspirin or two.

Assurance Maladie covers the cost of the home visit (€33), but even if you don't have insurance, there's no need to work up a sweat on top of your fever. You'll simply be charged the uninsured person's rate: €70 at the time of this writing. Don't the strength to write out a check? Relax: They'll send you a bill.

SOS Médecins was founded in 1966 by a Parisian M.D. after one of his patients died on a Saturday – a day when doctors didn't regularly make house-calls. He figured that if you could get a plumber at home on a weekend, you should be able to get life-saving care, too. Today, SOS Médecins has been adopted by other Francophone countries, including Tahiti, Senegal, and Switzerland. In France, the service is available in all the major cities, including Vannes, Antibes, Grenoble, and, of course, Paris.

its foundation is supported in part by member and public donations. You'll pay more here, and Assurance Maladie won't be able to reimburse you in the same generous way as if you'd gone to a public hospital. The benefit of private hospitals is that some specialize in specific types of services—maternity or oncology, for instance—and some also tout a bilingual staff, which can ease the stress of an already stressful situation for some.

Doctors don't go into the medical field because they want to get rich in France; they do it because they were fast-tracked on a science route during their *lycée* years (and possibly because the wanted a career in which they could help people). Because medical school costs next to nothing to attend in France, many choose this path despite its dearth of economic advantages. You will find that there are two types of doctors here, just to add another layer of complexity onto the process: *conventionnée* and *non-conventionnée*. *Conventionnée* doctors have contracted with the state to provide their services at a set cost that's reimbursable by Assurance Maladie; *non-conventionnée* practitioners have no contract with the state and set their own fees. You'll find this disparity especially among dermatologists and cosmetic surgeons, where fees can vary widely depending on the doctor, the location, and the services being rendered.

Pharmacies and Prescriptions

You can't miss the pharmacy; Just look for the flashing green cross, and *voilà!* You've arrived. French pharmacies are different from North American ones in many ways. First, a doctor is always on staff and has the authority to prescribe or recommend treatment at his discretion, without consulting your primary physician. These doctors are also authorized to administer first aid if you need it. Next, you'll notice that some over-the-counter drugs you take for granted back home—cough syrup, pain reliever, even sore-throat lozenges—are found behind the counter at the pharmacist's, and requesting them requires some basic working French. Need saline solution? Don't go looking for it at your local supermarket—you'll find it at the pharmacy, along with high-end face creams, diet pills and potions, homeopathic remedies, and multivitamins. (You'll also find saline solution for sale at eyeglasses shops, where it might be less expensive than at the pharmacy. It pays to compare.) Some pharmacies also vend veterinary medicines, so you can pick up Fluffy's heartworm medicine and your antibiotics at the same time.

Picking up your prescription at the pharmacy works in a way you're probably familiar with: Bring your prescription to the counter, ask any questions,

© AURELIA D'ANDREA

Don't look for your contact lens solution at the *supermarché;* you'll find it at a *pharmacie.*

listen to the pharmacist explain how to take your medicine, pay for it (standard practice is to ask for your Carte Vitale, so you can be reimbursed), and save your receipts if you intend to seek reimbursement.

By law, every community must have a pharmacy that's open on weekends, holidays, and during off-hours; the information for the one closest to you can be found posted in the window or on the door of your neighborhood pharmacy.

Preventive Measures

No special inoculations are required to enter France, but it doesn't hurt to be in top health before your move. As part of the *carte de séjour* process, you'll have to have your lungs X-rayed for tuberculosis, but this is the only medical requirement you'll find here.

Like everywhere else, waves of viruses come crashing through the population every season, and many opt for flu vaccines as a prophylactic measure. If you didn't get that flu shot before you moved, you can still find one here. In France, the flu is called *"la grippe"* and often *"la grippe* H1N1," and pharmacies can direct you to health clinics where inoculations are administered or sell you the vaccine to take to your doctor to be injected.

ALTERNATIVE THERAPIES

The French love their medicine, whether it's the pharmaceutical kind or the kind created exclusively by Mother Nature. Homeopathy is particularly popular in France, and pharmacies everywhere sell homeopathic remedies behind the counter. Boiron, headquartered in Lyon, is the most popular brand, producing "remedies" for everything from bruises (arnica) to mental fatigue (nux vomica). The little blue vials run about €2, and many people swear by their efficacy. If you're one of the millions around the world who prefer to take the natural approach to healthcare, you'll find many opportunities to heal thyself in France. Flower essences, acupuncture, and massage are all on the menu. Herbal weight-loss formulations are in high demand in France, and you'll have dozens of varieties of liquids, pills, lozenges, and creams to choose from if you're looking to shed a kilo or two before bikini-and-Speedo season. Many healthcare services that fall under the "natural" umbrella are covered in part by Assurance Maladie, including homeopathy, which is reimbursed at 30 percent; be sure to inquire when seeking out your treatment.

VIVE LA VENDING MACHINE!

What do condoms, hypodermic needles, and wine have in common? If you guessed that they're all sold from vending machines in France, you're right. The French appreciate convenience as much as anyone, which is why you can also find espresso, razors, and Speedo bathing suits in automated machines here. (Yes, really.)

As part of a nationwide campaign against HIV/AIDS, easy-access condom machines have been mounted outside nearly every pharmacy in the country, as well as inside most Métro stations. Syringe dispensers can be found in big cities like Marseille and Lyon, but unless you're trolling through the seedier parts of town, you probably won't even notice them. More eye-catching are the automated wine dispensers, which made their debut in 2007. At *hypermarchés* like Auchan, you can BYOB and fill 'er up, just like pumping gas at the gas station. Tend toward teetotalism? A few select Auchans have also begun dispensing raw milk by the liter.

© AURELIA D'ANDREA

a common sight: condom vending machines

Environmental Factors

AIR QUALITY

Each year in France, 11 million tons of pollutants are pumped into the air from cars, factories, agriculture, and people living their day-to-day lives. This fact is particularly noticeable when you're stuck on your bicycle behind a two-stroke motorbike at a stoplight. In some ways, France's big cities look like developing nations when it comes to the color and prodigiousness of what gets pumped out of some exhaust pipes. Your health can be affected by all that pollution, both out in the street and in your home. To see what the pollution levels are like in your town, visit www. airqualitynow.eu. In Paris and Bordeaux, the levels can look scary-high from time to time. Many city dwellers in France take the extra precautionary step of purchasing an air filter; try Darty (www.darty.fr) if you live on a particularly busy street or near a freeway on-ramp, where pollution levels are particularly high.

WATER QUALITY

The French are known for their love of bottled water, consuming 40 gallons of it per person per year. Stroll down the aisle at the nearest *hypermarché,* and you'll find yourself in a sea of drinking water. Do you like yours flat or still? Full of minerals or not? Are you on a diet? There's a bottled-water variety to help you through. Those who don't need fancy water (or who don't want to add to the waste-disposal problem) will be glad to know that tap water is safe throughout France, though it tends to have a very high calcium content. This necessitates the purchase of products that eliminate calcium buildup in your appliances, such as electric kettles and dishwashers. Public fountains are common throughout Paris—they're often green, and if it's a Wallace fountain, designed by 19th-century French sculptor Charles-August Lebourg, it might even look like a piece of art. Potable water is available in public fountains, and numerous filter options are available for those who want to lessen the calcium content in their glasses. Around the Alps and Pyrénées, it's not uncommon to see cars pulled over to the side of the road, with a line of people bearing water bottles to be filled at natural springs.

SMOKING

Though the café smoking ban went into effect in 2008, France's addiction to "cancer sticks" still clings like tar to an old Gitane fan's lungs. Where else will you find a pregnant mother-to-be puffing her hand-rolled cigarette, with nary a glance of disapproval from passersby? The good news is that the rates of stroke and heart attack have plummeted since the ban; the bad news is that it's still too late for too many. Lung cancer kills more people in France than any other type of cancer. Bad habits are hard to break, and that's particularly evident in the outdoor seating section of cafés, which tend to take on the air of a smoker's convention in wintertime when the heat lamps are activated and the plastic walls encase the once-outdoor terrace. Smoking is no longer legal in public places, including office buildings, hospitals, museums, and school campuses, but that doesn't mean everyone adheres to the law. Enforcement has been rather lax, and business owners are reluctant to ask clients to stub out their cigs if no one has lodged a complaint. If you're sensitive to cigarette

ORAL FIXATION

Stroll into any corner *tabac* and peer behind the counter. Whether you're a smoker or not, prepare to be overwhelmed by the sheer variety of nicotine-infused offerings. There's tobacco in cans, packs (small and standard size), and tins; short cigarettes and long; light and regular; imports and domestic brands; roll your own, with or without insertable filters; flavored and unflavored pipe tobacco, cigars – you get the idea. In spite of the wealth of puffable possibilities, the French have actually significantly reduced their tobacco consumption: Men in particular have whittled down their cigarette intake by 15 percent since the mid-'80s. A noteworthy decrease in heart attacks and strokes among the general population is credited to the café and restaurant smoking ban instituted in 2007, but the average price of a pack of cigarettes – €5.90 ($8.40) – is still high enough to cause a coronary in some.

© JENNIFER PICKENS/BLACKBIRDPHOTO.COM

If you're a smoker, you've come to the right place.

DAILY LIFE

smoke, avoid enclosed terraces at cafés and brasseries, and count your blessings that you didn't decide to move to France before 2008.

Disabled Access

Though disabled-access laws are now in place, France has a lot of catching up to do, beginning with ditching the word *handicapped,* which is the preferred term in France for people with any minor or major disability. This is not the most hospitable country for the wheelchair-bound. Despite a law passed in 2005 to make offices, businesses, and public spaces accessible to all, the changes are coming at an escargot-worthy pace. The government agency that oversees laws relating to disabled citizens, the Ministère des Solidarités et de la Cohésion Sociale, has busted out a PR campaign that tries hard to convince people that efforts are under way to make France more accessible—but those who have to navigate the cobbled streets, clogged sidewalks, and other public spaces will tell you it's not happening fast enough. The Métro is not worth the hassle: Not all stations are equipped with an elevator, and those that do have them can't ensure that they'll be functioning when you need to use them. Buses are more likely to have a wheelchair access. By 2015, all public spaces will be accessible to those with restricted mobility, but until then, extra care should be taken when planning any excursion.

Safety

There's no sugar-coating it: Crime is on the rise in France. Still, it's not likely you'll become a crime statistic while you're here. Strict gun-control laws do mean that you're more likely to get stabbed than shot, but the odds of either one are infinitesimally small. If you are the victim of a crime in France, it'll most likely be a pickpocketing or other theft. In Paris, Métro line 1 is notorious for pickpockets, who hunt for distracted tourists on their way to the Louvre, the Musée d'Orsay, and the Champs-Élysées.

Also growing in popularity among thieves previously resigned to wallets are smartphones, with iPhones being of particular value. A recent spate of phone thefts in train stations and on the streets—generally the purloined items are snatched directly from the hands of their rightful owners—warrants extra care with your electronic doodads. Also be aware that when you're traveling

Thousands of surveillance cameras are positioned in public areas nationwide.

by car, your license plate gives away your nonlocal status, and visitors in rental cars have reported break-ins at popular tourist sites. The key is not to leave anything of value in your car, and be sure to keep all the doors locked when you're driving.

One technique being employed to curb crime in public areas is the camera. A public surveillance system already in place expanded in 2011, when more than 1100 cameras were installed throughout the public streets of Paris, adding to the 60,000 cameras already in place throughout the rest of the country. If it feels like a futuristic police state, that's probably not too far off—but this system has proved effective in apprehending thieves in the Métro and otherwise identifying criminals in public places.

POLICE

French police can help with matters as varied as finding a lost animal to giving you directions to helping you when your pocket is picked on the Paris Métro. There are several different types of police: *police nationale,* those legions of men and women who keep order and protect the public in metropolitan areas throughout France; *gendarmes,* who keep the peace in rural areas, provide military security, and stroll the welcome halls at airports; *police de la circulation,* who'll ticket you for breaking one of the rules of the road and issue you those pesky parking citations; and *douanes,* who enforce the law when it comes to customs and taxes. For basic issues, either go to the local *commissariat* of police in your region or dial emergency number 17—it's the same throughout France—to speak with a law-enforcement agent equipped to help you. Note that French is the common language spoken, so be prepared to try and stumble through; if you get a nice person on the other end of the line, she may meet you halfway with some English.

© TOPDEQ/123RF.COM

You may see mounted *gendarmes* (police) in Paris.

EMERGENCIES

France is fully equipped to handle any emergency you may face, but you need to know where to call to get the care that you need. The fire department, or Pompiers/Sapeurs, is the go-to agency for most emergencies. The staff act as intermediaries to determine whether they should come to your aid themselves or send the police or a more urgent medical service. If they determine that you need a doctor at home right away, they'll direct you to SOS Medecins (or you can call them directly—in Paris, the number is tel. 01/47 07 77 77), who'll be at your home in less than an hour. Or they might send Urgences Médicales, who'll pay you a visit within 12 hours (in Paris, tel. 01/53 94 94 94). Once or twice a year, cards with all the municipal emergency numbers are distributed to homes and apartments throughout France. Ask the *gardien* of your building for a card or request one at your local *mairie.* The most common numbers you'll need in an emergency are:

- 15 - Ambulance (Service d'Aide Médicale d'Urgence/SAMU)
- 17 - Police (Police/Gendarmes)
- 18 - Firemen (Sapeurs/Pompiers).

EMPLOYMENT

In early 2011, president Nicolas Sarkozy reignited the heated debate over one of France's most controversial social issues by declaring, "The 35-hour workweek no longer exists." Threatening the status quo with this latest proclamation may have hurt Sarkozy's popularity ratings (recent polls show him limping behind contentious right wing party leader Marine Le Pen in the 2012 presidential race), but it hurt the national psyche even more—particularly the working class and those seated center left at the political table. The social perks that the French seem to take for granted are the same ones that leave many Americans slack-jawed with a combination of disbelief and envy: Free healthcare? A minimum of five weeks' paid vacation? Subsidized education? How can people gripe about a few increased work hours when they've got all that? Easy. The French work hard for their benefits and don't want to see them whittled away without a fight. So far, the 35-hour workweek—and the 218-day work year *and* the five weeks' worth of vacation—is safe from the meddling hands of politicos, but it promises to be a frequent topic of conversation as the election inches closer.

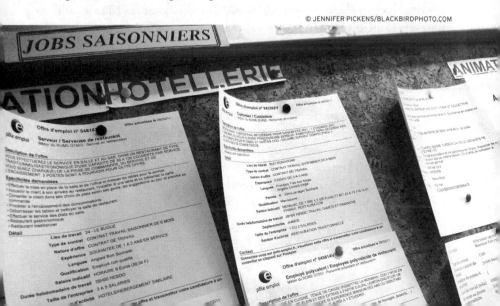

For expatriates arriving in France with hopes of laying down roots and actually earning a living, there are numerous possibilities, some more feasible than others. In a perfect situation, you'll be transferred here through your current job, settle into a cushy three-year contract complete with housing, travel, and food allowances. (This is a reality for many—your first social gathering in France with more than a handful of American expats will verify it.) American companies by the boatload have branched out with offices in France— American Express, Xerox, Hewlett-Packard, IBM, and Sanofi-Aventis—and if you've been employed with such a company for more than three months, you're eligible for an Employee on Assignment permit. Does your company have international offices? If so, it's worth checking with your HR department on the chances of an international transfer.

Teaching English has long been a popular way for Anglophone expats to earn a living in France, and it might be the one professional realm where Americans have an advantage over the French; employers often prefer native speakers and those with limited French because it reinforces the goal of the education process: teaching (and learning) English. Private language schools and individual private lessons are the two paths of least resistance, and opportunities are plentiful if you establish yourself as a niche teacher of children, perhaps, or of legal English to traveling attorneys.

For the lucky arrivals armed with a law degree, finding employment in France and securing that all-important work-sponsored visa will be much easier. The nonprofit sector—the International Chamber of Commerce, OECD, and UNESCO—are good places to start your hunt for a legal job in France. Not an *avocat* (lawyer) and don't plan to become one? There's still hope, especially if you're in possession of a student visa, which allows you to work up to 20 hours per week (and more during the summer semester). With a long-stay visa, you can continue your freelancing gigs abroad without worrying about breaking any employment laws—though if you plan to stay more than three months and intend to sign up for Assurance Maladie, you'll need to file an income tax return so the French government can determine how much to charge you for healthcare coverage.

The unemployment rate is high in France, currently hovering just below 10 percent, and unemployment among foreigners is even higher, at 22 percent. When a position opens up, a French employer will first look to the pool of French applicants to find a qualified candidate. That's some stiff competition, considering that the natives are already equipped with a solid (and predictably uniform) educational foundation and, presumably, an extremely high level of French fluency. Bundled with the fact that they are citizens and you are not, they will most likely trump your qualifications unless you have some tricks up your sleeve. (Or if the jobs you're applying for aren't desirable, meaning the qualified locals may pass and take unemployment or job offer *numéro deux* instead.)

Another option for anyone not averse to a bit of risk-taking is under-the-table work. Though it's not discussed much in the open, there is a thriving underground economy in France, supported primarily by expats here on legal visas, as well as illegal immigrants who haven't taken the steps to get their visa situations sorted out. From restaurant work to teaching English to watching children and giving tours, there are endless opportunities to earn some euros by working *sous la table* (under the table). Unsurprisingly, the big cities have the most opportunity, with Paris being the employment mecca of France. It's possible to tap into the diverse population and exploit it, if that's your thing. But be warned that getting caught could have dire consequences—including expulsion and being banned from returning for four years—not only for you but also for the person who hires you, who'll be slapped with a hefty fine.

Taxes run extremely high for employers in France; to cover your *cotisation,* or social benefits, they must pay the state an average of nearly a third of the wages they pay you, so the temptation is always there to add an extra undeclared body or two to the payroll. Surprisingly, even long-established companies, particularly those in the tourist trade whose day-to-day workings are limited mostly to foreign visitors, fly under the radar and employ people off the books. Either they have good lawyers, know the ropes, or are genuine roulette players willing to engage in the risks. Whatever the case may be, they're here, hiring people like you and me to our mutual advantage—but not without considerable hazards.

If all this talk of deportation, fines, and other risks have you reconsidering the illegal employment minefield, making your freelance status official or even starting your own business might be the solution. Be prepared to build a fat dossier of tax forms, *cotisation* papers, and endless copies of your *carte de séjour.* If your desire to make it work in France supersedes your fear of paperwork, prepare to investigate your moneymaking options.

Self-Employment

FREELANCING

Once you've been granted your visa and have either your *carte de séjour* or *recepisée* in hand, you'll need to register as an "auto-entrepreneur" with the Centre de Formalités des Entreprises des Autoentrepreneurs (www.lautoen-trepreneur.fr). This allows you to go legit by declaring your activity and subsequent income, then pay the taxes that help support that generous healthcare system you're now entitled to take advantage of. You'll create an online dossier that describes the sort of work you'll be doing and answer all the nosy questions the government wants to ask about you to make your status official. Then hit the *envoyer* (send) button. (This process can also be done in person at the Centre de Formalités des Entreprises (CFE), Chambre de Commerce, or Chambre des Métiers). A month or two later, you'll receive a Notification d'Affiliation au Statut Auto-Entrepreneur, the form you'll use to declare any earnings. You'll also receive a chart that will help you determine the taxes or *cotisation* that you need to remit, which will fall somewhere between 13 and 23 percent of your declared earnings, contingent on the type of work you perform. You'll do this three times a year, and you'll be glad to know that if you've earned nothing, you owe nothing.

STARTING A BUSINESS

Starting a business in France is a marvelous idea—if you have a solid plan, a healthy respect for paperwork, the patience of a saint, and, perhaps most importantly, a healthy bank account. Recent changes in French tax law have made it more feasible (and less expensive) for Average Jacques and Jacquelines to launch their moneymaking ventures here. But to get your foot through the self-employment door, you need to have it all worked out on paper first for the consular officials before you even get here: meaning a student visa, *visa de long séjour,* Carte Compétences et Talents, or other work-friendly visa.

If you can afford to hire a consultant before you get started, it's not a bad idea. She can help you with all the befuddling aspects of taxation, idiosyncrasies in labor law, and other formalities. The Agence Pour la Création d'Entreprises (www.apce.com) is a semiprivate organization—the government funds 60 percent of its budget—that helps entrepreneurs develop and launch their businesses in France. The APCE has devised a helpful checklist for prospective *auto-entrepreneurs* to determine the viability of their ideas and help them pick which *statut juridique* they'll need to register under once they decide to give it a go.

WORK IT

Normandy-based business adviser Valerie Lemiere is the Anglophone entrepreneur's best friend. Through her website, www.startbusinessinfrance.com, she gives aspiring Donald Trumps advice on how to launch a business in France, ideas for how to run it, and suggestions for avoiding the pitfalls that stand in the way of success. Here, she offers five tips for starting your own enterprise in *la belle France*.

1. Get the required documents to set up a business before you leave.
In France, you'll need a *titre de séjour vie privée et famille* in order to register your business. A tourist visa or short-term *carte de séjour* won't be enough. It is easier to get these papers in the U.S., where there is no language barrier. Get in touch with your French embassy or consulate. If you have special skills, you could look into the *carte de séjour compétences et talents,* which is valid for three years.

2. Take a copy of key administrative documents.
Birth certificates, marriage certificates, qualifications, and diplomas are required to set up health coverage for you and your family members. Some job titles, such as carpenter, builder, hairdresser, accountant, and lawyer, are considered regulated activities that require proof of qualification (or three years' experience for crafts activities).

3. Put together a basic business plan before you leave.
Do your market research online, assess your competition, and work on your services, products, suppliers, and prices. Draw up a provisional plan to assess how much money you'll need to get started, assess your running costs, and calculate your break-even point. Ask for help from an accountant, too.

4. Wait a few months after arrival before setting the business up.
Get to know the area and ensure this is where you want to live (moving from one department to another generates red tape and hassle by having to reregister with different bodies). Update your business plan with local information: competition, prices, delivery costs, taxes. Get in touch with local business advisors who will give you more background and feedback on the local economy and your activity: Chambre de Commerce et d'Industrie (for trade and tourism), Chambre de Métiers (for skilled manual activities and crafts), BGE (national network of nonprofit associations that help entrepreneurs).

5. Seek out advice to understand your liability and how much tax you will pay.
Your personal situation and your business activity are likely to dictate which legal structure is best for you. For instance, two partners will opt for a SARL/limited company, while a communication consultant with low investment and low expenses would be better off registering as an *auto-entrepreneur.* Meet with a business advisor and/or accountant to understand how much you will pay to set up your business, look at the yearly accountancy feesm and understand the social charges and income tax expected to be paid according to each business type. Find out your personal liability, and take measures to protect your assets if necessary (such as *acte insaisissabilité* to protect your home).

DAILY LIFE

Next, the process moves in much the same way as becoming an *auto-en-trepreneur*: You create a dossier with the Centre de Formalités des Entreprises des Autoentrepreneurs (www.lautoentrepreneur.fr). You'll be prompted to determine which category your new business falls into: Artisan/Industriel/Commerçant or Profession Libéral. If you're a commercial agent, you'll need to register with the Registre Spécial des Agents Commerciaux (RSAC). As an artisan entrepreneur, you must follow up with the Chambre de Métiers. If you choose to start your own dog-walking business, private English school, or bicycle touring company, will need to make your status as an Entrepreneur Individuel à Responsabilité Limitée (EIRL) formal at www.eirl.fr or www.guichet-entreprises.fr. Both of these agencies offer resources and services to aid you in your quest to become a successful entrepreneur in France.

Registering under some *statuts,* including the relatively new EIRL, allows you to defer the Contribution Foncière des Entreprises (CFE) tax for the first three years. However, if you don't report any earnings whatsoever within your first two years, your status will be reverted automatically to the not-so-budget-friendly *"entreprise individuelle"* designation, which means you'll be responsible for paying taxes on estimated revenue to the tune of €3,000 the first year. Investing in a tax accountant is a good idea if you want to avoid any potential financial surprises down the line.

TYPES OF BUSINESSES

The type of business you choose to undertake depends entirely on your skills, personal interests, demands, moneymaking potential, and location. Businesses that don't require retail space or office space are, from an economic perspective, easier than others. You might also consider buying an existing business—a *gîte,* a bed-and-breakfast, a retail shop, or perhaps a vineyard—and putting your own spin on it. But keep in mind that you'll inherit the previous owner's reputation, so if it wasn't a good one, you'll have some damage control to do. Still, it means an opportunity to take a good idea, improve on it, and integrate into the community.

As you consider your options, make use of some of the free and very handy services that are there for the asking—as long as you're asking in French. Your local *maire* (mayor), who wants to see new business flourish in his district—is a wonderful resource. He can tell you what has worked or hasn't worked in the past, prognosticate one whether your business idea has potential for success in the community, and direct you toward local resources to help you become a local success. Your local *chambre de commerce* serves much the same function; remember, it's in their interest for you to succeed, so it's worth taking advantage of the resources they have to offer.

The Job Hunt

EMPLOYERS

It's easy to get discouraged scouting the want ads on Craigslist or FUSAC: "Only those with working papers need apply." Well, don't take that at face value. Many companies publish similar phrasing in their ads to keep the government looking the other way, but when it comes down to interviewing and subsequently hiring, your lack of work permit may not be an issue at all. First and foremost, you'll find that you need to establish trust with your future employer. He doesn't want to offer you a job you're not legally entitled to take, only to get fined or, worse, forcibly ejected from France. If you do decide to take the below-board route, always be discreet and be honest with your employer, who is taking a risk to hire you. But don't be afraid to apply for that job, even if you're not 100 percent qualified. There may be an opportunity for a work sponsorship, or maybe your interviewer knows of another position at another company that needs someone with your skill set.

The job hunt in France begins much the same way it does in the U.S. Start by talking to everyone you know—friends of friends of friends, distant cousins, elementary-school classmates—because it really is all about who you know. Don't know anyone? That's OK. But don't even think about hitting the pavement without fluffing up your dossier first. You'll need one, and it should include copies of every spelling bee award and talent-show ribbon you've ever earned, because that stuff matters here. Include copies of your college diploma—ideally translated into French—and certificates of completion for any higher-education studies you've taken, including language courses. Have your letters of recommendation handy, too, and be prepared to tote them to your job interview along with the rest of your dossier documents.

INTERVIEWS

You've landed a coveted interview, and now you want to charm their socks off. How do you do it? Start by adhering to standard interview protocol—dress sharply, show up on time, and come prepared with a bit of background knowledge and questions for the person interviewing you—and end with a thank-you note. Take great care to tout your strengths and accomplishments without sounding like a braggart, and be prepared for questions that dip into personal territory; it's not unusual to be asked about your hobbies and whether your plans include starting a family.

French employment laws make it difficult for you to be fired once you've been hired, so expect the interview process to extend the limits of thoroughness.

This is so your future employer can get a full sense of what you're all about before she extends a potentially lifelong offer your way. You will be asked about your weaknesses and strengths and what you think makes you right for the job. Above all, you will be assessed for your French-speaking abilities—you must be conversational, at the very least, if you want to work for a French company. Don't expect special treatment as an *"exotique"* Anglophone, because you'll likely not get it.

LANDING THE JOB

If you've been offered a job contract in France, it will fall into one of a few categories. The *contrat à durée déterminée* (CDD), a fixed-term contract good for 18 to 36 months, might be the most popular. This is the usual "starter" agreement between an employer and a employee; if the work relationship is to be extended, the CDD is transformed into a *contrat à durée indéterminée* (CDI). The CDI is an open-ended contract that implies permanency, though it usually comes with a two-month probationary period. It is also possible to work without any sort of contract, in which case it is implied that you will be hired on an ongoing, open-ended basis. When you sign your contract—whether it's a CDI, CDD, *contrat de travail temporaire* (CTT) or *contrat jeunes en entreprise* (CJE)—make sure it clearly states your salary, as well as any monetary perks to which you've agreed or are entitled. Many employers offer staff an annual bonus known as the "13th month" check, which is, ostensibly, a holiday bonus—check your contract to see if it includes one.

BENEFITS

As with most jobs, a contract position entitles you to social benefits ranging from family healthcare to retirement pensions. The onus is on you to learn what all the perks are and to maximize your access to the ones that may take a bit of sleuthing, such as restaurant meal vouchers or commuter compensation. Like everyone else, you will earn 2.5 days of vacation for every month worked. Both women and men are entitled to leave after the birth of a child (for women, it's 16 weeks; for men, it's just two; but both parents can take additional time off at a decreased salary). A few different forms of sabbatical are also available to *salariés* (employees), including up to a year off to study in a field that will enhance your work performance.

One significant difference between the U.S. and France is the frequency of paychecks. In the U.S., getting paid every two weeks—and sometimes every week—is the norm. In France, you'll likely get one paycheck on the first of each month. And if that paycheck looks small, it might be because it is; you

WORK TO LIVE

Name: Amanda Nicole Zane
Age: 25
Hometown: New York, NY, and Portland, ME
Current city: Paris

Amanda is a practicing immigration attorney who also teaches legal English to French attorneys and law students. She did not, however, begin her Paris sojourn as an esteemed paid professional. After a short stint as a student at an elite university, she chucked it all and took a gamble on finding a coveted French job. With a little moxie and a whole lot of smarts, she landed her dream gig in the City of Light.

In her own words: "Pure chance brought me to Paris. I studied Spanish through middle school, high school, and university, but my law school only had exchange programs with French universities. So in spring 2009, I found myself 40 minutes to the west of Paris by RER-A at the Université de Cergy-Pontoise, studying French law.

Having fallen in love with the stereotypical things – cheese, language learning, pastries, etc. – I decided to return to pursue a French law master's. I returned merely two weeks after passing the Bar – and yes, many things are closed in August. Nevertheless, my classes at Sciences Po started shortly after, and perhaps from sheer fatigue, I fell ill and fell behind (11 classes in three languages!), and the rigidities of French education are such that nobody would work with me to salvage the situation. I had resigned myself to returning to the United States, as I only had a French visa valid for studies.

In a moment of desperation (was that the antibiotics or the steroids?), I sent résumés to every attorney specializing in immigration law recommended by the U.S. Embassy in Paris website. One morning in class, I had forgotten to turn off my mobile. It rang. I fumbled for "silence." During the break, I checked my messages – it was an attorney – and returned the call. Could I come that afternoon for an interview? He hired me conditionally, based on successful Bar results, which I have subsequently received. We are currently adjusting my status from *"étudiant"* to *"profession libérale"* and have already been accorded the permission of the French Bar for me to work as a foreign attorney.

This has been a path mired with complications. My medical visit was scheduled late (for February 2011), despite my having mailed the documents in August 2010 for scheduling, just as I was instructed by the French Consulate in Boston. Apparently, a change of status can be effectuated only three months after this medical visit, where one receives the passport stamp (*vignette*). This little hiccough is teaching me patience. Though I'm skeptical that this is a virtue, it is useful for dealing with bureaucracy (a word I only learned to spell in English after moving to France). The moral of the story is: Where there is a will, there is a way. If you want to be somewhere badly enough, you will find a way to make it happen."

DAILY LIFE

contribute a share of your salary—up to 40 percent in the highest income brackets—to support the social benefits you and your colleagues are entitled to. But your company is also contributing on your behalf, usually considerably more than what you pay, to offset the financial burden.

Labor Laws

WORKERS' RIGHTS

France has such strong laws in favor of the employee that getting fired is practically impossible here—but that doesn't mean you should show up an hour late for work, take two-hour lunch breaks, and leave at 3 every afternoon. Plenty of people do this, but some actually get fired for it, as former Paris-based secretary Catherine Sanderson did back in 2006. Sanderson, who blogs under the nom de plume "La Petite Anglaise," got the boot when her employers—an English law firm with offices in France—discovered she was blogging about her personal and professional life while on the job. She wound up winning a wrongful termination lawsuit, but you'll want to avoid that by simply showing up on time, taking the allotted hour-long break, focusing on your work, and leaving with the rest of your colleagues at the appointed hour. If you feel like you need a bit of support, you'll be able to find a trade union to advise you; though only 8 percent of French workers actually belong to a union (mostly those employed by multinational corporations), the unions still represent the entire workforce, so you can benefit from the strides they've made on your behalf without actually paying dues or participating in *grèves* during strike season.

By law, employers with more than 50 *salariés* on the payroll must create a *comité d'entreprise* (an employee's council), which acts as an intermediary between employees and staff on all issues affecting workers, and all companies with 11 or more employees must also have *délégués du personnel* (personnel representatives) that serve a similar function. Depending on the size of the company, there will be between one and nine elected *délégués,* each with an elected stand-in. Elections are held every two to four years, and *délégués* spend between 10 and 15 hours per month in their roles, which includes keeping employees abreast of changes in salaries, updated health and safety codes, modifications to the work code, and other changes in the workplace.

MINIMUM WAGE

If you're earning the French minimum wage, it will add up to €1,343.77 per month, which breaks down to €8.86 per hour. This wage increases when the

SURVIVING THE *GRÈVE*

Type As, prepare yourselves: You *will* have to wait in line at the grocery story as a slow-moving octogenarian counts change (those minutes feel like hours). You will *not* get "the customer is always right" service at the department store. And, at some point during your French sojourn, you will definitely experience the infamous *grève*.

A *grève*, otherwise known as a strike, is a part of the French political process that often precedes or immediately follows a legislative act. Like flu season, they come around every year – sometimes two or more of them. The key to surviving this inconvenience lies in planning: Be-cause most strikes are coordinated in advance, it's very possible to create a Plan B that'll get you to work or to the airport on time.

Euphemistically called "disruptions," transportation strikes rarely last more than 24 hours. For commuters, this means exploring alternative ways of getting to work: public bike-sharing, *co-voiturage*, or walking are common solutions. Should you have bigger travel plans during a planned strike, check with the airline for up-to-the-minute changes; if you're traveling on the French national railway lines, chances are your ticket will be valid on any train heading in the right direction after the strike is over.

Grèves (strikes) are a regular part of the French politcal experience.

© JENNIFER PICKENS/BLACKBIRDPHOTO.COM

cost of living index rises, ordinarily by 2 percent a year. Undocumented workers are clearly not protected by employment laws, adding extra risk to working under the table. Tipping for waitstaff and other service-industry jobs is not standard practice here, but it has come to be expected in heavily touristed areas. But don't feel obligated to leave a tip, and if you happen to find yourself employed in the service industry, don't expect to be tipped (but do expect a decent quality of life, even on your minimum-wage salary).

FINANCE

Whether you're a student, a work transfer, or a business entrepreneur, moving to France means getting intimately acquainted with your finances. Numbers not your thing? When all is said and done, they will be. From the moment you embark on this journey, you'll need to provide officials with financial data to prove your solvency in France; your visa application will ask for letters from your bank and proof of means of financial support. Once you arrive in France, you'll see how your previously prodigious peck of dollars morphs into a much smaller bundle of euros, which necessitates adjusting your way of thinking about your finances and your new currency.

France can feel expensive as a tourist, but as a resident, you won't have to worry about spending as much. You'll actually find some things to be a much better value for your money: food (even if you eat more of it) and wine and medical care, for example. You'll also come face to face with the startling realization that some products and services are much more costly, including gasoline, electricity, and even manicures (don't expect to find the $10 equivalent

anywhere in France, except at the local beauty academy). Sticker shock will happen, but not everywhere you go or with everything you buy.

You've probably heard of the VAT, or Value-Added Tax. Conceptualized by Frenchman Maurice Laure and implemented in 1954, it has since been adopted by many European countries, where the tax rate reaches as high as 25 percent on consumable goods such as clothing, electronic equipment, and wireless Internet and phone service. In France, the VAT rate was recently increased to 19.6 percent on most consumer goods; a smaller VAT tax is levied on the purchase of books, air and train travel, and food and drink. The tax is one of the key financial props holding France together, bringing in 45 percent of the country's tax revenue. The good news is that it is built into your purchases, so when you see something for sale for €20, that's exactly how much it will cost you.

THE EURO

France ushered in the euro era on January 1, 2002, and the new monetary unit has proved to be a stabilizing force in the French economy. But 2002 wasn't the end of the franc; in some shops throughout France, you'll find prices still listed in that old relic of a currency, and bank receipts often include the franc rate, too. In the little town of Le Blanc, in the Centre region, they just haven't been able to let go—30 local businesses have continued to trade in the franc. They only have a little time left, though, because the 10-year window for the global conversion of francs to euros closes this year.

Cost of Living

GROCERIES

Many a newcomer to *la belle France* is surprised to learn that the overall cost of living is less than in the United States. Locally produced fruits and vegetables are sold by the kilo (2.2 pounds), and when you break it down and compare it to the dollar, you'll see what a great deal you're getting. Carrots, potatoes, and onions run about €1 a kilo, tomatoes and peaches are about double that in peak season, and in wintertime, delicious little mandarin oranges and lychees imported from Madagascar will set you back about €2–3 per kilo. Much of the tastiest stuff (bread, wine) is subsidized or otherwise regulated by the government; a standard baguette costs about €0.85, and a perfectly quaffable bottle of bordeaux-supérieur can be had for €3–4. The key to shopping and saving is to do as the locals do: Patronize the outdoor markets for your produce, the *boucherie* for your meat, the *fromagerie* for your cheese, and the *caviste* for your wine. It's slightly more time intensive than hitting a *hypermarché* for an all-in-one experience, but when you factor in the travel time (big markets are almost always situated on the outskirts of town), fuel prices, and quality, those one-stop shops begin to lose their appeal. Besides, French refrigerators and freezers are so small that it doesn't make sense to stock up; if you're lucky to have a little *balcon,* it can do double duty as a cold-storage unit in wintertime. But otherwise, you'll have some serious food shuffling to do.

If you're going to shop like a local, it's worth investing in a *chariot*—a shopping bag on wheels—or a reusable basket or bag. A ban on nonrecyclable plastic bags has been in effect for a couple of years in France (though not everyone adheres to it), and you'll have to buy a recyclable bag on the spot if you come to the market unprepared. At outdoor markets, you'll still be given small plastic bags for your fruits and veggies, but not a bigger bag to shove the lot of them into.

DINING OUT

Eating out in France is also good value for your money. Wine is usually affordable—expect to pay €2–4 a glass at most restaurants. (Coca-Cola and that bottle of bubbly water will almost always cost you more than wine or beer.) Plats du jour at lunchtime run anywhere from €8 to €14, raised to €12–20 at dinner. Expect either an *entrée* (first course) and *plat* (main course) or *plat* and *dessert* for those prices; occasionally you'll be offered all three and a *café*

TIPPING TIPS

Some newcomers to France haven't gotten the memo: Tipping here is neither necessary nor expected. A 15 percent service charge is built into your bill at the café or restaurant, along with a VAT charge of 5.5 percent (recently reduced from 19.6 percent). You needn't try to calculate anything on top of your meal's stated price: All the extra taxes and fees are factored in, leaving you to focus on simply enjoying your meal. Can't break your tipping habit? Whatever coins you leave your service provider will be welcome, but remember: You don't have to.

An exception to the tipping rule can be found at an unexpected place: your home. In France, many of us live in apartment buildings, and most of these buildings have a live-in concierge-type person called a *gardien* (*gardienne* for a woman). It is customary to give a monetary gift at the holidays, but whether you give – and how much – is up to you. For some, €250 is about right; others think €25 is more than generous. If you choose to partake in the "season of sharing," your gesture will be received graciously and with gratitude.

or a *verre de vin* for that all-inclusive price. Meals are hearty and filling and uniformly tasty, and everyone in France takes advantage of these home-away-from-home-cooked meals. Recently, it's become trendy on brasserie sandwich boards around Paris to chalk a slash through the "normal" price and put an "economic hardship" price beside it, so your €12 lunch now costs €10. Even recessions have their perks. Ask around to find where the best—and best-tasting—deals can be had.

HOUSING

Both renters and buyers will find good housing values in France; you'll probably spend about as much putting a roof over your head as you will putting food in your mouth. Students—French and foreign alike—are entitled to special housing allowances that can cut the cost of living down considerably. In Paris, the résidences du Crous (www.crous-paris.fr) offer government-subsidized studios or one- and two-bedroom apartments exclusively for students for about €380 per month. If you're here to study and are based in a university town, check with the *mairie* to find out which options may be available to you.

If you're a homeowner or plan to invest in real estate, it's worth looking into the government-sponsored rebates for using alternative energy methods. Going solar has its perks—if you generate surplus energy, it could mean you get a check *back* from EDF instead of having to send one. Other energy-saving efforts homeowners make to increase efficiency are rewarded by way of tax deductions and write-offs.

TRANSPORTATION

It's *très cher* (very expensive) to own a car in France, particularly in the big cities, where forking out €50,000 for a permanent parking spot is not unheard of—and that's in addition to insurance and maintenance costs. Fuel, sold by the liter at big *hypermarchés* and at unassuming little street-side stations in cities, is seriously spendy. Expect to pay €1.20–1.60 per liter depending on the type of fuel, or as much as €100 every time you fill up your tank. For the best fuel prices, skip the big service stations off the freeways and opt for fill-up stations attached to supermarkets, where it's significantly cheaper.

Depending on where you live in France, you'll want to budget around €40 per month for public transportation; less if you're a student purchasing a youth pass, more if you're a party-hopping Parisian who's used to the convenience of taxis. Public bike-share systems nationwide average €28 per year plus any overtime fees (only the first half-hour is free), so buying your own bike will pay off over time if you use it as your primary means of transit.

From petrol to parking, owning a car in France can be pricey.

Beware, however, that bike theft is common in Paris and other big cities, so a good lock is worth the added expense. The national train system, SNCF, offers discount cards for an annual fee of between €49 and €79 for those who travel regularly by long-distance train. The discounts—always a minimum of 25 percent of the standard fare, and as much as 65 percent off—can make the yearly cost worthwhile.

CLOTHING

Unless you shop exclusively at discount stores like H&M, Etam, or Tati (or Monoprix during the semiannual sales), you'll probably find the cost of clothing in France to be considerably higher than what you're used to. There are many reasons for this: the VAT, which tacks nearly 20 percent on top of the base price; quality (French-made *everything* is built to last and priced accordingly); and salaries, which are higher here than in most countries even for minimum-wage workers, and therefore factored into the price of goods. You'll notice that at resale shops, called *"depôt-ventes,"* the sticker prices aren't all that discounted from what you'd pay for the same item brand-new in a department store or boutique. Eventually, you'll get used to paying more for things you used to take for granted, but in the meantime, let's set some reasonable expectations of average clothing prices:

- Shoes (men and women): €100

- Boots (men and women): €150

- Dress (department store): €120

- Dress (neighborhood boutique): €70

- Coat (men and women, department store): €200

- Jacket (men and women, neighborhood boutique): €80

- Underwear (women): €10

- Underwear (men): €7

- Socks (men and women): €7.

ELECTRONICS
Sticker shock is also bound to strike when you go computer shopping. When the time comes to invest in a new machine, you'll start asking yourself questions like, "I wonder if it's cheaper to buy a laptop on Amazon and spend $200 to have it shipped to me in France?" You'll grow accustomed to the steep prices, but if you have to get that *lave-linge* (washing machine) or *micro-onde* (microwave oven) right away, Darty, an electronics- and household-goods chain, is a good bet. From water-filter systems to American-style refrigerators, they can be found here—but it can't hurt to do a little comparison-shopping first. At www.prixmoinscher.com, you can compare goods by brand or product type and see who carries the most affordable version of the appliance you're looking for. A Sony 37-inch flat-screen television will set you back €500, a basic DVD player €50, and a Whirlpool electric oven around €400.

Banking

Opening a bank account in France is another exercise in red-tape aerobics, but it's a very necessary evil. If you're planning a reconnaissance trip to scope things out before you move, pencil in a visit to a bank and open an account so you'll be ready to roll with your *carte bleue* (debit card), checkbook, and French banking history when you need them, which will be right away. You'll need a checkbook for your home hunt, setting up house, paying utilities through *prélèvement* (automatic debit), and receiving Assurance Maladie reimbursements.

CHOOSING YOUR BANK
Deciding which bank to work with is the first hurdle in the dizzying adventure of finding a new home for your money. There are so many banks, and

who has time to check with each and every one to find out who has the most to offer? It's not just banks, either. Even La Poste—the post office—offers banking services. When making your choice, consider the minimum-balance requirements, English-language staff services (if you need them), and whether you need a savings or a checking account or both. Banks that can offer the services you need include Barclays France, BNP Paribas, Caisse d'Epargne, Crédit Agricole, Crédit Mutuel, HSBC France, La Banque Postale, and Société Générale, among others.

You will end up developing a familiar relationship with your French banker, who, along with the rest of the staff, will greet you with a friendly *bonjour* and often by name. You can expect personalized service and a warm formality at your bank, especially if you have a good chunk of money stored there.

As a student—and especially as a student under the age of 26—you'll be entitled to all sorts of banking perks and incentives that make it easy for you to function in French society. Your school can help you find the right bank that offers the best student benefits, the lowest *carte bleue* fees, and the most advantageous interest rates.

France is idiosyncratic in a number of ways, including its approach to personal-finance management. The bank branch where you opened your account becomes your "home" office, and any changes to your account must be made at that branch, even if it's across town. If you move to another city, you'll have to arrange with your current bank branch to have your home office changed; be prepared for the time and paperwork involved, as it could take an hour or more of your life to complete this transaction. Ditto for adding names to your account: If you opened it under your own name but want to add your husband's name, it isn't as straightforward as you'd hope. Your spouse will have to provide additional financial information, including letters from "his" bank in the U.S. testifying to his banking history, plus an *attestation d'hébergement,* copies of his ID, and possibly quite a bit more.

BANK CARDS AND BANKING PROTOCOL

Generally, you'll be charged a fee for your card that will be debited from your account. There are many types of *cartes bancaires*—commonly called *cartes bleues*—to choose from, and they all have a different price bracket. For €40 per year, you'll get a basic card that functions like most bank cards back home: withdrawals, basic traveler's insurance coverage, and supplemental car-rental insurance. For a little more—say, €130 per year—you could get a *carte* Visa Premier, with traveler's insurance that compensates you for late trains and canceled flights, as well as hospital stays in foreign countries. For €520 per

CHECKS AND BALANCES

It's one of those things we all take for granted: writing a check. Easy as pie, right? But in France, sending your monthly rent check to your landlord is a tad more complicated than you might imagine. First, you have to figure out what goes where.

The first blank space on a standard French check reads *"Payez contre ce chèque non endossable"* ("Pay against this nonendorsable check"). Here, you'll write out the amount of the check – in French. It might look something like *"deux-cent euros"* (€200). You have two lines available for spelling out the amount.

Next up is the space where you write the name of the person or institution

to whom the check is payable. This follows *"à"* ("to"). Just to the right of this, you'll find a little rectangular box. This is where you write the figure, using standard numbers. The French don't like it when you write outside the lines, so keep everything inside that little rectangle if you can.

Next are two short lines, one reading *"à"* – which in this case means "in," as in the city in which you are writing out the check – and the second reading *"le"* ("the"), which is prompting you for today's date. If you write the date in numeric format, be sure to do it the way the French do: date/month/year.

The last thing you'll need to do to make this check valid is sign it: Often there are no written prompts, only an empty space at the bottom. Go ahead and put your John Hancock there, but keep it contained! If your signature extends off the margins of the check, it may be rendered invalid.

year, you could get a fancy Carte Platinum American Express that earns you purchase points, covers legal fees in another country if you fall into trouble, and covers you with a new pair of glasses if yours are lost or stolen while you travel. You can also choose special colors and designs for your card for an additional €12–24 per year.

Be warned that banks also like to charge you for things you wouldn't necessarily consider charge-worthy, such as phone calls, paper bank statements, additional cards, and, of course, checkbooks. Ask your banker to fill you in on all those little things, because they do add up.

When you open your bank account, it will be assigned an RIB (Relevé d'Identité Bancaire) number, which you'll need to memorize or have on hand when you want to transfer funds from your American or Canadian account to your French one, and to set up the *prélèvement* for automatic debits. RIBs also come in handy on the first of the month, when rent is due. *Proprietaires* and *locataires* alike appreciate the easy rent-paying inherent in direct deposit.

Depositing checks here isn't as straightforward as it is in American and Canadian banks. In France, you can deposit cash into *guichets automatiques* (ATMs), but you'll have to deposit checks by visiting the bank, filling out a form, handing it to the person behind the counter, and taking a receipt.

Fiscal responsibility and integrity are taken very seriously here. If you bounce a check, the consequences include a check-writing ban for as long as five years—I'm not kidding. If you lose your card (or have it stolen), you are responsible for the charges unless you report the loss or theft immediately and better still, file a police report.

Banks won't charge you for using another bank's *guichet automatique* or *distributeur* for the first few withdrawals per month, but after the fourth, fifth, or sometimes sixth withdrawal, depending on the bank, they can—and often do—tack on a fee in the €1 range. If you're traveling outside the euro zone with your *carte bleue,* check with your bank beforehand to see which foreign banks it's partnered with. BNP Paribas, for instance, is partnered with Bank of America in the U.S. and Westpac in Australia, and therefore doesn't charge a withdrawal fee if you use *guichets automatiques* at those banks (but will charge you €3 per transaction, plus a percentage of the amount withdrawn, at other banks).

CREDIT CARDS

Credit cards aren't used in quite the same manner in France as they are in the rest of the world. People tend to live within their means, and that means paying with good old-fashioned cash, or using your *carte bleue* or check book to debit funds directly from your account. If this feels kind of 1953ish to you (even if your parents weren't born then), learn to appreciate the old-timeyness of it, because it has its perks. At many shops—particularly in small towns, but even in Paris—you'll be allowed to take things home on credit. We're not talking brand-new Renaults here, but a baguette and a bottle of *vin rouge* at those critical moments when you realize you've left your wallet at home.

French bank cards and credit cards are different from American ones in a very significant way: Instead of storing your information in a magnetic stripe, the card houses it in a tiny embedded *puce* (literally "flea," but better known as a microchip). When inserted into an ATM, automatic ticket kiosk, or credit card reader at restaurants, the card transmits your information through radio frequencies; to complete the transaction, you need to input your PIN code. This protects you and your card from unauthorized transactions, which is the main reason why Europe switched over to this credit card technology in 2004. As more and more countries switch to *puce* cards, the likelihood that North America will follow suit begins to increase.

It's important to have a card with a *puce* if you'll be spending a significant amount of time in France. For starters, many gas stations function at all hours without an attendant—you are expected to serve yourself and pay using a *puce* card. Most credit card machines can read American cards, but those cards are inserted into the machines differently than European *puce* cards, and if the person in charge of completing your transaction doesn't know how to do it, she is likely to tell you they don't accept those cards. (If your language skills permit, you can show her how it's done. Instead of inserting the card in the bottom of the machine, swipe it down a little trough on the left or right side.)

Taxes

FRENCH TAXES

It's been said that the only certain things in life are death and taxes, and that maxim doesn't lose any of its mojo just because you've moved to France. If you want to establish long-term residency, there's no way to make it more official than by declaring your earnings. For North Americans, this means double tax duty, since you'll still have to file taxes at home, too. In France, it means declaring all your income, regardless of where you earned it. Freelancers, now is the time to 'fess up, fully and completely. Don't know if you're obliged? If you've lived in France for more than 183 days out of the year, you're considered a resident in the eyes of the tax folks.

If you decide to go official with a small business and take advantage of Assurance Maladie, you'll need to begin paying French taxes. It's a complicated process that can be made a lot less confusing by enlisting the aid of a French tax specialist. The investment may be many hundreds of dollars, but isn't peace of mind worth it? If your answer is "no," it's still possible to work things out yourself through trial and error—hopefully not too much of the latter.

As an *auto-entrepreneur,* you're responsible for paying taxes three times per year. You'll receive the paperwork in the mail; you simply have to report your earnings, calculate the amount due, and include a check if necessary when you mail it off. For employees, social charges but not income tax will be deducted from your paycheck—you'll need to file your income tax by May 31 for the previous year. Income tax is determined by the total earnings of your household, which includes your spouse and children, who are all parts of a taxable whole and subject to deductibles even if they don't work. If your household collectively earned €5,963 or less, you owe nothing; but if you earned more than €70,830, you'll need to shell out a whopping 41 percent of your taxable income in federal fees. And, of course, there are different taxation rates for several income brackets in between.

There are resources available online (and it's wise to check in a few times a year, since laws change with disconcerting regularity), but ultimately, the weight of figuring it all out falls on your shoulders. You won't have much time to do that, since your 2042 form is mailed to you in April and must be filed the following month. You can, however, share the burden with a professional tax advisor. Programs like Click Impôts (www.clickimpots.com)—the French equivalent of Turbo Tax software—can be very helpful *if* you understand the language. If not, find a tax specialist who speaks English until you get the hang of it on your own. The French tax year begins on January 1 and ends on December 31.

For those residing in France whose fixed assets exceed €800,000, a wealth tax of between 0.55 and 1.8 percent, called the Impôt de Solidarité sur la Fortune (ISF), will be levied on those assets, payable before June 15 of each year. There are ways to get around the tax, or at least reduce the amount you owe, but it's worth soliciting the services of a tax expert to learn all the little tricks for shrinking your assets on paper.

AMERICAN AND CANADIAN TAXES

Thank goodness for the Internet: Without it, we'd be cajoling friends and family to send bulky IRS booklets to us overseas, and we'd be spending far too much time at La Poste mailing forms back when we could be relaxing beneath sunny skies at a terrace café. Because nearly everything is automated today, we get to benefit by filing taxes online from anywhere in the world. (You'll still need your W2 or 1099 forms, though, so have your employer send those to you at your French address.)

Even though you have to file your U.S. taxes as well as French taxes if you live in France, a treaty signed between the two countries means the taxes you pay in France are deductible on your U.S. tax forms. The IRS's online FreeFile program allows you to file online if your adjusted gross income (AGI) is less than $58,000. If you earned more than that, it's slightly more complicated: You'll need to purchase eFile software or go the old-fashioned paper route. Because of the potential hassles that filing at a distance can spawn, the nice folks at the IRS kindly extend a two-month filing extension to American taxpayers living abroad, so your paperwork isn't due until June 15. But note that if you owe money, the IRS still wants it on or before April 15. Refunds can be direct-deposited into your existing U.S. account. Canadians can also Telefile from abroad using a touch-tone phone, but do it before April 30 or face a 5 percent fine on whatever you owe.

Investing

France has embraced a free-market economy, and with it a culture of personal investing has emerged. The best source of information for no- or low-risk investing opportunities is your banker, who will be happy to explain your options and set you up with an investment program. If you have €20,000 in the bank, that's considered a pretty hefty sum, and any banker worth her salt will offer suggestions for earning money on those funds even without a prompt from you. Forty percent of France's stock exchange value is held by foreign investors, so you'll be in good company if you decide to take this route.

If stocks, bonds, and mutual funds don't make your heart sing but you still want to invest in France, consider a business enterprise. The nonprofit agency Invest in France (www.invest-in-france.org) is headquartered in the U.S. and offers free services and advice on setting up a corporation of 10 or more employees, taxation preparation, employment laws, and all the hidden benefits of launching a large-scale business enterprise in France. With the second-largest consumer market in Europe and a very healthy tourist trade, France is ripe with opportunity for those with an entrepreneurial spirit and the extra money necessary to put an idea into action.

The one area where investing in France is still a little iffy is real estate. So many people find themselves seduced by the rambling farmhouse covered in wild roses, so affordable at just €50,000! They buy it, fix it up, and expect to actually earn a living from the rental income it generates, and this is where things go awry. Unless you're in Paris or another metropolis with a year-round tourism base to pull from, you might be in for an unpleasant surprise. Furthermore, recent laws have affected the short-term residential housing market in Paris and other French cities, making it virtually illegal for owners to rent their properties for a less than a year at a stretch. This doesn't affect owners of commercial property, but the taxes they pay are considerably higher. Think twice before investing in property as a moneymaking venture, and be sure to check with a tax consultant who can help you sort out the particulars if you decide to take this adventurous route.

COMMUNICATIONS

Though there are still a handful of towns equipped with coin-operated public pay phones and utterly devoid of anything resembling high-speed Internet (hello, dial-up!), France has, for the most part, joined the 21st-century communications revolution. From subscription-service smartphones and surprisingly affordable Internet service to ubiquitous cybercafés and print-media *kiosques,* staying connected to the world at large—and our work and loved ones—is easy and, unlike most things in France, practically bureaucracy-free.

France is definitely a nation of mediaphiles, boasting one of the highest magazine readerships in the world. There are more than 100 local and national newspapers to choose from, so Sunday mornings at the corner café will never be idle. Television also figures prominently in the French leisure sphere, with the average person watching 3.5 hours per day. Expect access to the outside world in unexpected places—wireless hotspots at campgrounds, for instance—and, thanks to government subsidies, count on the cost of getting connected to be within reach.

Telephone Service

It's true that there are still a couple of places left in France where you're more likely to get reception using two cans and a piece of string than you are with your cell phone, but it's not likely that you'll be stranded without access. There's one thing most of us in France and abroad have come to rely on substantially, and that's the telephone. To meet the needs—and budgets—of a broad population, there are numerous options: pay-as-you-go mobile phones, private pay-by-the-unit *cabines* at cybercafés, corner public telephone booths, and numerous landline and cell-phone companies willing to sell you all manner of packages for chatting and texting your heart out.

But before you can start calling, you need to know how to do it. When you're placing a call to another French phone within France, the 10-digit number will always begin with a zero. Cell phones begin with 06 or 07, and landline prefixes differ depending on the region. In Paris/Île de France, the prefix is 01; in Brest, Cherbourg, Le Havre, Nantes, Orléans, Rouen, and other cities and towns in northwest France, the prefix is 02; in the north and northeast, it's 03; in the southeast, 04; and in the southwest, 05.

When calling France from the U.S. or Canada, you must follow a slightly different protocol, beginning with the international access code, 011, followed by the country code, 33. But wait, there's more: Before you dial the rest of the number, remember to leave off the zero at the beginning; it's necessary only when you're dialing inside France. So if you're calling Valence from Vancouver, you'll dial 011 33 3 XX XX XX XX. When you want to call the States or Canada from France, dial the international access code followed by the country code, the area code, and the seven-digit number. To call San Francisco from Strasbourg, you dial 00 1 415-XXX-XXXX.

When you need to find the telephone number of an individual or business, use the French version of the yellow and white pages, called *pages jaunes* and *pages blanches,* respectively. They operate the same way as back home, including online access. Hard copies are distributed by the nice people at La Poste once a year.

LAND LINES

In 2009, France Telecom ended its telecommunications monopoly, breathing new life—and new deals—into every corner of the market. Where there used to be just one long-distance carrier for landlines, now there are many, each of them offering great bargains on bundled Internet-phone–cable TV packages. They nearly all work the same way: You order your service online, receive confirmation for your order, then wait for your "box" to arrive. The box is your modem/cable hub, and once you have it—it can take between two days and two weeks to arrive—plug it in and start calling, viewing, and surfing. For around €30 per month for high-speed fiberoptic and ADSL internet, dozens of television channels, and no-cost calls to landlines throughout the world, it's pretty much worth the wait.

The top companies offering this bundled service are the same one providing cell phone service, and sometimes you can add mobile calling service onto your three-in-one "bouquet," making it a four-in-one. France Telecom owns the ubiquitous telecom company Orange (www.orange.fr), which seems to be leading the telecommunications race; for €37 a month, Orange offers a four-in-one Net Plus service that includes an hour of free mobile phone time in addition to cable TV, Internet, and landline service. Bouygues (www. bouyguestelecom.fr) offers a similar package, only with four hours of unlimited cell phone calls each month for €63. If you want something simpler, SFR (www.sfr.com) provides a three-in-one package including cable, free global landline calls, and high-speed Internet service for €32 per month. Students age 26 and younger get a 10 percent discount. Numericable (www.numericable. fr) is one of the newer companies to join the all-in-one game, with similar plans and less expensive monthly fees—but there's a one-time setup fee, so it makes sense only if you're looking for a long-term deal.

CELLULAR PHONES

Getting set up with a cellular phone, or "mobile" (as it's called here), poses challenges for Luddites and techno-wizards alike. The best solution is to carefully consider how often you'll use your phone and what you're willing to spend per month for those privileges. Quad-band smartphones, including BlackBerry and iPhone, can be great for the newbie in France, especially if you use the apps designed to help you find food, maps, train times, and more. But don't make the mistake of underestimating your American or Canadian carrier's roaming fees, which may be exorbitant—they have left many bewildered traveler or expat with a bill heavy on zeros. If you don't know what your call-abroad options are, check in with your service provider before leaving. There might be a simple solution that takes all the hassle out of communicating as soon as you land.

If you know you're going to be here for at least 12 to 18 months—the average length of time for most cell-phone contracts—you might choose to start from scratch and purchase a phone and calling plan here. At FNAC, you can get an iPhone or Android for free which if you sign up for an 18-month contract at €100 per month. Not sure you'll use your phone enough to warrant that kind of expenditure? Then a €20 pay-as-you-go phone might be the best possibility. These cheap phones are a good way to try out a service and see how much you use it. Phone House (www.phonehouse.fr) and FNAC (www.fnac.fr) both have big selections, and you can also find phones at *hypermarchés* like Auchan and Carrefour. Keep in mind that if you purchase the dual-band European phone, it won't work when you travel back to North America, but your tri- or quad-band phone will.

Another way to go is to invest in a second phone: Keep your U.S. cell phone for when you return stateside, and purchase another cheap one to use exclusively in France. This option makes the most economic sense if you're not a phone addict or you don't rely heavily on phones for work. At special phone shops and other electronics stores throughout France, you can buy a bundled phone-and-SIM-card combo for €15–30. When the time you've purchased runs out, you can buy additional minutes in increments of €5–10, starting at €5. The time is purchased in the form of a *carte prépayée* (prepaid card), or, if you purchase it from a *tabac*, you'll be handed a small printed receipt with an access code for you to punch into your phone.

THE LANGUAGE OF TELECOMMUNICATION

Without those little communication devices within an arm's reach, we're left feeling like we've been banished to life on Mars. What would we do with ourselves without mobile phones and Internet service? We might have to read a book or engage in a leisurely conversation over a *café* and croissant. If you're not quite ready for that, here are the terms you'll want to get acquainted with so you can plug in, turn on, and tune out.

abonnement subscription	**imprimeur** printer
appel telephone call	**livraison** delivery
cabine telephone booth	**mobile** cell phone
casque headset	**mot de passé** password
chaîne television channel	**ordinateur** computer
compte account	**promotion** sale
en ligne on line	**sans abonnement** without a subscription
facture bill	
fixe fixed landline	**SMS** text
forfait set price	**télécharge** download
frais fees	**téléphone** fixed landline
illimité unlimited	

This pay-as-you-go method is a little pricey when it comes to outgoing calls, but incoming calls and SMSs (texts or "textos") are free and unlimited. You can also purchase minutes exclusively reserved for texts, which are a lot more economical and just as far-reaching. Half-and-half time allotments are also available to those who want to keep their options open. The minutes you buy, whether for texting or calling or both, have an expiration date that's usually two weeks from the date of purchase. Keep in mind that if you don't purchase new minutes at least once every six months, you'll get a text from the SIM service provider alerting you that your account will be shut down if there's not some outgoing-call activity within a certain time frame. (You generally get a two-week warning.)

Another affordable option is to use your "unlocked" phone from home with a new France-compatible SIM card that you buy either before you depart or when you arrive in France (there are shops at the airport and in many cities and towns). In the United States and elsewhere, phones are sold "locked" by the telephone service provider to keep you roped into its service. ("Unlocking" shouldn't be be confused with "unblocking" phones that have been reported stolen, which isn't kosher on any continent.) You can use online unlocking companies like Remote Unlocks (www.remoteunlocks.com) and Unlock it Now (www.unlockitnow.com) wherever you happen to be, and while the service isn't free, it's cheapish enough—usually less than US$50.

If you make most or all of your phone calls to the U.S., some of the latest technology allows you to use your smartphone with programs like Line 2 and Toktumi (www.toktumi.com), which will assign you a local U.S. or Canada phone number that you can use throughout France to call home for free. These also allow you to use a texting option worldwide for a universal US$0.10 rate.

International and Domestic Rates

Even for starving students who don't have an extra €30 per month to pay for high-tech communication packages, it's still possible to make long-distance phone calls on the cheap. In all the major cities—Paris, Bordeaux, Lyon—you'll find "cybercafés," which aren't cafes in the traditional sense (you'll be lucky if they have a coffee vending machine) but often little DIY storefronts equipped with computers, printers, fax machines, and *cabines* of varying degrees of funkiness that allow you to make international calls for pennies. The phone's digital display lets you how much you're spending as you make the call, and it's usually more affordable than you'd imagine, especially if you call during off-hours.

In France, phone calling time is sold in units, which cost more during peak calling times (weekdays) and less during off-hours (evenings and weekends). Timing your calls for off-peak periods can save you a bundle over time.

Skype

By now, everyone knows about Skype: It's the traveler's best friend when it comes to staying in touch across oceans and continents, in a very *les* Jetsons sort of way. Skype is the next best thing to being there, since you can see the person you're chatting with in real time if your *ordinateur* (computer) is equipped with a camera. If you don't already have this super communications tool at your disposal, get thee to the Internet *tout de suite* and download the free software. The only real drawback is that you need a modicum of privacy to engage this way; talking to your beloved at the *bibliothèque* or cybercafé will make everyone uncomfortable. Skype's long-distance phone calling plans are worth a gander, too. You can purchase credit beginning at US$0.02 per minute, or you can opt for one of the bargain flat-rate fees, starting at US$1.25 per month.

Internet and Postal Service

France, like so many other countries, depends on the Internet to connect with the rest of the world. Eighty percent of the population uses an *ordinateur* at work, and more than 55 percent use one at home. If you purchase a package deal from one of the big-name telecom companies, you'll get an access code that allows you to tap into your Internet service outside your home, provided your FAI (Fournisseur d'Accès à Internet) service is available in the area. This comes in handy when you're traveling, and out-of-town guests are always happy to use it, too.

You'll find plenty of places out and about, from libraries and cafés to public parks and McDonald's, offering free "wee-fee" (Wi-Fi) access. Tap in using your own code or the one given to you by the service provider. Check in at the local *mairie* or tourist office for a list of local hotspots.

POST OFFICES

La Poste (www.laposte.fr) isn't just a post office: It's a bank, a bill-pay center, an Internet hotspot, and the place where naughty Frenchies hone their line-jumping skills. Branches are open six days a week (mail is delivered on all those days), and hours are usually 9:00 A.M. to 8:00 P.M., Monday through Friday, with reduced hours on Saturdays and during school holiday periods. Inside, expect to find DIY stamp machines with English-language instructions, boxes and padded envelopes for sale, and helpful staff to sell you dozens of different stamps and other services. Outside, you'll find cash *distributeurs* (ATMs) and *boîtes aux lettres* (mailboxes) for depositing your stamped envelopes and packages. A letter weighing less than 20 grams costs €0.53 to mail, and overseas postcard stamps will set you back €0.87.

© SOPHIA PAGAN/WWW.SOPHIAPAGAN.COM

Some mailboxes have a friendly look about them.

Media

NEWSPAPERS AND MAGAZINES

Want to feel like a true local? The place to begin your assimilation process is at *le kiosque,* aka the newsstand. Each of France's 10 national newspapers appeals to a specific segment of the politically oriented population, and to be able to talk about the 2012 presidential election with a modicum of savoir-faire, you'll need to align yourself with a reliable news source. On the left, there's *Libération;* in the center, *Le Monde;* and to the right, *Le Figaro.* You'll also find more than 100 other weekly or monthly journals to represent your viewpoint—and everyone else's. Don't know if your "left" is the same as your French compatriots'? Check out the online editions of each paper to see which news-delivery style resonates with you, then pick up a copy from the nearest *kiosque* and take it to the café for your afternoon coffee-and-civics lesson.

Popular free papers and journals include *ANous, Métro, Direct Matin* and *Direct Soir.* Look for them in Métro stations and *gares* (train stations);

© AURELIA D'ANDREA

The French flock to the ubiquitous sidewalk newsstands for their print-media fix.

occasionally you'll find them being distributed by real live humans in busy pedestrian areas.

France is a magazine-loving culture. News agents vend dozens of titles, from the standard fashion fare to a range of subgenres, such as detective tales, boating, video games, and gay culture. Unlike in the United States and Canada, you won't find much of a selection of reading material at most supermarkets orservice stations. But you will find them at the corner *kiosque,* in some *tabacs,* and any shop that has a sign reading "La Presse" on the outside. Some bookstores and FNACs throughout France also sell magazines. And if you're desperate for a fix, head to the nearest train station, which is always a reliable source of reading material for travelers on the go and anyone else seeking a little mental stimulation.

TELEVISION

The French consider television their number-one pastime, watching an average of 3.5 hours per day. This may seem a little high when you consider what's on: game shows, game shows, and the occasional game show. (It seems that way, anyway.) The truth is, there's a vast and varied world of television in France,

MEDIA MANIA

The French have cultivated a worldwide reputation for good taste, but if you flip on the television or survey the titles at your local newsstand, you might start to question the validity of this assertion.

Decidedly lowbrow game shows hold a particular appeal among French television viewers, and every channel has its own special offering. There's *Slam,* a crossword quiz show; *Qui Veut Gagner des Millions* (a *Who Wants to Be a Millionaire?* clone); the Jeopardy-esque *Questions pour Un Champion*; and *La Roue de la Fortune,* a *Wheel of Fortune* spinoff; among others. Game shows not your thing? How about hunting magazines?

At news kiosks, dozens of journals dedicated to blood sports sit alongside another dozen or so dedicated to fishing, the covers of which bear uniformly disturbing photos of frightened animals being stalked by dogs or men with guns. Titles run the gamut from *Le Chasseur de Sanglier* (*The Wild Boar Hunter*)to *Piegeur et Petit Gibier* (*Trapper and Small Prey*), but each shares the unifying theme: the celebration of the hunt.

And if your definition of good taste includes bare-breasted women on prime-time television, you're in luck! Puritanical attitudes toward the seminude female form aren't the norm, meaning you can expect to see topless women (but not often men) in print advertisements, during family-hour television broadcasts, and, of course, on beaches from La Rochelle to St. Tropez.

from cooking shows and cartoons (*Les Simpsons,* anyone?) to music videos and home-improvement programs. Expect lots of dubbed-into-French versions of American programs and films, plus a healthy smattering of police dramas. Documentaries are also popular. Basically, anything you'd want to watch at home is available here, only in French, without subtitles.

The major cable television providers will happily offer you English-language channel add-ons for a price, but experience says skip 'em. If you're committed to learning French, relying on Anglophone television channels for your news and amusement will only handicap your efforts in the long run. Instead, use French TV to your educational advantage; tuning in will help you adjust to the colloquialisms and idioms of modern French and keep you in the pop-culture loop. There are five national public television channels to flip through—France 2, 3, 4, 5, and Ô—and dozens of cable channels at your disposal.

RADIO

If you're one of the holdouts in the dwindling universe of radio listeners, there's no reason to stop tuning in just because the music is sung in a language other than your own. (At least 40 percent of the songs will be in French—that's a state mandate.) Whether you turn the dial over to hipster channel Le Mouv or überpopular mainstream station RTL, you'll be able to keep up on current events, discover the hot pop act du jour, and, perhaps most importantly, attune your ear to the language. Radio, like television, is great tool for helping you learn local dialects and colloquialisms, and with plenty of public and private options to choose from, all your listening needs will easily be met.

DAILY LIFE

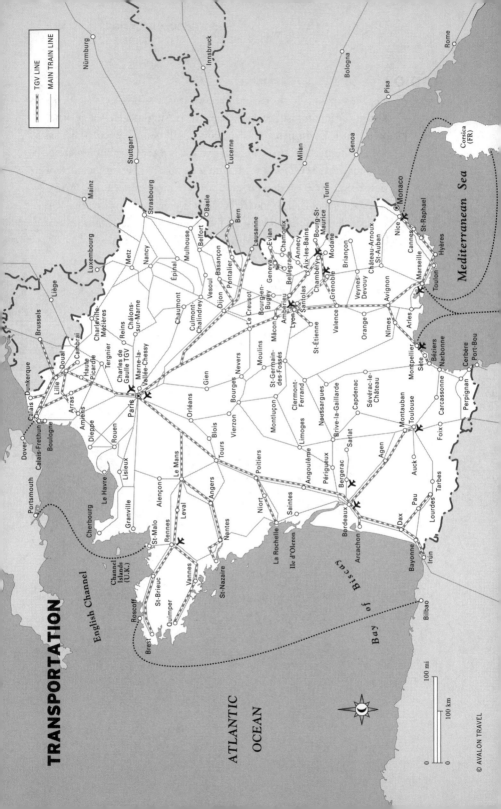

TRAVEL AND TRANSPORTATION

One of the best aspects of France's quality of life is a thorough, efficient, far-reaching transportation system. In cities, you can choose among trains, buses, public bicycles, trams, taxis, funiculars, and even human-powered pedal rickshaws to get you where you need to be. To reach rural destinations, there are more trains, plus rental cars, public ride share programs, buses, ferries, and, of course, regional airlines.

If there's one arena the French have perfected, it's rail travel. The world-renowned TGV (Train à Grande Vitesse, or high-speed train) is world-renowned for a reason: It propels you to your destination at 300 kilometers per hour, meaning you can leave Paris after breakfast and arrive in sun-drenched Nice in time to enjoy lunch at a terrace café. But the TGV isn't all France has to offer in terms of train travel. There are also normal long-distance trains, affordable regional trains, and—in Lyon, Lille, Marseille, Toulouse, and Paris—the Métro. Using any combination thereof, you could be skiing the Alps, biking

along a canal in Amsterdam, or shopping in London within just a few hours of leaving virtually any point in the country.

By Air

Nearly everyone arriving in France from North America lands at Paris's Charles de Gaulle (CDG) airport (known locally as Roissy), 25 kilometers northeast of the city. With nearly 60 million passengers moving through its three terminals each year, CDG is the second-busiest airport in Europe and the seventh-busiest in the world. It handles only international flights; domestic flights run out of Orly, which also serves routes to Africa, the Middle East, the Caribbean (including Cuba), and other points throughout Europe. Orly is also one of several airports serviced by those small, budget air carriers that sell almost-too-good-to-be-true cheap flights—EasyJet and Ryanair are the leaders—but more often than not, you'll end up have to schlep to a distant airport to catch that €29 flight to Marrakesh. (You'll also have to obey strict baggage limits, and it's wise to expect delays.) For flights within France, Air France (www.airfrance.fr) dominates with the most options, but there are plenty of others worth a look. Irish airline Aer Arann (www.aerarann.com) flies out of Rennes to the UK and Ireland; Swiss carrier Baboo (www.transavia.com) flies from Bordeaux and Toulouse to Hungary, Spain, and Switzerland; and Transavia (www.transavia.com) flies from Grenoble and Bergerac to Rotterdam, and from Paris to several North African destinations.

One of the great advantages to living in the heart of Europe is easy access to so many different countries and cultures. To find the best travel bargains, try websites such as Opodo (www.opodo.fr), which offers flights and affordable weekend package deals to destinations all over Europe, North Africa, and the rest of the world. You might also try Ebookers (www.ebookers.fr) and Promo Vacances (www.promovancances.com) for flights, hotels, and rental cars. Each of these sites allows you to compare prices and choose dates and flights that best suit your schedule and budget.

By Train

There's something romantic about train travel. It has a sense of adventure built into it that air travel lacks, and in France, it can even be a relaxing experience: No shoe-removal routines or liquid-toting restrictions apply (though if you're Chunneling over to London on the Eurostar, you'll need to go through a passport check). Between the roomyish bathrooms, generous legroom, and the café car—where a sandwich and a glass of wine are always within reach—train travel feels practically luxurious, even if it's designed for the proletariat.

The national railway line, SNCF (Société National des Chemins de Fer), links cities and towns via 7,000 stations all over the country to Paris, the railway hub. The TGV and other *grande ligne* trains take you on long-haul trips to major cities, and the TER (Train Express Régional) takes you to the smaller stations in between. Long-distance and local trains depart from the same stations, and there are several trains per day for most destinations, so if you miss the first one, you'll likely be able to find a seat on the next.

Train tickets can be purchased up to six months in advance (though most are available only three months in advance) and can be secured in person at the station and through travel agencies, or bought through the SNCF website (www.sncf.fr). Online, you can choose the English-language option if need be, and peruse all the options for the best deals and best amenities. Not all trains are bicycle friendly, for instance, but those that are will display a small bike icon next to the train details. You'll also be able to see which cars have wheelchair access and whether there's a café car. Using your credit card to pay online is a pretty straightforward process, and you can choose to print out your ticket at home, use your credit card to retrieve it from a kiosk at the station (but only with *puce* cards), or, with enough time, have it mailed to you. If you decide to use the phone to make your reservation, you'll be charged a premium rate of €0.34 per minute (as is common with many public services including banking, telecommunications, and electricity/gas.)

Train ticket prices fluctuate according to a number of criteria: time of day, whether or not you'll be traveling during a school holiday period, what age group you fall into, whether you have an SNCF membership card, whether you're traveling in first or second class, whether the ticket is refundable, and how far in advance you're buying. Spur-of-the-moment tickets are more expensive, so buying a week or two (or more) ahead of time will generally result in a price reduction. If you foresee doing a lot of train travel, forking over a few extra euros to get an SNCF membership card will pay for itself over time. The 12–25 membership card (referring to age) costs €40 per year and gives the under-25 set up to 60 percent off ticket prices. Those 60 and older are eligible for the €50 Senior card, good for reductions of up to 50 percent, and everyone else is eligible for the €70 Escapades card, which gives up to 40 percent discounts. Families with one or two children are eligible for discount train-travel cards valid for three years, but you have to apply for it, and it isn't necessarily a given that you'll be given one. To learn whether you qualify for the Carte Enfant

Famille, you must first create an on-line dossier and pay a nonrefundable €15 filing fee. Two outside social services agencies make the ultimate decision, which will be rendered within a week or two after you submit your dossier. Sample fares for everyday travelers without a discount card include Paris–Le Havre: €15; Nice–Grenoble: €57.30; Paris–Brussels: €45; Marseille–Bordeaux: €30.

On long-distance trains, a conductor will come through each car to stamp passengers' tickets; but on TER trains, you'll need to validate the *billet* (ticket) yourself. Most French train tickets are valid for two

Don't forget to *composter* (date-stamp) your ticket, or you might be fined.

months and not just for the date you're scheduled to travel, which is an invitation for some to try and cheat the system by using their tickets twice. To avoid getting slapped with a fee for riding on a nonvalidated *billet*, you'll need to run your ticket through one of the *composteurs* found on the quai. If you forget to do it, the onus is on you to seek out the conductor as soon as you board the train, so she can stamp your ticket for you.

French trains are nearly always on schedule, unless there's a *grève* (strike), in which case local, regional, and long-distance trains may be delayed or cancelled altogether. Usually *some* trains will be cancelled or delayed, but not all of them—for instance, there may be two trains running to Grenoble instead of six. This is uncommon, but when it does happen, you usually have plenty of forewarning from both the news media and the transportation officials. It's also important to remember that that France uses a 24-hour clock, so a train that leaves at 3:00 P.M. will read as 15:00 on your ticket.

By Métro

Even at its packed-in-like-sardines worst, the Paris Métro is still a life enhancer for commuters in the City of Light. Extensive, fast, relatively affordable, and generally safe, it gets you where you want to go—and you just feel so *Parisian* getting there. For visitors, the best Métro ticketing option is the €12 *carnet* of 10

MÉTRO BOULOT DODO

It started out as a patchwork of words borrowed from the 1951 poem "Couleurs d'Usine," by Pierre Béarn: *Métro, boulot, dodo*. Today, it has evolved into a 21st-century mantra for the overworked masses: commute, work, sleep; same-old, same-old; another day, another dollar. If you want to sound like a real Parisian – and echo the sentiments of the poem's author – sprinkle this expression into the conversation at your next end-of-the-week decompression gathering. Try something like: "This week has been rough – nothing but Métro, boulot, dodo. I'm ready for a vacay." (Now try it again, only this time in French!)

tickets. They have no expiration date and are also valid for bus travel. For those staying longer than a few weeks who expect to use the system regularly, a Navigo pass is a more cost-effective option. The Navigo is sort of like a credit card, only with your photo on it. Register online (www.navigo.fr), wait for your card to arrive in the mail, then add money to it using automated kiosks inside the station.

Other French cities besides Paris have Métro systems—Toulouse, Marseille, and Lyon, to name a few—and essentially they all work the same way. After entering the station by sliding your pass over the sensor or inserting your ticket, you follow the signs pointing to the final destination on your line. For instance, if you're traveling from the Louvre to Gare de Lyon, you'll take the train marked "Château de Vincennes," since Château de Vincennes is the last stop in that direction on that line. Hop on a train going the wrong direction? No problem. Disembark at the next station and cross over to the opposite platform to redirect yourself without having to purchase another ticket or exit the station.

© SOPHIA PAGAN/WWW.SOPHIAPAGAN.COM

Most commuters in Paris rely on the Métro for transportation.

When your train pulls up to the platform, stand clear of the doors to allow passengers to exit. You'll often see people exiting the train and standing near the doors; they're just getting out of the way temporarily to make the disembarking process easier for others. Once everyone is off, it's your turn to pile in. A buzzer will sound when the doors are about to close, usually giving you about five seconds to get moving. Once you're on the train, assess the situation—if it's packed, don't try to pull down and sit on the folding seats near the door. Instead, stand like everyone else. Though it's not mandatory, it's always nice to give up your seat to pregnant women, parents with small children, and the elderly, for which you'll be rewarded with that rare treasure: a smile from a French stranger.

By Bus

In Paris, you'll see them lined up along the Seine near Pont Alexandre III: long-distance bus after long-distance bus, their giant logos in languages that reveal their point of origin—Italy, Germany, Poland. While the most popular mode of intra-France public transportation is the train, there are international long-distance coaches that will ferry you to your destination in relative comfort for a not-too-shabby price. UK-based Eurolines (www.eurolines.fr) services most of Europe with uniformly comfortable coaches that run from multiple cities in France to Spain and Portugal. Busabout (www.busabout.com) is one of the newer bus companies geared toward care-free types who want to see the sights and have the flexibility of stopping and staying awhile. For around €400, you can get a six-day Flexi Pass that allows you to get off and on buses traversing the European continent. Unlike Eurail passes, they aren't limited to non-European residents. To travel long distances within France, you're better off making use of the efficient train system, but in rural areas, buses will become your best friend. Just don't expect them to take you great distances. To learn more about the buses in your *département,* check in at the *maire*'s office, where you'll be able to get a timetable and a bus-route map.

By Boat

If the plane, train, bike, Métro, and bus options don't meet your needs, you'll be relieved to know that France operates a few different ferry services heading to points south (Corsica and Spain), northwest (the UK), and even farther west (Ireland). Individual passengers or passengers with motorbikes, cars, and bicycles are welcome aboard, and some carriers allow companion animals. Sea France (www.seafrance.com) offers round-trips between Calais and Dover for €34; Société National Maritime Corse Méditerranée (SNCM) sails to Corsica, Algeria, Sardinia, and Tunisia. A round-trip ferry ride from Marseille to Scandola, Corsica, in a private cabin with two beds will cost you €110 or so, depending on the day of the week. More fares are available on SNCM's website (www.sncm.fr). Brittany Ferries (www.brittany-ferries.fr) is yet another company servicing France with big boats setting sail to Ireland, England, and Spain. Getting to Bilbao, Spain, from the port town of Roscoff, in Brittany, will surely be a seafaring adventure, but it doesn't come cheap: For the 23-hour voyage, expect to pay €200 each way for two passengers (but you can bring a car with you at that price).

By Bicycle

When Paris mayor Bertrand Delanoë rolled out the Vélib' bike-share program in 2007, the global media went gaga. What novelty! How very modern and innovative! What had gone overlooked, apparently, was that bike-share programs had already been established in other cities throughout France for years. Maverick transport system or not, Vélib' has spawned copycat programs throughout the world, and with good reason: It's a convenient way to get around, get your exercise, and help relieve the car congestion on busy city

© SOPHIA PAGAN/WWW.SOPHIAPAGAN.COM

Riding a bike is one of the easiest ways to get around in the city.

streets. Lyon, Grenoble, Nice, Bordeaux, Toulouse, and many other cities have their own versions of Vélib,' but if you want to make use them, you'll need to get yourself set up with a *carte bleue* (only those with a *puce* will work) or look into whether the local transportation pass—like Paris's Navigo—will give you access. The transport passes can be purchased using regular old *puce*-free credit cards from vendors at *gares* and Métro stations. Helmets aren't included in your community bike rental (but are recommended), but baskets and locks are part of the nominal fee.

By Car

COVOITURAGE (CAR-SHARING)

One well-kept secret among locals who want to get from here to there on the cheap is Covoiturage (www.covoiturage.fr), which translates to "car-sharing." Once you've register online for free, you can plug in your trip starting point and desired end point, hit the *"rechercher"* button, and see if you'll be matched up with someone who has a car who's also making that trip and wants passengers to help pay for gas. If you get a match (or two or three or more), you can read the driver reviews from other passengers, find out whether they allow dogs, music, or smoking in their cars, and see how much they're charging per passenger for the trip. Between Grenoble and Lyon, prices range €5–11; to Nice from Marseille, prices vary €10–35.

DRIVER'S LICENSES

By now, you should know that nothing comes particularly easy in France. They really make you work for it, whether it's getting your *carte de séjour* or opening a bank account. Expect more of the same when seeking a French driver's license. It's definitely possible to acquire one, but not necessarily simple and easy. The first confusing hurdle you'll have to jump over to get closer to your *permis de conduire* (driver's license) is determining whether your state (or province, for Canadians) is one of the dozens with a reciprocal driver's license agreement with France—British Columbia and California do not, but Pennsylvania and Prince Edward Island do. If your state is on the list, just go to your local *préfecture,* show your U.S. driver's license, fill out a form, and wait two weeks for your valid-forever French license to arrive. If your home state is not on the lucky list, then you'll have to take the figurative long route to be able to take the literal long route by *voiture* (car). That means finding a school, or *auto école.* They're everywhere: Type in *"auto école"* and the name of your city into your favorite search engine and see what comes up. Prices vary somewhat, but you can expect to pay between €700 and €1,500 for an extensive driver's education course that includes classes in theory and driving codes, plus 20 hours of actual driving time. Don't expect to get into the first school you approach right away. There is generally a waiting time of up to several months for these in-demand academies. You can see how popular they are by looking around the streets of your town and counting the cars with the illuminated *"école"* sign on top. Classes, as you might expect, are taught in French. Don't think your language skills are up to snuff? English-language classes do exist, but you'll pay a premium for that privilege or enlist the services of a translator for the written test.

Driving indefinitely on your valid U.S. driver's license—which is only valid in France for the first year you're here—might be a gamble worth taking if the thought of dealing with another layer of bureaucracy is just too much to bear. Some drivers interviewed for this book claim to never have had a problem related to driving with their non-French licenses, even after racking up countless speeding tickets. (Tickets are generally issued by mail, after a radar trap catches you exceeding the speed limit.) Still, there's nothing like the peace of mind that comes with living life aboveboard, so drive safely, with caution.

BUYING A CAR

Cars can be purchased in France at used-car lots and new-car lots, and through private parties on websites like ParuVendu (www.paruvendu.fr) and La Centrale (www.lacentrale.fr). You'll also see handwritten *"à vendre"* signs tacked to car windows. But you'll not likely see much in the way of junker *voitures* since the government offers financial incentives to people to trade in their environmentally hostile gas guzzlers for more modern, fuel-efficient Renaults, Peugeots, and Citroëns. Even then, the old, gross polluters tend to retain their value, which makes purchasing a new car in France look pretty wise from a fiscal perspective. Whatever path you take to buy a car, you'll need to get it registered immediately afterward.

How you secure your *carte grise,* or automobile registration card, depends on whether you bought a new or used vehicle. If you bought your car new from a dealer, the dealer will submit the paperwork to the *préfecture* on your behalf. When you buy a secondhand car, you can choose to fill out the registration forms in person at the *préfecture* and some *mairies,* or you can register online (www.cartegriseminute.fr) to get your *plaques d'immatriculation* (license plates) and *carte grise.*

Like the annual smog checks that are mandatory in some U.S. states, all cars in France are subject to a *contrôle technique* every two years. You bring your car to an authorized service station, where everything from your shock absorbers to your seatbelts will be tested for wear and functionality. Expect to pay around €40 for the service, plus any necessary fix-it fees that result from the diagnostic testing. Cars older than five years are also subjected to annual smog checks.

RULES OF THE ROAD

When traveling by car on French roads, you have several options: fast-moving toll highways; smaller, slower highways, and snail-strength surface roads. They'll all get you to your destination, but it's the toll (*péage*) roads that are most efficient and therefore worth the extra cost. Toll roads, or *autoroutes,* usually begin with an A (A1 through A89) but may begin with an E. Tolls vary depending on the road and the distance traveled, so expect to pay anywhere from €1.10 to €35.60. Payments can be made in cash or using a credit card, and some toll booths are staffed by humans who can make change and direct you on what to do if you don't have cash or cards. One thing you'll learn pretty quickly after driving on French highways is that the left lane is reserved exclusively for passing; it isn't meant to be a high-speed cruising lane. Use it to pass slower cars, then move back into the right lane until you exit the highway or need to pass another car.

DRIVING ME CRAZY

Circulation: Do you know what it means? In France, it has less to do with your cardiovascular system and more to do with driving. (It means "traffic.") Before you get behind the wheel of your *voiture* and become part of the *circulation,* you'd best brush up on your roadway lingo.

accident accident	**passage piétons** crosswalk
autoroute highway	**péage** toll road/booth
bande d'arrêt d'urgence emergency lane	**piéton(ne)** pedestrian
chaîs snow chains	**pont** bridge
conducteur(ice) driver	**ralentir** slow down
dépasser to pass	**rond-point** roundabout
embouteillage traffic jam	**route** road
feu de signalization traffic light	**sens interdit** no entry
limitation de vitesse speed limit	**sens unique** one way
	tomber en panne break down

Before you do any driving in France, you should familiarize yourself with French road signs.

Routes nationales ("N" roads) and *routes departementals* ("D" roads) will also get you where you need to go, albeit much more slowly. One feature of the smaller roads that hinders speed and efficiency is the roundabout. For the uninitiated, France's ubiquitous *ronds-points* can be dizzying. Drivers to the left always have the right of way, which means you may have to stop and wait for several cars to pass before you can enter. Only enter the roundabout when there are no cars to your left.

To avoid the radar-enforced speed traps, it's helpful to know the speed limits. On toll roads, the maximum speed is 130 kilometers per hour (km/h). In wet conditions, you must slow down to either 90 km/h or 110 km/h, depending on the road. On main roads, the limit is 90 km/h, and when driving through towns, reduce your speed to 50 km/h.

Beginning in 2008, it became mandatory to carry a reflective warning triangle and neon safety vest (*gilet*) for each passenger. Failing to do so could cost you €137—or worse, your life, if no one can see you changing the tire on the side of the road. You can buy the safety duo for about €20 at auto body shops, some gas stations, and the French equivalent of AAA, called Automobile Club (www.automobileclub.org). The Day-Glo reflective vests are also a common sight on the racks at French thrift stores.

In recent years, the government has launched a series of anti-drinking-and-driving campaigns to curb a growing problem in France. The legal blood alcohol limit is 0.5 grams per liter, or 0.25 milligrams in a breathalyzer, which is how you'll be tested. This is equivalent to two standard glasses of wine (10 cl) or beer (25 cl). If you're pulled over on suspicion of driving under the influence, you could receive a fine and lose six points off your 12-point driving record, lose your license for as many as three years, or end up in prison for up to two years, depending upon your level of intoxication. More information about driving laws can be found on the government's road-safety website, www.securite-routiere.gouv.fr.

Car insurance is mandatory and generally more affordable than in the United States or Canada, since personal health insurance is also mandatory and therefore an unnecessary component of your auto insurance. How much you pay depends on many factors, including the type of vehicle you're driving (motorcycle, caravan), how long you've been driving, and your driving record. Automobile Club offers free quotes, but you can also walk into any storefront offering *"assurances automobile"* and ask for a *devis* (quote).

PRIME LIVING LOCATIONS

OVERVIEW

From the Right Bank penthouse with the sweeping view of the Seine to the vine-covered *longère* in rural Brittany, France has an idyllic housing option for whatever the foreign heart fancies. But what exactly will you do with yourself once you find your dream home? The best places for expats to settle in France aren't just those where jobs can be found (or created), but those with a solid social infrastructure that ensures you'll never feel alienated or isolated. If it's solitude you crave, there are plentiful opportunities for it here, but most people come to France with the aim of steeping themselves in the local culture, meeting the natives, and indulging in a daily croissant (or two) washed down with a thimble-size *café express*.

The French are mobile bunch: The waiter at your favorite café in Paris, Marseille, or Lyon is likely from the *province*, as the rest of the country is called; when asked, he'll tell you, with a wistful, faraway look in his eyes, what a beautiful, special, warm, and inviting place his hometown is. He's here for the same

© ALAIN VIRNOT

reasons people everywhere move to big cities: work opportunities, education, culture. That doesn't mean the love of home has faded in any fashion.

At some point, you too will wax poetic about your adopted hometown. Before you know it, you'll be spouting facts about its long and illustrious history, defending it against any disparaging remarks, and otherwise behaving in the prideful manner befitting a local. "Oh, Sarlat has the area's most colorful Saturday morning market," you'll say. "And in truffle season—bah! It's absolute heaven!" or *"Oh la la!* Aix in the springtime, *c'est magnifique!* The chestnuts and cherry blossoms are in bloom, and we still have two months before the tourist glut!" You'll be boasting about your town's big cinema festival/specialty liqueur/locally produced cheese quicker than you can say *"Vive la France!"*

But you have to find before you flaunt, and where you settle can make or break your experience. The life you carve out in rural France will not be the same one you make for yourself in a big city. Regional idiosyncrasies abound, and so do attitudes. The most successful transitions result from careful planning and research. If settling into a thriving community with access to transportation, good food, culture, and friendly locals is on your agenda, here are some options you should get to know.

PARIS

Paris is a city of émigrés. We come from all over—North and West Africa, South East Asia, North America, the Middle East, Eastern Europe, and beyond. By far the country's most cosmopolitan locale, Paris boasts more foreigners than any

Street performers, like this ball-bouncing artist, give Parisian neighborhoods their own unique flavor.

other city in France. Anything you want—even a burrito, which makes some of us Californians extremely happy—can be sussed out here, and employment and housing opportunities trump those of anywhere else you could settle. Many nonnative Parisians say Paris does not represent "true France." Why? Because so many other dreamers have moseyed over it that it no longer looks "French." But trust me: It does, and it is. Even so, there's no denying the international flavor of that the capital exudes. In each of the 20 arrondissements, you'll notice distinct differences: Some are more congested, others more verdant; some, like the 16th, have a quiet and residential air, while the 18th hums with a more active, lively vibe. Wherever you are in Paris, expect French to be spoken (along with Arabic, Swahili, English, Hebrew, Italian, Portuguese, and Spanish), polite formality to reign, and nonstop opportunities for cultural diversion, educational opportunity, and macerating in a history-rich marinade while you're here.

BRITTANY

Affordable property and easy access to the United Kingdom and Northern Europe have long attracted foreigners to this temperate western outpost. With a rich history punctuated by Viking invasions, Celtic influence, and Roman conquests, this green and pleasant land has retained its seafaring tradition without shying away from modernity. Rennes, the regional capital, welcomes an

© MARY MARGARET CHAPPELL

Sunny outdoor cafés abound in Rennes.

international student community that spins past the city's 16th-century half-timbered buildings on definitively modern Le Vélo Star bicycles, one of the low-cost public transport options the city has to offer. With a socialist mayor governing a population of 210,000, Rennes has established itself as a modern city with a progressive outlook, which might explain the relatively recent influx of high-tech businesses to this former car-manufacturing region. Further south, on the Côtes d'Armor, Vannes perches above a conifer-hemmed seashore overlooking a handful of tiny, picturesque islands. In the old town, there's an open invitation to everyone who happens by to venture in and explore the ancient cobbled streets and step into a stone-built brasserie for an afternoon glass of the local cider. Tucked in among the area's bigger towns are pretty little villages where farming and fishing are still the dominant livelihoods. Throughout Brittany, you'll find small-town community and big-city conveniences, from theater to concerts and five-star dining. Because of the affordability of real estate in this corner of France, Brittany is popular among those on a budget.

BORDEAUX AND THE DORDOGNE VALLEY

This picturesque corner of France has so much going for it. It's a pretty, cosmopolitan regional capital with small-town ambience and a big heart, close proximity to the world's most famous wine-growing region (and all that it yields), and an übercharming river valley crammed with more castles than you could ever hope for. For centuries, this area has welcomed foreigners, from 16th-century Jews escaping religious persecution in Spain to 21st-century Englishmen and -women looking for an easy escape from London. Expect to hear English spoken in unexpected places—small-town brasseries, waiting areas outside elementary schools—and expect to be smitten by the fairytale feel. If you've come to France to evade your fellow Anglophones, this may not be the place to settle down: For years, the English have been ferrying over and snapping up land, which has, historically, been a great bargain. The recent global mortgage crisis put a slight damper on the house-buying spree, but the English-speaking community has put down roots and won't be going anywhere soon. Still, if truffles, wine, and rolling green countryside are your cup of tea, this corner of France has your name on it.

Bordeaux boasts a youthful population and thriving café scene.

Place de la Comédie sits at the heart of Montpellier's youthful *centre ville*.

TOULOUSE AND MONTPELLIER

From the gateway city of Toulouse to the university hub of Montpellier, the Languedoc region signals your proximity to the dazzling Mediterranean with palm trees and sunny skies. A decidedly non-French influence can be felt here, and decidedly non-French shopping bargains are within easy driving distance (there's no sales tax in nearby Andorra). Toulouse's international flavor is enhanced by the aerospace industry that has set up shop here, attracting skilled workers from around the world. Advancing toward the Mediterranean, past the medieval fortress town of Carcassonne and over the sand-colored hillsides specked with wind turbines sits the sunny, student-heavy city of Montpellier. In its giant main square, Place de la Comédie, locals young and old stroll around, sit by the fountain, and stop to listen to a guitarist playing flamenco tunes with understated perfection. Compared to Paris, Toulouse and Montpellier are bargains in the housing department, and there's no need to sacrifice cultural amenities to secure your place in the sun. Year-round art, theater, and workshops are on the to-do list, and within a one-hour train ride, you can be out the door of your city apartment and sitting on a beach chair facing the sparkling sea.

PROVENCE AND CÔTE D'AZUR

Even for experienced urbanites, France's second-largest city, Marseille, can feel overwhelming: Its crowded, graffiti-filled, labyrinthine streets seethe with a gritty energy that only intensifies with the summer heat. It's worth a visit, but Marseille can't really stake a claim as a "prime" living location. However, 30 miles north is the much calmer, quieter oasis of Aix-en-Provence. Best known as the birthplace of painter Paul Cézanne, the capital city of Provence occupies a strategic location between the sea and the rugged mountains and is blessed with that coveted Mediterranean climate. The Romans first settled here more than two millennia ago, and remnants of their civilization—bridges, arenas, fountains—still stand as reminders of that rich past. Today, this town of 150,000 attracts a diverse

PRIME LIVING LOCATIONS

You'll find plenty of sunshine and sea views along Nice's Promenade des Anglais.

student population, as well as artists, actors, and others who find the soft terra-cotta palette an alluring invitation to relax and stay awhile. Expect picture-perfect pedestrian promenades, colorful markets, and quaint shops vending everything from fresh-pressed juices to €300 shoes. But beauty has its price—Aix is not the cheapest place to settle in France. A two-hour train ride east will bring you in the little seaside oasis of Antibes. This charming town, population 75,000, has a summer-holiday atmosphere yet functions as any nontouristic destination would, with a busy year-round marketplace, plenty of restaurants, and friendly locals. The neighboring high-tech hub of Sophia Antipolis (known as the Silicon Valley of France), boosts a melting pot of expatriates, with international workers staffing its software companies and pharmaceutical labs. In the summer, the locals head out of town and rent their homes for astronomical sums that sometimes supplying the owners with enough income to live for the rest of the year. Just a 15-minute ride up the coast is the center of Nice, where broad boulevards, a sweeping seaside promenade, and a charming old town await. A truly livable city, Nice has historically attracted the silver-haired set, but its nearly idyllic position on the Cote d'Azur, a short hop from Monaco and Italy and the ski resorts of the Alpes-Maritimes, mean that the younger generation is catching on. More affordable than neighboring Antibes, Nice has a lot to offer the expat, including employment and outdoor-recreation opportunities.

LYON AND GRENOBLE

The first thing you'll notice about Grenoble is its stunning landscape. Tucked into a flat valley high in the hills amid the snow-capped alpine peaks of three mountain chains, the city attracts sporty types in droves. The city is diverse on many levels: It has thriving Vietnamese and Sri Lankan populations and also throws out the welcome mat to the gay and lesbian community. Students come here to learn, skiers to shoot the *pistes,* and high-tech profesionals to work their magic at Hewlett-Packard, Schneider Electric, and the numerous biotech companies that have made Grenoble the scientific capital of France. An hour up the road is beautiful Lyon, where medieval meets modern with an enchanting style. Though tourism is one of the city's official moneymakers, Lyon is a livable place where students, shop workers, and entrepreneurial types can build a rich and fulfilling life among the ancient Roman ruins, medieval churches, and Renaissance-era townhouses. The student population hovers around 100,000—second only to Paris—and with all that youth comes a certain vibrancy that helps keep Lyon feel current. Throughout the city, chic boutiques sidle up to quotidian *epiceries;* on any given day in the giant main square, you'll find all ages promenading about, dancers dancing, and tourists gawking at the mishmash of architectural eye candy. This town likes to have fun, too: Nightclubs and wine bars flourish here, and judging by the number of Irish pubs dotting Vieux Lyon's charming back alleyways, you might think you've accidentally stumbled into a James Joyce novel. Multicultural, food-oriented, and progressive, Lyon is a interesting, vibrant city in which to put down roots.

© TAOLMOR/123RF.COM

Lyon's Old Town and footbridge

PRIME LIVING LOCATIONS

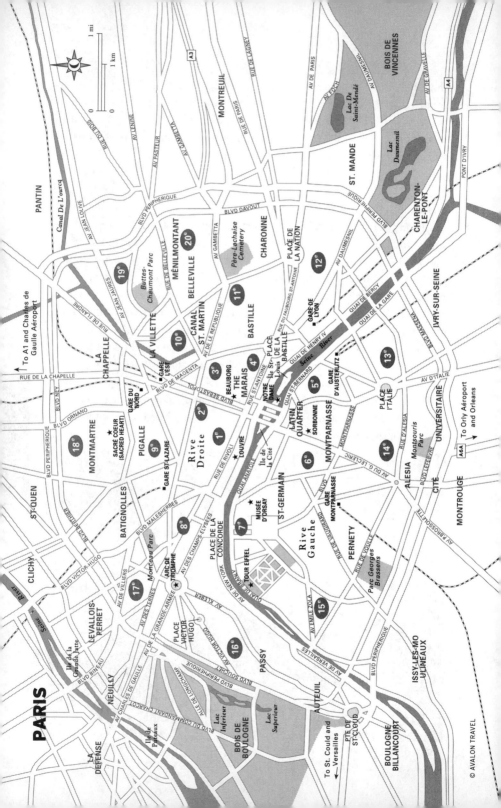

PARIS

Mention to anyone, anywhere, that you're planning a move to Paris and without fail, you'll be met with a torrent of envious commentary beginning with "How romantic!" and ending with "I've always wanted to live in Paris, too." For centuries, daring dreamers have flocked to this beautiful, history-rich city on the Seine in pursuit of education, to develop their art, and to simply to be able to say, "I used to live in Paris." There's a lot to love about this city, and many a writer—from Ernest Hemingway to David Sedaris—has taken pains to describe Paris in all its glory, the good and the bad. The good is easy to measure: You'll find it in the postage-stamp size-squares that mark every neighborhood; in the endless dining options that will take your taste buds on a journey from Alsace to Sri Lanka; in the corner *boulangeries,* where still-warm *viennoiseries* call out to you from inside a gleaming glass case; and in the dozens of museums offering up centuries of world-class art to overwhelm your senses. Paris is beautiful beyond belief, and even in the grittiest neighborhoods in the northern section of

the city, you need only look up at a building's façade to revel in a moment of aesthetic pleasure. Ornate curlicued balconies decorated with geraniums in full bloom, carved wooden doors hemmed by art nouveau sculpture, and 100-year-old advertisements peeking out from a faded brick wall never fail to tantalize the eyes.

Before Paris became the picture-perfect metropolis it is today, it was Lutèce—and before that, it was just a miniscule fishing village settled by the Parisii, a tribe of Celtic Gauls who first set up shop along the Seine in 250 B.C. The Parisii created their home here for economic reasons; the river provided a rich source of sustenance (and people can still be seen fishing on the banks of the Seine, though eating your catch isn't rec-

© SOPHIA PAGAN/WWW.SOPHIAPAGAN.COM

one of Paris's many secret corners

ommended), and its strategic positioning made the region ripe for developing trade. Julius Caesar and his colleagues conquered the city in 50 B.C., and Roman influences can still be seen here and there, but the later epochs—the Haussmann period and art nouveau—left a real visual legacy that continues to seduce visitors and immigrants today.

Paris is certainly not without its flaws. Petty crime is common—it's not unusual to see the torched remains of an unfortunate Vespa lying in the street, and graffiti is cropping up on edifices of even *maisons particulaires* in the bourgeois 16th. Traffic, particularly on Thursdays and Fridays at rush hour, when Parisians head for their weekend homes in the provinces, can be brutal. The pollution is so pervasive that it stains the sand-colored buildings a dirty gray, prompting a municipally mandated cleaning at least once a decade. And let's not forget the Métro, which resembles a human-packed sardine can during peak commute times. If you're driving, good luck finding a parking space. But even if you're crazy enough to hit the streets of Paris in a car, you'll find that the trade-off is worth all the hassle.

The Lay of the Land

ARRONDISSEMENTS

The first thing a newcomer learns when arriving in Paris is that it is carved into 20 distinct regions called arrondissements, each an administrative unit each its own mayor and town hall. These districts spiral out clockwise from the geographic center of the city, ending in the northwestern quadrant. The Tour Eiffel and Musée d'Orsay can be found in the 7th; the Louvre is just across the river in the 1st. Sacré Coeur is in the 18th, and Notre Dame is in the 4th. Studying a map of the city—or, better still, picking up the very handy pocket-size Michelin map atlas of Paris—will facilitate your orientation within each of the various districts.

Wherever you settle, you'll be within 45 minutes of anywhere else in the city. The thorough and efficient Métro system makes the distances less daunting,

PARIS: *FLÂNEUR'S* PARADISE

Nineteenth-century poet Charles Baudelaire brought the term *flâneur* to life, and there's little question that his hometown, Paris, was the inspiration. The *flâneur* – walk-about, stroller, urban explorer – thrives on the sensory experience of the city, absorbing its sights, smells, and sounds, synthesizing the disparate elements into a meaningful whole.

"For the perfect *flâneur*, for the passionate spectator, it is an immense joy to set up house in the heart of the multitude, amid the ebb and flow of movement, in the midst of the fugitive and the infinite," wrote Baudelaire in 1863. For modern-day *flâneurs*, Paris is the winning lotto ticket – the mother lode of *flâneurial* fodder.

Each of the city's 20 arrondissements is its own universe, with a unique breed of inhabitants and dynamic character. In the 1st arrondissement, you could sit for hours at the fountains in the courtyard of the Louvre, inhaling the cacophony of foreign languages until the sun sets over the Seine. In the 4th, men in black hats frame the doorways of the Jewish *boulangeries*, a Jerusalem street scene recreated in the City of Light. In the 16th, women of a certain age, dressed in fur and designer shoes, promenade their pooches in the bourgeois safety of this tidy neighborhood. What do they know of the *banlieue*, just over the *périphérique*, where cars sometimes burn and the police wear riot gear?

There's no such thing as a boring day in Paris; the visual stimulation and inspiration are endless. Whether or not you identify with the *flâneur's* philosophical perspective, you will not be able to help – as Baudelaire suggests – but experience the streets as you roam them, from Porte de Clignancourt to Porte d'Orléans.

though one of the benefits of Paris life is the bounty that your quartier offers (making it unnecessary to leave if you don't want to). With the exception of the 16th arrondissement, every neighborhood in Paris has, within a two-block radius of your apartment, a *boulangerie,* a butcher shop, an *épicerie* for buying vegetables and fruit, and a Métro or bus stop.

RIVE GAUCHE AND RIVE DROITE

Each of the two sides of Paris, *la rive gauche* and *la rive droite,* has its own special flavor, and locals feel passionate about the benefits of their side of the Seine. The Left Bank, or *la rive gauche,* is where you'll find the Sorbonne, the Eiffel Tower, the Catacombs, and those cafés and brasseries made famous by centuries of writers and philosophers: Brasserie Lipp, Les Deux Magots, Café de Flore. Today, more tourists than locals pull up a chair on the sidewalk terraces, but if you move just south off the St. Germain des Prés, you'll discover homey neighborhoods and a safe, child-friendly atmosphere. The Left Bank feels more sedate, more residential, and slightly less *populaire,* or working-class crowded. If it weren't for the tourists, you might not know you were in Paris.

© INGVAR BJORK/123RF.COM

a bird's eye view of Paris's business district, La Défense

On the other side of the river, you'll find the Champs-Elysées, the Marais, the Bastille, and Sacré Coeur. *La rive droite* feels hipper, younger, and edgier, particularly in up-and-coming neighborhoods like Belleville and La Villette. Paris's gay hub is here, in the old streets of the Marais; and just north of the Bastille, on rue de la Roquette, you'll find the highest concentration of pierced and tattooed locals. The entire city is in gentrification mode, and you can really feel that transition happening in Paris's northern half.

DOWNTOWN

Paris doesn't have a typical "downtown" in the way that, say, New York City has Lower Manhattan or San Francisco has its financial district. But what it does have is La Défense, a cluster of skyscrapers on the southwest edge of the city where more than 150,000 workers migrate seven days a

ag home to high-tech corporations, government offices,

inesses, La Défense also houses the region's largest shop-

atre Temps (open on Sundays), and a handful of resi-

ique features is its truly livable, well-integrated neigh-

tier in the city's 20 arrondissements is a self-contained

amenities you'd find in a big city compressed into a

While there are legions of commuters who live out-

city and drive or take public transport in each day, many more Parisians live and work within a short distance of their homes. For those who do traverse the city for *travail* (work), the efficient, relatively fast public transportation network means no point within the *périphérique* is more than 45 minutes away.

Daily Life

"Métro, boulot, dodo." It's the 9-to-5 worker's lament: commute, work, sleep. Rinse and repeat. We'd all rather be on permanent vacation, but if you must participate in the daily grind, Paris is the place to be. After you've been in town awhile, you'll discover that a lot of people really are here just for work—after university, the upwardly mobile move to Paris to earn enough money for all those vacations, and especially for retirement back in the village or city where they were raised. There's a sense of transience in this metropolis, made more palpable by the tourists who help shore up the city's financial infrastructure

and by the international working community here on short- and long-term (but rarely permanent) work contracts.

The standard workweek is 35 hours, but Parisians are notorious for working long, American-style hours. To compensate, they invest a comparable amount of time in urban leisure activities: eating and drinking; going to the cinema, concerts, and theater; and haunting the countless green spaces that have become a communal backyard for apartment dwellers whose dwellings aren't equipped with one (most aren't).

SCHOOLS AND COMMUNITY CENTERS

Like other livable cities, Paris is family friendly. Every neighborhood has a mix of state-sponsored childcare centers, schools, libraries, playgrounds, and community activity centers designed with youngsters' needs in mind. Likewise, senior centers in every arrondissement give the silver-hair set a place to dine, socialize, and generally find camaraderie with their peers.

For nearly 1,000 years, Paris has been a center of learning, with the Sorbonne taking the prize for oldest university in France. The main campus, in the 5th arrondissement on Paris's Rive Gauche, boasts a student population of 24,000 and employs a staff of nearly 800. Among the other dozen or so Paris universities are École Normale de Musique, in the 17th; Université de Paris-Vincennes-St. Denis, just over the *périphérique* in the suburb of St. Denis; and the Institut Catholic de Paris in the 6th. For any would-be university enrollee, the student-centric website www.etudiantdeparis.fr is worth investigating; it offers valuable insight on student life, academic scholarships, and student benefits.

CLIMATE

When this four-season city turns chilly and gray, around mid-November, people simply more dress warmly and continue their everyday outdoor activities: biking, trips to the market, Sunday strolls, and walks to the park. Outdoor cafés erect plastic walls and roll out the heat lamps, and life continues as usual. Then, in spring—especially after a rough winter with snow and freezing temperatures—the city springs to life with an unrivaled vibrancy that makes winter, even with all its holiday fanfare. look like a pretty dormant season. In summer, when the weather turns muggy and hot, Parisians make weekend escapes to their country abodes, leaving the city to the tourists during August, the standard vacation month.

The expat who stays citybound in the summer will find Paris perfectly pleasant, between Paris Plage—the temporary "beach" set up by the Seine—outdoor concerts and film festivals, and events sponsored by Anglophone

For most of the summer, the banks of Paris's Seine become a playground for *promeneurs.*

organizations like the American Church in Paris (www.acparis.org), Shakespeare and Company bookstore (www.shakespeareandcompany.com), and WICE (www.wice-paris.org).

PARIS TIME

Historically, on Sundays and often on Mondays, huge chunks of the city have felt like a ghost town, with iron gates pulled down over shop doorways, paper shades drawn across *boulangerie* displays, and supermarkets sitting dark, forlorn, and empty. But this is changing, with more and more businesses opening on Sundays, if only for limited hours (which are posted at the entrance). In neighborhoods with sizable Arab populations—the 18th, 19th, and the 20th, in particular—shops are closed on Fridays instead of Sundays, and the same neighborhoods are alive and open for business on Christmas Day. In Jewish districts, particularly the 4th and the 11th, many restaurants are closed on Saturday. If you happen to be in the hood and have the misfortune to lose a bicycle chain, don't expect the yarmulke-clad locals to help—work isn't allowed on the Sabbath.

PARKS AND GREEN SPACES

In the southwest and northeast sections of the city sit two gloriously verdant areas that also happen to be among the few green spaces in Paris where dogs are free to roam off leash. Both parks, Bois de Boulogne to the west and Bois de Vincennes to the east, are accessible by Métro, car, bike, or bus and are open 365 days a year. In the summer, paddle boats and canoes can be rented at each park's picturesque lake, and there are plenty of picnic tables, cafés, and other amenities available to help maximize your outdoor pleasure.

In Bois de Boulogne, prostitution has become a 24-hour phenomenon, so it's not uncommon to see women—and some men—teetering around in the woods wearing little more than high heels and underwear in the middle of the day. This practice becomes especially acute in the evening and during rush hour, and it seems to be relegated to the areas of the park with the most road traffic. Prostitution aside, both *bois* (woods) are a city slicker's oasis, as well as wonderful places to spend a spring, summer, or autumn afternoon.

Housing

During your house hunt, you'll start to get used to diminutive dimensions of Parisian homes. That 20-square-meter apartment in the 11th for €800 per month that looked so good on paper might take on a different hue when you realize the entire place is just 215 square feet, which is probably the size of your

© AURELIA D'ANDREA

You might find yourself an Art Nouveau apartment to call home in Paris.

(very small) living room back home. It's wise to sample a few different places before signing on the dotted line—you'll also notice that prices will drop if the place is on the market for more than a month. If you're renting directly from the owner, don't be afraid to negotiate. That doesn't mean trying to get your 60-square-meter flat with *un ascenseur* (an elevator) down from €2,000 to €1,000, but if the apartment needs work or is missing amenities, you have a bit of haggling room.

Unless you have a money's-no-object budget, finding a place to call home in Paris isn't as simple as choosing a neighborhood; many other factors come into play, including the local housing supply and the time of year. It's the same story in cities and towns around the world: A move in winter shrinks your options, because really, who wants to move house when there's snow on the ground? This big a transition is challenging enough in the warm months, so skip the winter move and plan for May, June, or July. Toward August, you begin to compete with college students and *rentrées* coming back from long summer holidays who also need to get down to the important task of finding accommodations.

Where to Live

In Paris's trendier right-bank arrondissements—the 11th, 10th, and 4th—you'll find that the hipsters have hogged up all the affordable places and sent the rent sky-high for what's left. Still, you may want to try your luck in these vibrant neighborhoods, especially the area around the Bastille (11th) and Canal St. Martin (10th), where a youthful vibe dominates and there's always a cheerful café for kicking back and people-watching. If you prefer a more sedate atmosphere with an aura of security, you'll love the 16th, which has a calm, homogenous ambience with a dash of Americana thrown in. (Step into the Starbucks on Victor Hugo, and you'll see what I mean.) Further south, in the 14th, it's practically suburban, though you're never far from critical amenities, including transportation, markets, and restaurants. If you can't imagine apartment living and don't even want to give it a whirl, consider a move to the burbs, where your options will run the gamut from apartments and lofts to single-family homes.

BASTILLE

The Bastille, in the northeast section of Paris, was once a forlorn, neglected neighborhood of working-class immigrant families and grungy youth hostels.

But in the past 20 years, new parks have been installed, boutiques have sprung up, cafés have blossomed on virtually every corner, and the neighborhood has became both more appealing and more expensive. If you can snag a place in your price range here, you'll find great outdoor markets, renowned restaurants, plenty of corner parks, excellent transportation, a well-respected public hospital, and plenty of shops to meet your daily needs.

Apartments rent a little higher here than in other quartiers—not because it's a chichi neighborhood (it isn't), but because it has hipster appeal. Expect to pay around €33 per square meter, or around €1200 per month for a 40-square-meter one-bedroom apartment. If you're looking to buy, you might be able to find something of a similar size for €300,000. Most Bastille housing comes in the form of apartments, but the recent trend has been to convert industrial *ateliers* (workshops) into open, airy, loftlike apartments of particular appeal to artists. If you find one of these unique dwellings, you may have to spend money on an internal revamp, since these spaces originally had toilets in the courtyard rather than indoors. For the light and the expansive feel, the investment might be worth it.

CANAL ST. MARTIN

Just north and slightly west of the Bastille is the Canal St. Martin neighborhood, in the 10th. One of the newest "it" zones, this pleasant, well-used canal is flanked by cafés, hair salons, clothing boutiques, and a pharmacy and supermarket or two. Move north or south of the canal, and funky, lived-in neighborhoods explode with color and vitality. Though you'll find plenty of children in this neighborhood—especially on Sundays, when the streets along the canal are blocked off so families on bikes, inline skates, and scooters hit the pavement en masse—it has a younger feel than the neighboring 11th. Apartment living is the norm here, and the prices are a little lower than in the 11th. Expect to pay around €1,000 for your one-bedroom apartment with beamed ceiling and fireplace, or invest €280,000 or so to purchase that one-bedroom and call it your own.

THE MARAIS

Although gay men and women feel at home throughout the city, the hub of Parisian gay life is the Marais (4th), which is the equivalent of San Francisco's Castro or Montreal's le Village. It's also the oldest neighborhood in Paris and, not surprisingly, one of the most stereotypically French in character, with crooked cobbled streets, half-timbered buildings, charming squares, and loads and loads of tourists. If you want to live in the heart of the city, with easy access to bars, restaurants, museums, and shopping, the Marais is your place.

Gentrification has changed the visage of all these neighborhoods, which now feel a lot more homogeneous (read: Caucasian) than mixed, but there's no denying the Marais' charm, accessibility, and cool quotient. Housing prices run the gamut here: Shared situations can be found in the low hundreds per month, and many a cash-strapped student or artist has learned to cohabitate in a handful of square meters by building a mezzanine in the living room or making good use of the *clic-clac* (pullout sofa). Besides, you'll be out spending all your time at museums, parks, cafés, and wandering around the neighborhood anyway. For a one-bedroom apartment of roughly 35 square meters, expect to pay between €800 and €1,500 per month. If buying is an option, there's still good value to be found here, with similarly sized one-bedrooms for €200,000 to €400,000.

BELLEVILLE, BATIGNOLLES, LA CHAPPELLE, AND LA VILLETTE

Better bargains can be found in the up-and-coming districts, including Belleville (20th), Batignolles (17th), La Chappelle (10th/18th) and La Villette (19th), which have all undergone some urban renewal of late but still have enough of a rough edge to keep the big-money investors out and the prices reasonable. As in the rest of Paris, the Métro or another form of public transportation is never more than a 10-minute walk away, and the usual amenities—schools, hospitals, restaurants, outdoor markets, launderettes, corner *épiceries,* shoe repair shops—are within easy reach.

Belleville, which sits on a hill in northeast Paris, is home to a large Asian community—especially Chinese and Vietnamese—and is one of the greenest arrondissements in Paris, with both Parc des Buttes-Chaumont and Parc de Belleville nearby. This quartier is favored by artists—and there are oodles of not-too-chic galleries here to prove it—and has a lively ambience. There's a distinct "inner city" feeling to the streets formerly walked by local hero Edith Piaf, and if you can live with graffiti, the sound of a guitar being strummed in the apartment across the courtyard at odd hours, and the unofficial Romany flea markets that take place in the early morning, you could find this neighborhood to be homey and welcoming.

A skip away to the west is La Villette, a former factory zone that's transmogrified into a hip, expansive neighborhood with a giant oasis—the Parc de la Villette—at its core. Like the other affordable hoods, this one is culturally diverse; you'll find kebab stands next to natural food stores next to trendy canalside bars, and a family- and dog-friendly green space that's almost as nice as having a real backyard.

The once-gritty Batignolles neighborhood in far northwest Paris is experiencing a major revamp: Its giant industrial zone is being transformed into an eco-habitat complete with parks, energy-efficient affordable housing and storefronts, art spaces, and subterranean parking. In 2012, the light-rail system currently operating on the ring road in the southern part of the city is expected to extend out here, which will give Parisians yet another smart and efficient way to traverse their city. With all this structural improvement, you can expect prices to increase, but right now it's still bargain-basement territory, especially when you cross north over avenue de Clichy—a one-bedroom, 50-square-meter apartment can be had in this area for €1,000 per month (or often less). Houses are similarly affordable; a 19th-century one-bedroom with a fireplace and balcony sells for €250,000. The neighborhood has some idiosyncrasies, such as a noticeable community of transgender people who are either attracted by the numerous wig shops, Lucite high-heel-shoe salons, and shiny-clothing stores or responsible for their proliferation. They mean no harm, and don't detract from the funky, multicultural vibe. Grab a kebab and watch the parade of humanity go by—you might like it.

Ditto for the La Chappelle neighborhood, slightly south of Sacré Coeur. Also known as Little Jaffna for the extensive Sri Lankan community that has settled here, La Chappelle is by turns grungy and quaint, depending on which street you happen to be walking down. Rue Louis Blanc, its plane trees sheltering pedestrians from the summer skies, has a welcoming allure, helped along by a generous sprinkling of South Asian restaurants and grocery stores. Nearby is the Gare du Nord, one of Paris's major train stations, which lends a permanent sense of transition to the neighborhood. Expect housing prices to drop as you cross the main drag, Boulevard de la Chappelle. It gets even grittier here, but for some, even a gritty Paris address still beats the burbs.

THE 16TH

The 16th arrondissement has long been a magnet for moneyed expatriates. Many embassies are situated here, and a handful of international schools makes it convenient for parents who want their kids educated nearby. At the two or three Starbucks in this neighborhood, you might be surprised to hear the teenage clientele yakking away in English. In other words, this arrondissement has a clean, safe, as-American-as-Paris-can-be feeling that might help you ease into big city living with more ease than elsewhere. The Trocadéro and La Muette neighborhoods are popular choices, where you'll find lots of ladies in fur coats roaming the *rues,* shopping bags in hand; a parade of pure-bred pooches being walked by the hired help; several museums; and cafés and brasseries galore. North toward the Arc de Triomphe are the Ternes and Parc Monceau (17th) neighborhoods, both of which have an upscale flair and a safe feel. All the amenities are nearby, including Monoprix and Darty; the Champs-Élysées is a short walk away; and you'll likely discover that your new neighbors are fellow North Americans or other expatriates who are also seeking a less colorful Parisian experience than other arrondissements might offer. If you can afford to spend €2,000 per month on your 40-square-meter, one-bedroom apartment, there's plenty to choose from. Buying here is priccy, too: Expect to fork out more than €300,000 for a small one bedroom. The prices go up, up, and up from there.

ALESIA

In the far south of the city, in the 14th, is the pleasant, family-friendly Alesia neighborhood. Slightly off the beaten path, this district still feels like true Paris. Expect to see lots of college-student spillover (the Sorbonne is not too far away); great neighborhood shopping, with plenty of outdoor markets and sweet neighborhood boutiques; and movie theaters, supermarkets, and a nice multicultural mix of inhabitants that represents the scope of Paris. The cost of living here is on par with the Bastille neighborhood, across the river, and transportation is good: the Métro, RER, bus, and the new tramway are all nearby.

SUBURBS

Why would anyone come to Paris only to end up living in a suburb? Well, with a few exceptions, it's considerably less expensive—and if you're the type who can't live without a car, you might actually find free(ish) parking instead of having to fork over €20,000 to buy a parking spot, as is the usual local custom. Another advantage that suburbia has to offer is excellent transportation: Paris's Métro extends far out into the hinterlands of the Île de France, so even if you choose to settle 30 kilometers away, you can still be in central Paris in 45 minutes.

St. Cloud

Just over the périphérique to the southwest of Paris is the suburb of St. Cloud, on a hilly spot next to the 460-hectare Parc de St. Cloud. Living in this quiet, upscale suburb, you'd never guess that Paris was a five-minute Métro ride away. Life here feels calm and sedate, and if you've dreamed of a house in the country, finding one in St. Cloud might be the next best thing. You could find a standalone dwelling—with a yard—for around €700,000. Rents are on par with the 16th.

Living in St. Cloud most likely means a commute into Paris, unless you work at the exclusive American School of Paris, which is based here. Métro, tramway, and bus will move you in and around the area, as well as to and from all the amenities you could ever hope for. This is one of Paris's wealthiest bedroom communities—your hard-earned euros will buy you convenience, so a trip to the big city is necessary only if you *want* to go.

Montreuil

Crossing the *périphérique* at the city's far eastern border is Montreuil, a slightly rough-around-the-edges *banelieue* that's popular with twentysomethings who aren't intimidated by a little funkiness. Many North and West African immigrants have settled here, giving the town a heady multiculturalism that blends well with the burgeoning arts scene. Nearby, you'll find the region's largest natural-foods store, Les Nouveaux Robinson, which attracts many Parisians who come for the organic bodycare products, free-range eggs, and vast array of faux meats. There are also a few huge *hypermarchés,* including multistory Auchan and Carrefour markets.

Montreuil particularly appeals to families for its affordability—you can actually find single-family homes for less than €250,000 here—and its schools, parks, and quick access to central Paris. The biggest downside is that Montreuil isn't as tidy-looking as many Parisian neighborhoods; some areas appear downright neglected. But if you can bear gentrification-in-progress in exchange for cheaper-than-average rent, Montreuil is worth a look.

St. Mandé

Just south of Montreuil is St. Mandé, a cute little suburb with a much less edgy feel than its neighbor to the north. Perfectly positioned between the Bois de Vincennes and the Porte de Paris, this neighborhood makes it possible to get the best of Paris for a discounted price. Expect a quaint downtown main drag with a centuries-old church, plenty of *boulangeries* and drugstores, and a weekly outdoor market. On weekends—especially Sundays—St. Mande can feel really, really sleepy—but Paris is a hop, skip, and a jump away.

Housing prices are better here than in the closest Parisian neighborhood; a one-bedroom apartment runs around €900 per month, and buying a 40-square-meter one-bedroom will cost in the vicinity of €300,000—if you can find an empty unit. Housing is at a premium, and there are fewer "À Vendre" signs perched on windowsills than elsewhere in the Île de France region.

Getting Around

One of Paris's finest features is its public transportation system. There is an option for everyone: Métro, bus, bike, boat, taxi, public car share. It's helpful to know that the Île de France is divided into six transportation zones, the most critical to the average Parisian being zones 1, 2, and 3. Zone 1 is Paris, and zone 2 includes the nearby suburbs. Zone 3 includes the suburb of St. Cloud, while Versailles and Orly Airport are in zone 4, and Charles de Gaulle Airport and Disneyland Paris are in zone 5. Way out in zone 6, you'll find plenty of rolling green farmland and small commuter towns.

TICKETS AND PASSES

The standard Metro tickets are known as the Ticket T+ and cost €1.70 at time of writing. They are valid on trains, buses, and tramways in zones 1, 2, and 3. If you buy a *carnet* of 10 tickets, you save 20 percent; this is a good deal if you'll be in Paris for just a day or two, and they never expire (though the prices always increase), so buying a bunch and saving them for future travel is a smart idea. Children younger than four travel for free, and those age nine and younger are entitled to *tarif réduit* tickets, which cost half as much as the adult fare. Adults 26 and younger are also entitled to reductions with *jeunes* tickets. If you're going to stay awhile, consider investing in the handy Navigo Pass. This laminated card that you purchase at human-staffed kiosks in Métro and other train stations allows unlimited weekly access on buses, Vélib' bikes, and Métro trains. The tricky aspect of this pass is that once you purchase it, it's only valid between Monday and Sunday. So, if you buy your weekly pass on a Saturday, you get two days of travel. Better to buy your card on Friday, Saturday, or Sunday for the following week. Once you have a card—you'll need to attach a passport-size photo—you can renew it weekly in automated machines in the station (provided you have a credit card with a *puce*).

THE FRENCH VÉLO-LUTION

© WAJAN/123RF.COM/123RF.COM

When it first launched, in July 2007, Vélib' – Paris's much-hyped public bicycle system – was hailed as the eco-friendly answer to a very profound Parisian problem: city traffic. In theory, the 20,000 shared bicycles installed at more than 1,200 stations throughout the city's 20 arrondissements would encourage Paris drivers to permanently park their cars; which, in turn, would help unclog the capital's streets. In practice, it has pretty much lived up to its potential, with a few hiccups here and there: Vandalism and theft have been ongoing issues, and, sadly, a handful of fatal Vélib' accidents have marred the system's otherwise glowing reputation.

It works like this: You sidle up to a kiosk (you'll find one every 900 feet throughout the city), tap a few buttons, slide your credit card (embedded with a *puce*), determine how many days' worth of service you want (1, 7, 30, or 365), *et voilà!* The machine spits out a card with your membership number, which you then use to rent bikes wherever and whenever you want. The first half-hour is free; after that, you're charged between €1 and €4 per half-hour, depending on how long you

keep the bike. Smart Vélib'ists have figured out a way around paying extra fees, which is to return your bike at the half-hour point, wait five minutes, then take out another bike. Thirty minutes zip by when you're having fun on two wheels, so wear a watch if you want to ride for free.

The system is not without its flaws. When you want a bicycle most, that is inevitably when there won't be a single one available – and in popular neighborhoods during peak commute times, it's sometimes impossible to find an empty spot to dock your bike. These little issues aside, Vélib' continues to cultivate a fan base while spawning copycat bike-share programs around the world. In France, all the major cities – Bordeaux, Lyon, Nice – have public bicycle systems that operate in the same fashion.

So what will they think of next? Autolib', an electric car-share program based on the Vélib' model. The first test phase of Île de France's newest transportation system took place in August 2011 and opened to the public two months later. By the end of March 2012, the project will be complete, with more than 1,100 active stations in Paris and its suburbs.

HOURS

During the week, Métro service begins at 5:30 A.M. and ends at 1:15 A.M.; on weekends, hours are extended to 2:15 A.M. Up until 2006, night owls had to rely on taxis to travel after hours, but the Noctilien bus system changed all that. From 12:30 A.M. to 5:30 A.M., these 42 different bus lines will get you most places you want to go in the city. You'll need to time your journey right, however—the buses come every 60 minutes or so, sometimes more frequently on weekends.

On New Year's Eve, all public transportation is free. For access to all the information you could ever hope for, you'll want to visit www.translilien.com. And hooray! It's all available in English. Transportation maps are free from ticket booths in the stations, and wall-mounted maps are plentiful too.

À PIED

Of course, there's always the tried-and-true mode that nearly everyone can use to navigate the city: two feet. Sure, Paris is a big city, but it's also compact. It's possible to walk from top to bottom if you've got several hours to devote to the task, and walking allows you to experience the city in a way you'll never find underground or from the seat on a bus.

Paris is a very walkable city.

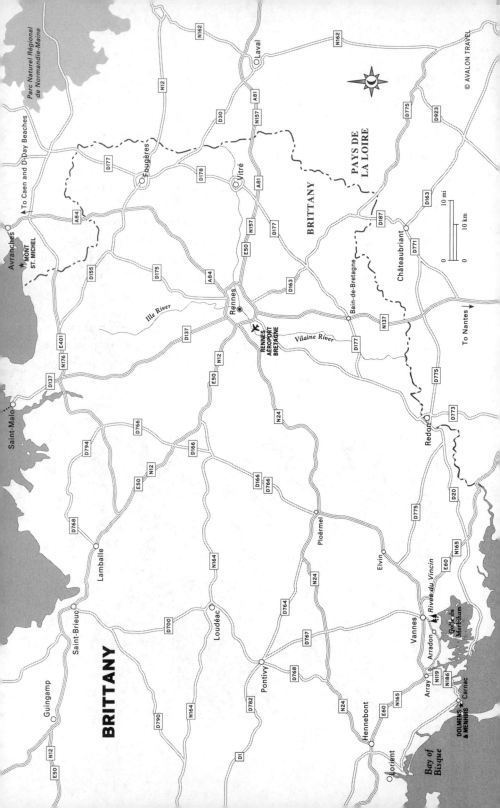

BRITTANY

Book a seat on the TGV heading in the direction of Quimper—that final outpost on the windswept wedge of western France jutting out into the Atlantic—and ride for two hours, and you'll find yourself in the middle of rolling green countryside, thick with conifers, chestnuts, and plane trees, rivers and streams, and beautifully preserved architecture dating back to the Middle Ages. There's an awful lot to like about this section of l'Hexagone, beginning with (but certainly not limited to) the relaxed atmosphere of even the region's big cities, like Rennes. Though Brittany is a short hop away from the French capital in terms of distance, it's worlds away when it comes to urban ambience. Where Paris is go-go-go, this region simply says "take it easy." You feel the difference at the train station, at the *mairie,* and especially in the parks, which aren't pocked with signs reading "No dogs allowed" or "Don't sit on the grass." This area is primarily agricultural in its economic output, but some manufacturing—automobiles and electronics—happens here, as does a whole lot of tourism. The academic community also helps shore up the local economy.

Rennes

As you've surely noticed, most of France's most livable cities are equipped
with a college campus or two (or seven), and Rennes is no different. This city
of 210,000 supports more than 60,000 students on its many campuses, with
roughly 23,000 of them working toward a degree or diploma at the University
of Rennes 1 and the University of Rennes 2. Each UR campus is dedicated
to a different sector within the academic spectrum: UR1 falls under the "sciences" rubric—life medicine, math, and life sciences—and UR2 focuses on
the arts, humanities, and social sciences. While this is definitely a city full of
young people, their presence is subtle. The urban panorama encompasses the
old, young, and middle-aged, all sharing the same beautiful, relaxed pace of
the Breton capital without eclipsing each other.

Rennes has an interesting history, remnants of which are still very visible
in the old city center. In the 9th century, Brittany became an autonomous
kingdom, complete with its own language, dress, cuisine, and social customs,
and it remained independent until integrating into the rest of France in the
16th century. Today, it still holds firm to its unique cultural roots, which are
celebrated through annual festivals, including Les Tombées de la Nuit, which
regales Rennois with a street-art fête twice each year.

Rennes is equally compelling from an architectural perspective, with its
18th-century *hôtel de ville,* its renowned 16th-century cathedral, and its 14th-
century half-timbered houses, called *colombages.* It's a wonder any of the latter

© MARY MARGARET CHAPPELL

Much of the Breton capital of Rennes was rebuilt after a major fire in 1720.

are still standing: In 1720, a devastating fire swept through the streets, burning long and hard for six nights. The fire, which started two days before Christmas, ravaged more than 900 homes on 33 streets in the center of town, leaving thousands homeless.

Today, the *centre ville* is a blend of old and older. Most of the newer architecture has been relegated to the periphery, where the growth holds steady to accommodate business as new students and families migrate in and out of the city. Rennes is a very much a city for walking; pedestrian zones dot the city center, and a multiuse path along the canal invites strollers, cyclists, and skaters. A solid public transportation system combined with a moderate-size *centre ville* means having a car isn't a must.

THE LAY OF THE LAND

Rennes sits 320 kilometers southwest of Paris, a two-hour train ride or three-and-a-half-hour drive away. The gateway to Brittany, this urban center is surrounded by sea and countryside, an ideal position for weekend getaways— 55 kilometers to the north is that much touristed, often waterless bay that holds Mont St. Michel. To the south, the Golfe du Morbihan—where ancient Celtic megaliths, sailboats, and buckwheat *galettes* washed down with *bolées* of cider reign—is approximately 100 kilometers away by car, an hour by train. Smack in the middle of rolling green farmland where cows, sheep, and donkeys graze, Rennes also boasts thick forests of sycamore, conifer, chestnut, and apple. Though Brittany is not exactly seaside, a maritime flavor that permeates the region—you'll find evidence of this at even the most landlocked *marchés,* where all manner of sea life (lobster, oysters, snails) is up for sale.

For the past two decades, Brittany has established itself as a favorite expat destination for Britons, who cite quality of life, a slowed-down pace, and affordable real estate as the main attractions. Proximity and ease of travel to the UK are another draw; ferries, planes, and trains are all possibilities for getting across the Channel. But even without ties to the UK, Brittany's central location has a particular appeal, especially for history buffs with a thing for the sea. The D-day beaches are near, dozens of Breton châteaux welcome visitors, and noteworthy lighthouses provide even more grist for the sightseer's mill.

Rennes sits at the confluence of the Ille and the Vilaine Rivers, in the *departement* of Ille-et-Vilaine. These two waterways are part of an important natural ecosystem and an important tourism infrastructure; the preservation of one supports the other. More than 5,000 kilometers of walking trails, bridle paths, and cycling trails encourage outdoor pursuits here, and the diverse flora

A TASTE OF BRETAGNE

Name Mary Margaret Chappell
Age: 43
Hometown: Richmond, VA
Current City: Cancale

Mary Margaret first moved to France in the 1990s and started teaching English to university students in the lovely regional capital of Rennes. Today, after stints as a pastry chef in New York City and a magazine editor in L.A., she's back in "le Panier de France" (the country's shopping basket), Brittany. She cooks (her latest book, *Le Tour de Bretagne en 80 Desserts Gourmands*, was published in 2007), writes (she's the local correspondent for the regional *Ouest-France* newspaper), and enjoys the pleasures of coastal life in northwest France. Here, she dishes on one of the Brittany's most delicious treasures: its food.

Sea Salt and Fleur de Sel
Both coarse sea salt and the finer fleur de sel are harvested in the salt marshes in Guérande, in southern Brittany, which means they are as easy to find in supermarket near me as Morton's or kosher salt are in the United States. I am absolutely ad-

dicted to fleur de sel because of the delicate flavor and slight crunch it gives foods when sprinkled on before serving.

Galettes
One of the first introductions any non-Breton has into the lexicon of Brittany (the region also has its own Celtic language, Breton) is the

© MARY MARGARET CHAPPELL

Galettes are the regional speciality.

and fauna—think egrets, otters, and wild boar—keep the terrain diverse and add to the area's natural allure. Accessing the city by car, you'll enter through one of the 15 *portes* that dot the ring road circumnavigating the city. Porte de Beaulieu (Paris) and Porte de St. Nazaire (Nantes) are two of the most common entry points.

DAILY LIFE

It's hard to describe the pace of a city that doesn't seem to really have one. Well, that's not fair: Rennes does have a pace, but it is slowed down to the point where it registers more as rhythm. In this center of learning, you can expect the usual helping of culture: music, art, theater, themed festivals. You'll word *galette*. Crêperies thrive all over Brittany thanks to *galettes*, traditional savory crêpes made with buckwheat flour and filled with everything from a simple sprinkling of cheese to gourmet-style compositions with vegetables and local seafood. Stands where you can buy freshly made *galettes* and crêpes are at every outdoor market. I usually buy a few each week for a quick dinner (throw a little cheese in, fold, top with a salad or some steamed veggies, and *voilà!*) or even breakfast.

Salted Butter

I'm one of those people who, when given a pat of sweet unsalted butter in a fancy restaurant, immediately asks for a salt shaker to doctor it up. So it's only natural that I'm thrilled to have chosen to live in a part of France where salted butter is the norm. Butter in general is the bread spread and cooking fat of choice here. Once, when I telling a neighbor about a recipe I was making with olive oil, she said to me, "Olive oil? Oh, I don't have any of that. *On est beurre ici*," which roughly translates to "We are all about butter here."

Artichokes

In spring and early fall, produce bins heaped with artichokes appear on the markets in Brittany, and the crazy-looking spiked plants turn up in fields along the road. I'd always thought of artichokes as a novelty vegetable you cook for guests, but after working on a feature about them for a magazine that required me to cook 40 or so to come up with six different recipes, I've come to think of them as a favorite seasonal addition to my cooking. I love the hearts in *galettes* (see above) and have learned to make *carciofi alla romana* from my Italian neighbor.

Cider

Oh, the luxury of being able to buy fruity, delicious, bottled hard cider (most often artisanally made) anywhere and everywhere I shop. The sparkling beverage – its alcohol content is a little lower than beer – goes exceptionally well with everything from *galettes* to a hunk of ripe camembert and tastes refreshing on a hot day. Plus it comes in a corked bottle that opens with a champagne-like pop, making any occasion feel like a celebration.

also find an easy-to-navigate public transit system and a user-friendly urban environment that feels very livable.

Rennes' University 1 (sciences) and University 2 (arts) are the two important axes of higher learning around which the city's student life revolves. These institutions are the main employers in Rennes, too. Outside the city, car-manufacturing plants and animal-agricultural factories employ thousands of Rennois. After Paris and Île-de-France, Brittany (and its capital) is the second most touristed region in France, which brings money into the community and adds to the cosmopolitan feel. It's not hard to see what people are coming in droves for: Between the tidy, attractive, walkable city center and the great green outdoors beyond the city limits, there's a bit of something for everyone.

© MARY MARGARET CHAPPELL

All manner of edibles can be found in Rennes's covered markets.

Rennes is the 10th-largest city in France, which is to say it's not really all that big, and that's a huge part of its appeal. You can get to know your neighbors here, though be warned: They often head to Paris and elsewhere once their education is out of the way. You'll also learn to invest in a lifestyle that's heavy on urban pleasures (markets, restaurants, art) and light on the bad stuff (Rennes has lower-than-the-national-average crime rates).

The city's primary drawback is that supermarkets are hard to come by; most are on the outskirts of the city center, though there is one giant Carrefour in the middle of town. The dearth of *hypermarchés* makes getting acquainted with the many daily (except Mondays) outdoor markets and covered *halles* mandatory.

WHERE TO LIVE

The city is carved into nearly a dozen different districts, some of which are popular with students, others with families, and others with the *bobo* ("bourgeois bohemian," the yuppies of France) population.

Villejean-Université and Pontchaillou

In the northwest quartiers of Villejean-Université and Pontchaillou, students will find easy access to student-oriented activities and amenities: *bibliothèques* (libraries), municipal swimming pools, a fully equipped sporting complex, a research hospital, and, of course, a university campus (University of Rennes 2). This area is undergoing a long-term urban-renewal overhaul that includes the creation of new apartment communities, expansion of transportation services, and the development of commercial zones. If you want room to breathe in a place that melds modernity and a young sensibility, the northwest is worth considering.

This quartier is more of a renter's zone than a buyer's oasis. When an apartment hits the market, it's often small, cheap (think €40,000 studios) and geared toward the student population. Renting here will yield better housing

TONGUE-TIED

Language is an important component of every culture, and it's no different in Brittany. The ancient local language, Breton, is alive and well here, as evidenced by road signs, regional television and radio (more than 10 shows are broadcast in Breton), and particularly in the streets, where 200,000 people speak the language fluently.

Breton's roots are Celtic. Looking at a map, you can see how proximity shaped the local tongue: Breizh (Brittany) sits just beneath western England, and in the 7th century, thousands of Britons – especially from Cornwall – migrated south across the sea to settle in France, bringing their language and customs with them.

At the turn of the 20th century, Breton was banned from schools and French was officially positioned as the dominant language by constitutional decree. Half a century later, the laws relaxed a little, allowing Breton culture and language to be taught once again in public schools and spawning the development of private language institutions throughout the region.

You won't need to understand Breton to get by in Brittany – by law, public signs must be written in both French and Breton – but still, it can't hurt to learn two important words imbued with deep cultural significance: *krampouez* (crêpe) and *chistr* (cider).

© MARY MARGARET CHAPPELL

Street signs throughout Brittany are written in both Breton and French.

options. An open, airy studio apartment within walking distance of campus costs €400; a bright and cheerful, 60-square-meter, two-bedroom apartment could be yours for €550 per month.

Sacré Coeur and Ste. Thérèse

Directly south of the city center, just beyond the *gare,* you'll find the quartiers of Sacré Coeur and Ste. Thérèse, both of which are highly sought-after neighborhoods for people with a little more money to spend on accommodations. Here, single-family houses hide behind green exteriors, sheltering little gardens that make coming home feel like you've entered an urban retreat. Rue des Omeaux is the hot place to buy right now, and the price tags match the demand. Expect to pay around €2,800 per square meter for a house here, half that to invest in an apartment. If you want to (or must) go the economical route, become a *locataire* (renter) and expect to fork out approximately €550 per month for a 40-square-meter apartment.

Thabor and Jeanne d'Arc

To the northwest of the city, you'll find the neighborhoods designated *"populaire,"* which is to say that yes, they are popular, but also in that other sense of the word: populous. In France, the descriptor *populaire* usually indicates a thicker population density and is often code for "ethnically diverse." In the local vernacular, this isn't always a positive connotation, but it's not derogatory in the case of Rennes. The neighborhoods of Thabor and Jeanne d'Arc are a mélange of students (University of Rennes 1 is here, too), immigrants from North Africa and elsewhere, and the working-class locals who staff factories around the city. You'll see lots of newish (1990s) construction here and find the cost of accommodation to be lower than elsewhere in the city. Buying a single-family house is also a possibility, especially in the Thabor neighborhood. Budget around €50,000 for a small but livable (for one or two) apartment here; a more spacious two-bedroom with a fireplace and a bit of old-world charm will cost about €175,000. Those coveted single-family dwellings tend to run large—upward of 150 square meters—and are priced accordingly. For €700,000, you could buy yourself enough space to raise all six of your children in their own rooms.

GETTING AROUND
Bus and Métro

Even though Rennes is a walkable city with well-maintained *trottoirs* (sidewalks) and a compact city center, the Métro and bus system, known as Star, comes in handy when you need to traverse the city quickly. Tickets cost €1.20 and are valid for unlimited journeys within an hour of validation. *Carnets* of 10 tickets cost €11.10, and with a rechargeable KorriGo card, you can choose from a generous handful of travel *formules*. Students, seniors, and *invalides* receive discounts as high as 80 percent, so it's worth exploring the Star website (www.star.fr) to peruse your options. Tickets can be purchased from bus conductors, at kiosks in Métro stations, or at business marked with a blue sign reading "Star Pointe de Vente." As you access the Métro, you'll pass small, yellow validation machines; it's imperative that you validate your ticket before entering by inserting it into the small reader. Otherwise, the transit authorities standing sentinel over the exit at your stop will slap you with a fine.

Bicycle

The royal-blue public VéloStar bicycles are available at 83 stations around the city, and they work the same way all the other bike-share programs do: by short- or long-term *abonnement*. As always, the first half-hour is free, and if you have a rechargeable KarriGo pass, you can use it to access these bikes 24/7, too. You'll find bikes outside the main *gare*, most Métro stations, and at other popular hubs around Rennes and its suburbs.

Train

The glass-paneled, *très* modern main train station, la Gare de Rennes, is on the south side of the city center, where it's connected to the Métro and several

© MARY MARGARET CHAPPELL

Rennes's public bike-share program makes it easy to get around.

bus lines. The *guichet* (ticket office) is open Monday through Thursday from 5:40 A.M. to 9:05 P.M. (9:15 P.M. on Fridays), with slightly reduced hours on the weekends. From here, you can take the TGV or regional trains to destinations across France and northern Europe. To get to the compact Rennes airport situated 10 kilometers southwest, take bus number 57, which runs to and from the République stop near the *mairie* every 10 to 30 minutes, seven days a week. It'll drop you off at the St. Jacques de la Lande stop, 300 meters or a five-minute walk to the airport.

Vannes

If Vannes were a North American city, it would be Hyannis, Massachusetts (on Cape Cod); or maybe Providence, Rhode Island; or Halifax, Nova Scotia, only without the skyscrapers. Clean, compact, and pretty in a seafaring way, Vannes is surrounded by a lovely body of water bobbing with sailboats and seagulls. With a population of 55,000, this little refuge from France's big-city hubbub has a definite charm. Maybe it's the cute harbor that brings the sea practically to the center of town, or the half-timbered houses pitched at odd angles and painted in candy colors. Whatever it is, you'll get a sense of it as soon as you arrive here. Life in Vannes feels manageable; traffic congestion is nil, drivers

© ELENA ELISSEEVA/123RF.COM

half-timbered houses in Vannes

Having the Golfe du Morbihan at your back door is one of the best reasons to live in Vannes.

stop for pedestrians at crosswalks, and the old town isn't so labyrinthine that you'll get lost trying to find the *boulangerie*. Come for a visit, sit down for a meal of the local specialty—a buckwheat *galette* with a *bolée* of cider—peruse the "À Louer" ads, and prepare yourself for a shock: Studios for €280? One-bedrooms for €350? Rental accommodations fall on the right side of affordable here, and with the Golfe du Morbihan staring you right in the face, just watch as Vannes' allure increases the deeper you dig into the classifieds.

THE LAY OF THE LAND

With 2,000 years of history and a fortified castle at its core, Vannes stares down at the sea from a thicket of medieval half-timbered townhouses that hem the old cobblestoned streets. This town is small, but you won't find it lacking in much—beyond the theater, cinema, and cafés, tucked in and among the pedestrian-friendly streets, there's even a Monoprix to fool you into thinking you're in a more populous metropolis. But no: This bright, orderly little town with a University of Bretagne-Sud (UBS) campus right in the *centre ville,* a wealth of restaurants and shops, daily markets, and outgoing neighbors—packs the best of France into 71 hectares.

The town, in the *departement* of Morbihan, has its own *gare* a 10-minute walk from the *centre ville,* which offers daily trains to Paris and beyond. To the south of the city, accessible by road, paved bike trail, or pebbly walking path, is the Golfe du Morbihan. As you look out to sea, series of small islands come into focus, beckoning you to pay a visit. This is entirely possible by either ferry or private boat, giving you access to campgrounds, castles, dolmens, and mega-liths, all of which are worth building a weekend getaway around. Footpaths for exploring the beautiful countryside abound, and you'll discover unexpected amenities, like cafés, hidden among the seaside greenery. North of the city lies the N165, a small highway that skirts the southern coast, connecting you with the many picturesque villages (including nearby Arradon and Carnac) that make this corner of the country a tourist mecca year-round. The city government oversees and administers the Rives du Vincin, a coastal nature preserve that attracts more than 12,000 visitors each month. They come to walk the groomed footpaths, amble over the rocky seashore, and explore the tidepools dotting the shore. Bird-watching is a popular pastime, too, and the nearby bird-protection zones are a feast for eyes, especially when aided by binoculars.

If you really must leave this little oasis by the sea, Nantes and Rennes are both an hour away by train, and Paris is reachable in three hours by train or in four hours by toll highway. From Vannes, you can also easily access the Loire Valley and its beautiful châteaux, as well as Normandy, with its D-Day beaches and pretty seaside villages.

DAILY LIFE

Even though it is home to a university, hotel-industry training school, and several *lycées, collèges,* and elementary-level *écoles,* Vannes doesn't possess the overtly youthful vibe of nearby Rennes. There are certainly young people to be found here, but the city center isn't teeming with them. You will notice the local population spans the age spectrum, and that there seems to be a healthy gay and lesbian community, but there's not a lot of cultural diversity here. (It does exist within Brittany, but not so much in Vannes.) What is most palpable is the influence of the Breton culture, which has Celtic roots and is proudly distinct from French culture. Road signs and street signs generally display both the French and Breton languages, and the number of shops vending Breton-specific products (salt, biscuits, edible seaweed) exhibit a pride in these locally produced, culturally significant goods.

Considering its proximity to the sea, it's not a shocker that Vannes' economy relies on this strategic location to provide locals with their livelihoods. Some of the world's top boating-industry design teams and builders are here—you'll see their headquarters clustered in modern low-rise office complexes along the waterway leading to the bay as you go for your morning jog. Fishing, sea-salt harvesting, and sea-vegetable harvesting also provide jobs within the community. Tourism is another major employer, and the service industry is a reliable source of jobs as well.

© ALAIN VIRNOT

The pace in Vannes is a bit more relaxed than in Rennes.

Like Rennes, Vannes isn't exactly brimming over with supermarkets, but all your fresh produce can be found at the local covered and open-air markets. At the Place des Lices, in the heart of the medieval city, jousting matches used to be a common spectacle—but now locals jockey for fruits and vegetables at the twice weekly (Wednesdays and Saturdays) market. As you meander the old town munching the ripe cherries you just bought at the *marché*, you might notice a selection of empty storefronts that, on the surface, seems to indicate a less-than-thriving economy. But the city's chamber of commerce wants you to launch your business there, so it encourages and enables local startups through several programs that offer financial and other kinds of support to would-be entrepreneurs. If becoming a retail business owner in France is something you've dreamed about, this might be a good place to let your dream set sail.

You might notice that Vannes isn't teeming with English speakers. The rest of Brittany is loaded with Anglophones, but somehow Vannes escaped the English invasion. If you're desperate for a conversation in your native tongue, a day trip to Redon or Josselin, where English Meetups are regularly held, might be in order. Better still, you might consider starting a language-exchange group to give your skills a workout and meet your new neighbors at the same time.

Weatherwise, the sun doesn't shine nearly as often here as it does in Nice, but Vannes still gets 2,000 hours of sunshine each year and counts itself among the few French regions with a true temperate climate, meaning it's never extremely hot or cold (though it did dip down to -11 degrees Celcius in 1963!). Summers are particularly glorious, when the afternoon warmth is tempered by cool sea breezes.

When the weather turns gray and drizzly, indoor entertainment options begin to look appealing, and there's plenty to choose from. The local *mediathèque*, in addition to providing the community with reading material, music, and DVDs, also serves as a center for cultural events, including book readings and live performances of the literary variety. At the Anne de Bretagne theater, invest in a membership to take advantage of year-round performances ranging from classical music to modern dance. A six-show *abonnement* (subscription) costs €91. When the weather becomes bright once again, not-to-be-missed outdoor events include an annual book festival, a jazz festival, and numerous art festivals.

WHERE TO LIVE

It's no secret among would-be home buyers in France that older homes are less expensive than new construction. New homes are more energy efficient, and in a country where electricity rates border on astronomical, this really means something. Herein lies the conundrum for the house hunter: Buy an affordable-right-now oldie or a newly constructed, affordable-over-the-long-term place? In Vannes, the choices seem limited to these two option, and nearly all the new buildings in town are houses (versus the older apartments).

Centre Ville

In the *centre ville,* finding a charming apartment with *colombages* will take some work. A better bet would be to settle for something newer—say, constructed within the last 200 years. Limiting your options to "modern" living opens up the possibility for more space, more light, and more energy efficiency. In the **St. Patern** district, a five-minute walk to the *gare* in one direction and five minutes to the medieval center going the opposite way, you could buy yourself an authentic 19th-century, two-bedroom apartment with southern exposure for less than €100,000. Renting that same apartment will cost you approximately €500 per month.

Vannes Ouest

In Vannes Ouest, modern apartment complexes—many constructed within the past five years—offer a bevy of living options for those who want more space and more modernity than the city center offers. Some of these places barely register on the appeal chart, but if it's both indoor and outdoor space you're after, this is your neighborhood. A 100-square-meter house with a spacious yard will cost around €300,000, while an apartment of the same size can be rented for €600 per month.

Tohannic

On the other side of town, near the university district, the Tohannic quartier is another option for accommodations near enough to the city center to be utterly convenient but far enough away so you don't feel claustrophobic in peak tourist season. The modern look of the apartment complexes here aren't to everyone's taste, but for students, proximity to the university and the lower prices hold a lot of appeal. A two-bedroom apartment with wood floors and a little balcony in a verdant, 12-unit complex costs €160,000. To rent, you'll need to budget approximately about €400 for a contemporary one-bedroom place with a balcony and parking.

GETTING AROUND

Vannes doesn't have a Métro, but it does have Vélocéa, a solar-powered public bike-share system that makes it easy to access the area's 50 kilometers of cycling paths with a daily, weekly, monthly, or annual membership. To travel greater distances, you'll want to familiarize yourself with TPV, the 10-line bus system. A mini-*carnet* of four voyages costs €4.40, and the standard 10-ticket *carnet* costs €9.80. Tickets are good for an hour's worth of travel after validation in a *composteur*. Monthly and annual Tango passes cost €33 and €330, respectively. Discounted Saxo (student) and Symphone (senior) passes are also available. If you foresee traveling regularly on the train, you'll want to investigate the Uzuël+ pass, which offers steep discounts (75 percent off) to those who travel regularly throughout Brittany by train.

PRIME LIVING LOCATIONS

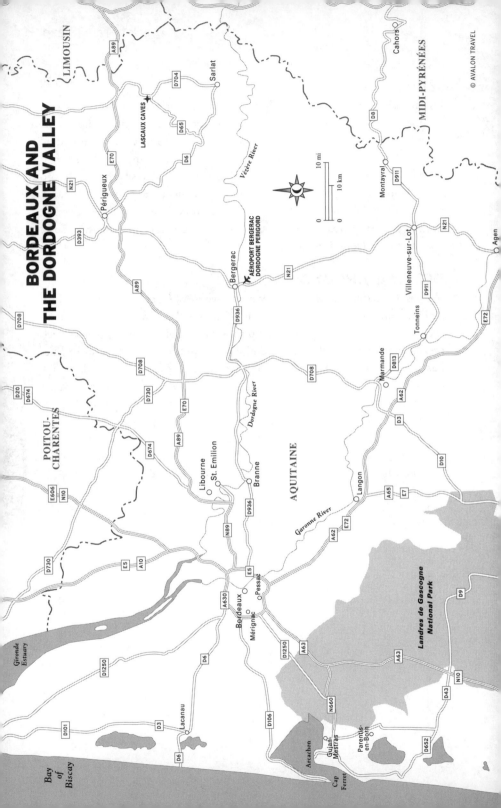

BORDEAUX AND THE DORDOGNE VALLEY

© AVALON TRAVEL

LIMOUSIN

MIDI-PYRÉNÉES

POITOU-CHARENTES

AQUITAINE

Landres de Gascogne National Park

Bay of Biscay

Gironde Estuary

Cahors

Sarlat

LASCAUX CAVES

Périgueux

Montayral

Villeneuve-sur-Lot

Agen

Bergerac

AÉROPORT BERGERAC DORDOGNE PÉRIGORD

Tonneins

Marmande

Libourne

St. Emilion

Branne

Langon

Bordeaux

Pessac

Mérignac

Lacanau

Arcachon

Gujan-Mestras

Cap Ferret

Parentis-en-Born

Vézère River

Dordogne River

Garonne River

10 mi

10 km

BORDEAUX AND THE DORDOGNE VALLEY

Perfectly positioned between the picturesque Atlantic coast and the rolling green hills of France's most renowned wine-growing region, Bordeaux has a lot to offer expats in terms of leisure activities—but there's more to this area than just fun in the sun with a glass of St. Emilion in hand. With seven universities, an international airport, and a revamped waterfront area that's attracting new businesses, Bordeaux feels young, hip, and alive in every language. This city also has proximity going for it: Just 80 kilometers east—an easy one-hour train ride away—sits Bergerac, a sweet old city with a 21st-century sensibility. The population of 27,000 feels about right, and you'll find all the cultural amenities—movie theaters, restaurants, museums—and an unintimidating small-town feel. Another hour east by train or car is the charming medieval village of Sarlat. Smaller than Bergerac, with a hint over 10,000 inhabitants, this little oasis smack in the middle of Dordogne castle country has old-world charm and modern-day functionality. This region is particularly well suited to

© JENNIFER PICKENS/BLACKBIRDPHOTO.COM

gastronomes who care about such things as fine wine, traditional cuisine (foie gras and truffles are big business around here), and the natural beauty of a riverine environment. The region has long held special appeal to the Brits, lured by cheap flights between the UK and the local airport in Bergerac, affordable land and housing, and abundant entrepreneurial opportunities. Thinking of opening a bed-and-breakfast? Great idea! Ditto for anything related to the seasonal tourist industry. But think year-round when you're hatching your business plan—tourism slows to a trickle in the wintertime.

Bordeaux

For more than 500 years, Bordeaux has been a magnet for foreign-born émigrés. In the late 15th century, Marranos—Jews who were forced to convert to Christianity but retained their culture and religious practice in private—migrated northward after being expelled from Spain and Portugal. They settled here and started businesses, built synagogues (including France's largest), and otherwise assimilated into the local community. Beginning in the 1600s, wine merchants from northern Europe—the Netherlands, England, and Ireland, in particular—came here to export that magic elixir back to their homelands. Maybe it was the climate, the work opportunities, or the potable potion itself, but these immigrant populations stayed and thrived (take one look at the number of Irish pubs, and you'll know this to be true). In another immigration boom in the '50s and '60s, waves of North Africans came by invitation from the French government to staff the automobile factories and take part in the great postwar economic revival, many staying long after the factories closed to open *épiceries* and other small businesses.

Today, the economy has slowed somewhat, but the city's sparkle

© JENNIFER PICKENS/BLACKBIRDPHOTO.COM

Try to find time to wander Bordeaux's interesting back streets.

You'll find halal butchers and Kurdish grocery stores in Bordeaux's quartier Victor Hugo.

hasn't dimmed a bit. Bordeaux is in the throes of an urban rejuvenation that has given it an injection of vitality. You see it when you first arrive at the Gare St. Jean: Step outside, and you'll take in backdrop of old and new buildings, with a brand-spanking-new tram in the foreground. Pile in with a mixed crowd of locals and out-of-town visitors, heading north toward the city center and its bars, restaurants, museums, and pedestrian shopping districts.

Medieval architecture continues to meet modernity along the riverside promenade, where joggers, cyclists, and flaneurs busy themselves along the photo-worthy vista for as far as the eye can see; and modern gardens contrast with the magnificent and massive 18th-century architectural marvel the Palais de la Bourse. With all the architectural glory mixed with contemporary functionality, it's no wonder Bordeaux was designated a UNESCO world heritage site in 2007. Today, this city of 240,000 is coming down from the high of that honorable designation and doing its best to live up to its revamped image as a livable modern are.

Diversity is Bordeaux's middle name, and nowhere is this more evident than in the dining scene. From Spanish tapas to Indian biryanis, Brazilian feijoadas and even savory vegan tarts, there's a culinary destination to fit your craving. Bars—tapas bars, wine bars, and the ubiquitous Irish bars—welcome a hip college crowd and even let the old folks feel OK about hanging out for *un verre* and a morsel or two. Bordeaux has its own special nightlife, and it feels a tad more laid-back than Paris' amped-up version. Relax, sip your elixir of choice, and enjoy the friendly ambience in one of the city's many café-hemmed squares.

You can expect to pay a lot less for more a living space here than you would in Paris: a one-bedroom (*deux-pièces*) a five-minute walk from the train station and a 15-minute walk to the center of town costs about €600 per month. A two-bedroom in the shadow of that gothic looker, Cathédrale Saint-André, will set you back about €900. Looking to buy? In the heart of the city, in the waterfront Chartrons district, one-bedroom flats start at about €130,000. Prices drop as you move out of the city center and away from the three primary tram lines.

THE LAY OF THE LAND

Bordeaux hugs both sides of the Garonne River, which spills out into a brackish estuary before it reaches the windswept Atlantic 100 kilometers northwest. Less than 50 kilometers west as the crow flies, sandy and swimmable beaches await, reachable by car and train. Wine country begins as soon as you reach Bordeaux's eastern border and continues for hundreds of square kilometers to the north, east, and south.

Bordeaux is divided into eight quartiers, each with its own flavor: **Centre,** the administrative heart of the city; **St. Michel,** an up-and-coming residential district not far from the train station; **Bordeaux Maritime,** a giant swath of the city to the far north that encompasses the trendy Chartrons neighborhood; **Grand Parc,** near—you guessed it—the city's largest park; **La Bastide,** a neighborhood in transition from industrial to residential, which sits across the river from the rest of the city; **Victor Hugo,** a lively section with cafés and gay-friendly establishments; and **Caudéron,** north and west of the city center. It's worth spending a day or two wandering each neighborhood to get a reading on what makes it special: Try the cafés, visit the local greengrocer, and, if you're brave enough, talk to the locals about what they like best about their quartier.

DAILY LIFE

Roughly 50 percent of Bordeaux's population is younger than 30, which isn't surprising when you consider there are a dozen universities and other institutions of higher learning in and around the city, and an equal number of primary and secondary schools. Young people have a real stake in this community, and the city has developed programs to ensure that all voices are heard. A recent municipal campaign called "Je Participe" ("I Participate"), encourages civic engagement by soliciting opinions on local campaigns and keeping residents

AOC ABCS

Drink enough French wine, and eventually you'll sip a vintage stamped with the letters AOC: Appellation d'Origine Contrôlée. Simply put, this is a pride-of-place stamp indicating that a wine's grapes were grown in a recognized wine-growing region, and that the elixir itself will bear predictable characteristics unique to that area. AOC wines are held to a regimented set of standards that exceeds the average wine-production criteria, and experienced palates can taste the subtle differences. The AOC standard is also what prevents the erroneous naming of any bubbly wine as "champagne." Being carbonated isn't enough – call it sparkling wine or plain old bubbly, but unless it was produced in the Champagne region of France, it's not champagne.

If you spend enough time at your local *caviste*, you'll notice a trend among AOC wines: They are more expensive than their non-AOC counterparts. In theory, the AOC designation ensures a certain quality – not a "perfect" wine, mind you, but something uniformly and predictably produced – and supports the perpetuation of that national point of pride, *terroir*, which is essentially the flavor that the land lends to a food or drink. The only way to really understand what AOC wines are all about is by tasting them, and these are all good starting points:

Alsace riesling: Riesling grapes are grown in the Rhine River Valley of eastern France, where the soil has a strong clay and limestone component that gives the wine its delicate mineral flavor. Peachy, fruity flavors round out these refreshing wines.

Beaujolais: Fruity and meant to be sipped while young, these wines are produced in Burgundy using the Gamay grape. The new year's vintage makes its debut every November – the exact date is decided by the growers – and festivals celebrating its release take place throughout France.

Châteauneuf-du-Pape: The Beastie Boys mention it in their song "Body Movin'" (from the album *Hello, Nasty*), which might be enough to put you off from this most famous Côtes du Rhône wine, but that would be a mistake. Produced with grapes first cultivated by French popes, this red Provençal wine is worth the spendy price.

abreast of proposed changes that would affect the community, before, during, and after implementation. A recently instituted program called "Fais Ta Ville" solicited the opinions of local youth to discover what changes should be made to make their lives better as Bordelais. They responded, and the city made those changes, including creating an online job board for teens, a public venue where youth could meet to socialize indoors, and activities and events for those young people who don't leave town in August.

For the over-30 segment of the population, life in Bordeaux has the potential to be equally as rich and interesting as it is for the young ones. Besides all the adult pleasures that abound here—especially wine and gastronomy—there are niche opportunities for enjoyment at every turn. Love the outdoors?

Bordeaux is within easy reach of forests, lakes, and the seashore, and there are nearly 1,000 kilometers of bike paths in and around the city. Mountains and rivers with all manner of sporty activities are within easy reach, too, and the Spanish border is just two hours away. The temperate climate resembles that of the San Francisco Bay Area (but with more sunshine and less fog), so year-round outdoor activities are a very real possibility. Whether it's kayaking the Garonne, jogging along the riverside path, or swimming in one of the municipal pools, there's something for everyone. In the culture department, you can choose among film festivals, music festivals, oyster festivals, wine festivals—if you can make a festival out of it, there probably is one in Bordeaux. Can all this fun possibly be part of everyday life? Around here, it can indeed.

Climate

In addition to its UNESCO-designated architecture and rich wine history, Bordeaux has a moderate climate that adds to its overall appeal. It's never too hot nor too cold; snowfall is rare but sunshine is not. Expect rainfall in the summertime, above-freezing days in winter, and a pleasant humidity, thanks to the city's proximity to the Atlantic. Again, if you've spent any time in San Francisco, you'll have an idea of what to expect weather-wise.

Employment

Unemployment in the region hovers around 10 percent, but new jobs are being created (nearly 20,000 each year) and the climate is ripe for entrepreneurship. The Bordelais are a happy, welcoming bunch, and why shouldn't they be? There's a lot to be happy about here, even if you're between jobs. When you do land that new position, odds are that your workplace will be within a 10-kilometer journey of your front door, as is the case for 75 percent of the people who live here.

The prospects look good in Bordeaux for jobs, and that's no accident. A big "Invest in Bordeaux" campaign has put the city on the map as a destination for new industry, and it is currently a national leader in biotechnology (especially R&D), high-tech development, education, and, of course, agriculture—more specifically, viticulture. More than 400 international businesses are located here, a third of them American-owned, which opens up possibilities for work transfers if you're already employed by McKesson, IBM, or Sanofi-Aventis. The international student population is significant, and if you arrive as a student, you'll automatically be granted work privileges; whether you choose to sling beer in a pub, teach English, or invent a cure for cancer is up to you.

Healthcare

Bordeaux wouldn't be such a livable city without top-notch medical facilities. If you ever get sick or require medical attention here, you'll see what really great healthcare looks like. The local public healthcare network has won Best French Hospital awards, and Hôpital Saint-André is celebrated for its cancer-treatment facilities.

Resources

To help Anglophone newcomers ease into life here, groups such as the Bordeaux Women's Club (www.bordeauxwomensclub.com), Association Bordeaux-USA (www.bordeaux-usa.com), and the Bordeaux British Community (www.bordeauxbritish.com) host more potlucks, pub crawls, book clubs, and country-side excursions than you could ever hope to attend.

WHERE TO LIVE

Bordeaux's population is expected to increase by 30,000 between 2010 and 2019. To meet the housing needs of this expanding population, city planners are building 10,000 new units to accommodate them. The city also offers financial aid to first-time homebuyers who want to make Bordeaux their primary place of residence through its Passeport 1er Logement program. (A program that offers tax breaks and other financial incentives to new homeowners is worth investigating wherever you choose to settle.) But before you sign up, get to know a sampling of the city's diverse residential neighborhoods—you'll find a mélange of housing, from single-family dwellings to modern, energy-efficient lofts and everything in between.

Chartrons

Northeast of the city center sits Chartrons, the city's onetime industrial hub, transformed today into a pleasant neighborhood with lots of antiques shops, cafés, and residential housing. For centuries, the wine trade lived and breathed here. Ships from England, Ireland, and the far reaches of Northern Europe would sail up the Garonne, park in the docks, and load up with that locally grown elixir of the gods, *vin,* before setting sail back down the river toward home. The edifices of local buildings are decorated with wine motifs—clusters of grapes, curlicued vines—and locals and visitors alike relish walking around to ogle the architecture. Residents of this quartier have the benefit of being positioned between tramlines B and C and close to several museums, a skate park for kids, and a popular covered market. On Thursdays along the quay, an open-air organic market welcomes shoppers to pick out plums, tomatoes, and grapes.

Laying down roots here is a smart idea. At least 60 percent of the Bordeaux population thinks so: That's the percentage of residents who own their own homes, several points above the national average. In Chartrons, housing prices are slightly higher than in bordering neighborhoods, but then, this is prime Bordeaux. For €300,000, you could buy a spacious, 100-square-meter renovated loft space with views of the water and a palm tree providing shade in your backyard garden. A slightly smaller three-bedroom apartment in a pristine 19th-century building with wood floors and bike parking rents for around €900.

Victor Hugo-St. Michel

Since medieval times, this quartier has housed the bulk of Bordeaux's small specialty businesses. Bordered by the Stade Chaban-Delmas to the west and the Garonne to the east, this neighborhood has a strong Spanish influence that you'll feel in the streets from shops and restaurants, the chatter that fills the air, and the cosmopolitan vibe. Try smoking a hookah in a Moroccan tea salon, sipping mint tea in a Turkish café, and shopping at North African markets. Six days a week, in front of the St. Michel church at the Place de Cantaloup, there's a funky flea market where clothes, books, records, chandeliers, garden tools, and just about anything else you might want is on sale and ready to be bargained for. Surrounded by cafés, this cute square has several eating and drinking spots where you can sit outside and watch the parade of people as you dine on tapas and sip a cool rosé.

Finding a place to settle in this neighborhood is easier than in Chartrons. It's slightly younger and more mixed, but that's bound to change with the gentrification that hits most neighborhoods at some point. Living spaces here are older and haven't been renovated to the same extent as those in Chartrons. This means they're smaller, but the prices are considerably lower. You could rent a light-filled, 40-square-meter one-bedroom apartment for around €450 or buy a similar-size space for around €150,000.

La Bastide

La Bastide could be called the Park Slope, Brooklyn, of Bordeaux, only much less expensive and with a smaller, prettier waterfront view. La Bastide wasn't incorporated into the city of Bordeaux until the 19th century. In its earlier incarnation, this section of town was looked down upon by the inhabitants of the other side of the river; for a long time, it was a factory-clogged quartier with a raucous reputation for shady cabarets and prostitution. Today, the *rive droite* neighborhood is a lot less disorderly and a lot more tame. Newcomers will find La Bastide making a name for itself as a pleasant residential oasis.

Just a 10-minute walk, five-minute bike ride, or two-minute tram trip across the pedestrian- and cycle-friendly Pont de Pierre, this former warehouse neighborhood is now home to cute bistros, little boutiques, and a beautifully landscaped botanical garden full of modern sculpture. For families, La Bastide is a welcoming place with schools for children of every age; the riverside Parc des Berges, with plenty of room for play and family picnics; and enough shops and services to keep you on your side of the river for weeks on end.

If you want a lot of space for not a lot of money, this is the place to launch your search. It's possible to find a three-bedroom 1930s house on a quiet street but close to the tramway and schools for €250,000. And did I mention the backyard? There's room for a swing set and a dog (or two or three). A two-bedroom apartment with a fireplace and balconies will set you back about €650 per month.

GETTING AROUND

A major component of Bordeaux's urban renewal project was the installation of a modern tram system, inaugurated in 2003. The tramway crisscrosses the city from north to south and east to west in three simple lines: A, B, and C. Trains run as early as 4:20 A.M. until as late as 1 A.M., and single tickets can be purchased from manual kiosks at the tram stops and directly from the driver if you have cash. Daily, weekly, and bulk-journey passes called Tickartes can be purchased at automated kiosks, at *tabacs,* or by mail directly from the local transport system, TBC (Tram et Bus de la CUB). A seven-consecutive-day pass will cost you €10.60, the same price as a *carnet* of tickets good for 10 trips. A yearly pass costs €378. Discounted passes are available to job seekers, senior citizens, people age 26 and younger, and *familles nombreuses* (families with multiple children).

A bus system with nearly 90 different lines—connected to the tram system—is another option for getting around. You can travel on the same tickets as you use for the tramline, and the buses go further afield. Transportation maps are available on the TBC website, www.infotbc.com. Don't forget to validate your card when you get on the tram. Like a lot of things in France, the transportation network is run on the honor system, so do the right thing! The penalty for riding ticketless or for not validating your ticket is only €5, but you don't want to have to go there—or pay that—if you don't have to.

If you're feeling spunky, you might want to try out Bordeaux's public bicycle system, V3, with 140 stations positioned near tram and bus stops and at the train station. Like Paris's Vélib,' V3 is both convenient and affordable: It's free for the first half-hour of use, then costs €1 for a day membership.

PRIME LIVING LOCATIONS

Bergerac

Hop on the train at Bordeaux's Gare St. Jean, and €15 and an hour and 15 minutes later, you'll be in Bergerac, a hospitable little town of 20,000 on the banks of the Dordogne River. While not the prettiest town in the Dordogne, Bergerac does have its charm, and because of its wealth of amenities, it has established itself as an important hub in this picturesque and highly touristed river valley.

THE LAY OF THE LAND

Bergerac, the gateway to the beautiful châteaux country of the Dordogne Valley, is surrounded by tobacco farms and vineyards. It straddles two sides of the Dordogne, but the city's heart rests on the north side of the river, where you'll find the train station, *mairie,* tourism office, and oodles of restaurants and cafés. Venturing outside the city limits, you'll find yourself in verdant countryside dotted with lakes, streams, and farmland. In town, there are friendly neighbors and plenty of diversions to keep you occupied all year round.

Hopefully this won't burst any bubbles, but you will definitely *not* be the first Anglophone to make your mark in this corner of France. Expect to find a surprising degree of multiculturalism and cosmopolitanism, but with an alluring small-town feel. Winding little backstreets with half-timbered medieval houses will make you feel like you're wandering around Disneyland France, but the skateboarding teenagers remind you that this is no fantasyland. The

The Cyrano Cinema in Bergerac shows all the latest films.

British invasion that peaked here in the '90s has calmed down quite a bit, though you'll likely hear English spoken in unexpected places, like the tailor shop, on the bus, or in a quiet bistro. The town movie theater is popular but, sadly, plays dubbed versions of English blockbusters more often that it does VOs (*versions originales,* i.e., English-language films) with subtitles. This might be just the impetus you need to get serious about your French lessons once and for all.

Bergerac's twice-weekly (Wednesday and Saturday) outdoor organic markets aren't only for picking up fresh flowers, fruit, vegetables, cheeses, and other edibles, but also for community socializing. It's here that you'll learn who your new neighbors are, what their current preoccupations are, and be caught up on all the local gossip. If your new hometown ever starts feel too small, hop a train to Bordeaux or Toulouse to get your city fix, then return with a newfound appreciation for your little village in the valley.

DAILY LIFE
Climate
Never mind truffles, wine, and natural beauty: The Dordogne Valley's weather is really something to get excited about. One of four distinct seasons rises up to greet you every three months, and each seems nicer than the next. Summers are bright and warm, with breezy afternoons and beautiful sunsets. The occasional thunderstorm brings a cool blast of meteorological excitement to a typically balmy summer day, but they're generally short-lived, blowing in and out before your picnic is completely ruined. Snow isn't common, but frosty winter mornings are. Pack your gloves and your caps; you'll learn to cherish them come January.

Employment
As in any small town, employment opportunities aren't as common here as in the in the big cities. Still, work can be found. There are seasonal jobs in tourism, as well as in agriculture. A job board outside the Centre Information Jeunesse, at Place de la République, has listings for all kinds of employment, and you can visit the center's website for more leads: www.info-jeune.net. Construction workers and skilled laborers in that arena are in luck—that's is one stable area of employment for the entire region. Independent professionals whose office consists of a laptop and a cell phone will be happy to know that Bergerac has a reliable telecommunications system to help you and the rest of the mobile workforce get the job done.

Healthcare

You'll never be too far from a medical professional in Bergerac, whatever your diagnosis—the city has three hospitals and countless dentists, opthamologists, kinesiologists, and ear, nose, and throat specialists. At the Clinique Pasteur in the *centre ville,* surgery is the specialty, particularly orthopedics. For more pedestrian maladies, the public Centre Hospitalier Samuel Pozzi is the place to go. Babies are birthed here, X-rays are administered and examined, and laboratory tests are analyzed. Long-term care is also offered.

Resources

The best resources for expats settling in Bergerac can be found at the *mairie,* where the staff can tell you about home-buying tax breaks and other incentives, provide you with printed information about the city's services, and answer all of your questions about relocating here.

The Dordogne section of French Entrée (www.frenchentree.com) is packed with interesting and informative articles on life in this area, including information on local real estate, putting your kids in local schools, adapting to the region as an Anglophone, and how to find the best local services.

Schools

From sliding-scale *crèches* to private music lessons, all of your children's educational needs will be met in Bergerac. Of the 10 elementary schools, two are private; one of the two *lycées* is also private, as is one of the four *collèges.* Yoga, painting, swimming, and horseback riding are just a few of the other educational possibilities. The one exception here is higher education: To start—or finish—your university degree, you'll have to commute to Bordeaux.

WHERE TO LIVE

One of the nice things about this patch of France is that even in the city center, you can still *tell* you're surrounded by countryside. It's practically guaranteed you won't feel that suffocating "Get me out of here!" panic that some Parisians are prone to after a long workweek. Life in this region has a perpetual vacation feel, partly due to the green and pleasant surroundings, and partly due to all that wine. Settling in the heart of the city rather than in the rather suburban-feeling outskirts frees you of dependence on automobiles—the local bus system and SNCF train can take you all the places you need to go. You become more integrated with your community when you view it on two feet rather than from the inside of your *voiture* (car).

The most quaint and interesting part of town to be the *centre ville,* northwest

Bergerac's pedestrian shopping district turns sleepy in the heart of winter.

of the river. The medieval backstreets lean into each other over quiet pedestrian walkways, and neighbors greet each other with a familiar *"Bonjour!"* on their way to and from the *boulangerie.* You'll learn to appreciate the ancient architecture—the arched doorways, the solid stone edifices, the fountains—and feel at home. If you want to make friends and feel part of a cozy community, restrict your home search to the center of town rather than the outskirts. When you want more breathing room, bring the dog out for a run along the green stretches at the river's edge. Perhaps you'll even take up kayaking and make use of the famous river.

The cost of living in the center of town borders on affordable. For around €500, you could have yourself a roomy two-bedroom apartment perched over a quaint medieval alleyway, close to all amenities. Don't forget, though: You've got to find something to do to *pay* that bargain-basement rent once you're here. If you're in the market to buy, you could have a spacious home with a big backyard and maybe even a swimming pool on the edge of town for around €200,000; for half that price, you could have a three-bedroom apartment in the center. Deciding whether or not you want to depend on a car should factor highly into your house-hunting decision. The bus system is OK here, but it's definitely not the Paris Métro.

GETTING AROUND

The local *gare* (train station) is a 10-minute walk from the *mairie* in the town center. From here, trains running west to Bordeaux depart nearly every hour, with the final train leaving at 7 P.M. Heading east toward Sarlat, trains leave every three hours. Taxis and rental cars can also be hired at the station. Aeroport Bergerac is four kilometers outside of town and offers direct flights to London and Paris. Footloose and car-free? Bergerac has three TransBus lines to get you where you need to go. Tickets cost €1 individually or €6.50 for a *carnet* of 10. Students and underemployed folks get a steep discount, paying just €1.50 for 10 tickets. Weekly, monthly, and annual passes are also available. Single tickets can be purchased on the bus, and you can buy your pass at the tourist office, *mairie,* or youth center.

Sarlat

Sarlat is mobbed with tourists in the summertime, and it's no wonder: This town of 10,000, founded in the 9th century, is charm central. Its earliest community was anchored to the Benedictine monastery, but populations dwindled during the Hundred Years' War, followed by the Black Plague. In the 1960s, Sarlat got a major makeover to bring back its shine after years of neglect, and after 25 years of ongoing structural revamps, the town grew into a major tourist hub.

With 500-year-old cobblestones paving the streets and modern suburban convenience on the periphery, Sarlat has everything you need—plus wine and truffles, a festive Saturday-morning market, and a Thursday afternoon organic market that lures shoppers from kilometers around. In the summertime, the place crawls with tourists who come to ogle the medieval architecture, sit and sip a foamy beer in one of the many quintessentially French cafés erected on the ancient squares, and luxuriate in the heady ambience of this pleasing village. If you live here, you'll find that the tourists are a mixed blessing. On the bad side, it can feel suffocatingly crowded; but on the good side, if you happen to run a tourism-related business, your income can multiply many times over throughout June, July, and August.

THE LAY OF THE LAND

Two hours north of Toulouse and two-and-a-half hours from Bordeaux, Sarlat is well positioned for those who like the feeling of living in a rural small town but like to have big-city conveniences within reach. Just outside town, you'll find yourself surrounded by lots of greenery, full of walking paths suited to every fitness level. The Dordogne River is a good 10-kilometer drive south, and that other picturesque river, the Vézère, is equidistant to the north. The terrain rolls gently in these parts, making it superb cycling territory.

Family-run shops line the streets of Sarlat.

Sarlat is small. *Really* small. There aren't neighborhoods as such, simply "in town" and "outside of town." Living *in* town affords you all the benefits this beautiful part of France has to offer: delicious, locally grown food; arts and entertainment; cafés and shops; and the quintessential outdoor market experience. Why live outside of town when you can hop on your bike and get your nature fix anytime you want it? One of the joys of living here is getting to know your neighbors and involving yourself in civic life, but if Green Acres is what you want, that can be found here, too.

Sarlat's city center is compact and oh-so-charming. What's not to love about medieval cobblestone squares hemmed in by umbrella-shaded café chairs, occupied in turn by happy locals sipping an afternoon *bière pression*? The town may be diminutive, but there's a subtle sophistication here, and a friendliness among locals that hasn't been diminished by the swarms of summer tourists who invade each year. The farther you move away from the *centre ville,* the more modern the architecture becomes, losing a bit (but by no means all) of its allure. If you want a slice of vintage, postcard-perfect Sarlat, confine your house hunt to the center of town, moving out if you must—but not too far.

The area north and west of Sarlat is equally beautiful, with castles, adorable restaurants, and touristy little shops wedged in among the more utilitarian butcher shops and *fromageries.* Exploring the rich historical heritage of the surrounding communities is a weekend activity that never turns mundane or boring.

MUSHROOM MADNESS

Every now and again, you hear a cautionary tale: The hapless mushroom gatherer – or was he a stealthy bandit? – in search of the gold nugget of the fungi family, the truffle, meanders a little too far over on property that doesn't belong to him. The next thing he knows, an angry, occasionally firearm-wielding neighbor is standing before him, ready to take it to the next level. (The latest incident, in 2010, resulted in the death of one such truffle hunter.)

The business of truffles and other fancy fungi is big in the southwest of France. Each winter in the Dordogne Valley town of Sarlat, a truffle festival launches the seasonal truffle market, where the "black diamonds" can fetch as much as €1,000 a kilo. The region has its own *trufficulteurs* union, and it depends on truffles and other mushrooms to keep the local economy afloat. Trespassers who've been caught foraging on land that does not belong to them have had to answer to the local authorities – something you definitely don't want to do, whether you're on vacation or living in your new hometown.

If you haven't been frightened away from the idea of hunting for your own wild 'shrooms, follow these rules for drama-free foraging.

Seek permission.
- If you're unsure whom the property where you'd like to forage belongs to, go to the mairie and ask.

Make sure your mushrooms are mature.
- In order to reproduce, fungi have to release their spores, which they can't do if they're picked prematurely.

Pack a knife.
- You'll need it to cut your 'shrooms. (Pulling is not allowed.) Tools other than knives are interdit (forbidden) by the mushroom-hunting rulebook.

Carry a basket.
- Putting your freshly foraged gems in a basket allows the spores to escape and reseed the earth for future generations of fungi.

mushroom tarts

© JENNIFER PICKENS/BLACKBIRDPHOTO.COM

WHERE TO LIVE

If you've come up with the brilliant idea of buying an old stone cottage, fixing it up, and opening a quaint little B&B in this corner of the Dordogne, you wouldn't be the first. That doesn't mean there isn't room for one more, but choosing where you settle should—as always—be done with great care; after all, how can you welcome guests at your abode if they can't find it out there in the countryside? Choosing to live in the center of town opens up the possibility of integrating with the local community, making friends you'll see on a daily basis, and feeling, well, more French. Settling farther afield in this lush and fertile area is tempting; who wouldn't want a place with a big garden, swimming pool, and barbecue for summer grilling? If you decide to chuck village life in favor of Green Acres, you'll need a car, and investing in a bike for short trips to the *boulangerie* isn't a bad idea either.

In Sarlat's historic *centre ville*, properties tend to be a little more expensive than in some neighboring areas, probably because there's only so much to choose from. You'll pay about the same for a four-bedroom home inside the city's old fortified walls as you would for a house with a pool and huge yard in the surrounding countryside. For a two-bedroom apartment, expect to spend about €100,000, and throw in another €50,000 for a house. It's still possible to find fixer-uppers in the €30,000 range, but know what you're getting into before you plunk down your hard-earned cash, or you may end up spending double that to make it livable. If you go the city-center route rather than the more rural one, you'll have excellent renting potential in July and August, when tourist accommodations are at a premium and weekly rents are as high as you'd pay per month the rest of the year. Renters lucky enough to find a long-term rental in the medieval city center can expect to pay €500 per month for a one-bedroom apartment.

GETTING AROUND

If you move to Sarlat, you'll want a bicycle, motorbike, or car to explore the lovely areas outside city limits: Lascaux and its famous prehistoric cave; the Dordogne and Vézère Rivers for swimming, canoeing, and picnicking; nearby castle towns Beynac, La Roque-Gageac, and Domme for cobblestone rambling. If you're a homebody, you can rely on the local bus system to ferry you around. Buses leave from the Place Pasteur and a few other spots in town, heading north toward Perigueax (1 hour) and Souillac (40 minutes) to the west, stopping at towns and hamlets along the way. Tickets cost €2 per trip, €1 for those 25 and younger. You can buy a *carnet* of 10 trips for €14, or opt for the monthly pass for €40.

PRIME LIVING LOCATIONS

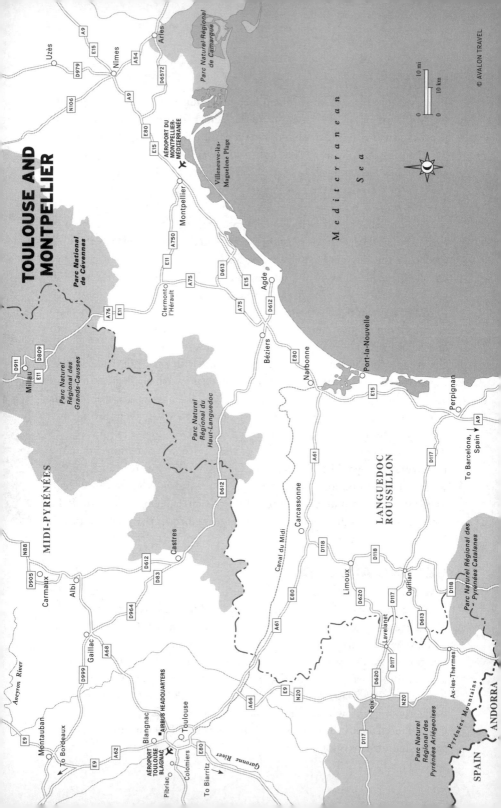

TOULOUSE AND MONTPELLIER

One of the most alluring features of city living in France is the possibility of finding a villagelike community smack in the center of a teeming metropolis. Two urban hubs in the southwest of the country provide opportunities for carving out a life enhanced by good neighbors, fresh food, efficient public transportation, and that small-town-within-a-city feel. On the eastern edge of the Midi-Pyrénées region, in the *département* of Haute-Garonne, Toulouse awaits. Sandwiched between giant expanses of undeveloped wilderness and the craggy peaks of the Pyrénées, this regional capital city boasts a population of nearly 500,000 (a fifth of whom are students at Toulouse's many higher-education institutions) and hosts an enormous expat population. Many of these newer arrivals are employed in the aeronautics industry, especially at Airbus, which has its headquarters just outside the city in the northwest suburb of Blagnac. Weekly language Meetups in town draw droves of Anglophones and their French friends in the high-tech community, plus students and others who like

© JENNIFER PICKENS/BLACKBIRDPHOTO.COM

the international flavor of the group gabfest. If you must live among fellow English speakers, you'll find yourself surrounded and content here.

Cross into the Languedoc-Roussillon region into the *département* of Herault, and inch over in the direction of the Mediterranean, where Montpellier welcomes with its bright, cheerful, youthful energy. This isn't the picture-postcard Mediterranean (the coastline is interrupted by kilometers of brackish ponds and the occasional power plant), but never mind. It's still gorgeous, sunny, and not too hilly, which makes it perfect for rambling, ambling, and exploring. For cyclists, students, and wine aficionados, Montpellier is an ideal base for the short or long term.

Toulouse

Close your eyes. Now open them. Look around, and you'll think that Toulouse could *almost* be Paris. It's not just the socialist mayor, the river that runs through it, or the traffic that the city has in common with the French capital—there's a certain spark in the air here. It feels like things are happening, and that's because they are. Dubbed la Ville Rose (the Pink City) for the rosy hue cast by the unique-to-Toulouse brick used in most of the city's architecture, this is the fastest-growing community in France, with a river of 12,000 new residents flowing into the population each year. Bisected by the Garonne River and dotted with tens of thousands of trees, the area is home to

The beauty of Toulouse is in the details.

several universities and a major airplane manufacturing industry that attracts *beaucoup de* (many) foreigners to Toulouse, giving an already cosmopolitan city a welcoming international flavor. From here, the Mediterranean is a little over over an hour away by car or train, and the ski resorts of the Pyrénées are similarly close. Sun, mild temperatures, and friendly locals invite you to linger, and the lively pace, international community, and work potential make this a viable destination for setting up a life in France.

THE LAY OF THE LAND

Toulouse is flat as a pancake and shaped like a giant vertical rectangle, with the Garonne meandering through its west side and a smaller but historically significant body of water, the Canal du Midi, skirting its eastern edge. Most of the action—museums, hotels, train station, *mairie*—lie on the east side of the river, where you'll also find a cluster of five university campuses. On the west side, accessible by bus, Métro, or bicycle or on foot, the streets are wide and airy, and new housing developments are being built among the old orangey-pink stone buildings. The riverside park, Prairie des Filtres, was once Toulouse's original rugby-playing field, and today you can still toss a ball around and have a picnic *sur l'herbe* (on the grass) on a sizzling summer day.

Point your compass south and sally forth for an hour, and you'll hit the Pyrénées. In the summer, Alpine lakes and hiking trails beckon, and during the winter, the ski train ferries you to the mountains for stress-free snow time. To the southeast of Toulouse, past the splendid medieval castle city of Carcassonne, lies Narbonne, the nearest swimmable Mediterranean beach. To the west, the Atlantic coastal city of Biarritz is reachable by train in four hours and Bordeaux in two, and Paris—590 kilometers to the north—is a six-hour journey.

Andorra, that teeny-tiny principality nestled in the Pyrénées, is a favorite destination of Toulousain shoppers on a budget. Because there's no sales tax or VAT, prices are much lower than in France—much, *much* lower. It's not unusual to see cars with French license plates loading up on a year's worth of toilet paper and canned goods at Andorran supermarkets. Many also make this their electronics- and sports-equipment-buying destination, but it's also possible to take a bus from Toulouse to merely enjoy the scenery and change of pace.

DAILY LIFE

The cosmopolitan feel of Toulouse is due in large part to its international student population and the international community fueling the workforce at the numerous high-tech companies in the area. Biotechnology is big business here, but the aerospace industry is the dominant economic force: In the Midi-Pyrénées region, it employs 140,000 people. Many of Airbus's 16,000 employees are Anglophones from the UK, Canada, and the United States.

The arts play a major part in local culture, and live music is an especially popular form of entertainment. Summer music festivals, including the riverside Rio Loco celebration, draw big crowds outdoors, and year-round you can find indoor musical offerings ranging from punk and flamenco to opera and classical. The city has its own orchestra, and taking in a performance at the Théâtre du Capitole is a rite of passage for every Toulousain.

In spite of the waterways flowing through it, Toulouse can feel a bit

HAVING A BALL IN TOULOUSE

They sound like mythical creatures out of a Harry Potter novel: Scrum-half. Wing. Fly-half. Fullback.

They're creatures, alright, but of the perfectly human variety – though if you've ever seen a game of rugby, you'd swear they were, perhaps, half bovine. The players really are that big. Rugby, that sport revered by he-men (and women) around the globe, is particularly well loved in Toulouse, the undisputed rugby capital of France. The hometown team, Stade Toulousain, has earned many ardent fans, which you'll no doubt discover if you're within proximity of the *stade* (stadium) after any home-game win. Though Toulouse has two stadiums, the home team plays its matches at Stade Ernest Wellon, the smaller of the two, with "just" 19,000 seats. If you decide to brave the crowds and see what a game is all about, it's advisable to bring earplugs – it can get plenty noisy in the observer's trenches)-.

Rugby is different from American football in that it's played on a pitch, not a field. Another major difference between is that those big, beefy fellows playing the game aren't allowed to wear protective gear. When someone gets tackled, the whole team joins in the pileup. This fact alone can be disturbing for first-time viewers. Be prepared for some serious physical pummeling to take place right before your eyes. It can be painful for more than just the players. You've been forewarned.

In rugby, the ball is never thrown forward but rather tossed from side to side between each team's 15 players. (Kicking the ball forward is allowed.) And if a player is tackled while holding the ball, he must release it or risk a penalty. The object of the game, as in football, is the touchdown, which is worth five points. Points are also scored through various kicks – conversion place kicks and drop kicks – and the winning team is the one that has scored the most points when the two 40-minute halves are up.

Not the slightest bit interested in sports or the testosterone-fueled before-and-after parties that erupt around the stadium on match nights? You might want to follow the local season matches in the newspaper anyway, so you know who's playing when, if only to make sure you don't accidentally find yourself in the midst of a winning team's revelry (or, worse, the losing team's ire).

suffocating in the summer. It gets hot, and pollution from the factories dotting the greater suburban area only help thicken the air, which can settle over the city like a brown blanket. Driving less and relying more on public transport is one way to support cleaner air, but there's nothing like a bike ride along the verdant Canal du Midi to make you feel like you're breathing oxygen-rich country air. Because Toulouse is so flat, cycling is an ideal way to get around. The city's popular public bicycle-share program, VélôToulouse—coupled with an expansive network of bike lanes—facilitates two-wheel travel. The Association Vélo Toulouse (AVT) also works to promote cycling in the area by hosting events and group rides, as well as advocating for safer, rideable streets. When the mercury on that thermometer begins its summer ascent, you could hop in a car or on a train and head for the Mediterranean, or you could stay closer to home and become a local at one of Toulouse's eight public swimming pools. Tariffs are low—€2.80 per visit, or you can purchase a discount card of 10 for €22.70-and discounts are given to students.

The locals work hard for a living, but like the rest of their compatriots, they know how to find balance between work and personal life. Weekends are sacrosanct among Toulousains, who congregate at sidewalk cafés for long lunches with family and friends, flock to the scads of cinemas for an afternoon flick, hit one of nearly 20 open-air markets, and wander the cool corridors of the city's many museums.

Like most big cities, Toulouse has its share of homeless people, and here the demographic appears to consist solely of young vagabonds, with their dogs and backpacks and sidewalk drinking. They're harmless, but panhandling can be annoying—still, you can expect those asking for change to be polite about it. Don't feel compelled to hand over your hard-earned cash unless you're really motivated.

WHERE TO LIVE
Centre Ville

This shouldn't come as a surprise, but the *centre ville,* encompassing the Place du Capitole, is the city's most desirable place to live—and therefore its most expensive. It's no wonder: The area boasts beautiful architecture, museums, restaurants, several shopping districts, and the giant, attractive square of la Capitole at its heart. If you're looking for access to the best of city living 24/7, take out your checkbook and prepare to pay considerably more for that privilege than you would in any other quartier. One-bedroom apartments, if you can find them, begin at €700 here, but elsewhere in the city you can get the same space for around €500. Buying a roomy two-bedroom flat with a little

© JENNIFER PICKENS/BLACKBIRDPHOTO.COM

The Capitole quartier is one of Toulouse's most popular places to live.

balcon will cost about €150,000 here. Home prices in Toulouse are lower than the national average. Thought that a studio apartment for €50,000 was a misprint? Not in Toulouse, where one-bedrooms average €85,000 and two-bedroom flats can be had for €115,000. But those prices do tend to inch higher in this hot hood.

St. Pierre

Students tend to congregate in a very specific quartier of Toulouse just to the west of the city center: St. Pierre. Wedged between the Université Toulouse 1 Capitole (UT1) campus and the Garonne River, St. Pierre's streets are crammed with the one thing that seems integral to student life the world over: bars. Nevertheless, this quartier has its own special appeal, with its pedestrian path, strolling lovers, and riverview location. On Thursdays—the unofficial "students-go-out" night—the population swells and the revelers take over with zeal. Moving away from the bars a bit, you can find some charming places to call home within walking distance, bus, or Métro to the *centre ville*. Rental prices are what you might refer to as "student-friendly," ranging from €300 for a flavorless, nothing-special studio to €550 for a 40-square-meter one-bedroom with beamed ceilings and a private courtyard. Buying a similar-size one-bedroom in a modern building (with sliding doors leading onto a balcony big enough for a table and chairs) will cost in the neighborhood of €100,000.

St. Cyprien

A five-minute walk or two-minute bike ride over the *pont* (bridge) St. Pierre will take you to one of Toulouse's newly trendy areas. St. Cyprien used to have an edge to it, with its Arab and Asian markets and multiethnic population, but these days it's looking a lot less up-and-coming and a lot more *bobo* (bourgeois bohemian), as twentysomethings who want to settle down are confronted with the reality of housing costs in the more central districts across the river. This neighborhood has everything the other *côté* has—markets, friendly neighbors, Métro, parks—but with a smaller price tag. It's also one neighborhood where buying a single-family dwelling with a pool is a possibility—it was built in the 1930s, and the interior has been given a full modern makeover. The lovely pool is surrounded by a grassy lawn that will feel magnificent underfoot on a hot summer day. The price tag? €400,000. A three-bedroom, 65-square-meter apartment can be had for €140,000, and renting something similar will cost around €850 per month.

Suburbs

Many expats moving to the area settle in the suburbs, particularly **Blagnac, Colomiers,** and **Pibriac** to the northwest. They are equally pleasant, if a bit staid, and accessible by car or by bus. Housing in Blagnac is most often new and relatively affordable, with three- and four-bedroom villas selling for around €200,000. (They'll come with the suburban perk of front and backyards, too.) A somewhat pedestrian, 21st-century 50-square-meter apartment here rents for €500. To the southwest, over on *l'autre côté* (the other side) of the Aéroport Blagnac-Toulouse, modern Colomiers offers affordable housing, decent public transportation, and a short commute to Toulouse. A big (70-square-meter) two-bedroom apartment lacking in charm but close to amenities rents for about €600, and it might even include access to an enclosed communal swimming pool. If you're in the market to buy, you'll have plenty of options for something roomy—say, four bedrooms for less than €175,000. Pibriac is a bit more expensive: Houses in the four-bedroom range sell for about €300,000 (with pool), and a similar-size rental will run you about €1,200 a month.

The southwest corner of Toulouse, including the Reynerie and Basso Campo districts at the end of Métro Line A, can feel a bit rough around the edges and probably aren't the most welcoming areas on the periphery of the city. For ideas on where to settle, it's worth talking to other local expats to learn from their experiences. Try English in Toulouse's Friday-night gatherings (www.englishintoulouse.com), and visit the Americans in Toulouse International Club (AIT I/C) online guide (www.americansintoulouse.com) for newbies in la Ville Rose.

PRIME LIVING LOCATIONS

GETTING AROUND
Public Transportation

Tisséo, the local transport system, encompasses Toulouse's bus, Métro, and single tramway line, which together can take you deep into the core of suburbia and beyond. The bus, called TAD—short for "Transport à la Demande"—offers 80 different routes that weave through every nook and cranny of the Toulouse *agglomeration* (greater urban area). The two Métro lines are not as far-reaching but ferry travelers to the southwestern *banlieue* quickly. Both Lines A and B operate from 5:15 A.M. to midnight (12:45 A.M. on weekends). A newish tram line leaves the city center and hits 18 stops all the way out to the Airbus headquarters in suburban Blagnac. Ticket costs for bus, Métro, and tram are the same: €1.50 individually and €12.50 for a *carnet* of 10.

On rugby and football match nights at the Stade de Toulouse and Stade Ernest Wallon, special *navettes* (shuttles) whisk sports fans from the closest Métro and bus stops to the arenas for free, and yet another free ride can be had on the electricity-powered city-center *navette*. To get to the Aéroport Toulouse-Blagnac 30 minutes away, a shuttle bus (€5) departs from the *autogare* next to Gare Matabiau every 20 minutes. From the airport, EasyJet and Air France fly to Paris's Orly Airport several times a day.

By Bicycle

VélôToulouse, with 253 stations and nearly 5,000 bicycles, operates like any other public bike system in France, with the exception that you don't have

© JENNIFER PICKENS/BLACKBIRDPHOTO.COM

Bike-friendly Toulouse is also supported by a Métro system.

24-hour access to bikes: The rental cutoff point is 2 A.M. (though you can return them 24 hours a day).

By Train

From Gare SNCF Matabiau in the northwest of town, just across the Canal du Midi, trains depart daily for Paris, Bordeaux, and other points in France and Spain. Station hours are 4:45 A.M. to 12:45 A.M.

Montpellier

Walking the sun-drenched, palm-tree-dotted streets of this vibrant city of 260,000, you almost feel like you're not in France. And you almost aren't—the Spanish border is a little more than an hour's drive down the A9 toll road. You feel the difference in the architecture, with its arched doorways and squared balconies; you smell it in the hint-of-salt air; and you sense it in the relaxed attitude of the local population. Montpellier is a pleasant place to visit, a popular place to study, and vibrant community you can really put down roots in.

Montpellier has also been a center of learning since the 11th century, when it was established as a trading zone for wine, olive oil, and spices. In the 12th century, the first universities opened here, including a medical school and a law school, modern incarnations of which still exist. A student body numbering

© JENNIFER PICKENS/BLACKBIRDPHOTO.COM

Vintage carousels can be found in Montpellier, as well as in most cities throughout France.

70,000 divides itself among Montpellier's four primary university campuses (including one of France's Ivy League-esque *grande écoles*), and lends to the city's youthful, dynamic feel. Forty-three percent of residents here are younger than 30, and that's not a bad thing. You'll always find a musical performance, theater production, or art exhibit featuring the work of these youngsters—and their older siblings (and parents), too.

Another contributing factor to the small-town cosmopolitan air in Montpellier is the presence of IBM and Dell, which both have campuses here. IBM is the single largest private employer in town, with 1,000 locals on the payroll, many of whom are non-French. And even though the wine-growing region east of Bordeaux gets all the attention, Languedoc—and the areas surrounding Montpellier—is not just France's but the world's top wine-producing region. If you've always dreamed of working in viticulture, there's great potential for getting your foot in the door here, though you may have to start from the bottom and work your way up (harvesting grapes, in other words). One of the perks of the grape harvester's job? Yes, of course! Free wine.

THE LAY OF THE LAND

Montpellier sits on a gently rolling swath of terrain 12 kilometers north of the Mediterranean. Flowing through the east of the city is the flood-prone Lez River, which dumps out into the Mediterranean 12 kilometers south of the city. Outside of Montpellier to the northeast and northwest, vineyards stretch across the bright, sunny hills as far as the eye can see. Two hours north of the city via the A75 is the Parc National de Cevennes, an outdoor lover's oasis where you can hike, mountain bike, camp, and otherwise get your nature fix. South of the city, about a 15-minute drive or 45-minute bike ride away, is the Mediterranean. You can swim, sunbathe (sans suit, if you want; there's a nudist beach here), or kite-surf here, and public transportation will carry you if you're not in the mood for cycling. Heading eastward up the coast by train, you can be in Arles in an hour. The former stomping grounds of Van Gogh are also the gateway to the Parc Naturel Regional de Camargue, with its pink flamingos, wild horses, and unique marshland landscape. Head south along the coastline, and within four hours, you could be sipping sangria and eating tapas at a bar in Barcelona.

DAILY LIFE

This city is powered on gray matter. Look around at the number of university campuses, and you can clearly see that intellectual pursuits are the order of the day in Montpellier. A medical school transforms student residents into

SEA TO SHINING SEA: THE CANAL DU MIDI

The idea was relatively straightforward and unquestionably clever: Construct an inland waterway linking the Mediterranean with the Atlantic, and boom! The trip from sea to sea is whittled down to a few days instead of four weeks, plus there are no more pesky pirates to contend with. Well, this simple idea took more than 15 years and the work of many hands and brilliant minds (including Leonardo da Vinci's) to bring to fruition, and today it stands as one of history's brilliant feats of engineering.

The Canal du Midi project, launched during the reign of Louis XIV in 1666, changed the physical, economic, and cultural landscape of the Languedoc region. To dig this 10-meter-wide, 240-kilometer-long canal, thousands of migrant workers were enlisted, with an unprecedented number of women joining their ranks. Contemporary French labor laws that determine fair wages, sick leave, and paid vacation days were born out of this long project.

The canal officially "opened" in 1681, not long after the project's mastermind and chief engineer, Pierre-Paul Riquet, died. Though Riquet never got to see his project's completion, his life and work are celebrated throughout Languedoc with statues, streets named in his honor, and an annual Canal du Midi fête in the city of Beziers.

Designated a UNESCO World Heritage site in 1996, Europe's oldest operating canal still functions as transport waterway for a few barges ferrying goods from the Mediterranean to the Atlantic. More importantly, it has morphed into a tourist zone, welcoming pleasure boaters who cruise from lock to lock in private vessels, stopping along the way to enjoy wineries, castles, and a bit of culture beneath the southern sunshine.

If you don't happen to have your own boat, you can rent one here; or stay overnight at one of the many hotels-on-water; or just enjoy the canal from the shoreline. A path, sometimes paved but often not, skirts its entire length, making it a favorite among cycle tourists and *promeneurs*. Adding to the canal's picturesque allure are 250,000 plane trees that grow in a shady arc over the water. This is postcard-perfect France, that ideal mélange of function and beauty.

healthcare specialists at the area's seven hospitals, which employ more than 8,000 medical and nonmedical staff combined. High-tech business complexes have mushroomed around town in the past couple of decades, attracting a blend of local cyberintelligentsia and techno-savvy expats. Life in Montpellier is many things, but one thing it never is, is dull. Life in Montpellier is many things, but it's never dull.

Adding to the eclectic, exuberant feel of the city is the mixed population of North African, West African, Spanish, and American immigrants. Notably, beginning in the 1960s, thousands of Algerians came to Montpellier to seek asylum during their country's War of Independence. They changed the literal and figurative flavor of the city, bringing in new restaurants, bakeries, and *épiceries,* and a cosmopolitan vitality. To meet the needs of this diverse

Follow rue Maguelone to Place de la Comédie, Montpellier's scenic hub.

population, Montpellier has nightclubs that close at 5:00 A.M. and open-air markets that start business at the same hour; preschools, art schools, and law schools; fine art and street art. Family-friendly and open-minded, Montpellier is livable, lively, and welcoming, and particularly suited to those in pursuit of higher learning.

The French-American Center of Montpellier (www.frenchamericancenter.com) exists in part to help students get settled in France by introducing them to locals, sharing job leads, and inviting newcomers to social events. Getting in touch with the organization after you land can enhance your first impression of the city for the better.

The Anglophone Group of Languedoc-Roussillon, or AGLR (www.anglophone-group-languedoc-roussillon.com), was launched in 2011 by a Canadian and an American with the aim of helping other Anglophone expats integrate and feel welcome. They're also a solid resource for all things related to a move to the Languedoc-Rousillon region.

HOUSING

Brand-new neighborhoods sprout up with regularity, usually featuring the hallmarks of 21st-century French construction: energy-efficient housing, children's recreation areas, and commercial spaces that add value to the livability quotient. By 2015, 20,000 new dwellings will have been constructed throughout the city to accommodate expected growth. Overall, real-estate prices run below the national average in Montpellier, at around €3,000 per square meter. Likewise, renting here is less expensive than many other big cities.

WHERE TO LIVE
Centre Ville

Montpellier is divided into seven primary districts, each with its own personality: hypermodern, utterly ancient, and everything in between. Not surprisingly, the *centre ville,* also called **l'Ecusson,** is where all the main action happens. At the core of this core is the Place de la Comédie, a *promeneur's* paradise embellished with umbrella-shaded terrace cafés, fountains, and a magnificent opera house, Théâtre de la Comédie. Even if you don't have a backyard or a terrace at your *centre* apartment, it's no bother; the square is a communal front yard. Children zip around on razor scooters, cyclists weave in and out of pedestrian traffic, and inline skaters glide by on their way north to the old city. Living here means living in the heart of Montpellier life, and if there's a *manifestation* (demonstration) or a parade, you can't help but hear about it first. This all-access location means you can mosey over to the covered market and fill up your wine bottles at the central vintner, shop for bread and cheese, and enjoy your picnic in the nearby Jardin du Champ de Mars. Anywhere you settle in this prime hub affords you the luxury of mobility and access—a winning combination when you're looking for a place to call home. So what will that home cost? If you can imagine living in a ground-floor, one-bedroom apartment with a small kitchen and a living-room fireplace, you might be able to imagine paying €500 per month for it. Purchasing an apartment of the same size costs just a *tad* more: around €200,000.

Antigone

Butted up against the northeast corner of the Place, just beyond the tourist office, is the Antigone district, a 1970s experiment in architectural modernity that some call a failed endeavor and others an urban redevelopment success. Designed to resemble ancient Greece, the quartier is broad and airy, with good access to public transportation and all the important amenities. A newly constructed, energy-efficient apartment near the giant public swimming pool and grand public library will run about €90,000 for a studio and €200,000 for a one-bedroom. To rent those same dwellings, you'll need to budget €400 and €600, respectively.

Croix d'Argent

Southwest of the city center is a neighborhood that holds a lot of appeal for newcomers: Croix d'Argent. It has a well-worn, lived-in feel and a laid-back attitude that feels homey, and it's within easy reach of the city center (15 minutes by bus or tramway), so you can get the best of the city framed in green. This quartier is family-friendly but it can get a little crowded on match nights; two stadiums are located, so if you haven't learned to love rugby or football yet, this might be the time. Real estate is more affordable in this neck of the woods: Expect to pay around €200,000 for a two-bedroom apartment or approximately €500 to rent a roomy, modern one-bedroom with a balcony.

GETTING AROUND
By Bicycle
The gently rolling landscape is perfect for biking, and the city bike paths—140 kilometers of them in total—make it easy for cyclists to get out of town for a day at the beach, at the vineyard, or in the countryside. If you don't have a bicycle, you can rent one from Vélomagg', which, unlike most of France's public bike-share systems, offers special rates for extended-use bicycles.

By Tram, Bus, or Car
To use the tram and bus systems (trams run every five minutes from 5:00 A.M. to 1:00 A.M., 2:00 A.M. on weekends; buses run roughly 7 A.M.–9:00 P.M.), investing in a monthly or annual pass will save you some serious change. First buy in a rechargeable card, which costs €5; you'll also be charged €3.50 to

Montpellier's tramway is cheery and efficient.

establish your dossier (and you'll need to provide a passport-size photo). Once that's out of the way, you can opt for a 30-trip pass, 31-day pass, or annual pass, for €32.30, €43, or €390, respectively. For job seekers, students, and seniors, special tariffs are available.

For €35 per month, you get an all-access Modulauto pass good for the tramway, Vélomagg', bus, and Montpellier's Modulauto car-share program. With 18 car-rental stations throughout Montpellier, this is a convenient option for those who need the use of a car only every once in a while. For more information, visit www.modulauto.fr.

By Train

Montpellier's St. Roche train station is conveniently located a 10-minute walk from the Place de la Comédie. From here, you can board direct trains to Paris (three-and-a-half hours) and Marseille (two hours), as well as local day-trip destinations such as Nîmes, Carcassonne, and Perpignan. Ticket windows are open from 6:00 A.M. to 9:00 P.M. The nearest airport is the Aéroport de Montpellier-Mediterranée, with flights to Paris, Madrid, Lyon, and Copenhagen. Recently added destinations include Tangiers and Manchester.

PRIME LIVING LOCATIONS

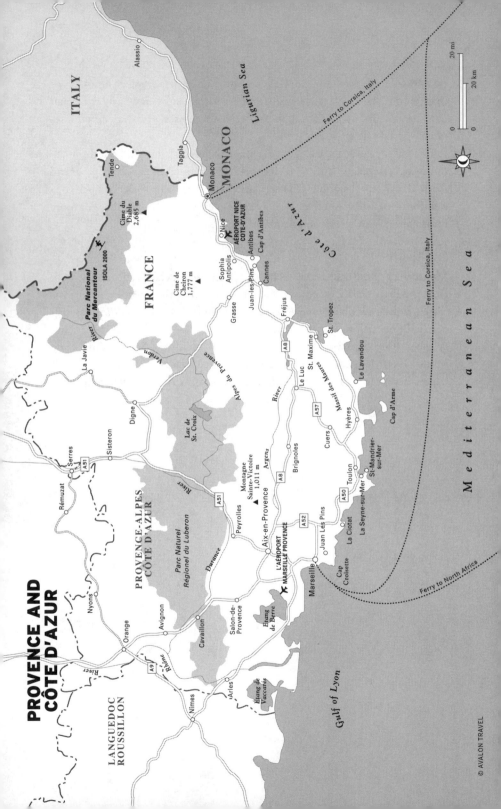

PROVENCE AND CÔTE D'AZUR

In the southeast, you'll find the sun-drenched, lavender-fields-and-olive-groves vision of France that romantics have long dreamed about. This is the land of palm trees and sparkling seas, tanned locals sunning themselves on café terraces with fluffy dogs at their heels, and shaded outdoor markets where women in wide-brimmed hats fill their wicker baskets with the summer's harvest. Living in a year-round vacation spot comes at a price (Oh, the tourists during the summertime! Oh, how overpriced that stone farmhouse is!), but it comes with unbeatable weather, education and employment opportunities, and easy access to southern Europe—so you might very well find Provence and the Côte d'Azur worth the price of admission. If you choose to settle here, expect to live among an eclectic expat mélange of students, retirees, and adventurous sun seekers, as well as a relaxed local population that includes Italians, Spanish, North Africans, and natives of southern France. Everyone is here for a slice of that legendary quality of life that includes breathtaking scenery,

relaxed local attitudes, deliciously unique cuisine, and year-round access to the sea and the mountains.

Those familiar with Paul Cézanne's work will already have a visual sense of Provence's varied geography, composed of craggy mountains, scrubby foot-hills, olive groves, and vineyards that stretch for miles. As the hills tumble to-ward the Mediterranean, the green gives way to definitive signs of civilization that include tourist hotels, oceanfront apartments, and busy harbors bobbing with pleasure boats and massive ferries shuttling passengers back and forth from Corsica, Sicily, and North Africa. A boat ride out to sea to explore the Mediterranean fjords, known as *calanques,* is an ideal way to spend a week-end afternoon. Further east along the water toward Italy, the Côte d'Azur calls out to those who find inspiration in maritime scenery. Henri Matisse, who lived just outside Nice in the early part of the 20th century, worked the captivating beauty of the Riviera onto many of his canvases, bringing the sea, mountains, and palm-tree-fringed hillsides into focus with his muted palette. Even in the dead of winter, the turquoise Mediterranean captivates: Its haunt-ing hue, framed by the snow-capped Alps rising up in the distance, turns the landscape magical.

Aix-en-Provence

Thirty kilometers north of bustling Marseille and a virtual world away sits Aix-en-Provence, better known as the birthplace of Cézanne and the onetime capital of Provence. The Romans first settled here in 125 B.C., building their aqueducts, forums (examples of which can still be found in nearby Arles and Nimes), and public baths over the town's thermal hot springs. Today, a thriv-ing arts community has taken root here, inspiring would-be Van Goghs and Chagalls (both of whom spent time painting in this area) with its rugged vistas and unspoiled natural beauty. In the city center, the ochre-and-sand-colored Provençal architecture is interspersed with buildings that have dis-tinctly Italianate flourishes, and there's no missing the dozens of sculptural hot- and cold-water fountains that bubble up in the many picturesque squares and quiet corners. When the towering plane trees are in full bloom, this city of 135,000 takes on dreamy appearance best appreciated from the vantage point of a seat at an outdoor café.

In 1904, Frédéric Mistral won the Nobel Prize in Literature for capturing the essence of this area and its people in his body of poetry written in the Provençal language. While the regional dialect—a subdialect of Occitan that more closely resembles Italian and Catalan than French—has been in steady decline over the past 100 years, it is still spoken by some here and understood by many more. A local movement to resurrect the language in the public domain via road signs and media has gained strength in recent years.

Today, Aix attracts thousands of international students each year to its many public universities and private art schools (nearly a third of the entire population is made up of students), and, thanks in part to Peter Mayle's bestselling book *A Year in Provence,* the area also draws dreamers who hanker for a simple life spent restoring one of those elusive old affordable stone cottages, growing vegetables, and perhaps becoming a beekeeper or a vintner in the process. Wherever you fit into the spectrum, Aix and the surrounding countryside are guaranteed to cast their balmy Mediterranean spell on you.

THE LAY OF THE LAND

Whether you arrive in the town center by car, train, or bus, you'll know you're in the right place when you spot the town's major fountain, La Rotonde. This round, multitiered beauty is a utilitarian traffic circle and art piece in one, surrounded by pairs of sculpted lions and topped by three female figures representing art, agriculture, and justice. To get your bearings from here, look up to Cours Mirabeau, the wide, plane-tree-hemmed boulevard and pedestrian promenade fringed with pop-up art galleries and outdoor cafés.

Heading north on foot takes you into old Aix, a tangle of pedestrian promenades crammed with boutiques, restaurants, *épiceries,* cafés, churches, and

Cours Mirabeau is as dramatic in winter as it is in spring.

small squares. Here is where you'll find the *mairie,* the main post office, and nearly a dozen fountains. South of Cours Mirabeau sits the Mazarin quartier, the "new" part of the city, designed in the mid-17th century by multitasker Michel Mazarin, who was then the archbishop of Aix. With its magnificently muted *hotels particuliers* (mansions) that once housed Aix's aristocratic population, Mazarin has seen those beautiful buildings carved into multifamily dwellings, boutique hotels, museums, and chichi boutiques. Nearby is the international bookstore Paradoxe, near Place des Quatre Dauphins, where you can peruse ads from people looking for roommates or landlords looking for renters. Several cinemas can also be found here.

As you move further south and west from the *centre ville,* you reach the student district, where university life reigns. Here, housing prices tend to be more affordable, but the charm factor decreases: The lovely Renaissance-era architecture has given way to late-20th-century high-rise apartment complexes. Still, for students and others on a budget, settling here makes a lot of practical sense.

Crossing the ring road that circles Aix brings you to a vast and varied world of the great outdoors. Day trips within a 10-kilometer radius will bring you to rivers, hiking trails, olive oil–tasting rooms, ancient chapels, wineries, and prime bird-watching spots. In springtime, wildflowers in bloom make for eye candy on day hikes, and if you mosey east, you can picnic in the shadow of 3,000-foot Montagne Sainte-Victoire, which presides over Aix from its vantage point just north of the city proper and has featuree prominently in many a painting over the centuries.

DAILY LIFE

In the summer, Aix belongs to the tourists; the rest of the year, you might say it belongs to students. Academia is the axis upon which this community spins, and you sense it at every turn. Bookstores, student cafés, and the students themselves are reminders that this is an important center of learning. If you haven't come here to study or teach, you're probably a high-tech contract worker or maybe a lucky retiree. Whatever the case may be, you'll need a reliable income to live here, because housing costs are higher than the national average—and the cafés seem to be more alluring than the national average, too.

Climate

Wherever you are in Aix, rest assured it'll be sunny and mild, with a year-round average of 17 degrees Celsius (62 degrees Fahrenheit). Winters rarely

ALMOND JOY

You see them at markets all over Provence: *fruits confits* (candied fruits) in a rainbow of colors, looking sweet and luscious and mysterious. What are you supposed to do with them? Many hundreds of years ago, some clever people got the idea to put two of Provence's greatest locally produced flavors – almonds and candied fruit – together to create the sweet regional delicacy known as *calisson*.

Legend has it that *calisson*, an almond-based confection flavored with crystallized melon and topped with a sugary glaze, made its first public appearance at a 15th-century royal wedding banquet held in honor of beloved king Réné d'Anjou to his second wife, Jeanne de Laval. The pair was betrothed in Aix, and the sweet gift was thought to have been bestowed by an Italian guest. Apparently, it was a hit, even though the treat wasn't manufactured locally until the 19th century, when the first *usines* (factories) opened in town.

Aix claims the top position for the most *calisson* artisans in the world: More than a dozen producers are officially registered with the Union Fabricant de Calissons Aix. A traditional Christmastime treat, *calissons* are served at Provençal dessert tables with the 12 other *desserts provençaux de Noël* (nougat, dried fruits, and nuts in their shells among them).

The teardrop shaped treats taste sweet and marzipan-y, and once you bite past the crunchy glazed coating, *calisson* are less crunchy and more moist, with a toothsome texture. One well-known fabricator,

Réné Roy, has developed a semi-sweet, semisalty version in flavors that include basil, ratatouille, and tomato, which earned a coveted prize at the Salon International de l'Alimentation in 2010.

So revered are these local confections that every first Sunday in the month of September, a benediction in their honor is held at Aix's church of St. Jean of Malta to ward off almond blight and to appeal to the heavens for the *calisson*'s continued longevity. You needn't be Catholic nor wait for Christmastime to enjoy it, though. *Calissons* can be found year-round at *confiseries* throughout France.

© JENNIFER PICKENS/BLACKBIRDPHOTO.COM

candied fruit for sale

dip below freezing, and Aix's sheltered position away from the sea means it's protected from that rough mistral winds that whip through this part of the Mediterranean every winter.

Employment

Aix's universities are an obvious channel to explore for jobs here. The robust student body is eager to polish its bilingual proficiency, so marketing yourself as an English-language instructor or tutor could yield some results, if you're motivated to hit the pavement in search of your first clients. Independent-minded techno-whizzes will want to explore all possibilities in Aix's thriving high-tech industry; contract consulting positions are there for the taking if do your homework and start flexing your networking muscles early. Check in with American companies with offices here, blanket the city with your CV, and think creatively. Any business ideas you might be stewing on that are related to tourism have potential to take root and thrive. Contact the Chamber of Commerce (www.ccimp.com) and Invest in Provence (www.investinprovence.com) for support in the creation and development of your brilliant idea.

Healthcare

Healthcare options abound in Aix, making it easy for you to find a hospital or a doctor, dentist, or other medical professional when you need it. The tourist office (www.aixenprovencetourism.com) offers a comprehensive list of health-related services to visitors and residents alike, but when in doubt, call any of these numbers for immediate assistance:

- Emergency medical services: 15

- Police: 17

- Fire Department: 18

Resources

Before you move, join a few expat organizations so you'll have a welcome wagon there to greet you when you arrive. The Anglo-American Group of Provence (www.aagp-provence.com) is an established networking association of 700 expat families who'll show you the ropes and answer your questions, and the Aix-en-Provence Expat Meetup group (www.meetup.com) offers you the chance to catch up with other nonnatives in a casual atmosphere.

Schools

Aix has a higher-than-average concentration of both public and private bilingual and international schools, which can be a burden or a blessing for a parent. Do more choices make the decision about where to enroll your child easier or harder? Joining a parents' group to help you sort out all those niggling questions is a good way to make new friends and be productive in one fell swoop. Try International Parents (www.internationalparents.net) and the English Bubble (www.englishbubble.fr).

WHERE TO LIVE
University Area
Where you choose to settle in Aix depends largely on two things: your budget and your livelihood. If you're a student, lucky you—there's a tremendous selection of student housing here, and landlords love you because they know you won't be staying for more than a year or two. Students on a budget will find the best (read: cheapest) accommodations on the southern periphery of town, where the universities are clustered together. Nearby is the pleasant Parc Jourdan, where you can kick back on a bench and read beneath an shady umbrella of trees or wander among the busts of local dignitaries, including Émile Zola and Frédéric Mistral. A 25-square-meter studio apartment that would fetch €400 to €700 a month in the city center will set you back about €500 here.

City Center
The obvious choice for a heady Aix experience is the city center, and because the town is compact, you'll have access to all cultural and other amenities whether you choose to settle in Old Aix, Mazarin, or Sextius. For old-world charm—and heaping helpings of tourists in the summer months—confine your search to **Old Aix.** Here, you could wake up and stroll the flower market in front of the Hotel de Ville, sit for a leisurely *café* at a café on a square tucked deep in the maze of pedestrian-only streets, then get your hair cut at a modern salon. Further east, in the brand-spanking-new **Sextius-Mirabeau** quartier, you could stare out the window of your modern building (painted in the same sandy hues as the nearby 17th-century townhouses) and see Montagne Saint Victoire. In the evenings, you might play billiards at the local pool hall or head to the local nightclub, and weekends might mean poking around for treasures at a *vide-grenier* (communal garage sale) on Cours Sextius. In the quartier **Mazarin,** you could live the chic life among fountains, bookstores, cinemas, and museums, and have easy access to both the train station and the La Provençal toll road, which will take you to the Mediterranean beaches in no time flat.

If you're hoping to buy a dreamy stone villa with a thicket of bougainvillea, be prepared for a bit of sticker shock; in Aix city limits, private homes are not uncommon (as they are in Paris or Lyon, where nearly everyone lives in an apartment), but they sell for a premium: We're talking €700,000 to more than €1,000,000 for a slice of the Provençal homeowner's pie. Expect a good-size yard for your million euros, likely with a pool plunked in the middle of it. Smaller villas can be found in the €300,000 to €500,000 range, but they go fast, so if you have your heart set on a two-story stone home with periwinkle shutters and room enough for a dog and kids, have that mortgage in order and be prepared to strike a deal *tout de suite* or simply "settle" for a pretty terra-cotta colored apartment in the heart of the city instead.

GETTING AROUND
By Bicycle

Like most livable cities in France, Aix has its own public bike system, called V'hello, which works much the same way Vélib' does in Paris, only on a much smaller scale (V'hello has only 200 bikes at 16 stations). You'll need a *puce* credit card to activate a temporary *abonnement* (membership). Weekly memberships cost €3 and annual memberships cost €25. With a yearly membership, the first half-hour of each rental is free, the second is €0.50, and subsequent hours run €1. Double those prices for weekly memberships.

By Train

The Gare SNCF (ww.aix-marseille-ter.com) at Place Victor Hugo is a leisurely 10-minute walk from La Rotonde. The ticket office opens at 7 A.M., but you can access the automatic ticket machines between 5:30 A.M. and midnight. From here, you can go as far as Pertuis to the north and Marseille to the south; at other stops, you can take connecting trains to get to other stations throughout France. The nearest TGV station, where you can take direct trains to Brussels or Geneva, is a 15-minute bus ride minutes outside of Aix. To get there, take the Line 40 Navette Aix TGV-Aéroport from the *gare routière* (bus station) on Avenue d'Europe. Tickets are €3.70 to the TGV stop, or pay €7.20 to go to Ikea in Vitrolles and €7.80 to get to the airport right outside Marseille. The Navette Aix-Marseille (www.navetteaixmarseille.com) will take you from Aix to Marseille for €5, where you can also connect with high-speed trains. Tickets can be purchased at the *gare routiere,* where you'll also catch your departing bus. Monthly and weekly passes are also available at discounted rates; discounts are also available to students and seniors.

© JENNIFER PICKENS/BLACKBIRDPHOTO.COM

Aix-en-Provence's La Rotonde fountain

By Bus

Aix en bus (www.aixenbus.com), the local bus system, has more than 20 different bus lines to transport you virtually anywhere you need to go in and around Aix, including the suburbs and areas that border on rural (making it convenient for getting to nature areas for day hikes). Most buses run from 6:30 A.M. to 10:30 P.M., with reduced hours on Sundays and holidays. You can either buy a €1 ticket for each leg of your journey from the driver on the bus, or a rechargeable card in advance from the tourist office, kiosks at the Hotel de Ville and Place Joan de Arc, and at many *tabacs*. A *carnet* of 10 tickets costs €7; don't forget to validate your ticket once you enter the bus. Maps and schedules are available at the tourist office.

Car Sharing

Aix also has its own co-*voiturage* program run through the local automobile association, called Auto Club Aix (www.autoclubaix.com). Using the association's online service, you can find cheap (starting at €2) rides to Marseille and elsewhere throughout the region.

Antibes

Wandering around the narrow back-streets of old Antibes, it's not hard to see why Picasso parlayed a week-end getaway here into a two-month painter's retreat. (He later moved to Vallauris, a few miles north of An-tibes, where he raised two children with Françoise Gilot.) The town is quaint in an ancient, seafaring sort of way, with a tiny old town dotted with little restaurants and shops, a pretty harbor and city-center beach, and plenty of cobblestones to sup-port the authentic old-world vibe. The Greeks first settled in Anti-bes—which they dubbed Antipo-lis—way back in 1000 B.C., choos-ing this spot among all the others because of its strategic position, perched on an outcrop of rock that

a narrow backstreet in Antibes

rises out of the Mediterranean and shelters the town's harbor. Today, Antibes is a haven for holidaygoers (the population increases dramatically during the summer) and, thanks to the number of vacationing and expat Brits, it defi-nitely feels more English than Greek (but still more French than English!). This means you'll never be without a lifeline to the Anglophone community, if you really need one.

Though Antibes has a village-y feel about it, its population of 76,000 quali-fies it as a true city, albeit one with a small-town heart. If France without the hustle and bustle is what you're after, and the idea of a know-thy-neighbor community holds appeal, Antibes is worth a gander.

THE LAY OF THE LAND

Antibes sits 695 kilometers southeast of Paris, but it feels like you're a moon ride away from the capital. The sunny seaside town is joined at the hip with Juan-les-Pins, its virtual fraternal twin to the southwest. Whereas Antibes is all cobblestones and history, Juan-les-Pins is a youthful explosion of modernity, complete with nightclubs, bars, and 21st-century architecture. Further south

SOCCA TO ME

The lucky locals on the Côte d'Azur have the *Sarrasins* to thank for their local delicacy, *socca*. At the base of this rich, savory snack is the chickpea, which was brought to Europe from Egypt in the Middle Ages by Arab traders, eventually working its way up through Italy's boot to settle deliciously where the sea meets the southeast corner of France.

Once the working person's breakfast and a menu staple of the poor, *socca* has morphed into a popular street food in Nice, where it is made the traditional way with just four ingredients – chickpea flour, olive oil, salt, and water – blended together to form a batter, then fried on a flat, round griddle. Its final appearance resembles something like a messy crêpe, and the best way to experience it is to visit a restaurant – or several – specializing in *socca*. Ask the nearest Niçois for a recommendation, then sample till your stomach says *"Arrêt!"*

If you're roaming around Vieux Nice (Old Nice), the first place you might happen to stumble upon is Chez Theresa, in the middle of the busy Saturday market on Cours Saleya. Here, a crowd gathers around as the *très maquillagée* (elaborately made-up) proprietress pours the rich batter onto a rustic open griddle, barking out the French equivalent of "Who's eating?" before scraping up a serving or two, plopping it on a sheet of paper, and setting it before you with an overzealous hand.

The salt and pepper shakers taking up residence on each of the 10 or so tables are the only condiments on offer, and they're all the *socca* really needs. Season, then eat with your fingers. The taste is savory, rich, and vaguely custardy – the consistency of the *socca* is crunchy at the thinnest sections and spongy at the thickest. It goes down best with Madame Theresa's €2 plastic cupfuls of rosé.

© JENNIFER PICKENS/BLACKBIRDPHOTO.COM

Made from chickpea flour and olive oil, this simple street food called *socca* is addictive.

PRIME LIVING LOCATIONS

still is Cap d'Antibes, the Beverly Hills East of the Riviera (Cannes is Beverly Hills West). Think yachts, tans, and pretty little beaches with gorgeous views in every direction. If the Cap feels exclusive, that's because it is.

In Antibes proper, you'll orient yourself by finding the tourist office at Place Charles de Gaulle. The heart is positioned in *vieil* Antibes, the old city, with its narrow, crooked pedestrian passageways, *boulangeries,* and brasseries. In the spring, Antibes' appeal skyrockets as balconies, church walls, and public green spaces erupt in a fragrant riot of bright, colorful blooms—jasmine, wisteria, mimosa—changing the look of the town from lovely to over-the-top gorgeous. Adding to this tangible vision of heaven are the beaches, which sit south and east of the city center; Plage de la Gravette, the closest beach to the *centre ville,* is, fortunately, a gorgeous little arc of white sand, though many of the *plages* (beaches) around Antibes are of the stone-pebble sort rather than the desirable sable. If you're moving to Antibes with the thought of summer-evening jogs on the beach with Fido, now's the time to cast those dreams aside. Dogs are not allowed on any Antibes beaches, although the fine for getting caught is only €11, should you decide to take the risk.

To the north and a bit west, across the A8 toll road (also known as La Provençale) is Sophia Antipolis, the Silicon Valley of France. Hewlett-Packard, IBM, Air France, American Express, Honeywell, and France Telecom are just a few of the dozens of big-name businesses that have set up shop here since the area was first developed in the late 1960s. Nearby, there's also a campus of the University of Nice, giving the area an interesting mix of young professionals and students. Heading back south toward Antibes, you'll likely see the giant shopping complex with big-box stores like Conforama (hardware), Darty (electronics), and Carrefour (food and household products), plus car dealerships and, of course, a McDonald's, where the Wi-Fi is always free. Within a two-hour drive of Antibes are a host of interesting destinations, including Cannes, 10 kilometers to the west, where you can hit a nude beach *and* an antiques show in one day. To the north is Mercantour, a national park with day hikes amid colorful wildflowers near alpine lakes, deer, and other wildlife (but be sure to bring binoculars if you want to see golden eagles and marmots). In Monaco, 30 kilometers to the east, you can gamble an afternoon (and a week's wages) away at the casino and ogle the parade of fancy cars driving by. The ski resort of Isola 2000 is reachable in 90 minutes by ski bus, and the €37 round-trip ticket includes the cost of a day lift ticket.

© JENNIFER PICKENS/BLACKBIRDPHOTO.COM

Antibes oozes charm in any season.

DAILY LIFE

Antibes definitely qualifies as a "living the dream" city. It's gorgeous in a bright, sunshiny, Mediterranean way and neither too big nor too small, with a nearly ideal climate, good schools, hospitals, and amenities galore. Your days here might begin with a jog along the sea, then a morning shopping excursion at the *marché* followed by a leisurely *crème* at your favorite café. Next, you might take a Pilates class before you start your afternoon shift as a server on a tourist yacht docked in the harbor. In the evening, after dinner at an organic restaurant in the old city, you'll head home to your modern, roomy apartment with a view of the hills north of the city to see if any new clients have responded to your ad for an English instructor posted at the local English pub. If it's summer, count on this "average" day to take a little longer to get through; you'll be sharing your village with mobs of tourists who'll crowd the market and take your favorite spot at the café. But with that view of the sea, you really can't complain.

Climate

The climate is extremely attractive, with short, wet winters and that fabled Côte d'Azur sunshine that blasts bright 300-plus days of the year. Summers are long—think April to October—and warm enough to allow for continuous outdoor living on your terrace from the beginning of spring straight through to autumn.

Employment

Finding work in and around Antibes probably won't be an epic challenge, provided you speak a bit of French—and, better still, that you have work papers. This area is notorious for its au pair opportunities and its yacht jobs, which run the gamut from cook to server to housekeeper. Tune in to Riviera Radio (106.5) to hear the latest listings on the Crew Review segment, and check the station's website for more up-to-the-minute job openings: office assistant, international project manager, and everything in between (www.rivieraradio.mc). Seasonal employment at cafés and restaurants is another option, but if service-industry work isn't your thing, don't give up. With your high-tech skills, you could land a job at one of those big-name corporations who've set up shop at Sophia Antipolis: Intel, Dell, IBM. Openings are posted at www.sophia-job.fr.

WHERE TO LIVE

One of the many nice things about Antibes is its size: It's small enough to navigate on foot but big enough to support all the amenities you'd want in a town—theater, cinema, museums, restaurants, daily market, and shops. Nearly 80 percent of the homes here are apartments, so wherever you live, whether in the old town or even ritzy Cap d'Antibes, you'll likely have very close neighbors, and with luck, a sea or mountain view to complete the rosy picture.

© JENNIFER PICKENS/BLACKBIRDPHOTO.COM

Searching for a little slice of Antibes to call home is worth the effort.

Antibes Centre

Antibes Centre, which encompasses *vieil* Antibes, is where all the quotidian action takes place. There are cafés, *boulangeries,* schools, doctors' offices, a bus station, and a train station just to the north of the center. From the center, you can access a swimmable beach in five minutes or hop a train or bus to the national parks to the north, Marseille to the west, or Nice to the east. It's pretty, not at all overwhelming, and an obvious choice for those looking for a sense of community on the Riviera. Every day *sauf* (except) Monday is market day in Antibes; vendors and buyers crowd the *marché couvert* on Cours Massena, catercorner to the *mairie*. You'll find the usual foodstuffs, as well as products unique to Provence, including olive-oil soaps and candied fruits. On Saturdays, Place National hosts an antiques market, and during the summer, concerts at the Cathédrale Notre-Dame mean free entertainment for the whole family.

In the center of town, finding a bright studio with a terrace and a communal swimming pool for less than €600 per month is utterly feasible; a similar-size apartment in the old town with a view of the harbor will average approximately €700. Spend a bit more, and you'll get significantly more. For around €1,000, you could get a three-bedroom flat with a terrace, garden, tennis court, and sea views. If you're going to invest in real estate here, expect to spend about €300,000 for a bright and sunny two-bedroom apartment in a modern complex with a pool and views. Apartments on the *rez-de-chaussée* (ground floor) sell for considerably less than their elevated counterparts, but keep in mind that if it's a sea view you're after, you won't find it down there.

Antibes Ouest

Residential Antibes Ouest has a sleepy feel, away from the hubbub of the city center, and hosts a mix of independent *maisons* and the standard apartments in myriad architectural styles, with a distinctly suburban vibe. If you're coming to Antibes with kids and want them to have room to run around, this is your hood. Don't expect to find anything too "quaint" or "charming" in these parts, but count on roomy, functional, late-20th century modernity—quite possibly with a sea view.

Juan-les-Pins

If you've sought out the Riviera so you can sit on a beach and tan yourself silly 300 days a year, you'll likely *not* want to settle in neighboring Juan-les-Pins, where the beaches have been hijacked by hotel chaise longues and giant beach umbrellas (which you too can use—for a fee). However, if you like amazing sunsets, jazz, and gambling, Juan-les-Pins may be just what you're looking for. Pretty 1960s tower apartment complexes will be your likely choice of accommodations; for a sea-view apartment with a terrace in the 75-square-meter range, you can expect to invest around €350,000. Looking to rent? Studios run around €600 per month, one-bedrooms around €800, and two-bedrooms around €1,100.

Cap d'Antibes

The closer you inch toward Cap d'Antibes, the more expensive the real estate and the fewer choices you'll have. The people who call Cap d'Antibes home are the reason the harbor is loaded with yachts—the rocky hillside overlooking the far southern tip of the Cap secrets away luxury villas that only a select few can afford, unless you happen to have an extra €4 million in the bank. Don't have that many zeros on the end of your asking price? Consider a modest, 45-square-meter, one-bedroom apartment facing the sea for €450,000, or about €150,000 more than the beach-view apartments in the areas to the north. Rentals are hard to come by. But if you restrict your search to the equally lovely areas to the north, you can have your beach and swim in it, too.

GETTING AROUND
By Bus

Envibus (www.envibus.fr), the local transport system, holds the title of cheapest transport in the region. Tickets are €1 and valid for three hours. A *carnet* of 10 tickets costs €8, and monthly passes are €22. Seniors ride for a reduced fare. You have the choice of purchasing a rechargeable "sans contact" card or a traditional "magnetique," both of which can be purchased at the *gare routière* in the center of town or at the *mairie*. Buses run from 7 A.M. to 10 P.M., and there are 31 bus routes to choose from. If the bus will be your primary form of transport and you foresee using it at least once a day, the newly unveiled Carte Azur pass (€365) makes a lot of sense. It allows you to ride buses and trams along the coast and inland, as far down the coast as Monaco, and it offers unlimited access on the tramways. Monthly passes cost €45.

By Train

Trains depart the hard-to-miss brick-red Gare d'Antibes at Place Pierre Sémard hourly for Nice, costing an average of €4 euro for the 20-minute journey and between €20 and €30 for the two-hour trip to Marseille's St. Charles station. You can also take direct trains to Paris and Bordeaux from Gare d'Antibes by purchasing tickets directly from station agents (between 5:45 A.M. and 10:30 P.M.), from station kiosks, or online at www.sncf.fr.

By Bicycle

Bike lanes aren't as prolific here as in other French cities, and there is no communal bike system—but getting about on two wheels makes a lot of sense here, since it's not too hilly nor too big. Public works projects to widen streets and create both bike and pedestrian paths are ongoing, but for now, you'll need to pack your sense of adventure (and your helmet) to *faire des courses* (run errands) by bicycle.

By Air

Whether you fly by private jet or EasyJet, you'll be glad to know there's an international airport 13 kilometers north east of Antibes. From the Aéroport Nice-Côte d'Azur, you can fly direct to Sweden, Portugal, or Greece. And if you happen to be flying during the Cannes Film Festival, you can expect to see a French cinema star or two sitting in the departure lounge awaiting a flight back to Paris.

Nice

There's no getting around the cliché: Nice really is nice. What makes France's fifth-largest city so special is that it has the best of big-city living packed into an easy-to-navigate, pretty-to-look-at, midsize *ville*. Adding to Nice's niceness is that marvelous stretch of beach that attracts Speedo-clad swimmers even in

© JENNIFER PICKENS/BLACKBIRDPHOTO.COM

Like baroque guitar? Keep on the lookout for street performers in Nice.

the heart of wintertime. It's hard to suppress a smile here, what with all that sunshine, the belle époque architecture, and the fabulous panorama to keep you cheery. What's more, Nice is within reach for all manner of budgets, from the penny-pinching student set straight through to high-rollin' bigwigs. Once the exclusive domain of wealthy holidaymakers and silver-haired sunbirds, Nice has morphed into an all-ages city with a lively old town, a chic city center, and a not-too-shabby selection of outlying neighborhoods where real-estate prices drop but transportation and amenities are still close at hand.

The Greeks first laid claim to Nice in the 4th century B.C., but a few centuries later, the Romans staked their own claim to the area, building baths, forums, and amphitheaters, remnants of which can still be found around Nice, primarily in the Cimiez quartier to the northeast. The amalgamation of so many influences is part of what makes Nice so vibrant and interesting. While this city isn't quite a center of learning, there are two universities here, one of which has a strong international student population (University of Nice Sophia Antipolis). What it lacks in adult-learning opportunities, it makes up for in weather, access to leisure activities, and a high quality of life. You'll learn a lot just by exploring the city's many museums and visiting the towns and green oases that skirt the region.

THE LAY OF THE LAND

If you're heading into town by car via La Provençale, you'll likely find yourself pulling off the highway in northern Nice and heading south on avenue Jean-Médecin, which bisects the city center. You'll pass the train station on your way in, as well as Basilique Notre-Dame and the commercial center of modern Nice, with its five-story shopping mall and street-level midrange boutiques. Continuing *tout droit* (straight ahead), you slice right through the area's most desirable living spot, the Carré d'Or (Golden Square), ending up at Place Massena, a pedestrian zone separated from Old Nice by boulevard Jean Jaurès, with its sleek tramway and expansive public promenade.

Cross over into the *vieux ville,* a pie-wedge shape of prime real estate where you'll find Nice's nicest outdoor market, groovy after-hours bars, and ethnic and regional restaurants galore. The ambience feels vaguely Italian here—not that odd, considering Nice's proximity to the Italian border and who those early local settlers were. Along the coast to the west is the beautiful promenade des Anglais, with its hotels and high-rise apartment complexes overlooking the spectacular Baie des Anges (Bay of Angels), where a steady parade of in-line skaters, joggers, and cyclists work up a sweat on the multiuse path skirting the seashore.

People swim in the turquoise Mediterranean Sea year-round.

Heading back east along the shore past the old town and around the Colline du Château, which bears the crumbling ruins of an old castle and a park with a view, you'll discover the Port de Nice, a picturesque rectangle of water showcasing some pretty swell little boats. If you continue eastward, you'll eventually hit Monaco, then Italy, with some gorgeous towns perched above the sea in between. Tucked into the northern *collines* (hills) behind Nice are charming medieval villages, as well as nature areas with plentiful hiking and wildlife-viewing. Go a little further still and you'll get to winter-sports country, easily accessible by "ski bus" and car.

DAILY LIFE

After a gray December in Paris, a train ride to Nice is a lot like a twister ride to Oz after wintering in Kansas: bright, full of color, and a joy to look at. The sun shines bright here roughly 300 days a year, which means you can put those full-spectrum lights back in the closet and pull up a beach chair as you activate your vitamin D receptors and send the seasonal blues a-packin.' Bustling and vibrant and much cleaner than Paris, Nice has a lot going for it. The Francophone community is friendly and welcoming—they've seen your type here for centuries—and the English-speaking infrastructure will give you a nearly instant sense of security, knowing others have put down roots here and made it work.

NICE NIÇOISE

Name: Cassandra Tanti
Age: 32
Hometown: Melbourne, Australia
Current city: Nice

Cassandra moved to the Cote d'Azur on a whim after traveling through the area and falling under Nice's spell. As the founder of a local Anglophone magazine, it's her job to share what she loves best about the city. Here, she offers an insider's look at oh-so-nice Nice.

In her own words: "Nice is one of those magical cities that you visit and inevitably want to live there. I've seen it happen many times over the years to travelers just like me. My sister and I were simply passing through Nice on our way to Italy. Five years later, we are still here.

With a career in journalism in Australia and an overwhelming need to stay in my adopted city, I started a tourism-entertainment magazine (www.thatsnicemagazine.com) for English speakers two years ago. My aim was to help people maximize their time in this beautiful part of the world. I, in turn, have experienced many of the wonderful things this city and region have to offer. Here are my top tips for living in Nice:

One of the main reasons why Nice is so captivating is the social attitude of the close-knit English community. Getting a job at or frequenting one of the English-speaking bars is the best way to integrate. The wages are not spectacular in this part of the world, but that is balanced by the fact that you are living in the beautiful French Riviera. Make sure you also take advantage of the fantastic healthcare system by getting a *carte vitale*. Your employer is legally required to do this for you, but many do not.

The most treasured pastime in Nice is coffee or a glass of rosé in the sun, along with long lunches and dinners. My favorite terraces can be found at Place Garibaldi, which captures the sun all day long, and the famous Cours Saleya, which is always bustling with like-minded people. Avoid the Cours Saleya for cuisine, though – wander the

Climate

Because its temperature is regulated by the ocean breezes, Nice doesn't get as blisteringly hot in the summer months as cities sitting further inland do. The average temperatures is 60 degrees Fahrenheit, and 80 is the norm in summer. When a hankering for snow hits, you'll have to travel for it, but not too far; in 90 minutes, you could be zipping up your ski suit and hitting the slopes. Most don't come here for the winter sports, however, unless your idea of "winter sports" includes swimming laps in the Mediterranean.

Employment

Finding work in Nice probably won't be too challenging, provided you're outgoing, speak a spot of French, and aren't put off by the thought of working in a service-industry job. Tourism brings a lot of money into the region, so there streets of the old town and just to the north, where you will find more authentic restaurants that don't just cater to the tourist trade.

Try to speak French. It is easy to survive in Nice on very limited French, but if you really want to understand and enjoy this city, learning the language is vital.

If the summer crowds and annoying pebbles on Nice's public beaches get to be too much, head to one of the private beaches. For around €15, you can laze around on a comfortable sun lounge and enjoy personalized service, easy access to the water, and an umbrella if needed.

While Nice is a fantastic base, there is so much surrounding the city that deserves to be explored, and I'm not talking about Monaco and Cannes. Forty minutes east is St. Jean Cap Ferrat, a breathtaking inlet with spectacular mountain views and crystal-clear waters. To the west are Golfe-Juan and St. Raphael, with many beautiful beaches in between. There are so many perched medieval villages and small townships that also encapsulate the French Riviera lifestyle. It can be easy to never leave Nice, but don't fall into that trap. Make the most of the regular services offered by buses (€1 to anywhere, including the French Alps in winter) and trains (around €5) all along the coast.

Finding an apartment in the summer months can be very difficult. Most people begin their Nice experience in May, so many of the apartments are taken come June and July. The best place to find an apartment is at www.anglohifo .com.

Finally, stay safe. Nice is not a particularly dangerous city, but Anglophones make perfect prey for thieves. Never leave your bags unattended at a restaurant, bar, or especially the beach. If you go to the beach at night, remember that thieves will distract you with conversation while swiping your bag right from under your nose. It's happened to me three times. And always leave your passport and expensive items, like iPods and phones, at home.

are myriad opportunities for tapping into that resource. For yacht-staffing gigs, listen to Riviera Radio; for other jobs of particular appeal to expats, read the *Riviera Reporter* (www.rivierareporter.com) and pick up a copy of *That's Nice* magazine (www.thatsnicemagazine.com) for leads.

Healthcare

If you should fall sick or suffer an injury while you're in Nice, you're likely to fall into good hands at one of the city's five hospitals. Surgical clinics, *maternités,* and private doctor's offices are plentiful, and there's a medical university here: Centre Hospitalier Universitaire de Nice (www.chu-nice. fr) where doctors trained in the latest cutting-edge medical technologies are at your service. In an emergency, dial 15—but do your research before disaster strikes.

Resources

The expatriate scene is varied and sizeable in Nice. English speakers congregate at the usual places—the English pub, yoga classes, the American-themed bar—but they're integrated into the French-speaking community, too, so don't be surprised of the woman serving you at the local juice joint is also from Cincinnati. To up your chances of meeting more people like you and learning from their experiences, find a Meetup, join the English-American library (www.nice-english-library.org), and tap into the local blogging community to begin your networking journey.

Schools

For families with school-age children, Nice is a hospitable scholastic environment outfitted with the standard *maternelles, lycées,* and *colleges,* plus private preparatory schools offering bilingual instruction (Lycée Albert Calmette), an international elementary school (Auber Elementaire), and a primary school equipped to handle physically disabled students (Acacias Maternelle). The sprawling University of Nice Sophia Antipolis is here as well, making it theoretically possible for the whole family to attend school in Nice.

WHERE TO LIVE
Carré d'Or

The city's modern hub has its heart in the desirable Carré d'Or, bordered by Victor Hugo to the north, promenade des Anglais to the south, rue Gubernatis to the east, and rue Congrès to the west. Punctuated by healthy-looking palm trees, these neat and tidy streets beckon with their pretty apartment buildings in Easter-egg hues, some festooned with belle époque flourishes, others simpler in design with blue or green shutters. What they all have in common is their pleasing aesthetics and their desirability. When people talk about moving to Nice, this is what they're talking about. Sea views? Not necessarily, but your

a typical Niçoise apartment building

© JENNIFER PICKENS/BLACKBIRDPHOTO.COM

accommodations are guaranteed to be bright and cheerful, with room to breathe and access to all the usual amenities. To rent a one-bedroom, 40-square-meter apartment in this hood, you'll need to budget about €700 per month; to buy something of a similar size, €250,000 should afford you a few possibilities. Within a 10-minute walk, you can be throwing down you beach towel on Lido Plage or shopping for olives at the open-air market on Cours Saleya, in the old town. A 10-minute tram ride will get you to the Gare Nice-Ville or the Musee d'Art Modern.

Quartier des Musiciens

Just north of the Carre d'Or is the Quartier des Musiciens, a similarly at-tractive neighborhood—think wedding-cake architecture with intricate iron *balcons*—farther from the beach but offering more affordable real estate. Look for vintage one-bedroom apartments with revamped interiors to sell in the €250,000 range. If you prefer to rent before committing, you could easily find something here in the 40-square-meter range with a balcony for €600 per month.

Vieux Nice

In Vieux Nice, the architecture turns moody and dramatic, colorwise; the buildings erupt in reds and oranges, their contrasting turquoise-blue shutters giving the eye a whole lot of stimulus. This is where the young go to socialize, eat, drink, and be merry. The 35-and-up crowd is welcome also, but there is a distinctly youthful atmosphere here, surely encouraged by the copious drink-ing establishments. Amid the baroque churches and modern art galleries are doorways leading to some prime apartment living, if ancient character (stairs instead of an elevator, in other words) is your thing. A roomy one-bedroom with big windows and a balcony can be had for less than €200,000, and a similar rental will run around €650 per month.

Cimiez

If money is no object and high-rise living on the promenade des Anglais holds no appeal, the Cimiez neighborhood might be right up your alley. Perched on a hill northeast of the *gare,* oh-so-close to Nice's Roman ruins and archeol-ogy museum, Cimiez is green, pleasant, and family-friendly. It also sits on a main bus line that will take you to the city center, train station, and beaches. Apartments tend to be a little roomier here, and, as you've been warned, more expensive. For 60 square meters of modern apartment living, plus a balcony with room for a bistro table and two chairs, you'll pay between €900 and €1,000 per month. To buy something to call your own, expect to invest at least €400,000 for a 60-square-meter apartment with views, balconies, an open kitchen, and a communal backyard.

GETTING AROUND
By Bike

Nice can be hilly in spots, which makes its public bicycle system, Vélo Bleu, a challenge for those with less than Olympian athletic abilities. Still, the network of 1,200 bikes spread across 120 stations comes in handy for navigating the seaside promenade, as well as the Carre d'Or and broader city center. To subscribe to the service by the day, week, or year, call tel. 04/30 00 30 01, type in your credit card details, and you're off! Rates are €25 per year, €10 per month, €5 per week, or €1 per day. Like all the other public bike-share systems, Vélo Bleu is free for the first half-hour but begins charging €1–2 for subsequent one-hour increments.

By Tram and Bus

A wonderfully efficient tramway glides around Nice, connecting riders with bus lines in areas the tram doesn't reach, which includes more than 20 cities and towns around the Nice area. A 31-day adult pass good for unlimited travel on trams and buses throughout the Lignes Azur network costs €40, with discounts for students and seniors. Passes are available for purchase at *tabacs* and libraries around the city, and the cards are rechargeable. Whether you're using a temporary ticket or a permanent card, you must validate it on every journey or risk getting slapped with a fine of €30, payable on the spot (it costs even more if you don't have a ticket at all). Slide your ticket into the machine when you enter the bus or tram—or, if it's a card, wave it across the machine until you hear a beep. *Noctambules* (night owls) will be happy to know that the Lignes Azur pass is also valid for transport on the five Noctambus bus lines and one tramline that run after hours, meaning 9:30 P.M. to 1:15 A.M. For a timetable and route, visit www.lignesdazur.com.

To get to the Nice Côte d'Azur Airport, take bus 99, which departs from the main *gare,* and bus 98, from Gare Riquire on the east side of town. Tickets are €4 (not included in the price of your Lignes Azur pass), and buses depart every 20 to 30 minutes, depending on the station.

Parking

Nice's broad-reaching network of buses and trams means relying on a car here is a nonissue, but if you decide to invest in a scooter or automobile, you might want to take advantage of Parcazur, the secure parking zones next to tramlines and bus stops. The Las Planas station is just off the A8 toll road, so you can park and go without having to worry about parking tickets or exorbitant fees. You'll find another Parcazur zone at the Vauban tram stop and another at the Pont-Michel terminus. It's free to park here, but you have to use the local transit system for the privilege.

By Train

There are four SNCF train stations spread across Nice, with the main station being the Gare Nice-Ville. The ticket windows at the *gare* are open from 6:00 A.M. to 9:00 P.M. every day, and tickets can be purchased from automated kiosks during off hours. From here, you can take the 35-minute train to the lovely town of Menton on the Italian border, or plot a five-hour journey to Grenoble (train change required). For more destinations and ideas, scope out the local train network at www.ter-sncf.com.

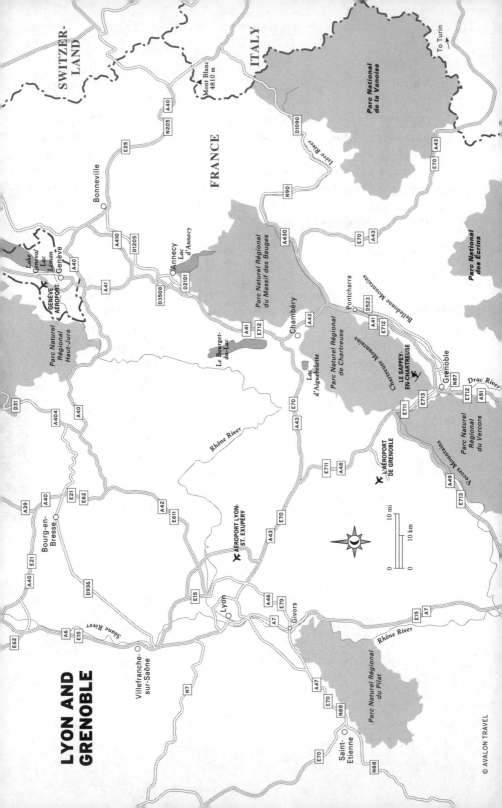

LYON AND GRENOBLE

With the exception of the Alps, eastern France doesn't attract the same kind of attention from the global travel media as its regional neighbors to the west, north, and south. It's true that there's no sparkling sea here, no star-studded film festival, and no Tour Eiffel, but what they do have here they have in spades: the great outdoors. From snow-capped ski slopes to rugged, wildflower-festooned foothills and verdant glacial valleys, southeast France holds particular appeal for athletic types who crave access to nature. Skiing, rock climbing, downhill mountain biking, hiking, river rafting, swimming—all of it and more can be found right here, 365 days a year.

Grenoble is a real winter-sports haven—ski slopes are accessible within 15 minutes of the city center—but outdoor sports aren't the region's only draw. Lyon, France's third-largest city and perhaps one of its prettiest, has long been known as a food lover's paradise. The local specialty? Simple, honest meals prepared with regional ingredients—and *lots* of meat. But the city is cosmopolitan, and even vegans can find something to nosh on here without any fuss.

© JENNIFER PICKENS/BLACKBIRDPHOTO.COM

Roman ruins, perfectly preserved Renaissance-era neighborhoods, and exceptional outdoor terrain keep this swath of l'Hexagone intriguing and inviting, and the recreation possibilities invite the adventurous to stay and explore.

Lyon

The first humans to settle in Lyon were the Romans, who built the city they called Lugdunom on top of Fourvière Hill back in 43 B.C. Today, this city of 500,000 still attracts nonnatives in droves. Thirty-eight percent of the population migrated here from elsewhere, and one out of every two nonnatives comes from outside the Rhône *département* altogether. This says a lot about the city: Its population is diverse, there is opportunity to be found, and Lyon natives are tolerant of newcomers. In the past decade, the city has grown younger, fueled by an increase in the number of students (currently at 60,000), while the over-60 population has dwindled as retirees move away.

For much of the 18th and 19th centuries, Lyon was a manufacturing center for silk and other textiles, but the factories have long closed down, replaced by banks, high-tech office complexes, and schools. Expats tend to gravitate toward the universities here as sources of both education and employment. Lyon also welcomes millions of visitors every year, so the tourism infrastructure lends itself to job creation within that sector. Many tourists come as pilgrims of sorts, to pay a visit and their respects to the many churches, cathedrals, and *basiliques* throughout the city, including the most famous, Basilique Notre-Dame de Fourvière. This city also cares about aesthetics; even Lyon's old slaughterhouse was designed by a famous local architect, Tony Garnier. The structure has since been transformed into Halle Tony Garnier, one of the city's most popular concert halls.

THE LAY OF THE LAND

From the grassy courtyard beside the Basilique Notre-Dame du Fourvière, 300 meters high on an east-facing hillside, unparalleled views of Lyon bring red-tile roofs and the city's two rivers into focus. Beyond the urban limits, rolling hills stretch as far as the eye can see (a few of them dotted with those towering symbols of poor planning and rapid growth, the *cité*). Further still, the Alps and western Europe's highest peak, Mont Blanc, preside over the countryside's many mountains and valleys. Italy and Switzerland are right there, too; Geneva is 160 kilometers due east, and the Italian city of Turin is 230.

Rivers, mountains, and proximity to neighboring European nations make

dancers in Lyon's 17th-century Place Bellecour

Lyon's position particularly strategic. Since the Middle Ages, this regional capital in the heart of the Rhône River Valley has been an important trade hub, and the city continues to thrive as a center of commerce, trade, and industry. Economically, Lyon is robust: Its citizens have larger-than-the-national-average incomes, and the region is number two in France for job creation through international investment. Lyon also embraces new industry, and even has its own Wall Street equivalent and school of economics.

For hundreds of years, Lyon has been an important religious and academic center, and today it draws thousands of international students to its many universities every year. Many come to study but end up staying long past graduation, seduced by the Gallo-Roman architecture; the thriving arts scene, which includes its own opera and theater companies; the world-class cuisine; and the lovely landscape. Some of the loveliest neighborhoods are the oldest—in the St. Jean and St. Paul quartiers, on the west side of the Sôane, the cobblestone alleyways are lined with 17th- and 18th-century *maisons particuliers* that have been transformed into modern storefronts, galleries, restaurants, and neighborhood *épicieries* without losing an ounce of their medieval charm. Hovering overhead is Fourvière Hill, where an ancient Roman amphitheater still welcomes performers onto its thousand-year-old stage.

In the center of town, straddled by the Sôane and the Rhône, the Presqu'ile quartier welcomes strollers and cafégoers to its many picturesque squares, especially Place Bellecour and Place des Terreaux, the city's onetime guillotine

PR ME LIVING LOCATIONS

grounds. Wherever you are in Lyon, groomed streets lined with perfectly mani-cured trees, dotted with tidy parks, and—it must be admitted— embellished by a rather generous graffiti presence, give the city its unique accessibility.

DAILY LIFE

Weekday mornings and evenings on Lyon's Métro resemble Paris's rush hour: Students, office staff, doctors, biotech professionals, bankers, and service in-dustry workers crisscross the city, keeping it civil in the crowded confines of public transport. Like Paris, 480 kilometers to the northwest, Lyon is fast-paced, as you might expect of the country's number-two business capital. Lyon is also a multicultural community—almost 10 percent of its residents are foreign born—with a strong Anglophone presence.

Several Lyon language-exchange groups supplement the French-immersion and university-level language courses available to nonnative French speakers. Anglophones à Lyon, an informal group of friendly twentysomethings, meets once or twice a month over drinks for language and cultural exchange. The group's Facebook page is the best source of meet-up information. The Ameri-can Club of Lyon is a more formal association that hosts many themed events throughout the year, usually tied in with an American national holiday. Its an-nual International Expat Expo is a prime networking zone that's popular with the English-speaking set. For employment opportunities, the website www.francejobs77.com lists English-language or bilingual job openings, mostly in the high-tech sector. For an apartment hunt, Craigslist Lyon has a decent se-lection of housing options in realistic price categories.

On Sundays in Lyon, the only businesses that seem to welcome commerce are the open-air *marchés* and McDonald's—still, you don't have to spend money to enjoy yourself. The Opéra de Lyon regularly hosts free midday concerts, several free museums are open on weekends, and a stroll through one of the city's many parks and plazas reveals sculpture, fountains, and all the gratis people-watching you could want. Wander Lyon's *traboules* (public covered stairways), visit its Roman ruins, or step over the *périphérique* to me-ander the *marché aux puces* along the Canal de Jonage for a no-cost, visually stimulating Sunday experience.

In Lyon, you can expect four very distinct seasons: hot summers; nippy au-tumns; cold, snowy winters; and brisk, colorful springs. During the warmest months, locals flock to the area's 10 public swimming pools or make the 45-minute drive east to Lac d'Aiguebelette, at the foot of the Alps, for swimming, hiking, and relaxing. In wintertime, everybody heads to the mountains; the nearest ski slopes are 90 minutes away by *voiture* (car). If sports aren't your thing,

some of Lyon's riverside habitats

look for plentiful indoor diversions year-round: theater, cinema, dance, museums, and music.

WHERE TO LIVE

Like Paris, Lyon is carved into small administrative districts—nine in total—called arrondissements. However, unlike Paris, the arrondissements seem to be randomly scattered throughout the *ville* in no particular order, rather than spiraling out in a neat and tidy fashion. The first five districts were created by decree in 1852, and they have retained the most historic flavor. Between 1867 and 1964, the remaining four districts were mapped out, giving the city its present-day look of ancient-meets-modern.

3rd Arrondissement

The 3rd arrondissement, especially the quartiers of Villette and Paul Bert, have seen the biggest shift in the past few years in terms of influx of new residents. There's something to be said for this part of town: It's spacious and easy to navigate, it has all the usual amenities and services, and it has one of Lyon's two major *gares* smack in its center. You'll see a noticeable number of aesthetically challenged modern apartment complexes here, but just the right amount of attractive older buildings keep it balanced. There's also a lot of commercial activity in this part of town, including Lyon's biggest shopping mall, and it's within spitting distance of the Université Jean-Moulin campus. The trend has been toward families moving in, rather than singletons and university-student types, and the number of schools, *crèches* (nursery schools), and outdoor play areas for children support the family-friendly atmosphere. Living in a popular neighborhood has its price: You'll pay a few more of your hard-earned euros per month here than you will in the 7th or 4th arrondissements, but finding a space for around €20 per square meter is entirely possible. A light-filled, 70-square-meter two-bedroom flat on kid-friendly Place Ferrandière costs €250,000. A little farther south, closer to the busy boulevard Honoré de Balzac and near all manner of public transportation, an apartment of the same size will cost €200,000.

4th Arrondissement

North of the city, on a hill in the 4th arrondissment, the Croix-Rousse quartier's rough, artsy charm isn't a result only of the graffitied walls. This neighborhood has been home to Lyon's labor force for millennia: first the Romans, who built an amphitheater here; then, in more modern times, the factory workers at the city's silk mills and textile manufacturing plants and the builders of the grand *basilique* across the river. This is a prime spot to live if you want to save money on the gym by walking to and from the bus and Métro stops at the bottom of the hill each day. Croix-Rousse is sandwiched between two pleasant green spaces, and the bars, theaters, and art galleries make leaving the neighborhood on weekends a nonstarter. Housing is in demand here, as it has been for a few hundred years, but when you do find those rare "À Louer" signs, you'll get good value for your money. Roomy one-bedrooms rent for around €650.

6th Arrondissement

The 6th arrondissement is a bit *bobo* (yuppie), but if the words *safe, calm,* and *quiet* strike a chord, then focusing your house hunt around well-to-do **les Brotteaux,** near the pretty Parc Tete de l'Or, will likely yield pleasant results. The atmosphere here is not dissimilar to Paris's 16th—if you've been there, you'll know what to expect here in terms of ambience and amenities. Within a five-minute walk of the park, which you'll come to appreciate on hot summer days for its cooling shade trees and leisure lake, you could find a two-bedroom apartment with a fireplace and skylights for €250,000. A similar apartment on the ground floor will cost about €175,000. To rent, budget about €900 for a two-bedroom, 70-square-meter apartment in a building with bike parking and communal garden space.

7th Arrondissement

For something a bit livelier, the 7th arrondissement, particularly the quartier called **la Guillotiere,** is an interesting possibility. Just across the Rhône from Place Bellecour, la Guillotiere is one of the city's most ethnically diverse neighborhoods, with a strong Jewish, Indian, and Chinese presence. There's a bit of urban scourge here—an SDF (homeless person) here and there, the occasional intoxicated corner-dweller—but if you can handle the blight, the prices are right, especially considering the easy access to the *centre ville.* Rents average about €15 per square meter, which means a 50-square-meter apartment with a new kitchen and a *balcon* will cost you €800 per month. Investing in an apartment of a similar size means spending about €2,700 per square meter; a pretty one-bedroom with a fireplace and oodles of 19th-century charm sells for €150,000.

GETTING AROUND
Public Transportation

Lyon's public transport system, TCL, includes the tramway, Métro, Cristalls trolleybus, and funicular lines that zip passengers up the city's steepest hillsides. Each station, with the exception of Croix-Pacquet on the C Metro line, is handicapped-accessible. Tickets cost €1.60 individually, but you must buy them from a station agent or automated kiosk to get that rate. If you need to board the bus and don't have a ticket, the price of buying one from the conductor increases to €2. As always, buying a *carnet* of 10 tickets is more economical, costing €14. If you plan to use public transport daily, consider investing in a monthly pass for €49.10. Starting at €66 per month, passes are available to everyone that include both local transport and regional train travel on the TER system. Discounts are given to students, seniors, couples buying passes together, and big families. It's worth investigating all the possibilities to see if you're eligible for a discount. Once you've settled on the pass or ticket option, point your compass in the direction of the nearest main Métro station, one of the two train stations, or the *gare routière,* where you'll find ticket agents who can sell you what you need. *Tabacs* and *papateries* are the other possibilities.

In Paris, it's not uncommon to see smokers lighting up as they wait on the platform for their trains, but these infractions are treated seriously in Lyon. Smoking is not advisable here—the fine for lighting up on the train or in a station is €81. Also, traveling without a validated ticket falls under the legal description of "fraud" in Lyon, so don't forget to stick your ticket in the *composteur.* The fines for failing to do so is €5, and you'll be charged €43.50 for riding without a ticket.

Bicycle

Now some good news: The Vélo'v bike-share program allows anyone—even newcomers who haven't opened a bank account or received a French bank card—to use one of the 4,000 spiffy red-and-silver bikes with any credit card, not just those with a *puce*. Hundreds of bike stations are scattered around the city, and the *abonnement* process is pretty straightforward. When renting a bike, you agree to uphold traffic laws and obey the Vélo'v rules, which include not talking on your cell phone while riding, not riding against one-way traffic, and not riding with more than one person per bike.

Train

To leave Lyon by train, you'll likely depart from the Gare PRT-Dieu station, on the right side of the Rhône, or Gare de Perrache, on the south end of Presqu'ile. Both are TGV and SNCF stations. Trains depart daily for Paris, Geneva, Grenoble, and other destinations within France and neighboring countries. To get to Lyon's international Aéroport St. Exupéry, 25 kilometers southeast of the city center, take the Rhône Express trambus from the Part-Dieux station (€13); in 30 minutes, you'll be standing in line at the check-in counter. Trams run every 15 minutes between 6 A.M. and 10 P.M., 365 days a year.

Grenoble

Grenoble has one of those illustrious, richly transformative histories replete with multiple incarnations, from glove-manufacturing town to revolutionary stewpot to winter-sports mecca and high-tech hub. But what really put Grenoble on the modern-day map was the 1968 Winter Olympics. In anticipation of an unprecedented influx of tourists and athletes from around the globe, the city shored up its tourism infrastructure, built new housing, and cleaned up its center, giving Grenoble a bit of well-deserved sparkle. Since then, the city has continued to grow and expand southward, with suburban-looking malls, 21st-century apartment complexes, and *hypermarchés*. Grenoble is a practical town, and the landscape reflects that. It's not fussy or overtly embellished, but rather simple and functional to meet the needs of its citizens.

The pitched roofs and the mountain peaks towering over the landscape will probably give it away: Grenoble is the gateway to the snow country, specifically the Alps. Access to snow sports is as easy and convenient as hopping on a local bus for the 15-minute ride to the nearest resort. In the summer, those same mountains morph into a lollapalooza of a wildflower show, where hiking and mountain biking reign.

Balancing out the ski-bum element is a brainpower contingency. Three University of Grenoble campuses are located here, plus an international graduate

JENNIFER PICKENS/BLACKBIRDPHOTO.COM

Grenoble architecture

school of business, a science research campus (Université Jean Fourier), and several private institutes of higher learning. If life nestled within a community of intellectuals who like to ski on weekends sounds like your cup of tea, you've come to the right place.

Grenoble is neat and tidy but could use a bit of polishing up. Some parts have a well-worn look that might be classified as neglect, and some of the architecture has a definitive Eastern Bloc sensibility. But dig a little deeper, and you'll discover an eclectic community of immigrants, adventurers, outdoor enthusiasts, and left-brain professionals. And if you move here, it helps if you aren't lactose intolerant: *Fromage*—in the form of fondue, raclette, and pizza—seems to play an integral role in most café and restaurant menus.

THE LAY OF THE LAND

Wedged between the Drac and Isère Rivers in a high mountain valley in southeastern France, Grenoble reeks of outdoorsiness in a deliciously invigorating way. Everywhere you look, mountains, trees, and blue sky dominate. To the north are the Chartreuse mountains (the birthplace of that licorice-tasting liqueur); to the south and west, the Vercors; and to the east, the Belledonne, each range resplendent in its own way.

In the *centre ville,* perched above the Isère River, the Bastille fortress looms. Slate-gray ramparts stand 300 meters high against the green hillside , and instead of keeping invading armies out, the Bastille now welcomes hundreds of

FROM MISSISSIPPI TO THE MOUNTAINS

Name: Christina Rebuffet-Broadus
Age: 29
Hometown: Pascagoula, MS
Current city : Grenoble

Christina moved to Grenoble in 2004 and hasn't looked back. A writer, English teacher, and skiing aficionado, this former Mississippian shares her wealth of insider's knowledge about her adopted city in the mountains.

"If there's one thing that sets Grenoble apart from other French cities, it has to be the surroundings. You'll often hear people talk about the *Y grenoblois*. It's not some existential question but a picturesque description of the landscape. The Belledonne, Chartreuse, and Vercors Mountains converge on a Y-shaped valley, and Grenoble spreads over that flat Y – just look at a map!

This means that, although the Alps dominate, the city itself is one of France's flattest, which means that cycling or even Rollerblading to work is a comfortable option. Plus it cuts down on the traffic jams and pollution and is good conditioning for weekend activities. It's surprising how sporty this city is. It seems almost everyone either hikes, bikes, skis, climbs, or runs. Heck, I'm from Mississippi and I've even come to like cross-country skiing, downhill skiing, snowshoeing, and hiking for entire weekends.

But Grenoble isn't all muscle. A hefty science-based industry – the city proudly nicknamed itself "the French Silicon Valley" – means that Grenoble's got more than its fair share of eggheads. And that means good salaries, an active cultural life, and a large expat community. Although French is by far the common language, you'll regularly hear English on the streets. Foreign students flock here and, of course, so do working expatriates. With a trained eye, you'll even learn to spot the expats before they open their mouths.

If I had to sum up the experience, I'd say moving to Grenoble feels a bit like having a safety net. There's all the thrill of changing countries, but if you ever need it, a strong sense of community among the Anglophones means that you have someone to fall back on. Many people are more than willing to share tips on how best to enjoy this great city!"

thousands of visitors each year. Feeling spunky? You could head here instead of the gym, huffing it up the mountain on foot (there are stairs and groomed trails for the fearless), or go the relaxed route and climb into one of *les bubbles,* the cable-line transport pods that shuttle passengers up and down the hill. In either case, magical bird's-eye views of the city await.

To the east of the *centre-ville,* the 21-hectare Parc Mistral resembles a bright-green welcome mat. This is the place to go for Bastille Day fireworks, spring picnics beneath the magnolia trees, and leaf-peeping on a cool autumn afternoon. This is also where you'll find the Stade des Alpes, the go-to venue for local football (soccer) matches. Cultural events include the Nature and Environment Film Festival, tai-chi classes, free concerts, and other festivals.

The city's high-tech hood, Polygone Scientifique, with its nuclear research institute, nanotech research lab, and molecular biology labs, is squeezed between the two rivers to the north and west of the city center, off the A48 leading to Lyon. This *technopole* isn't particularly attractive, looking very much like any contemporary office complex off the freeways of Los Angeles, but it's hard to knock one of the region's biggest employers based on aesthetics alone. More than 10,000 locals are employed here, with many an expat among them.

College campuses are spread throughout the city, including the three University of Grenoble campuses: the art university, the architecture school, and the graduate school of business.

DAILY LIFE

Life in Grenoble is centered on three primary industries: high-tech, academic, and sporting. That's not to say that you couldn't come to Grenoble with the idea of selling homemade soap, freelance writing, or working as a carpenter, but employment opportunities here reveal themselves most often in those three particular genres. Of the dozen or so English-language academies, about half are hiring on a regular basis,

English is widely spoken, and you'll likely hear it in accents that suggest Ireland, England, and the United States. The Anglophone community is strong and thriving: It's not hard to find a cultural event produced by English speakers but geared toward all. An annual Irish film festival, an English-language radio show, an Anglophone knitting bee, English libraries and literary

Prepare to see – and smell – chicken roasting in Grenoble.

ALPINE NETWORKING

Christina Rebuffet-Broadus has eight years of expat life in Grenoble under her belt – plenty of time to suss out all the most valuable resources available to new-to-town Anglophones. These are her recommended contacts:

The Working Women's Network of Grenoble (WWNG): Networking American-style, with help on getting the right professional contacts, developing your skills, or just finding a good hair stylist.

France-États Unis: A group of French and Americans who like to meet for monthly *apéros,* organize outings, and promote friendly Franco-American relations.

Open House: A social group that helps newcomers transition to Grenoble, as well as give them opportunities to meet people, make friends, and participate in interest groups like wine-tasting or book clubs.

GrenobleLife.com: It's like getting into the heads of Grenoble's expats. Many different people contribute to the website, which has articles on everything from what's to love about the city to quirky things about French society to great places to eat. A must for anyone thinking of moving here.

The Bookworm Café: Located in the charmingly gritty old Italian neighborhood, this cozy café has a wide selection of used English books, English newspapers, and a children's area. Plus, according to one English friend, it's the only place in town to get a "cuppa" proper English tea.

events (mostly book readings), and an American-theme restaurant are just a small sampling of the resources that will help you get your fix when the homesickness kicks in.

Perhaps the number-one reason people are drawn to this area is access to outdoor recreation: skiing, mountain biking, hiking, rock climbing. The possibilities for amusing yourself *en plein air* are vastly varied and accessible to all ages. Dozens of ski resorts are within a two-hour drive of Grenoble, and the closest—the family-friendly Le Sappey-en-Chartreuse—is just 15 minutes away. Short-term seasonal jobs at the resorts are plentiful, and students and others with valid work papers will have no trouble finding work if they're qualified. Being bilingual helps, too, so start practicing your French!

WHERE TO LIVE
Centre Ville

The historic *centre ville* of Grenoble, situated on the south banks of the Isère, is the place to be if you hanker for a thriving community with interesting, cosmopolitan neighbors and access to markets and restaurants. In the side-by-side Championnet and Notre-Dame quartiers, near the river and *gare de télépherique* that takes you up the mountain to the Bastille, a studio apartment in a 19th- or early-20th century building averages €400 per month. In this area, you'll find the Place Saint André, called la Place du Trib' by locals (the old courthouse used to be here), a popular destination for leisurely café breaks followed by or preceding an art-film screening at the Cinémathèque de Grenoble. This is Stendhal's (who, like Balzac, Zola, and Moliere, needs only one name for recognition) home zone, and the area oozes with his era's old-timey charm. On the Championnet side, you'll find the pleasant Place Victor Hugo, a comfortable nice-weather hangout with free wireless Internet, statues, and benches.

Chorier-Berriat

A bit farther south and west, moving in the direction of the Drac River, you'll come to the colorful Chorier-Berriat neighborhood. Once the dwelling place of the factory workers who breathed life into the local glove-making industry (try a guided tour at the Musée du Gant), it has become a warm residential neighborhood with a multiethnic population. This is where you'll go to find your halal hamburger, Vietnamese spring rolls, and tofu. The daily (except Mondays) Marché de l'Estecade, on avenue de Vizille, is a fun and practical place to pick up your daily food supply and acquire a sense of the local characters. Renting here is slightly less expensive than in Notre-Dame; a one-bedroom in Chorier-Berriat costs the same as a studio in that neighboring quartier, so expanding your search to encompass this area means more bang for your buck. Renting a big one-bedroom with two fireplaces, a bathtub, and excellent access to transportation means spending around €600 per month. A budget of €150,000 will buy you a flat in a late-20th century apartment building with parking, an elevator, and a balcony, but you'll probably need to budget a thousand more euros to strip off that dated wallpaper and give the whole place a freshening-up.

St. Laurent

If you've always fantasized about what life might be like in Italy, you may like to settle in the right-bank quartier of St. Laurent. Over the centuries, this neighborhood has been home to waves of Italian immigrants, and it still has a decidedly Italian sensibility, enhanced by the many pizzerias along the river. You'll hear a lot of *bon giornos,* and not just in restaurants; there's even an Italian-language radio station broadcast from here. There's something sweet about this neighborhood—the art galleries, cafés, and restaurants snug beneath the shadow of the Bastille. The tramline doesn't reach this part of town, which might be why the cost of living is equal to those of less charming neighborhoods on the other side of the river. Look to pay about €450 for a studio.

Île Verte

Tucked into the northeast crook of the Isère River is another hospitable quartier called Île Verte. This neighborhood is indeed green (*verte*), as well as a friendly, attractive place to settle down for a while. The architecture is noteworthy: Towering above the 19th- and early-20th-century apartment buildings are three ultramodern high-rises that were constructed in anticipation of the '68 Olympic Games. Depending on your sense of aesthetics, they're either an eyesore or retro-hip, but there's no denying their eye-catchiness. Studios are roomier and more affordable here than in St. Laurent, and public transport is excellent, with tram Line B slicing straight through the middle of the neighborhood. If your budget can stretch to €150,000, you could have yourself a two-bedroom place with a huge kitchen and views looking out over the neighboring mountains. Renters have a lot to choose from, including bright studios for €400 and one-bedrooms for €550.

GETTING AROUND

Even if you're not a tourist, the tourist office (14, rue de la République) in the Notre-Dame district is a good place to start your Grenoble adventure. You can buy bus passes and find maps, bus schedules, and tips on accommodations and dining here.

Public Transportation

Besides walking and cycling on private or public Métrovélo bikes (www.metrovelo.fr), the easiest way to get around Grenoble is by tram and bus, which are grouped together under the city's TAG transport system. The tramways four lines (A, B, C, and D) are efficient and far-reaching, and the system's two dozen or so local and regional bus lines fill in the gaps. Single voyages cost €1.40. You can buy tickets from the conductor, automated kiosks, and 140 different *tabacs* and other agents around town. Weekly, monthly, and annual passes are available for a slight discount, as are senior and student passes; purchase these at *tabacs,* from agents at the *gare routière,* or online. Remember to get your ticket validated—the fine for forgetting to do so is €43.50 and must be paid on the spot (or else the fine increases).

Grenoble's Soviet Republic–style *gare,* on rue Emile Gueymard, sits next door to the *gare routière* on the west side of the city, a 10-minute walk from center. Ticket windows are open 4:30 A.M. to 11:05 P.M. Monday to Saturday,

public tram in Grenoble

and from 5:30 A.M. on Sundays and holidays. Tickets to Lyon average about €20, depending on the day and time, and the trip takes 90 minutes. For the three-hour trip to Paris, ticket prices vary considerably, but bargain prices run as low as €22. The two-hour journey to Geneva costs €25.

Air Travel

Low-cost airlines Ryanair and EasyJet fly out of Grenoble-Isere Airport, located about 45 kilometers northwest of the city, to destinations including London and Stockholm. Getting there means a 35-minute bus ride on the airport *navettes* that leave from the *gare routière*. Hours are odd and trips infrequent—be sure to plan in advance. One-way tickets cost €12.50.

PRIME LIVING LOCATIONS

RESOURCES

Consulates and Embassies

UNITED STATES AND CANADA

There are 11 French consulate bureaus in the United States and six in Canada, each presiding over a consular region. Where you go for your in-person appointment depends on which state or province you live in; to figure out which one is your regional HQ, begin your search at the French embassy in Washington, DC, or Ottawa, Canada.

French Embassy in the United States

FRENCH EMBASSY
4101 Reservoir Rd. NW
Washington, DC 20007
tel. 202/944-6000
www.ambafrance-us.org

French Consulates in the United States

ATLANTA
The Lenox Building
3399 Peachtree Rd. NE, Ste. 500
Atlanta, GA 30326
tel. 404/495-1660 _
www.consulfrance-atlanta.org
Jurisdiction: Alabama, Georgia, Mississippi, North Carolina, South Carolina, Tennessee

BOSTON
Park Square Building
31 Saint James Ave., Ste. 750
Boston, MA 02116
tel. 617/435-0418
www.consulfrance-boston.org
Jurisdiction: Massachusetts, Maine, New Hampshire, Rhode Island, Vermont

CHICAGO
205 North Michigan Ave., Ste. 3700
Chicago, IL 60601
tel. 312/327-5200
www.consulfrance-chicago.org

Jurisdiction: Illinois, Indiana, Iowa, Kansas, Kentucky, Missouri, Michigan, Minnesota, Nebraska, North Dakota, Ohio, South Dakota, Wisconsin

HONOLULU
Alii Place, Ste. 1800
1099 Alakea St.
Honolulu, HI 96813|
tel. 808/547-5852
Jurisdiction: Hawaii and the U.S. Pacific Islands

HOUSTON
777 Post Oak Blvd., Ste. 600,
Houston, TX 77056
tel. 713/572-2799
www.consulfrance-houston.org
Jurisdiction: Arkansas, Oklahoma, Texas

LOS ANGELES
10390 Santa Monica Blvd., Ste. 410
Los Angeles, CA 90025
tel. 310/235-3200
www.consulfrance-losangeles.org
Jurisdiction: Arizona, Colorado, New Mexico, Southern California, Southern Nevada

MIAMI
Espirito Santo Plaza, Ste. 1050
1395 Brickell Ave.
Miami, FL 33131
tel. 305/403-4150
www.consulfrance-miami.org
Jurisdiction: Florida

NEW ORLEANS
1340 Poydras St.
Ste. 1710
New Orleans, LA 70112
tel. 504/569-2870
www.consulfrance-nouvelleorleans.org
Jurisdiction: Louisiana

NEW YORK
934 5th Ave.
New York, NY 10021
tel. 212/606-3600

www.consulfrance-newyork.org
Jurisdiction: Connecticut, New Jersey,
New York

SAN FRANCISCO
40 Bush St.
San Francisco, CA 94108
tel. 415/397-4330
www.consulfrance-sanfrancisco.org
Jurisdiction: Idaho, Montana, Northern
California, Northern Nevada, Oregon,
Utah, Washington, Wyoming

WASHINGTON, DC
101 Reservoir Rd. NW
Washington DC 20007-2185
tel. 202/944-6195
www.consulfrance-washington.org
Jurisdiction: Delaware, Maryland,
Pennsylvania, Washington, DC, West
Virginia, Virginia.

French Consulates in Canada

CALGARY
525 11th Ave. SW, Ste. 500
Calgary, AB T2R 0C9
tel. 403-264-1777
www.ambafrance-ca.org
Jurisdiction: Alberta, Saskatchewan.
Embassy services are available here.

MONCTON
77 Rue Main, Ste. 800
Moncton, New Brunswick E1C 1E9
tel. 506/857-4191
Jurisdiction: New Brunswick,
Nova Scotia, Prince Edward Island,
Newfoundland, and Labrador. Visa
applications are processed at the general
consulate in Montréal.

MONTRÉAL
1501 McGill College, Bureau 1000
Montréal, QC, H3A 3M8
tel. 514/878-4385
www.consulfrance-montreal.org
Jurisdiction: Québec, Nuvanuk

QUÉBEC CITY
25 Rue Saint-Louis
Québec City, QC G1R 3Y8
tel. 418/266-2500
www.consulfrance-quebec.org
Jurisdiction: Québec City. Visa
applications are processed at the general
consulate in Montréal.

TORONTO
2 Bloor St. E, Ste. 2200
Toronto ON M4W 1A8
tel. 416/847-1900
www.consulfrance-toronto.org
Jurisdiction: Manitoba, Ontario

VANCOUVER
1130 West Pender St., Ste. #1100
Vancouver, BC, V6E 4A4
tel. 604/637-5300
www.consulfrance-vancouver.org
Jurisdiction: Alberta, British Columbia,
Saskatchewan, Yukon, and North West
Territories

French Embassies in France

Both the American and Canadian
embassies in France are good sources
of information for new residents in
France, offering referrals, services, and
information on such topics as how to
avoid pickpockets and how to report a
lost or stolen passport.

AMERICAN EMBASSY
2, avenue Gabriel
75008 Paris
tel. 01/43 12 22 22
www.France.usembassy.gov

CANADIAN EMBASSY
37, avenue Montaigne
75008 Paris
tel. 01/44 43 29 00
www.canadainternational.gc.ca

RESOURCES

Planning Your Fact-Finding Trip

FRENCH ENTRÉE
www.frenchentree.com
An online guide to living, working, and vacationing in France.

FRENCH GOVERNMENT TOURIST OFFICE
www.us.franceguide.com.
A useful site with current information on all things related to tourism in France.

FUSAC (FRANCE USA CONTACTS)
www.fusac.org
A good starting point for finding a short-term rental during your stay in Paris and beyond.

SNCF
www.sncf.fr
The French national railway website, where you can purchase train and airplane tickets, book rental cars, and more.

Making the Move

IMMIGRATION AND VISAS

THE CALCULUS GROUP
www.calculusgroup.org
An agency that will file your visa paperwork on your behalf.

CRÉDIT AGRICOLE
www.credit-agricole.fr
This popular French bank's website has a thorough section on moving to France, including immigration and visas.

FRENCH LAW
www.frenchlaw.com
A basic site explaining French immigration law.

GLOBAL VISAS
www.globalvisas.com
Immigration specialists who will handle all your paperwork for a fee.

OFII (OFFICE FRANÇAIS DE L'IMMIGRATION ET DE L'INTÉGRATION)
www.ofii.fr
New arrivals in France will need to register with this office to complete the temporary residency process.

WORK AND STUDY PERMITS

Working in France

ASSOCIATION FOR INTERNATIONAL PRACTICAL TRAINING
www.aipt.org
The Americans Abroad program helps U.S. citizens who have found jobs in France to acquire work permits.

COUNCIL ON INTERNATIONAL EDUCATIONAL EXCHANGE (CIEE)
www.ciee.org
Offers information for students on working in France.

EUROPEAN-AMERICAN CHAMBER OF COMMERCE (EACC)
www.eaccfrance.com
Provides would-be investors and entrepreneurs with advice and resources for launching a business in France.

JUST LANDED
www.justlanded.com
A useful website that extensively explains the work permit process.

TRANSITIONS ABROAD
www.transitionsabroad.com
This established publication is an excellent resource for job seekers in France.

Studying in France

FRENCH MINISTRY OF FOREIGN AFFAIRS
www.diplomatie.gouv.fr
This government website offers an English-language guide to studying in France.

IES ABROAD
www.iesabroad.com
An informative study-abroad site.

STUDY ABROAD
www.studyabroad.com
A handy, thorough site for anyone thinking of studying in France.

CUSTOMS AND SHIPPING COMPANIES

ERC (EMPLOYEE RELOCATION COUNCIL)
www.erc.org

EURA (EUROPEAN RELOCATION ASSOCIATION)
www.eura-relocation.com

FIDI (INTERNATIONAL FEDERATION OF INTERNATIONAL FURNITURE REMOVALS)
www.fidi.com

GROSPIRON
www.grospiron.com/fr/lien

OMNI (OVERSEAS MOVING NETWORK INTERNATIONAL)
www.omnimoving.com

BLOGS

AN ALIEN PARISIENNE
www.analienparisienne.wordpress.com
The offbeat, humorous blog by a woman who moves to France to be with the man she loves—and gets a lot more than she bargained for.

BRETON DIARY
www.bretondiary.com
Football-loving Englishman Keith lives the good life in rural Brittany and shares his exploits with the world at large.

CHEZ LOULOU
www.chezlouloufrance.blogspot.com
Cheese-crazy "Loulou" started her blog in 2006, chronicling her love of the the beautiful south of France. You'll find lots of valuable material here, plus good photography.

PARIS MISSIVES
www.parismissives.blogspot.com
Randy Diaz moved to France from San Francisco in 2008, but don't you dare call him a Francophile. This blog details his experiences in Paris and beyond, always with a dose of humor and insight.

GETTING SETTLED

ANGLO INFO
www.france.angloinfo.com
A comprehensive site for expats, including information on jobs, housing, buying a car, having a baby, and finding a builder who speaks English.

THE ESCAPE ARTIST
www.escapeartist.com
Plenty of good, basic information on retiring or otherwise settling abroad can be found here. The site also has a job-search section with employment listings in France.

EXPATICA
www.expatica.com
Detailed job listings, plus useful forums to answer all your move-to-France questions.

FRENCH ENTRÉE
www.frenchentree.com
This site will become your move-abroad bible. It covers everything you'd want to know about life in France, from buying a home to putting your kids in school to dealing with local bureaucracy.

JUST LANDED
www.justlanded.com
As its title suggests, this website offers practical information related to every facet of your move, as well as links to other sites.

TRANSITIONS ABROAD
www.transitionsabroad.com
This established magazine has a thorough, well-organized website loaded with resources for those who want to live, work, or study in France.

Housing Considerations

RENTING

COLOCATION
www.colocation.fr
This is France's top roommate-finding database for renters. Includes detailed information about roommates, such as whether they smoke, keep late hours, or have pets.

CRAIGSLIST
www.paris.fr.craigslist.org
Craigslist is the number-one source for finding almost-no-hassle rental housing. Other cities around France don't have as strong a Craigslist community as Paris does, but it's worth investigating their outposts of the site anyway.

FUSAC
www.fusac.fr
The go-to resource for the Paris Anglophone community for more than 20 years has advertisements for housing, jobs, and other services, plus household items and other things for sale.

PARTICULIER À PARTICULIER
www.pap.fr
This source of for-rent ads is extremely popular, so start making those calls on Thursday morning as soon as the new issue comes out.

RENT A PLACE IN FRANCE
www.rentaplaceinfrance.com
Small but excellent selection of long-term housing for English-speaking renters through English-speaking proprietors.

BUYING

CENTURY 21
www.century21.fr
This well-known name in real estate has a strong presence in France. In addition to buying and selling, the company also lists rentals.

FRANCE THIS WAY
www.property.francethisway.com
Another thorough, easy-to-navigate real-estate database targeting the English-speaking community and encompassing every region of France.

FRENCH ENTRÉE
www.frenchentree.com
This English-language site offers regional listings and detailed articles on buying or renting a home or apartment.

FRENCH PROPERTY
www.french-property.com
This website, which has been providing extensive information for years, offers an excellent database of houses for sale, usually by the Anglophone community for the Anglophone community.

SELOGER
www.seloger.fr
A popular online real-estate service that gives home seekers access to nationwide listings of studios apartments, villas, and even châteaux, along with rental listings.

Language and Education

GENERAL RESOURCES

APPRENDRE LE FRANÇAIS EN FRANCE
www.fle.fr
A comprehensive list of all the public and private French language-learning institutions in France.

FRENCH UNIVERSITIES DATABASE
www.dr.education.fr/Serveurs_Etab/Univ_alpha.html
A complete listing of all the French universities that accept international students.

INTERNATIONAL GRADUATE
www.internationalgraduate.net/eurofrance.htm
Helpful information for students planning to enroll in graduate school in France.

LANGUAGE SCHOOLS
Paris
ALLIANCE FRANÇAISE
www.alliancefr.org
Nonprofit language school and cultural center offers classes at every level, plus events and expositions.

ATELIER 9
www.latelier9.com
A stellar reputation and small classes (no more than nine students per class) are the hallmarks of Atelier 9.

MAIRIE DE PARIS
www.cours-municipal-d-adultes-cma.cma-paris.org
The affordable French language courses offered through the Mairie are in high demand. Plan ahead to snag a seat.

THE SORBONNE
www.english.paris-sorbonne.fr
If you learn by doing, enroll in a program at the Sorbonne. Classes are in French, so it's sink or swim.

Brittany
INSA RENNES (INSTITUT NATIONAL DES SCIENCES APPLIQUÉES DE RENNES)
www.insa-rennes.fr
This *grande école* offers intensive French-language courses in the summer for incoming students.

OFII (OFFICE FRANÇAIS DE L'IMMIGRATION ET DE L'INTÉGRATION)
www.ofii.fr
Offices throughout France offer referrals for French-language courses.

UNIVERSITÉ DE RENNES 2
www.sites.univ-rennes2.fr/cirefe/
The university runs a popular full-time course for international students who want to learn French.

SPEAK UP FORMATION
www.speak-up-formation.com
Intensive French-language courses for adults and children.

Bordeaux and the Dordogne Valley
ALLIANCE FRANÇAISE BORDEAUX
www.alliance-bordeaux.org
The nonprofit organization has a branch in Bordeaux offering language courses and cultural events year-round.

FRENCH FACTORY
www.ffbordeaux.fr
Small class sizes and a variety of levels to choose from.

UNIVERSITÉ DE BORDEAUX 2
www.langues-vivantes.u-bordeaux2.fr
The university offers courses for doctoral diplomas in life sciences, medicine, and social sciences.

UNIVERSITÉ DE BORDEAUX 3
www.u-bordeaux3.fr
French language courses for international students are available.

Toulouse and Montpellier

ALLIANCE FRANÇAISE TOULOUSE
www.en.alliance-toulouse.org
Nonprofit French language and culture institute offers classes for children and adults.

APRE (ASSOCIATION FOR THE PROMOTION OF FRIENDSHIP BETWEEN FRENCH AND FOREIGN STUDENTS)
www.institutfrancaismontpellier.com
For nearly 50 years, APRE has provided French immersion classes in Montpellier. All levels welcome.

INSA (INSTITUT NATIONAL DES SCIENCES APPLIQUÉES DE TOULOUSE)
www.insa-toulouse.fr
One of France's *grandes écoles* teaches intensive French-language courses to international students.

INSTITUT LINGUISTIC ADENET
www.ila-france.com
French taught at all levels; housing and meals offered in some curricula.

LANGUE ONZE TOULOUSE
www. langueonze.com
Intensive training courses year-round, and students have access to a multimedia lab that includes books, magazines, and DVDs.

MONTPELLIER ESPACE LANGUES
www.cours-francais-montpellier.com
Offers job placement as well as language training.

Provence and Côte d'Azur

ALLIANCE FRANÇAISE NICE
www.alliance-francaise-nice.com
Language and culture classes for every level at affordable prices.

CENTRE INTERNATIONAL D'ANTIBES
Antibes
www.cia-france.com
Popular French-language school on the Riviera offers summer courses for teens, adults, and families.

ÉCOLE FRANCE LANGUE
www.france-langue.fr
Offers classes in business French, hotel and tourism industry French, and art history.

INSTITUT D'ÉTUDES FRANÇAISES POUR ÉTUDIANTS ÉTRANGERS
Aix-en-Provence
www.iefee.com
French language and cultural institute welcoming students from around the world.

IS INSTITUTE DE LANGUE
Aix-en-Provence
www.is-aix.com
Long-established language school offers language courses as well as cultural activities.

LANGUAGE INTERNATIONAL
www.languageinternational.fr
Advertises itself as a low-cost alternative to other local language academies.

LANGUE À NICE
www.langanice.fr
Offers semester-, trimester-, and year-long courses at private-college tuition prices.

SCEFEE (SERVICE COMMUN D'ENSEIGNEMENT DU FRANÇAIS AUX ÉTUDIANTS ÉTRANGERS)
Aix-en-Provence
www.sites.univ-provence.fr/wscefee
Multilevel language courses run through the Université de Provence.

Lyon and Grenoble

ALLIANCE FRANÇAISE DE GRENOBLE
www.afgrenoble.org
Five different courses, as well as cultural events and workshops, including cooking classes.

CENTRE INTERNATIONAL D'ÉTUDES FRANÇAISE
cief.univ-lyon2.fr
This international-language institute, run out of the Université de Lyon 2, provides diploma courses in French.

GRENOBLE INP
www.grenoble-inp.fr
This technical institute has French-language courses for students enrolled in diploma programs.

INFLEXYON
www.inflexyon.com
Language center popular with the under-30 set with affordable French lessons at all levels.

INSA LYON
fle.insa-lyon.fr
This *grande école* offers language courses for international students pursuing degrees in other fields.

UNIVERSITÉ STENDHAL GRENOBLE 3
w3.u-grenoble3.fr/cuef/accueil.php3
This university of Grenoble teaches intensive day and evening courses, plus cooking classes in French.

COLLEGES AND UNIVERSITIES

Paris

AMERICAN GRADUATE SCHOOL IN PARIS
www.ags.edu

AMERICAN UNIVERSITY OF PARIS
www.aup.edu

ÉCOLE SUPÉRIEUR DE CUISINE FRANCAISE
www.egf.ccip.fr

INSTITUT CATHOLIC DE PARIS
www.icp.fr

LE CORDON BLEU PARIS
www.lcbparis.com

SCIENCES PO
www.sciencespo.fr/en

THE SORBONNE
www.english.paris-sorbonne.fr

Brittany

ÉCOLE DES BEAUX ARTS DE RENNES
www.erba-rennes.fr

ESC RENNES SCHOOL OF BUSINESS
www.esc-rennes.fr

L'INSTITUT SUPÉRIEUR DES ARTS APPLIQUÉS
www.lisaa.com

INSTITUT UNIVERSITAIRE DE TECHNOLOGIE
www.iu-vannes.fr

UNIVERSITÉ DE BRETAGNE-SUD
www.univ-ubs.fr

UNIVERSITÉ DE RENNES 1
www.univ-rennes1.fr

UNIVERSITÉ DE RENNES 2
www.univ-rennes2.fr

Bordeaux and the Dordogne Valley

INSEEC BUSINESS SCHOOL
grandeecole.inseec-france.com

UNIVERSITÉ DE BORDEAUX MONTESQUIEU
www.u-bordeaux4.fr

UNIVERSITÉ DE BORDEAUX SEGALEN
www.u-bordeaux2.fr

UNIVERSITÉ MICHEL DE MONTAIGNE BORDEAUX 3
www.iut.u-bordeaux3.fr

Toulouse and Montpellier

ÉCOLE SUPÉRIEUR DES BEAUX ARTS
esbama.free.fr

UNIVERSITÉ MONTPELLIER 1
www.en.www.univ-montp1.fr

UNIVERSITÉ MONTPELLIER 2
www.univ-montp2.fr

UNIVERSITÉ PAUL VALÉRY MONTPELLIER 3
www.univ-montp3.fr

UNIVERSITÉ TOULOUSE 1 CAPITOLE
www.univ-tlse1.fr

UNIVERSITÉ TOULOUSE 2
www.univ-tlse2.fr

UNIVERSITÉ TOULOUSE 3 PAUL SABATIER
www.univ-tlse3.fr

Provence and Côte d'Azur

CENTRE UNIVERSITÉ MEDITERRANÉE
www.cum-nice.org

ÉCOLE SUPÉRIEUR D'ART
www.ecole-art-aix.fr

ÉCOLE SUPÉRIEUR DE COMMERCE
www.espeme.com

INSTITUTE FOR AMERICAN UNIVERSITIES
www.iaufrance.org

UNIVERSITÉ DE LA MEDITERRANÉE D'AIX-MARSEILLE 2
www.univmed.fr

UNIVERSITÉ DE NICE SOPHIA-ANTIPOLIS
www.unice.fr

UNIVERSITÉ DE PROVENCE D'AIX-MARSEILLE 1
www.univ-provence.fr

UNIVERSITÉ PAUL CÉZANNE D'AIX-MARSEILLE 3
www.unicaen.fr

Lyon and Grenoble

UNIVERSITÉ CATHOLIC DE LYON
www.univ-catholyon.fr

UNIVERSITÉ CLAUDE BERNARD LYON 1
www.univ-lyon1.fr

UNIVERSITÉ DE GRENOBLE
www.grenoble-univ.fr

UNIVERSITÉ JEAN MOULIN LYON 3
www.univ-lyon3.fr

UNIVERSITÉ JOSEPH FOURIER
www.ujf-grenoble.fr

UNIVERSITÉ LUMIÈRE LYON 2
www.univ-lyon2.fr

UNIVERSITÉ PIERRE-MENDES FRANCE
www.iut2.upmf-grenoble.fr

UNIVERSITÉ POPULAIRE DE LYON
uplyon.free.fr

UNIVERSITÉ STENDHAL GRENOBLE 3
www.u-grenoble3.fr

Health

GENERAL HEALTH AND INSURANCE

ASSOCIATION DENTAIRE FRANÇAISE
7, rue Mariotte
75017 Paris
tel. 01/58 22 17 10
www.adf.asso.fr

ASSURANCE MALADIE
www.ameli.fr

FEDERATION HOSPITALIÈRE DE FRANCE
1 bis, rue Cabanis
75014 Paris
tel. 01/44 06 84 44
www.fhf.fr

FRENCH HOSPITAL GUIDE
www.hopital.fr

SANTÉCLAIR
www.santeclair.fr

EMERGENCY CONTACTS

AMBULANCE
Dial 15

EUROPE-WIDE EMERGENCY NUMBER
Dial 112

FIRE
Dial 18

POLICE
Dial 17

HOSPITALS AND PHARMACIES

Paris

AMERICAN HOSPITAL OF PARIS
63, boulevard Victor Hugo
92200 Neuilly-sur-Seine
tel. 01/46 41 25 25
www.american-hospital.org

ASSISTANCE PUBLIQUE HÔPITAUX DE PARIS
Hopital St. Antoine
184, rue du Faubourg Saint-Antoine
75012 Paris
tel. 01/49 28 20 00

BRITISH AND AMERICAN PHARMACY
1, rue Auber
75009 Paris
tel. 01/42 65 88 29

GRANDE PHARMACIE INTERNATIONALE DE PARIS
17 bis, boulevard de Rochechouart
75009 Paris
tel. 01/48 78 03 01

HÔPITAL ST. LOUIS
1, avenue Claude Vellefaux
75010 Paris
tel. 01/42 49 49 49

PHARMACIE DU DRUGSTORE DES CHAMPS-ÉLYSÉES
133, avenue des Champs-Élysées
tel. 01/47 20 39 25

Brittany

HÔPITAL PONTCHAILLOU/CENTRE HOSPITALIER UNIVERSITÉ DE RENNES
2, rue Henri le Guilloux
35033 Rennes
02 99 28 43 21
www.chu-rennes.fr

HÔPITAL PROSPER SCHUBERT
20, boulevard du Général Guillaudot
76017 Vannes
tel. 02/97 01 41 41
www.fhf-bretagne.fr

HÔPITAL SUD/CENTRE HOSPITALIER UNIVERSITÉ DE RENNES
16, boulevard de Bulgarie
35203 Rennes
tel. 02/99 28 43 21

SOS MEDECINS
Clinique Océane
11, rue du Dr Joseph Audic
56000 Vannes
tel. 08/25 89 89 94

Bordeaux and the Dordogne Valley

CENTRE HOSPITALIER JEAN LECLAIRE
rue Jean Leclaire
24200 Sarlat
tel. 05/53 31 75 75

CENTRE HOSPITALIER SAMUEL POZZI
9, avenue Prof Albert Calmette
24100 Bergerac
tel. 05/53 63 88 88
www.hopital-bergerac-samuelpozzi.fr

CLINIQUE PASTEUR
54, rue Professeur Pozzi 24100 Bergerac
tel. 05/53 61 56 56
www.medi-partenaires.com/clinique-pasteur

GROUP HOSPITALIER PELLEGRIN
Place Amélie Raba-Léon
33000 Bordeaux
tel. 05/56 79 56 79
www.chu-bordeaux.fr

GROUP HOSPITALIER ST. ANDRE
1, rue Jean Burguet
33000 Bordeaux
tel. 05/56 79 56 79
www.chu-bordeaux.fr

PHARMACIE DES CAPUCINS
30, place des Capucins
33000 Bordeaux
Open 24 hours.

SOS MEDECINS BORDEAUX
www.sosmedecins-bordeaux.com
Dial - 3624

Toulouse and Montpellier

CENTRE HOSPITALIER UNIVERSITAIRE DE TOULOUSE
www.chu-toulouse.fr
Network of nine hospitals in the Toulouse region.

CHU DE MONTPELLIER
191, avenue Doyen Gaston Giraud
34090 Montpellier
04 67 33 05 55

CLINIQUE CLÉMENTVILLE
25, rue de Clémentville
34070 Montpellier
tel. 08/26 88 88 84

SOS MÉDECINS TOULOUSE
24, route d'Espagne
31100 Toulouse
tel. 05 61 33 00 00

Provence and Côte d'Azur

CENTRE HOSPITALIER D'ANTIBES JUAN-LE-PINS
107, avenue de Nice
06600 Antibes
www.ch-antibes.fr

CENTRE HOSPITALIER DE NICE
www.chu-nice.fr
Network of five hospitals in the Nice area.

CENTRE HOSPITALIER DU PAYS D'AIX
avenue des Tamaris
13616 Aix-en-Provence
tel. 04/42 33 50 00

POLYCLINIQUE DU PARC RAMBOT
74 bis, cours Gambetta
13100 Aix-en-Provence
tel. 04/42 23 99 99

SOS MÉDECINS
tel. 04/42 26 24 00 or 04/93 67 20 00

SOS MÉDECINS NICE
tel. 08/10 85 01 01

Lyon and Grenoble

CENTRE HOSPITALIER DE GRENOBLE
tel. 04/76 76 75 75
Network of four hospitals in the Grenoble area.

HÔPITAL DE LA CROIX-ROUSSE
103, grande rue de la Croix-Rousse
69004 Lyon
tel. 08/20 08 20 69

HÔPITAL EDOUARD HERRIOT
5, place d'Arsonval
69003 Lyon
tel. 08/20 08 20 69

HÔPITAL NORD HOTEL-DIEU
1, place de l'Hôpital
69002 Lyon
tel. 08/20 08 20 69

SOS MÉDECINS
5, chemin des Couvents
38 100 Grenoble
tel. 04/38 70 17 01

DISABLED ACCESS

**ASSOCIATION DES
PARALYSÉS DE FRANCE**
www.apf.asso.fr
Advocacy organization for people living with paralysis.

AUTISME FRANCE
www.autisme.france.free.fr
Support and resource organizations for families living with autism.

CAISSE NATIONAL DE SOLIDARITÉ POUR AUTONOMIE
www.cnsa.fr
Government-run association promoting independent living for the elderly and disabled.

PERSONNES HANDICAPPES
www.fondationdefrance.org
Organization working to support and uphold French disability laws and better the lives of the disabled public.

Employment

STARTING A BUSINESS

THE AMERICAN CHAMBER OF COMMERCE IN FRANCE
www.amchamfrance.org

APCA (ASSOCIATION POUR LA CRÉATION D'ENTERPRISES)
www.apce.com

BOUTIQUES DE GESTION
www.boutiques-de-gestion.com

CHAMBRE DE COMMERCE ET L'INDUSTRIE DE PARIS
www.ccip.fr

INVEST IN FRANCE
www.invest-in-france.org

NACRE (NOUVEL ACCOMPAGNEMENT POUR LA CRÉATION ET LA REPRISE D'ENTERPRISE)
www.emploi.gouv.fr/nacre

JOB SEARCHES

APEC
www.apec.fr
French-language job-seeking website with listings in multiple industries.

BERLITZ
www.berlitz.fr
An established English-language institute that's always looking for new recruits.

CRAIGSLIST
www.paris.en.craigslist.org
The Paris focused Craigslist site offers the most employment-related ads of all the French regional sites.

RESOURCES

EUROJOBS
www.eurojobs.com
Search engine for job seekers throughout France and the rest of Europe. Emphasis on high-tech industry opportunities.

FUSAC (FRANCE USA CONTACTS)
www.fusac.org
Job listings for English teachers, hotel and restaurant workers, and tourism-related industries.

PÔLE EMPLOI
www.pole-emploi.fr
French portal for job seekers in France.

WALL STREET INSTITUTE
www.wallstreetinstitute.fr
Each of the institutes 70 centers throughout France accepts résumés year-round.

VOLUNTEERING

CADIP (CANADIAN ALLIANCE FOR DEVELOPMENT INITIATIVES

AND PROJECTS)
www.cadip.org
This Vancouver-based nonprofit aims to support volunteering abroad with humanitarian projects.

CARE FRANCE
www.carefrance.org
Nonprofit French volunteer organization with projects all over the world.

GO ABROAD
www.goabroad.com
This U.S.-based database of volunteer programs includes an extensive selection of possibilities in France.

WWOOF (WORLD WIDE OPPORTUNITIES ON ORGANIC FARMS)
www.wwoof.com
Free food and lodging in exchange for your work on organic farms throughout France. Always welcoming new members.

Finance

BNP PARIBAS
www.bnpparibas.com

CAISSE D'EPARGNE
www.caisse-epargne.fr

CRÉDIT AGRICOLE
www.credit-agricole.fr

LA BANQUE POSTAL
www.labanquepostale.fr

Communications

PHONE AND INTERNET SERVICE

BOUYGUES TELECOM
www.bouyguestelecom.fr
Internet, television, and telephone service.

FNAC
www.fnac.fr
This chain sells a wide variety of mobile phones and other communication devices.

ORANGE
www.orange.fr
Internet, television, and telephone service.

PHONEHOUSE
www.phonehouse.fra
The leading mobile-phone store in France, where you can also buy your *puces*.

SFR
www.SFR.fr
Internet, television, and telephone
service.

NEWSPAPERS

LE CANARD ENCHAINÉ
www.lecanardenchaine.fr

THE CONNEXION
www.connexionfrance.com

LA DÉPÊCHE DU MIDI
www.ladepeche.fr

DORDOGNE TODAY
www.dordognetoday.com

LE FIGARO
www.lefigaro.fr

FRANCE SOIR
www.francesoir.fr

LIBÉRATION
www.liberation.fr

MÉTRO
www.metrofrance.com

LE MONDE
www.lemonde.fr

NICE MATIN
www.nicematin.com

NOUVEL OBSERVATEUR
www.tempsreel.nouvelobs.com

OUEST-FRANCE
www.ouest-france.fr

LE PARISIEN
www.leparisien.com

THE RIVIERA TIMES
www.rivieratimes.com

SUD-OUEST
www.sudouest.fr

MAGAZINES

A NOUS
www.anous.fr

A TOULOUSE
www.toulouse.fr

L'EXPRESS
www.lexpress.fr

MARIANNE
www.marianne2.fr

PARISCOPE
spectacles.premiere.fr

PARIS MATCH
www.parismatch.com

LE POINT
www.lepoint.fr

THAT'S NICE
www.thatsnicemagazine.com

Travel and Transportation

GENERAL RESOURCES

AIR FRANCE
www.airfrance.fr
France's national airline.

COVOITURAGE
www.covoiturage.fr
National public ride-share program.

EUROLINES
www.eurolines.fr
Long-distance bus company.

EUROPECAR
www.europecar.fr
Nationwide car-rental agency.

OPODO
www.opodo.fr
Popular online travel agency.

SNCF
www.sncf.fr
French national railway lines.

REGIONAL TRANSPORTATION

Paris

RATP (RÉGIE AUTONOME DES TRANSPORTS PARISIENS)
www.ratp.fr
Information in English for the bus, Métro, regional trains, and transport passes.

VÉLIB'
www.velib.paris.fr
Paris's public bike-sharing system.

Brittany

STAR (LE SERVICE DE TRANSPORT EN COMMUN DE RENNES MÉTROPOLE)
www.star.fr
Information on Rennes' Métro, bus, and other transportation lines.

LE VÉLO STAR
www.levelostar.fr
Rennes' public bike-sharing system.

Bordeaux and the Dordogne Valley

LA CUB (COMMUNITÉ URBAINE DE BORDEAUX)
www.lacub.fr
Portal to Bordeaux's bus, tram, and public-bicycle system.

TRANS'PERIGORD
www.cg24.fr
Public-transportation hub for the Sarlat region.

TUB (LES TRANSPORTS URBAINS BERGERACOIS)
tel. 05/53 63 96 97

Hours, fares, and other information for Bergerac's bus system.

Toulouse and Montpellier

TAM (TRANSPORTS DE L'AGGLOMERATION DE MONTPELLIER)
www.montpellier-agglo.com
Public-transportation hub for Montpellier's bus, tram, bike, and car networks.

TISSÉO
www.tisseo.fr
Public-transportation hub for the Toulouse region.

VÉLÔTOULOUSE
www.velo.toulouse.fr
Toulouse's public bike-sharing site.

Provence and Côte d'Azur

AIX EN BUS
www.aixenbus.com
Hours, schedules, and tariffs for buses throughout the Aix region.

ENVIBUS
www.envibus.fr
Portal to the Antibes area public-transportation network.

LIGNES D'AZUR
www.lignesdazur.com
Bus and tram information for the greater Nice area.

VÉLO BLEU
www.velobleu.org
Nice's public bike-sharing system.

V'HELLO
www.vhello.fr
Information for Aix's public bike-sharing program.

Lyon and Grenoble

MÉTROVÉLO
www.metrovelo.fr
Grenoble's public bike-sharing system.

TAG (TRANSPORTS AGGLOMERATION DE GRENOBLE)
www.semitag.com
Public-transportation hub for the Grenoble area.

TCL (TRANSPORTS COMMUNAL DE LYON)
www.tcl.fr

Public-transportation hub with information on Lyon's tram, Métro, and bus systems.

VÉLO'V
www.velov.grandlyon.com
Lyon's public bike-sharing system.

Prime Living Locations

PARIS

General

PARIS CONVENTION AND VISITORS BUREAU
www.en.parisinfo.com

PARIS MAIRIE DIRECTORY
www.paris.fr

PARIS TOURIST BOARD
www.parisinfo.com

Schools

AMERICAN SCHOOL OF PARIS
www.asparis.org

BILINGUAL INTERNATIONAL SCHOOL OF PARIS
www.bilingualschoolparis.com

LYCÉE HONORÉ DE BALZAC
www.balzac-apesa.org

PARIS.FR
www.equipements.paris.fr/?tid=41
City of Paris's official list of primary schools.

PARIS.FR
www.equipements.paris.fr/?tid=44,55,56
City of Paris's list of lycées.

BRITTANY

Rennes General

RENNES MAIRIE
www.rennes.fr

RENNES METROPOLITAN
www.ca-rennes-metropole.
demarchesenligne.fr

RENNES OFFICE OF TOURISM
www.tourisme-rennes.com

Rennes Schools

ACADEMIE DE RENNES INTERNATIONAL SCHOOL
www.ac-rennes.fr

LES ÉCOLES
http://lesecoles.fr/rennes-35000
Comprehensive list of public and private primary and secondary schools in Rennes.

Vannes General

VANNES OFFICE OF TOURISM
www.tourisme-vannes.com

Vannes Schools

VANNES MAIRIE
www.mairie-vannes.fr
The office of the *maire* has a comprehensive list of all public and private schools in the Vannes region.

BORDEAUX AND THE DORDOGNE VALLEY

Bordeaux General

BORDEAUX OFFICE OF TOURISM
www.bordeaux-tourisme.com

RESOURCES

PERIGORD NOIR-DORDOGNE VALLEY OFFICE OF TOURISM
www.perigordnoir.com

Bordeaux Schools

BERGERAC MAIRIE
www.bergerac.fr
The *mairie* of the city of Bordeaux provides a comprehensive list of public and private schools.

BORDEAUX INTERNATIONAL SCHOOL
www.bordeaux-school.com

Bergerac General

BERGERAC MAIRIE
www.bergerac.fr

BERGERAC OFFICE OF TOURISM
www.bergerac-tourisme.com

Bergerac Schools

PAYS DE BERGERAC
www.pays-de-bergerac.com
The official site of the greater Bergerac area provides a comprehensive listing of public and private schools throughout the Bergerac area.

Sarlat General

SARLAT OFFICE OF TOURISM
www.sarlat-tourisme.com

Sarlat Schools

SARLAT MAIRIE
www.sarlat.fr/edito.asp?Scolarite
Sarlat's office of the *maire* offers a comprehensive listing of the area's public and private schools.

TOULOUSE AND MONTPELLIER

Toulouse General

TOULOUSE CONVENTION AND VISITORS BUREAU
www.sotoulouse.com

TOULOUSE MAIRIE
www.toulouse.fr

TOULOUSE OFFICE OF TOURISM
www.toulouse-tourisme.com

Toulouse Schools

LES ENFANTS TOULOUSE
www.enfant-toulouse.com/scolaire/
ecolesprimairestoulouse.php
The city of Toulouse's official list of public and private schools.

INTERNATIONAL SCHOOL OF TOULOUSE
www.intst.eu

Montpellier General

MONTPELLIER MAIRIE
www.montpellier.fr

MONTPELLIER OFFICE OF TOURISM
www.ot-montpellier.fr

Montpelier Schools

ECOLE PRIVÉE INTERNATIONAL BILINGUE
www.ecole-privee-bilingue.fr

VILLE DE MONTPELIER
www.montpellier.fr/24-l-enseignement-et-la-
recherche-a-montpellier-toutes-les-ecoles-
de-montpellier.htm
The Montpellier *maire*'s office offers a comprehensive list of schools throughout the region.

PROVENCE AND CÔTE D'AZUR

Aix-en-Provence General

AIX OFFICE OF TOURISM
www.aixenprovencetourism.com

Aix-en-Provence Schools

AIX-EN-PROVENCE MAIRIE
www.mairie-aixenprovence.fr/-Education
The *mairie*'s official list of public and private schools.

INTERNATIONAL BILINGUAL SCHOOL OF PROVENCE
www.ibsofprovence.com

INTERNATIONAL PRIVATE SCHOOL OF PROVENCE
www.epim-mis.com

Antibes General

ANTIBES MAIRIE AND OFFICE OF TOURISM
www.antibesjuanlespins.com

Antibes Schools

ACADÉMIE DE NICE
www.ac-nice.fr/ienantibes/admin/ecoles/
ecolant.htm
A comprehensive list of all the public schools in Antibes.

L'ANNUAIRE OFFICIEL DE L'ENSEIGNEMENT PRIVÉ
www.enseignement-prive.info/ecoles/
departement/alpes-maritimes/06/1
A comprehensive list of all the private schools in Antibes.

Nice General

NICE MAIRIE
www.nice.fr

NICE OFFICE OF TOURISM
www.nicetourisme.com

Nice Schools

SITE DE LA VILLE DE NICE
www.nice.fr/Education-recherche
The city of Nice's official list of public and private schools.

LYON AND GRENOBLE

Lyon General

LYON MAIRIE
www.lyon.fr

LYON OFFICE OF TOURISM
www.lyon-france.com

RHÔNE-ALPES DEPARTMENT OF TOURISM
www.rhonealpes-tourisme.com

Lyon Schools

CITY OF LYON
www.lyon.fr/vdl/sections/en/enseignement
The city's official list of public and private schools.

THE INTERNATIONAL SCHOOL OF LYON
www.islyon.org

Grenoble General

GRENOBLE LIFE
www.grenoblelife.com

GRENOBLE MAIRIE
www.grenoble.fr

GRENOBLE TOURISM
www.grenoble-tourism.com

Grenoble Schools

THE AMERICAN SCHOOL OF GRENOBLE
www.americanschoolgrenoble.com

CITY OF GRENOBLE
www.grenoble.fr/7-education.htm
The city of Grenoble's education site.

ÉCOLE ST. JOSEPH
www.ecolestjoseph.fr

Glossary

aller-rétour   round trip

apéro   snack eaten with an drink before dinner

ascenseur   elevator

assurance   insurance

attestation   written and signed statement or testimonial

auberge   inn

banlieue   suburbs

billet   ticket

bisou   kiss

bobo   "*bo*urgeois *bo*hemian," yuppie

boulangerie   bread shop where pastries and other baked goods are often sold

bricolage   DIY, do-it-yourself

brocante   antiques and collectibles sale

café   cup of coffee; establishment where you drink coffee

carte de séjour   residency card

caviste   wineseller

chariot   personal shopping cart on wheels

chien(ne)   male/female dog

cinéma   movie theater

clic-clac   foldout couch-bed

clinique   private hospital

collège   middle school

composteur   ticket stamping machine at train stations, on buses, and at Métro stations

crèmerie   shop that sells dairy products

déménager   to move house

demi   half-pint of beer

dossier   file (n)

école élémentaire   elementary school

encore   again

enfant   child

épicerie   grocery shop

étudiant(e)   male/female student

facture   bill (n)

gare   train station

gratuit   free/no cost

grève   strike (n)

ici   here

immobilière   real-estate agent

libre   open/available

lycée   high school

maire   mayor

mairie   mayor's office, town hall

maison particulier   independent house, usually of grand standing

manifestation   demonstration

marché aux puces   flea market

maternelle   preschool

maternité   maternity hospital

notaire   notary

ordinateur   computer

panier   shopping basket

patisserie   pastry shop

permis de conduire   driver's license

petit(e) ami(e)   boyfriend/girlfriend

populaire   working-class/crowded

préfecture   regional headquarters for the Ministry of the Interior

préfecture de police   police headquarters

presque   almost

La Presse   newsstand

quartier   neighborhood

rendezvous   appointment

rentrée   the start of a new school year

rosé   pink wine

rue   street

sac   plastic shopping bag

salariée   employee

sans papiers   undocumented workers

SDF   "sans domicile fixe," homeless

SVP   "s'il vous plaît," please

syndicat   union or association

tabac   tobacco shop that also sells bus tickets, lottery tickets, and sometimes magazines and beverages

tartine   slice of bread

travail   work

verre   a glass (usually of wine or beer)

vide-grenier   community rummage sale

viennoiserie   breakfast pastry

voiture   car

French Phrasebook

French is an intimidating language. It isn't so much the rolling *R*s and figuring out how the accents work that makes it so—it's the fear of sounding silly, saying things "wrong," and ultimately not being understood. But rest assured that the French will always meet you halfway if you at least *try*, even if your response to *"merci"* ends up as *"beaucoup."* Set those feelings of vulnerability aside and let 'er rip. You'll be rewarded for your efforts! Remember to begin all requests and queries with *"Excusez-moi, s'il vous plaît"* (Ex-CUE-zay mwa, see voo play) and end them with *"Merci, madame/monsieur"* (MARE-see, MAD-ahm/MUH-syer)

PRONUNCIATION

Before you start practicing your French, relax. This isn't rocket science, though it does take a bit of diligent practice. Getting a grip on French accents will help you read the language—as will pronouncing the consonants and vowels—and let you avoid ordering a cold meat terrine (*paté*, pah-TAY) when you really want pasta (*pâte*, paht).

Vowels

Accents do not always change the sound of the vowel. French is tricky like that.

é: accent *aigu*

à, è, ù: accent *grave*

â, ê, î, ô, û: accent *circonflexe*

ë, ï, ü: accent *tréma*

a, as the **"a"** in **"also"**
　Example: grave **GRAHv (serious)**

ai, as **"ai"** in **"aisle"**
　Example: ail **EYE (garlic)**

e, as **"e"** in **"bed"**
　Example: femme **FEMM (woman)**

é, as **"ay"** in **"bay"**
　Example: café **CAF-ay**

eau, as **"o"** in **"oh"**
　Example: bâteau **bat-OH (boat)**

er/et, as **"ay"** in **"stay"**
　Examples: regarder **ray-GAR-day (to look),** complet **comPLAY ("full")**

i, as **"ie"** in **"piece"**
　Example: minute **MEE-noot (minute)**
　Exception: the **"-in"** suffix changes the **"i"** sound to a nasal **"ahn"**
　Example: vin **VAHN (wine)**

o, as **"o"** in **"pope"**
　Example: stop **STOPE (stop)**

oi, as **"wa"** in **"water"**
　Example: oiseau **WAH-zo (bird)**

ou, as **"oo"** in **"tool"**
　Example: bouche **BOOSH (mouth)**

u, as **"oo"** in **("stoop")**
　Example: prune **PROOn (plum)**

ui, pronounced **"oo-ee"**
　Example: fruit **FROO-ee (fruit)**

Consonants

With a few exceptions, French consonants are pronounced as they are in English. Exceptions: The letters *d, n, p, r, s, t,* and *x* are generally not pronounced at the end of a word.

ç: accent *cédille*

c, when preceding an e or an i, sounds like **"s"** as in **"salad"**
　Example: céréale **say-ray-AL (cereal)**

ch, as **"sh"** as in **"shower."**
　Examples: chat **SHAH (cat),** champignon **shahm-peen-YON (mushroom)**

g, when followed by a, o, or u, g is as the **"g"** in **"game."** If followed by e **or** i, it is as the second **"g"** in **"language."**
　Examples: gare **GAHr (train station),** géant **jhay-AHNT (gigantic)**

RESOURCES

gn, as **"ny"** as in the Spanish word **"piñata"**
   Example: mignon **meen-NYO** **("cute")**

j, as the **"j"** in **"jump"**
   Example: jus **joo (juice)**

h, silent when it's the first letter in a word
   Examples: hôpital **OH-pee-tal (hospital),** *horloge* **or-LOGE (clock)**

ph, as **"f"** as in **"film"**
   Examples: pharmacie **farm-a-SEE (pharmacy),** *philosophe* **FEE-lo-soff (philosopher)**

s, not pronounced at the end of a plural word
   Example: lettres **LETT-ruh (letters)**

th, as **"t"** as in **"tuna"** (note that there is no "th" sound in French)
   Examples: thé **TAY (tea),** *théâtre* **tay-AH-tra (theater)**

NUMBERS

0 *zéro*		**31** *trente-et-un*
1 *un*		**32** *trente-deux*
2 *deux*		**40** *quarante*
3 *trois*		**41** *quarante-et-un*
4 *quatre*		**50** *cinquante*
5 *cinq*		**51** *cinquante etun*
6 *six*		**60** *soixante*
7 *sept*		**61** *soixante-et-un*
8 *huit*		**62** *soixante-deux*
9 *neuf*		**63** *soixante-trois*
10 *dix*		**64** *soixante-quatre*
11 *onze*		**65** *soixante-cinq*
12 *douze*		**66** *soixante-six*
13 *treize*		**67** *soixante-sept*
14 *quatorze*		**68** *soixante-huit*
15 *quinze*		**69** *soixante-neuf*
16 *seize*		**70** *soixante-dix*
17 *dix-sept*		**71** *soixante-et-onze*
18 *dix-huit*		**72** *soixante-douze*
19 *dix-neuf*		**73** *soixante-treize*
20 *vingt*		**74** *soixante-quatorze*
21 *vingt-et-un*		**75** *soixante-quinze*
22 *vingt-deux*		**76** *soixante-seize*
23 *vingt-trois*		**77** *soixante-dix-sept*
30 *trente*		**78** *soixante-dix-huit*

79 *soixante-dix-neuf*
80 *quatre-vingts*
81 *quatre-vingt-un*
82 *quatre-vingt-deux*
83 *quatre-vingt-trois*
84 *quatre-vingt-quatre*
85 *quatre-vingt-cinq*
86 *quatre-vingt-six*
87 *quatre-vingt-sept*
88 *quatre-vingt-huit*
89 *quatre-vingt-neuf*
90 *quatre-vingt-dix*
91 *quatre-vingt-onze*
92 *quatre-vingt-douze*
93 *quatre-vingt-treize*
94 *quatre-vingt-quatorze*
95 *quatre-vingt-quinze*
96 *quatre-vingt-seize*
97 *quatre-vingt-dix-sept*
98 *quatre-vingt-dix-huit*
99 *quatre-vingt-dix-neuf*
100 *cent*
101 *cent un*
125 *cent vingt-cinq*
200 *deux cents*
300 *trois cents*

1,000 *mille*
2,000 *deux mille*
1,000,000 *un million*
2,000,000 *deux millions*
one billion *un milliard*
one quarter *un quart*
one third *un tiers*
one half *un demi*
three-fourths *trois-quatre*

DAYS AND MONTHS
Neither the days of the week nor the months of the year are capitalized in French.

Monday *lundi*
Tuesday *mardi*
Wednesday *mercredi*
Thursday *jeudi*
Friday *vendredi*
Saturday *samedi*
Sunday *dimanche*
today *aujourd'hui*
yesterday *hier*
tomorrow *demain*
January *janvier*
February *février*
March *mars*
April *avril*
May *mai*
June *juin*
July *juillet*
August *août*
September *septembre*
October *octobre*
November *novembre*
December *décembre*
spring *printemps*
summer *été*
autumn *automne*
winter *hiver*

TIME
France uses the 24-hour clock. Instead of a colon, an "h" is used; so 1:00 A.M. appears as 1h00 and 11:30 P.M. appears as 23h30.

1:00 A.M. *une heure*
2:00 A.M. *deux heures*
3:00 A.M. *trois heures*
4:00 A.M. *quatre heures*
5:00 A.M. *cinq heures*
6:00 A.M. *six heures*
7:00 A.M. *sept heures*
8:00 A.M. *huit heures*
9:00 A.M. *neuf heures*
10:00 A.M. *dix heures*
11:00 A.M. *onze heures*
noon *midi*
1:00 P.M. *treize heures*
2:00 P.M. *quatorze heures*
3:00 P.M. *quinze heures*
4:00 P.M. *seize heures*
5:00 P.M. *dix-sept heures*
6:00 P.M. *dix-huit heures*
7:00 P.M. *dix-neuf heures*
8:00 P.M. *vignt heures*
9:00 P.M. *vignt-et-un heures*
10:00 P.M. *vignt-deux heures*
11:00 P.M. *vignt-trois heures*
morning *le matin*
afternoon *l'après-midi*
evening *le soir*
night *la nuit*
midnight *minuit*
What time is it? *Quelle heure est-il?*
one minute *une minute*
two minutes *deux minutes*
early *tôt*
late *en retard*
10 minutes late *dix minutes de retard*

THE BASICS
"Please" and "thank you" are the first steps toward making yourself welcome in France. Once you've mastered those niceties, expand your vocabulary with these quotidian basics.

yes *oui*
no *non*
OK *d'accord*
maybe *peut-être*
I *je*
me *moi*
you *vous (formal)/renouveler un ordonnance (informal)*
him *lui*
her *elle*
his *son/sa/ses*
her(s) *son/sa/ses*
their *leur(s)*

RESOURCES

who *qui*
what *quoi*
when *quand*
why *pourquoi*
where *où*
how many *combien*
because *parce-que*
thank you *merci*
thank you very much *merci bien*
you're welcome (formal) *je vous en prie*
you're welcome (informal) *de rien*
I'm sorry *je suis desolé(e)*
I don't understand *je ne comprends pas*
open *Ouvert*
closed *Fermé*
closed on Sundays *Fermé le Dimanche*
push *Poussez*
pull *Tirez*
stop *Arrêt!*
post office *la poste*
bank *la banque*
empty *vide*
full *complet/complète*
happy *heureux*
sad *triste*

GREETINGS

Greetings are an important formality and many-times-a-day ritual. It's imperative that you master these common salutations for successful living in France.

Hello *Bonjour*
Hi! *Salut!*
Good evening *Bon soir*
Good day *Bonne journée*
Good night *Bonne soirée*
Good weekend *Bon weekend*
My name is . . . *Je m'appelle...*
What's your name? *Comment-vous appelez-vous?*
I'd like to introduce you to . . . *Je vous présente...*
Nice to meet you *Enchanté(e)*
goodbye *au revoir*
See you later *À tout à l'heure*
See you soon *À bientôt*
How are you? *Comment allez-vous?*

How's it going? *Comment ça va?*
It's going well, thanks *Ça va bien, merci*
It's going well, and you? *Ça va bien, et vous? (et toi, if informal)*
Enjoy your meal *Bon appétit*

GETTING AROUND

Where is . . . *Où est...*
a hotel *un hôtel*
the airport *l'aèroport*
the train station *la gare*
the bus station *la gare routière*
the Métro *le Métro*
the bus stop *arrêt du bus*
right *à droite*
left *à gauche*
straight ahead *tout droit*
on the corner *au coin*
here *ici*
there *là*
nearby *près d'ici*
for rent *à louer*
for sale *à vendre*
deposit *caution*
available *disponible*

ACCOMMODATIONS

Do you have a room available? *Avez-vous un chambre libre?*
We're full *Nous sommes complet*
I have a reservation *J'ai un réservation*
Combien de nuits? *How many nights?*
I'd like to stay three nights *Je voudrais rester trois nuits*
double room *avec un grand lit*
bed *lit*
key *clé*
the price *la prix*
cheap *pas cher*

FOOD

to eat *manger*
to drink *boire*
breakfast *petit-déjeuner*
lunch *déjeuner*
dinner *dîner*
snack *casse-croûte*

water *l'eaucarafe d'eau*
wine *vin*
beer *bière*
menu *la carte*
first course *entrée*
main course *plat or plat principal*
I'd like . . . *Je voudrais...*
I'm vegetarian/vegan *Je suis vegetarian(ne)/vegetalien(ne)*
without . . . *sans*
with . . . *avec*
the check *l'addition*
supermarket *supermarché/ hypermarché*
fruit *fruit*
vegetables *légumes*
cheese *fromage*
butter *beurre*
milk *lait*
soy milk *lait de soja*
coffee *café*
tea *thé*
hot water *eau chaud*
jam *confiture*
egg *oeuf*
meat *viande*
bread *pain*
noodles *nouilles*
pasta *pâte*
rice *riz*
salt *sel*
pepper *poivre*
ketchup *sauce de tomate*

SHOPPING

Fruits and vegetables are sold by the kilo at French outdoor *marchés* and supermarkets. If you want less than a kilo, ask for *un demi* (a half-kilo) or *un quatre* (a quarter-kilo).

to go shopping *faire les courses*
How much does this cost? *C'est combien?*
I'm looking for . . . *Je cherche...*
I'd like to buy . . . *Je voudrais acheter...*
I'd like a half-kilo, please *Je voudrais un demi, s'il vous plaît*
That's too much *C'est trop*
It's too small/big *C'est trop petit/grand*

Do you have any others? *Vous en avez d'autres?*
Do you accept bank cards/credit cards? *Est-ce que je peux payer avec une carte bancaire/carte de crédit?*

SHOE SIZES

5 35
6 36
7 37½
8 38½
9 40
10 42
12 44

NATIONAL HOLIDAYS

The French celebrate a handful of national holidays, or *jours feriérs*, throughout the year (and despite the country's claim to be utterly secular, many are religious holidays). They include:

- New Year's Day *(Jour de l'an)* January 1
- Easter *(Pâques)* April, date varies
- Labor Day *(Fête de premier mai)* May 1
- WWII Victory Day *(Fête de la Victoire)* May 8
- Pentecost *(la Pentecôte)* Date varies
- Bastille Day *(Fête nationale)* July 14
- All Saints' Day *(Toussaints)* November 1
- Armistice Day *(Jour d'armistice)* November 11
- Christmas Day *(Noël)* December 25

RESOURCES

BANKING

bank card *carte bancaire (CB)c*
savings account *Compte d'épargne*
checkbook *carnet de chèque/chèquier*
account *compte*
checking account *compte chèque*
overdraft *découvert*
withdrawal *prélèvement*
bank statement *relevé bancaire*

HEALTH

an emergency *un urgence*
pain *douleur*
I'm sick *Je suis malade*
sharp pain *douleur vive*
swelling *des oedèmes*
flu *grippe*
stomach *flu gastro*
prescription *un ordonnance*

to refill a prescription *renouveler un ordonnance*
diagnosis *diagnostic*
X-ray *une radio*
ultrasound/sonogram *une échographie*
examination of heart, lungs, ears *l'auscultation du cĭur, des poumons, des oreilles*
pap smear *un frottis*
pregnancy/pregnant *grossesse/enceinte*
midwife *sage-femme*
ophthalmologist *opthalmologiste*
cardiologist *cardiologue*
physiotherapist *kinésithérapeute*
dentist *dentiste*
homeopathy *homéopathie*

Suggested Reading

Ernest Hemingway did it best: write about the French experience from an American's perspective, albeit with a candid pen fueled by copious amounts of alcohol. Honest yet romantic, he made legions of dreamers yearn for their own Lost Generation era in Paris's Left Bank. Hemingway left big shoes for others to fill—and boy, have they tried. These tomes, written by scholars, cultural and social critics, cooks, and other France aficionados, will get you revved up (and duly warned) in anticipation of your move.

HISTORY AND CULTURE

These will help prep you for the culture shock you're likely to experience after you move, even if you've visited France a hundred times before.

Leibowitz, David. *The Sweet Life in Paris.* New York: Broadway Books, 2009. A delicious introduction to France from a top blogger, cookbook author, and Paris expat.

Nadeaux, Jean-Benoît and Julie Barlow. *Sixty Million Frenchmen Can't Be Wrong.* Chicago: Sourcebooks, Inc., 2003. An insightful look at French history and contemporary French society.

Platt, Polly. *French or Foe?* Skokie, IL: Distribooks, 2003. French cultural idiosyncrasies explained with a dash of humor.

Timoney, Charles. *Pardon My French.* New York: Gotham, 2008. A funny look at all the French-language errors you'll probably make during your stay in France.

MEMOIRS

First-person memoirs written by Anglophones who've up and moved to France are officially a genre unto themselves. Some of the most popular are:

Baldwin, James. *Notes of a Native Son.* Boston: Beacon Press, 1984. Among these essays by the revered American writer are tales of his years in France.

Beach, Sylvia. *Shakespeare and Company.* New York: Harcourt, 1959. The owner of the famous Paris bookstore reminisces about her exciting literary life in Paris's Left Bank and beyond.

Corbett, Bryce. *A Town Called Paris.* New York: Broadway Books, 2008. A saucy Australian finds true love—with a showgirl—in the City of Light.

Gershman, Suzy. *C'est La Vie.* New York: Viking, 2004. A woman of a certain age moves to France and begins anew after her husband's death.

Gopnik, Adam.*Paris to the Moon.* New York: Random House, 2001. A *New Yorker* writer spent several years in Paris with his family; these are his memories.

Hemingway, Ernest. *A Moveable Feast.* New York: Scribner, 1964. Classic Hemingway about writing, writers, drinking, and adventure in France.

Mayle, Peter. *A Year in Provence.* New York: Knopf, 1990. The quintessential move-to-rural-France tale, full of humor and insight.

Rochefort, Harriet Welty. *French Toast.* New York: St. Martin's Press, 1997. An American moves to France, marries a Frenchman, and pens the delicious details.

Sedaris, David. *Me Talk Pretty One Day.* Boston: Back Bay Books, 2001. Humorous essays detailing Sedaris's language foibles and other funny disasters in France.

Stein, Gertrude. *Paris, France.* New York: Liveright, 1970. The famous 20th-century author's homage to life in France.

Turnbull, Sarah. *Almost French.* New York: Gotham Books, 2002. Another Australian moves to France, settles in Paris, and shares the witty details.

FICTION

Clarke, Stephen. *A Year in the Merde.* New York: Bloomsbury, 2005. The goofy tale of a middle-aged Englishman's adventures in the City of Light.

Guene, Faiza. *Kiffe Kiffe Tomorrow.* Orlando: Harcourt, 2006. The story of a young North African immigrant girl's life in the Paris suburbs.

Hugo, Victor. *The Hunchback of Notre Dame.* A dramatic, sorrowful tale of lives intertwined in the heart of medieval Paris.

Hugo, Victor. *Les Misérables.* A riveting story of perseverance, revenge, and survival by one of France's most revered writers.

Nemirovsky, Irene. *Suite Française.* An edge of your seat story set in Paris and the French countryside during World War II.

IF YOUR FRENCH IS UP TO SNUFF...

You should really try reading some of these authors' works in their own language—but if you can't tell your *voilà* from your viola, you can still find semi-decent translations of some of France's most revered writers.

André Breton

Albert Camus

Colette

Simone de Beauvoir

Guy de Maupassant

Jean de La Varende

Alexandre Dumas

Victor Hugo

Anaïs Nin

Marcel Proust

Jean-Paul Sartre

Voltaire

RESOURCES

Suggested Films

The Lumière brothers are credited with inventing the final link in cinema technology, bringing the art form to life in France at the turn of the 19th century. (The Institut Lumière, dedicated to the work of the Lyon-born siblings, should not be missed.) Since then, French filmmaking has evolved into an honored and honorable tradition, and France boasts a long list of directors whose films are consistently compelling: Jacques Demy, Jean-Luc Godard, François Ozon, Jacques Chabral, Marcel Pagnol, Jean Renoir, François Truffaut, Ousman Sembène, Louis Malle, Agnes Varda, and many more. A (very) short list of must-sees includes:

DRAMAS AND COMEDIES

Amélie. Directed by Jean-Pierre Jeunet, 2001. Burbank, CA: Buena Vista Home Entertainment, 2002.

Betty Blue. Directed by Jean-Jacques Beineix, 1986. United States: Cinema Libre Studio, 2009.

Breathless. Directed by Jean-Luc Godard, 1960. Livingston, NY: Criterion Collection, 2007.

Le Cercle Rouge. Directed by Jean-Pierre Melville, 1970. New York: Criterion Collection, 2004.

City of Lost Children. Directed by Marc Caro and Jean-Pierre Jeunet. Culver City, CA: Columbia Tri-Star Home Video, 1995.

Delicatessen. Directed by Marc Caro and Jean-Pierre Jeunet, 1991. Hollywood, CA: Paramount Home Video, 1992.

Elevator to the Gallows. Directed by Louis Malle, 1958. New York: Criterion Collection, 2006.

The Grand Illusion. Directed by Jean Renoir, 1937. Chicago, IL: Home Vision Cinema, 1999.

La Haine. Directed by Mathieu Kossovits, 1995. Irvington, NY: Criterion Collection, 2007.

Paris, je t'aime. Directed by Olivier Assayas et al, 2006. Los Angeles: First Look Home Entertainment, 2007.

SUGGESTED MUSIC

There's nothing like the sound of Edith Piaf's warbling to put you in the mood for France. Here are other French musical "arteests" worth getting to know:

- Air
- Arielle Dombasle
- Ben l'Oncle Soul
- Blossom Dearie
- Daft Punk
- Françoise Hardy
- Serge Gainsbourg
- Keren Ann
- Les Innocents
- Louise Attack
- Nouvelle Vague
- Les Nubians
- Paris Combo
- Phoenix
- Rhinôçérôse
- Superbus

Pauline at the Beach. Directed by Eric Rohmer, 1983. Santa Monica, CA: MGM Home Entertainment, 2003.

The Red Balloon. Directed by Albert Lamorisse, 1956. New York: Janus Films, 2008.

The Triplets of Belleville. Directed by Sylvain Chomet, 2003. New York: Sony Picture Classics, 2004.

The Town Is Quiet. Directed by Robert Guédiguian, 2002. Agat Films & Cie/ Canal+, 2000.

Umbrellas of Cherbourg. Directed by Jacques Demy, 1964. Port Washington, NY: Koch Vision, 2004.

DOCUMENTARIES

The Gleaners and I. Directed by Agnès Varda, 2000. New York: Zeitgeist Video, 2002.

Kings of Pastry. Directed by Frazer Pennebaker and Flora Lazar, 2009. New York: First Run Features, 2011.

Man on Wire. Directed by James Marsh, 2008. United States: Magnolia Home Entertainment, 2008.

Index

Acknowledgments

I'm so grateful to the many talented, generous, and patient people who supported this project in so many wonderful ways: Jeff Rogers, Jennifer Pickens, Sophia Pagan, Alain Virnot, Mary Margaret Chappell, Owen Peery, Claudia Delman, Philippe Nicolitch, Christina Rebuffet-Broadus, Cedric Holz, Mariel Chatman, Jane Lunn, Ross Husband, Sheila Johnson, Cassandra Tanti, Karin Bates Prescott, Jennifer Kildee, Amanda Zane, Emoke Tarnay, Randy Diaz, Joe Kissell, and Janet Hasson. If I've forgotten anybody, let's work the oversight out over a bottle of Bordeaux (my treat)!

www.moon.com

DESTINATIONS | ACTIVITIES | BLOGS | MAPS | BOOKS

MOON.COM is all new, and ready to help plan your next trip! Filled with fresh trip ideas and strategies, author interviews, informative blogs, a detailed map library, and descriptions of all the Moon guidebooks, Moon.com is all you need to get out and explore the world—or even places in your own backyard. As always, when you travel with Moon, expect an experience that is uncommon and truly unique.

MOON LIVING ABROAD IN FRANCE

Avalon Travel
a member of the Perseus Books Group
1700 Fourth Street
Berkeley, CA 94710, USA
www.moon.com

Editor: Elizabeth Hansen
Series Manager: Elizabeth Hansen
Copy Editor: Mia Lipman
Graphics Coordinator: Elizabeth Jang
Production Coordinator: Elizabeth Jang
Cover Designer: Elizabeth Jang
Map Editor: Kat Bennett
Cartographers: Kat Bennett, Kaitlin Jaffe
Indexer: Rachel Kuhn

ISBN-13: 978-1-59880-972-5
ISSN: 1534-5890

Printing History
1st Edition – 2005
2nd Edition – January 2012
5 4 3 2 1

KEEPING CURRENT

Although we strive to produce the most up-to-date guidebook that we possibly can, change is unavoidable. Between the time this book goes to print and the time you read it, the cost of goods and services may have increased, and a handful of the businesses noted in these pages will undoubtedly move, alter their prices, or close their doors forever. Exchange rates fluctuate – sometimes dramatically – on a daily basis. Federal and local legal requirements and restrictions are also subject to change, so be sure to check with the appropriate authorities before making the move. If you see anything in this book that needs updating, clarification, or correction, please drop us a line. Send your comments via email to feedback@moon.com, or use the address above.

MAP SYMBOLS

▦▦▦ Expressway	○ City/Town	✈ Airfield
▦▦ Primary Road	◉ State Capital	✈ Airport
▦▦ Secondary Road	⊛ National Capital	▲ Mountain
▪ ▪ ▪ ▪ Unpaved Road	★ Point of Interest	♠♠ Park
▪▪▪▪▪ Ferry	▪ Other Location	🎿 Skiing Area
▬▬ Railroad		

- ▲ Archaeological Site
- ⚱ Church
- ⛽ Gas Station
- Mangrove
- Reef
- Swamp

CONVERSION TABLES

°C = (°F - 32) / 1.8
°F = (°C x 1.8) + 32
1 inch = 2.54 centimeters (cm)
1 foot = 0.304 meters (m)
1 yard = 0.914 meters
1 mile = 1.6093 kilometers (km)
1 km = 0.6214 miles
1 fathom = 1.8288 m
1 chain = 20.1168 m
1 furlong = 201.168 m
1 acre = 0.4047 hectares
1 sq km = 100 hectares
1 sq mile = 2.59 square km
1 ounce = 28.35 grams
1 pound = 0.4536 kilograms
1 short ton = 0.90718 metric ton
1 short ton = 2,000 pounds
1 long ton = 1.016 metric tons
1 long ton = 2,240 pounds
1 metric ton = 1,000 kilograms
1 quart = 0.94635 liters
1 US gallon = 3.7854 liters
1 Imperial gallon = 4.5459 liters
1 nautical mile = 1.852 km

°FAHRENHEIT	°CELSIUS	
230	110	
220		
210	100	WATER BOILS
200		
190	90	
180	80	
170		
160	70	
150		
140	60	
130		
120	50	
110		
100	40	
90	30	
80		
70	20	
60		
50	10	
40		
30	0	WATER FREEZES
20	-10	
10		
0	-20	
-10		
-20	-30	
-30		
-40	-40	

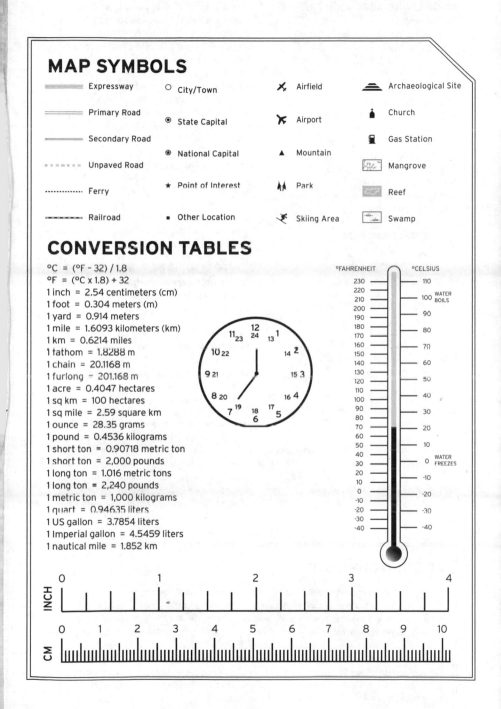